The Pulitzer Prize-winning author of *TALES OF THE SOUTH PACIFIC* returns to the scenes of those tales that won him world recognition. Once again he evokes the magic of the blessed isles in the Pacific with stories and accounts glowing with color and alive with adventure. *RETURN TO PARADISE* is a new visit to a land of enchantment by one of the most gifted story tellers of our time.

RETURN
to
PARADISE

James A. Michener

FAWCETT CREST • NEW YORK

RETURN TO PARADISE

THIS BOOK CONTAINS THE COMPLETE TEXT OF
THE ORIGINAL HARDCOVER EDITION.

Published by Fawcett Crest Books, a unit of
CBS Publications, the Consumer Publishing Division of CBS Inc.,
by arrangement with Random House, Inc.

ISBN: 0-449-23831-8

Printed in the United States of America

20 19 18 17 16 15

CONTENTS

To

The Mighty Ocean

In 1948 I addressed some students at Washington and Lee University, and in the question-answer period one young man observed with asperity, "But it's easy for you to write. You've traveled."

I became angry and replied that it was my intention never again to write about foreign lands. I added, "The writer's job is to dig down where he is. He must write about the solid, simple things of his own land."

I believed this when I spoke, and I believe it now. And yet less than a year after my public confession, I was on my way back to the South Pacific to write another book on that languid retreat. How did this happen?

There was within me the abiding, deep and growing conviction that what happened in Asia was of sovereign importance to my country. I reasoned, "We understand the basic motivations of Europe. What takes place there may or may not please us, but at least we know how to interpret what does happen and how to build bulwarks against calamity. But in Asia most of what occurs we do not even vaguely understand, and what happens in Asia is vital." I was therefore eager to revisit Australia, New Zealand and New Guinea to find how things were going with our forward friends. If there is anything any of us can do to encourage an understanding of Asia and its Pacific approaches, we should do it.

But not even my preoccupation with the Pacific could justify my returning merely to grind out another batch of stories upon the old theme. It is true that several immense talents spent large portions of their lives chronicling the Pacific, and no writer need be ashamed of punishing his legs while trying to reach the footsteps of Conrad, Melville, Maugham or James Norman Hall. But a writer's artistic life is a most delicate adjustment of many factors, and I simply refused to waste mine sailing after fresh Pacific yarns.

Then it occurred to me that the trip would be justified if I attempted to write a kind of book that—so far as I knew—had never been tried before. Such an adventure would make the return to the Pacific intellectually honorable.

So I write a series of jammed-crammed essays containing

all I knew about this ocean. I endeavored to make the essays both evocative and provocative. Then, when each was finished, I wrote a story growing out of the theme of the essay. Thus, the reader could see from the essay what I thought about a given island; while from the fictional story he could determine what the island thought about itself. Furthermore, this procedure would throw illumination upon the relationship between fiction and fact. Thus the first essay, "The Atoll" is a statement of fact in which each item is literally true, so far as I can ascertain. But what follows, "Mr. Morgan," is fiction, and none of it is true except that when I read it now it seems more truthful than the essay.

There was one final problem. Would this long journey prove to be merely another of those heartbreak trips of disillusion into a past that cannot be recovered? I was apprehensive about this, for I knew that virgin impressions of great events can rarely be recaptured; but when our plane rose above the bridges of San Francisco and I saw below me this vast and mighty ocean, my heart expanded.

J. A. M.

The Atoll

Ages ago, when the world was different, the South Pacific contained many islands we have never known. Then as now the floor of the ocean rose and fell when volcanic pressures fluctuated. A violent up-thrusting that created new islands would be followed by an imperceptible subsidence which slowly dragged the newborn lands back below the surface of the sea.

About 10,000 years ago one such mountainous island rose above the warm waters near the equator. Around its edges swarmed a multitude of remarkable animals, the coral polyps, taking refuge in deep water. Slowly they began to build a calciferous reef, each new polyp adding his tiny limestone skeleton to those that had died before.

The polyps had chosen their new home with studied care. The water temperature must never go below 68 degrees, or the tiny animals would freeze. The base of their building could be no deeper than 120 feet, or they would drown. The water must be salty, but not too salty, and it had to contain an abundance of plankton, that microscopic marine life on which coral feeds. Most important of all, the water had to be fresh and free of sand, for any kind of sedimentation would suffocate the polyps.

Working slowly, dying by the multiple billions so that their limestone structures could become rock, the polyps clung to the shores of the new island and in some years raised their reef as much as three inches. Of course, the highest point was still far under water and no eye could have discerned that a miracle had already begun to take place.

For now the ever-violent ocean bed began steadily to subside. In a thousand years it fell perhaps three feet, but slowly the island was settling into the sea. Unseen, the coral continued building. Now it was less than fifty feet below the surface.

Then one day the dying island exploded into cataclysmic fury. Its volcanic flames lighted the sky for many years, but as the fierce heat died out the entire ocean bed—island, reefs, coral and all—shivered and sank deeper into the sea.

The coral was not drowned. Through many centuries it continued to build until a final day when, with some unchronicled gasp, the last fragment of the original island disappeared forever.

More than a thousand years elapsed and in that time the coral on the sunken reef continued its patient growth. It was now close to the surface and one day a solitary limestone pinnacle no bigger than a pencil broke the waves. A score of decades passed. A bird skimming the empty wastes of ocean could have seen a thin shining ribbon of white coral. A piece of driftwood caught fast and rotted. Sand began to collect and finally a seed drifted two thousand miles across the waves and found lodgment. A casuarina tree began to grow.

It was washed away. More soil collected. Igneous rock from some recent volcano floated mysteriously to the almost-born island. Sand edged the inner shore of the reef. A coconut arrived, a pandanus. In two thousand years a new fragment of earth had been created.

Now the entire reef, miles in circumference, threatened to break the surface. Within the circle the sea water became dirty and all polyps on the inner shore died. Those on the outside now did the work, building the reef ever outward from its center.

A new violence, a new upheaval of the ocean floor and the entire reef was lifted twenty feet into the air. Here and there weak portions crumbled into the pounding sea, leaving narrow channels into the lagoon. At other points, where coral skeletons had been piled highest, substantial islands rose like a cluster of jewels strung along the golden strands of the reef.

At last the miracle was complete! A coral atoll, circular in form, subtended a shallow lagoon. On the outer edge giant green combers of the Pacific thundered in majestic fury. Inside, the water was blue and calm. Along the shore of the lagoon palm trees bent their towering heads as the wind directed, and after a thousand more years brown men in frail canoes came to the atoll and decided it should be their home.

The world contains certain patterns of beauty that impress the mind forever. They might be termed the sovereign sights and most men will agree as to what they are: the Pyramids at dawn, the Grand Tetons at dusk, a Rembrandt self-portrait, the Arctic wastes. The list need not be long, but to be inclusive it must contain a coral atoll with its placid lagoon, the terrifyingly brilliant sands and the outer reef shooting great spires of spindrift a hundred feet into the air. Such a sight is one of the incomparable visual images of the world.

10

This is the wonder of an atoll, that you are safe within the lagoon while outside the tempest rages. The atoll becomes a symbol of all men seeking refuge, the security of home, the warmth of love. Lost in a wilderness of ocean, the atoll is a haven that captivates the mind and rests the human spirit.

More than a symbol, however, the atoll is a reservoir of tangible beauty. Fleecy clouds hang over it, so that in the dawn it wears a flaming crest of gold. At midday it seems to dream in the baking heat, its colors uncompromisingly brilliant. At sunset the clouds once more reflect a shimmering brilliance. At night stars seem to hover just out of reach, and if there is a moon it does not dance upon the waters. Its reflection lies there passively like a silvered causeway to the opposite shore.

Each of the motus along the reef—the independent islands with trees—has its own characteristic charm. Some have beaches a mile wide of such dazzling sand as to blind the unprotected eye. Others contain coral gardens that delight the imagination. Still others are the home of a thousand birds, the prowling ground of sharks, the keepers of the caverns where pearls grow.

The coral itself is infinitely colored. Most startling are the bright, untempered hues: radiant blacks, garish greens, bright blues, enviable yellows and brooding purples. But after the shock of seeing such prodigal brilliance, it is the pastels that continue to invite the eye. There are delicate pinks, soft blues and airy greens. Sometimes a single patch of coral will contain a dozen shades. Again there will be an acre of one primitive color alone. Only on a living reef can you see the pageantry of coral, for once dead and exposed to air, its color fades and vanishes.

Also infinite are the forms of coral. Most spectacular are the branching arms that seem to clutch outward toward the ocean. Most unforgettable is the brain coral which reproduces in arresting likeness the shape and convolutions of the human brain. There are shelves of coral, trees of coral, great globes of it, angular skeletons, and even delicate flowers. Each is composed of the dead remnants of millions of polyps.

But to savor the true miracle of coral, you must go to the outer edge of the reef. There, suspended by ropes from a small boat, you push yourself down, down along the living face of the majestic structure. Whereas the lagoon waters were delicate and sprinkled with sunlight, the brooding waters at the reef face are sullen and black. Below you, as

11

far as the eye can penetrate, there is nothing but great chunks of mysterious forms jutting into the breaking sea. Sometimes the reef has broken away and left small caverns. Your hand explores one and draws back in terror! An octopus hides there. Then your eye becomes accustomed to the mournful darkness and you see about your face a myriad of brilliant fish. You look in amazement, for never have you even guessed such creatures could exist. In every possible form and color these astonishing fish drift by. When you think you have seen all the wonders a reef can hold, a monstrous coral fish goes past. It has a dozen silky tails, streamers from each fin, a face like a pig's, a striped body like a zebra's and such colors as no artist would dare combine. Off into the caverns it goes, and your eye lingers on a dark shape gliding through the mysterious waters. Was it a shark? It turns on its side and disappears. And always at your elbow the fantastic shapes of coral, the brilliant colors, the provocative textures. Above you the great surf pounds, and now your lungs throb with pain. You pull upon the rope and lunge toward the surface, up past the glorious fish, the murky caverns and the living coral. You break the waves and catch a comber full in the face. Exhausted, you climb back into the boat. You have seen the face of the reef, the battleground from which the atoll rose, and you will never forget what you have seen.

This is how an atoll looks. Along the outer edge toward the sea—nothing. A few trees perhaps, a stretch of blinding sand, some bird nests. Along the inner shore of the largest motu a string of thatched huts, each with its share of beach. Next, three or four shacks built of wood and corrugated iron. Then a trading store with a verandah for the loafers. Then a European house painted white and red, the government quarters. Finally a big church, whitewashed, with sloping roof leading to three huge concrete tanks, also whitewashed. These are for the collection of rain, since no atoll ever has enough fresh water for cooking and drinking.

And everywhere there are coconut palms. This amazing tree is the life blood of the atoll. Its wood makes furniture. Its plaited leaves make fine baskets or hats or carpeting or partitions. A silky lace-like growth about the crown yields good mats. The heart of the palm makes the world's best salad, the husk is perfect insulating material, and the hard shell of the nut makes good charcoal.

As if this were not enough, the liquid within the nut is a delicious substitute for drinking water and is moreover so pure that it can be used medically as a completely sterile saline solution. With safety it can be injected even into the blood stream, for in the hard shell there is always a soft eye through which a needle can be passed.

As for the meat itself, its uses are manifold. Few nuts are allowed to ripen into the hard, unpalatable stuff sold in American markets. If they do reach that age, when the milk is bitter and useless, they are made into copra for their oil, which is manufactured into soap and margarine. Most nuts are picked young, when the meat is so soft that it can be eaten with a spoon. There are six stages in the ripening of a coconut, each with its own name, each with its peculiar cooking possibilities.

The best dish is this: Take a fish caught that afternoon on the reef and cut it into strips, raw. Soak them overnight in lime juice and sea water. Pick some young coconuts and add their milk to the fish. Stand the pot in the sun for five hours. Grate up the coconut meat, add two onions and mix it with the fish. Add some salt. The result is a kind of bitter-sweet dish which tastes completely different from any other food. There is no smell of fish, no taste of sea water, no bite of lime. It is a delicious feast.

But more than the beauty, more than the coral, more than the subtle food, it is the native people who make an atoll so strange and yet so attractive. By some curious chance the natives on most Pacific atolls are Polynesians. These brown navigators consistently bypassed the commodious islands like New Guinea or the Solomons to seek out tiny atolls. Along the north coast of New Guinea there are many specks in the ocean populated by Polynesians. And scattered through the Solomons there are others. But to see atoll life at its best you must go farther east beyond Tahiti, where there are so many low-lying islands that they seem to form clouds along the horizon. There the Polynesians have built a true island culture.

Eager to share in its simplicities, many white men have also come to the atolls. A longing for solitude, an obsession about lost islands, a yearning for the relaxation of native life have combined to lure men onto even the most desolate islands.

Have they found happiness? Many have not. I think of Bunner Langdale as the typical atoll man. A brilliant artist in pen and ink, a gifted observer, a fine storyteller, he developed a passion for the low islands that cling to the bosom of the

13

sea. Year after year he wandered among them, taking his boat from one landfall to the next.

He was alternately a wonderful conversationalist, a moody recluse. He developed toothache, that dreaded affliction where dentists or doctors are available only once a year. He knocked off the top of the tooth and each day rammed in two drops of carbolic acid. His pain was sometimes unbearable but finally a ship put into the atoll. The doctor said he wouldn't risk pulling the tooth while Bunner was conscious and he had no anaesthesia, so the captain sorrowfully gave Bunner the only bottle of whiskey on board and the atoll man got steaming drunk. Then the pain was numbed and he felt fine. Brandishing a chair he cried, "I'll kill the man that touches me." His friends tried to take him by trickery, but he outguessed them and all night roared his joy at the sudden relief from pain. In the morning he was sober with the same old tooth. Now he promised to kill the doctor if he so much as touched the tooth with the forceps. The ship sailed. Bunner went back to his carbolic acid.

He was a man you couldn't argue with. Just before starting on a long boat trip to New Zealand he scratched himself on coral—a half-inch wound, no more—and by sailing date his leg had festered. The doctor, a different one this time, warned him that it was risky to chance such a long trip before the coral poisoning had healed. Bunner told him to go to hell, but the last eight days of the voyage were mortal agony and when he landed the leg was immediately amputated.

Still he loved the atolls and with his peg leg went back to them. Again he scratched himself on coral, the other leg this time, and again the dreadful poisoning set in. This time he doctored himself with care and for a time reduced the infection, but finally it broke into violent corruption and only a miraculous operation saved his life.

Now he had no legs, but still he would not leave the atolls. Fitted with crutches, he became a cherished figure about the Pacific, a man with wonderful humor and delicate insights into beauty. Small government jobs were found for him, always on some distant island, and there he lived, tramping the deck of his boat, studying the charts of new atolls across the world.

One night a storm came and Bunner Langdale swung his crutches across the wet deck. They slipped. Unseen, he plunged toward the railing and fell noiselessly into the deep waters of the lagoon. I found out later they recovered the body.

14

One of the old hands in the atolls said to me, "They're dreadful places, really. They house diseases you've never heard of. They are lonely and desolate. If the white men who live there told the truth they'd admit the islands are hellish. I've watched such men go crazy. What's worse, I've seen them die on their feet. There isn't one who wouldn't leave if he had the money and the chance."

Captain Bobby Crookshank, a sea dog if there ever was one, is an honest judge of atoll life. An officer in the Royal Navy, he came at last to the Pacific where his bright Scotch-Irish wit made him famous. As a youngster he was boxing champion of the British Navy and carries with him a silver beer mug inscribed with the details of his championship. If he runs into trouble with some contentious character, he quietly serves a mug of beer, inscription-side toward the face. "Suddenly," he says, "the chap begins to see things my way."

Bobby has shipped into many of the atolls and vows he never yet has seen one a decent man could live on. "They're low dirty places. If you get enough rain, you also get malaria. If you escape the fever, there's no water to drink. A single kitchen can hold a million flies. Land crabs pester you, and if you kill them, they stink up the atmosphere. Rats are as big as coconuts. Why, the average motu is less than a mile wide and you can walk all over it in one afternoon. There are no pretty birds, only the cawing kind, damned few flowers and no meat. I tell you, a man's already half crazy when he first steps onto such a place."

Recalling certain atolls I had known, I challenged Captain Bobby and said, "You're spreading it a bit thick, aren't you? Admit it. You've seen at least one atoll you considered beautiful."

He rubbed his white hair for a moment, ordered me a beer and laughed. "You've got me there," he confessed. "There was such an island. One evening I saw it at sunset. I remarked at the time that it looked right pretty lying there astern of the ship. Because I was leaving the goddamned place."

The American who best knew the atolls was a tragic man, the novelist Robert Dean Frisbie. During the war I heard of him many times. Wherever I went east of Fiji, people would say, "If you're interested in the islands, you must meet Frisbie." It was astonishing how much I learned about this strange man. He had been thrown out of several islands. He had infuriated governments and encouraged native rebellion. In the midst of his world weariness he married a magnificent

15

Polynesian girl who bore him five children and then died. He had protected his children through an atoll hurricane when the giant seas poured over the motus, and he had written as perceptively about atoll life as any modern writer.

One day we heard he was dying in Tongareva, a thousand miles from anywhere. The Navy sent a plane up to bring him back to the American hospital in Samoa. I remember the trip because we picked up a Chinaman in Tahiti, bound for Honolulu. As we neared Tongareva we got into difficulty and had to ditch the cargo. Out went the Chinaman's gear, out went the food, everything. When we closed the hatch we were astounded to find that the Chinaman, too, was gone. A frantic search disclosed him jammed into a corner. He came out praying, and approached us with resignation. He assumed that we would pitch him out next.

Well, we found Frisbie in terrible condition. He was totally emaciated, and with his deep eyes and protruding lower jaw he looked like the dying Robert Louis Stevenson. He pleaded for morphine to ease the pain, but we were warned that it was forbidden him.

He was tended solely by his daughter Johnnie, a thirteen-year-old girl. We discussed with her what must be done, and she agreed to stay on the atoll and care for her younger brothers and sisters. She said brokenly that she did not think her father would live, and in the morning the children gathered at the plane to bid him a weeping good-bye.

We packed him into the baggage compartment, spreading three blankets on the floor to keep him warm. On the long, bitterly cold flight I sat with him and became convinced that he would not die. We even planned a book we would one day write together and he told me of his feelings about atolls.

We were over Manihiki, one of the most lovely. It lay below us like embracing arms enclosing a lake of placid wonder. "I saw Manihiki first about twenty years ago," he said. "They can joke about white men in the islands, but out here I've experienced the full meaning of life. Believe me, when you're on an atoll and the hurricane piles the seas over ... You've seen about all nature can show.

"And I've liked the people. Pettiness seems to be on a smaller scale. Goodness on a more generous one. In America I suppose you hear a lot of nonsense about the alluring women. Actually the men are more to be wondered at. They have the courage of heroes, but they can weep like children. As crew on a small ship in trouble they can't be beat."

Frisbie was in great pain, aggravated by the unaccustomed

16

cold. He spoke of the reading he had done on the atolls, of his essays in the *Atlantic Monthly* which made him famous, and of the sales of his latest books. His great problem was the future of his children. Since they were half-caste Polynesians he had to get them back to school in America if he' wanted them to become American citizens. He said his oldest girl was quite intelligent and wondered how he could afford to send her to the States. He said he thought she might be able to write a book that would be a best seller, and even though he knew how rarely anyone gets rich from writing books, he insisted upon dreaming of that chance.

Then he grew moody and said, "It's a hell of a life, by God it is. You sit on those damned islands with no one to talk to. You read till your eyes are sore and when you try to write, all you can do is 'chronicle small beer.' I tell you, I've been so lonely down there I'd have talked with a fish, if he'd had a grain of intelligence." He was silent for a while and then laughed. "I felt the same way in California," he admitted.

The doctors in Samoa fixed him up and to everybody's surprise he got a job teaching school. Half a year later I found him under a pandanus tree drinking bush beer while his daughter Johnnie taught his classes, "because she can keep discipline better than I can." Each night he instructed her in the next day's lesson and she would stand barefooted in a sarong hammering English at the heads of nineteen-year-old oafs.

"If she can do that," I said, "she can write a book."

"She will, too!" Frisbie insisted.

"If she does," I said impulsively, "I'll get it published."

Frisbie was eager to discuss the book he and I were going to write. "We'll limit it to Polynesia and we'll describe everything as the eye of God might see it. We'll tell about the beauty, yes, but we'll also speak honestly of the desolate bitterness." He was well now and became excited, for he wanted to narrate the simple truths of island life.

I last saw Frisbie in Samoa. Already he was beginning to get into trouble. He fled from Pago to Apia to Tahiti and back to Rarotonga, from which he had been exiled years before. I received aching letters from him. His grand dreams were fading in the daylight. Only once did he speak of our book but there was no glow of hope and he never referred to it again.

His ambitions now centered in Johnnie's work, and to my astonishment—for one is always meeting people who "are going to write a book" but who never do—one day it arrived. I read it with great nostalgia, for Frisbie had obviously poured all his energies into correcting and polishing his daughter's naiad remembrances of atoll life. It was good, very good, and within a week I found a publisher. Now Frisbie's letters were full of the things he would do. With the money Johnnie would make from her book the children would come to America, where he would write a great novel about a ship.

But when his daughter's book was published—even as the reviews were reporting it to be a delightful evocation of atoll life—Frisbie with the jutting jaw was dead in Rarotonga. His children were destitute. There was no money, no home, no legacy but debt. Friends took up a collection to bury him. After his death I received a letter he had posted long before. He was now uncertain about the books he had planned. Things seemed more difficult than they used to be. He thought another book by Johnnie might be the thing. Certainly he would do his part and help her with the spelling. I read the letter with dull pain, for already I had been told that he had been responsible for his own death. He had used once too often a rusty hypodermic needle.

I liked Frisbie, I respected his basic honesty. If ever I knew a man who destroyed himself through the search for beauty, Frisbie was that man. I can respect the uncompromising artist, and I never once met Frisbie but what I pitied him and liked him, too. There were other atoll men of whom I could not say as much.

Let's call him Rackham. He was forty-eight, a scrawny fellow who had sailed more than fifty miles to see me. He thought I had an authority which was not mine, that I could somehow find him passage to the States. "I came out here twenty years ago," he complained. "I didn't get the breaks. This is my woman. The kids are mine, too. Now get me straight, Lieutenant. I wouldn't desert this woman and those kids for anything. But I was wondering if you could . . . That is, perhaps there might be a place . . . Maybe I . . . But you understand, I won't leave the woman behind."

He pestered me for days. He was a real wreck of the islands, a no-good, forlorn bum. He had sponged on one native family after another, debauching their daughters, making drunken sots of the sons. The Pacific war brought powerful memories to Rackham. He saw Americans again, clean men with money of their own. For six years he had been without teeth. Now he wheedled an Army dentist into whipping him up a set. He told me of the wonderful things he was

18

going to do, but he always ended by saying he wouldn't desert the woman.

When he talked with me this woman stood in a corner, or behind a tree. Usually she had one of the children with her, and in time she came to hate me, because she knew what I didn't know.

Finally Rackham came out with it. "Lieutenant," he whined, "so help me God, I wouldn't desert the woman. But I'm an American." He dropped his head on the table and mumbled, "So help me God, I want to go home."

. There was a long silence. Then he looked up and began to plead: "I've got to get back. A plane. A cargo ship. Maybe a destroyer? You've got to help me!" He gripped his knuckles in anguish. "I'm an American citizen," he said.

There was nothing we could do. We had an aching compassion for this fellow countryman, but there was nothing we could do. The atolls had ruined him. He was beyond help. I last saw him leaving the lagoon, his woman and the two children with him in the boat.

But I must not cite Rackham as representative of the island white man. I know many men who have led wonderful lives out there. Matt Wells, for example. I hope I look half as good at fifty as he does at sixty-three. He has a full head of hair, strong teeth, a tremendous appetite for life. How many children he has had no one can say, but during the war he became famous because our soldiers started the rumor that he was the illegitimate son of H. G. Wells. If such speculation ever reached Matt, he didn't bother to deny it, a fact which I had to forgive, for many American naval officers were convinced that I was the son—illegitimate or otherwise—of Admiral Marc Mitscher. I corrected neither their error nor their spelling, for it was because of my supposed kinship to the great aviation tactician that I was allowed the privilege of traveling to so many islands in search of characters like Matt.

We disagreed on only one point. Matt considered missionaries the lowest form of animal life, whereas I insisted that I had known some who were a greater credit to the white race than any other men who had invaded the islands.

"Name one!" Matt roared.

"Bishop Jones," I suggested.

Grudgingly Matt said, "You've got me there. Bishop Jones is one of the finest men I ever knew. Clean-spoken, honest, I'd trust that man anywhere—except with small boys."

My favorite atoll man, however, is Fred Archer. He has

19

lived on the lonely islands for many years, a lean, handsome, courageous man. He told me, "Certainly, I've watched six or seven of my friends go mad on atolls. They get a glassy look in the eye. They retreat farther and farther into a dream world. I recall one atoll in the Ninigos where my two predecessors had died. The last one disappeared mysteriously. On gloomy nights, as trading vessels left the lagoon, captains would cry, 'Mark my words, Fred. He didn't die. The natives murdered him. They've got his body in the bush. You watch out, Fred. They'll do you in next!' "

He said that reading and sport had kept him happy, plus the fact that he was an accomplished seamstress. "Every meal I'd have a red dictionary by my plate, a novel and a shotgun. I once heard my native boy instructing his assistant. 'Suppose Mastuh he got red book here, green book here, rifle here. Then table he set good too much.' I never took less than an hour for meals, because I frequently looked up to study the beach. Gray cranes eat chicken eggs, and whenever I saw one at the water's edge, I'd put down the novel, lift up the rifle and pot him."

Archer had a house bordered with flowers, walks lined with croton and whitewashed rocks. He had a dinner service for eight and received each month a shipment of new books from Sydney. As for the sewing, a dear old lady in England got his name under the totally mistaken idea that he was a missionary. She sent him a life subscription to what she considered an appropriate magazine: a monthly devoted to wholesome family living with an insert containing a pattern and full sewing instructions. Fred was amused by the patterns until one day he needed some new pajamas and remembered that some months back there had been a pattern for a "radical new idea of night clothes that would not bind in the crotch." He rummaged through the recent issues until he found the instructions and then discovered that he had a knack for cutting out garments. He bought a sewing machine and taught a Polynesian girl to use it. He adds, "There used to be some embarrassment when visiting women asked the girl where she had learned to make such beautiful clothes. 'Mastuh, he teach me,' the girl said proudly, whereupon I had to produce the magazine by way of explanation."

Archer says the most perfect atoll he ever heard of was Maty in the Ninigos. It was owned by a meticulous German and managed by an expansive Swede. "It was magnificent. Every stone was in place. The house was a thing of beauty. The Swede used to invite maybe a dozen planters from various islands. A native lay under the table with a switch to drive mosquitoes away from ankles. Behind each guest stood a Polynesian girl to serve the meal and to spend the night if necessary. Life on Maty was simple and beautiful and placid."

But even Fred Archer bears witness to the ultimate desolation of atoll living. "This Battersby was a planter who had made a multitude of enemies. He was afflicted by what the natives call 'the big cross.' He hated everybody. But as he grew older he decided that he must erase his bitterness. Accordingly he planned a great feast, and in careful longhand wrote out more than thirty invitations to his past enemies. He gave them to his boy to take by pinnace to all the nearby islands.

" 'But Mastuh . . .' the boy protested.

" 'Take them all!' Battersby cried in exultation. 'Tell all fellow men big cross he stop long me no more!'

"In sad bewilderment the native took the letters and buried them under a rock by the lagoon. He said nothing, even helped prepare the feast.

"But when Battersby stood anxiously by the shore waiting for the craft that would never come, the native could bear it no longer and cried out, 'Mastuh! All fellow he no come!'

"Battersby looked up in bewilderment. 'No come? You took the letters, didn't you?'

" 'No, Mastuh. Me no take. Me put here.'

"In anguish Battersby dug up the invitations and looked at the faded addresses. With a great curse he began to beat the native who cried, 'Mastuh, no! Me no take letters because men he all dead finish!'

"One by one the belated invitations fell from Battersby's trembling hands. He looked at the names. 'Master Friedhoffer?' he mumbled.

" 'He dead finish long time, Mastuh.'

" 'Master Kleinschmidt?'

" 'He stop long dead long time too, Mastuh.'

"The old man let out a scream. 'They're all dead?' he cried.

" 'They all dead finish true, Mastuh,' the native said. Gently the black man tried to lead the old planter to the verandah where the feast was spread, but Battersby would not go.

" 'You run long,' he said in a despairing whisper. 'Tell all boy they kai kai meat, wine, all thing.' And so as the natives feasted, the white man blew out his brains."

The atolls are beautiful. They are among the most beautiful features of this earth, and it is no wonder they have lured many men. Not even the wild hurricanes, the loneliness, the stinging flies or the bitterness of a life slipped past can subtract one portion of the crystal beauty of these miraculous circles in the sea. In spite of all the men who have died of atoll fever, the lagoon and the pounding surf are incomparably wonderful.

Much romantic nonsense has been written about the atolls. Even the word lagoon has been debased far below its true currency. On the motus the beautiful girls have been ridiculed; the patient native men have been burlesqued. A thousand wastrels have befouled the islands; a hundred sentimentalists have defamed them.

But there still remains this fact: when the great seas pound upon the reef, when the stars shine down upon the lagoon, there is a mysterious, fragile something that no amount of misrepresentation can destroy. To say that men have died in such places, engulfed in disillusion and despair, is merely to point out that on a lonely atoll, as in most cities, good men find loveliness, weak men find evil.

Mr. Morgan

The atolls are beautiful. . . . Not even the wild hurricanes . . . or the bitterness of a life slipped past can subtract one portion of the crystal beauty of these miraculous circles in the sea.

When I was a boy we lived in this manner. At six each morning the church bell summoned us to prayer and wardens stood by the entrance checking our names. If a man were missing other wardens were sent running to find him, and if a man and girl were both missing we trembled until they were found, for we knew what the penalty would be if they had been together.

After church we were allowed to go about our duties, except that wardens could summon us to jail at any time if we had broken rules. One day a week we had to work on church land making copra or we fished for pearl shell in the lagoon, turning over all we found to the pastor. We had also to keep careful records of any money we made from schooners, for of this the wardens collected one share in ten, as the Bible directs.

At sunset the bell rang again, and we gathered for prayer. After that we could eat when we wished, but in the evening began the most troublesome of our rules. All young men and all unmarried girls had to carry lighted lanterns wherever they went. This was to help the wardens keep track of what was happening on the island, and if two lanterns were seen heading toward the bush in back of Matareva, the wardens ran there to see that no indecencies took place. Of course, some young men were smart enough to put out their lights and wait for girls, but if they were caught the wardens beat them. The girl was further humiliated next morning in church, after which both the offenders were sent to jail.

At nine each night the church bell rang again and everyone had to be indoors. Sometimes it was very beautiful at that hour. The moon would shine down upon the lagoon and through the village of Matareva pale lights would move mysteriously from house to house. Those were the wardens, checking up to see that all families were behaving themselves properly. The wardens had a right to enter any house at any time for an accounting of what each person inside had been doing for the past day, but on week nights the wardens did not abuse this privilege, unless one of them became attracted to some girl, and then he would break into her house almost every night, whether she wished him to or not. It was useless to protest, for the pastor knew that his control of Matareva depended upon the absolute loyalty of his wardens, whom he excused of even the most brutal behavior.

On Saturday nights the wardens became especially active, for no frivolity was allowed from then until Monday at daybreak. No husband must sleep with his wife. There must be no kissing, no singing, no reading of books. The rules were strictly observed in most homes because on these nights the wardens gave no warning. There was a rush at the door, a clatter of clubs and people moaning from cracked heads.

On Sunday we prayed three times and had a procession led by the wardens. We marched from the lagoon to the church and stood at solemn attention while the pastor, in a black suit, walked slowly from his house to the church. Then we entered behind him. This took place only at the eleven-o'clock service, but even if it was pouring rain we marched as usual, the wardens with umbrellas, the pastor under a canopy held by four boys.

One Sunday, at the end of an unprecedented spell when fish deserted our lagoon, a school of tunny dashed in through the channel, driven by sharks. They arrived just as the procession started and fishermen who had been without food for days looked passionately at the leaping fish, but wardens dashed up and down striking the men with clubs to keep them from breaking line. On Monday the tunny were gone.

Our law, our parliament, our judge and our business dictator were all one man: the pastor. His name was Thomas Cobbett and he came from some unidentified rural village, perhaps in New Zealand or Northern England. In appearance he was ordinary, a small man with watery blue eyes. Actually he was an inspired prophet right from the latter pages of the Old Testament with a penetrating voice and a sure faith that God personally guided him in the government of our atoll. He appeared always in a black suit and, when surrounded by his burly wardens, was a terrifying symbol of God's wrath in Matareva.

Often we puzzled why the Government permitted him to usurp its powers, but many years later an official explained that there had been so much clamor about Christianizing the islands that it was decided to leave one forgotten atoll exclusively to missionaries so as to test what they could accomplish.

Pastor Cobbett accomplished miracles. Even today many people will say there was never a finer island than Matareva in the old days. We were forced to bathe each afternoon. We had to kill the land crabs that burrowed in our gardens, buy screens for our kitchens and nail tin around our coconut trees to keep rats from eating the young nuts. We had to burn coral to make lime for painting our houses, and our walks had to be lined with white shells. Every woman worked one day a week at the church, so that the gardens there were the most beautiful in the Pacific.

The pastor was equally relentless regarding our spiritual lives. The old music, which everyone knows to have been lascivious, was forbidden and replaced by church hymns. Dancing was completely taboo and wardens could arrest anyone who dared to start the lewd old hulas. Everyone had to get married, widows must not talk with men except in the presence of other women and the number of illegitimate babies—a phrase never used on our island before Pastor Cobbett's time—was much reduced. There were some, of course, for in the old days girls had babies before they were married as proof that they would make good wives, but Pastor Cobbett raved against the practice and the penalties were brutally severe except when the father proved to be a warden. If the warden was unmarried, he had to marry the girl right away. If he already had a wife, he was reprimanded in private and the girl was publicly humiliated before the entire village on Sunday morning. She had to march from the rear of the big church up to the altar, fall upon the floor, put a black cloth over her head and walk back past all of us. It was always surprising to me that any girl would have the courage to risk such public shame, but many did and it was found that old women of the village supported them in their behavior, but as the old women died off, the girls found no consolation and some of them committed suicide, a thing never before heard of in our village.

Did no one revolt against this tyranny? As I said, some old women tried, because not even the wardens were cowardly enough to beat an old woman. Nor was the pastor able to quell them, for when he preached against them they stared back with implacable hatred. He solved the impasse by having his wardens spy on the family of the offending woman until a son or husband was detected breaking some trivial rule. Then the old women learned that no one could get the better of Pastor Cobbett. Once a man tried, but he was thrashed so often and spent so much time in jail that he fled to

Tongareva, but his canoe was fragile. It capsized and he was eaten by sharks. After that Pastor Cobbett ruled our lives inflexibly.

But in 1919 a small schooner from Suva put into our lagoon and landed a man who was to revolutionize Matareva. He was a tall thin man with stooped shoulders and a dark complexion. He wore a dirty shirt, unbuttoned, and white cotton pants that seemed always about to slip off his hips. He had no shoes, a battered hat, a small suitcase. He stood on the wharf and stared at our village. Then he hitched up his pants with his wrists and said, "Just what I expected. I'll stop here."

The pastor hurried up and said, "There are no houses."

"I'll build one," the stranger replied.

"We have no materials. None."

"Those leaf huts look OK to me," the man said.

The pastor grew red in the face and said bluntly, "We don't want white men on this island."

So the stranger dropped his suitcase, planted his hands on his hips and growled, "You sound like a sergeant."

The pastor shouted for his wardens, who ran up with clubs, but the barefooted stranger sidestepped them, searching for some weapon of his own. An old woman kicked him a board, and with it he fairly flew at the astonished wardens, who were accustomed to punishing men afraid to strike back.

The stranger fought with such fury as we had not seen before, and soon the fat bullies retreated with bad bruises, leaving the amazed pastor alone by the wharf. The visitor walked up to him and said, "The name's Morgan. I'll build my house over here."

That night he stayed with my father, and at great risk to themselves, four men of the village crept into our house after midnight. "Morgan Tane," they whispered, "that was a good fight you did!"

"We were proud to see the wardens run," another whispered.

"Morgan Tane," said the spokesman, "you were brave to challenge the pastor. No one has ever been so brave before." There was a long silence and then the spokesman said in a hushed voice, "We have been waiting for a man like you. Will you help us to fight against the wardens?"

The stranger answered promptly. "Me? I didn't come down here to fight. I had enough of that."

"But Morgan Tane," the spokesman whispered, "here you

26

will find no peace. The wardens will never let you spend one night in peace."

The stranger lit a cigarette, puffed on it several times and said, "Then I'll have to do something about it."

"Good!" the men cried. "We'll have a great rebellion."

"You don't understand," Mr. Morgan corrected them. "I'm not interested in trouble. I'm not going to be your leader. I'm not going to fight the wardens. I came down here for rest and quiet."

"But if the wardens ..."

"It looks to me as if each man has got to handle them his own way. I'm going to bed."

He started building his house next day, and by Sunday he was completely involved in our struggle against the pastor, for as we prepared for the customary procession, it was noticed with hushed surprise that Mr. Morgan, bare to the waist, was hammering on his roof-tree. Two wardens were sent to haul him into church, but they retreated in dismay when he produced a shotgun and said, "This thing is loaded."

They rushed off to report the crisis to the pastor, who came out into the road and studied the infidel from a safe distance. Then he wiped his face and waited for the congregation to reach the church. When the procession passed the uncompleted house, Mr. Morgan stopped his hammering and sat cross-legged on a barrel, weaving pandanus during the service. After the closing hymn he went back to the roof-tree.

Pastor Cobbett knew that if he let this insult go unpunished, his hold upon Matareva was doomed, so when church was over he gathered his wardens and strode to the place where the white man was working.

"Mr. Morgan!" the pastor cried in his sepulchral voice. "Do you intend to desecrate the Sabbath?"

"Go away!" Mr. Morgan growled.

"You have spoken," Pastor Cobbett cried in terrible tones. "Now God shall destroy this sacrilege."

The pastor stepped up to the nearest pole and began to shake it as Samson shook the pillars of the temple. "Don't be a damned fool," Mr. Morgan called down from the roof-tree.

"Come! Wardens! Everybody! Pull down the house of evil." The wardens, who knew of the shotgun, refused, but there were many natives who believed that Cobbett's voice was the voice of God, and these sprang into action, pulling down one of the posts so that a corner of the new house collapsed, tossing Mr. Morgan into the dust.

There was a moment of fateful silence as he slowly picked himself up, brushed off his pants and stood with his feet apart in the dust, studying the pastor. Finally he asked, "Reverend, are you crazy?"

"God has spoken," the missionary cried in his Old-Testament voice. "Men, destroy the blasphemy!"

The hypnotized natives rushed to the remaining poles and ripped them from the ground. Mr. Morgan remained with his head cocked to one side, staring with amazement at the impassioned scene. Still he did nothing and Pastor Cobbett exulted in victory, crying, "The devil in our midst has been cast out."

That was enough. Mr. Morgan looked at the pastor with disgust and said, "They shouldn't of let you out of the booby hatch." He rummaged among the ruins of his house and then walked doggedly to a spot some thirty feet away. There he raised his shotgun and with six cold, deliberate blasts destroyed each of the stained-glass windows in the church. They had been the glory of Matareva, and as they crashed an anguished sob arose from the watchers.

Pastor Cobbett stood like a man who has seen death striding across the motus. When he finally found strength to speak, a last fragment of window fell into the dust. He threw his hands over his face and gave an animal-like wail: "Sodom and Gomorrah have come! Surely God will strike this island with pestilence and evil." So powerful was his cry that true believers started to quake as if the day of judgment were at hand.

Mr. Morgan stalked back through the trembling crowd and hitched up his dirty pants. "Pastor," he said firmly, "if you want to hold prayer meeting, do it on your own land. Get off mine." He flourished the empty gun and the fearful natives drew back in horror as if he were truly cursed. Pastor Cobbett, still staring at the mutilated windows, made incoherent sounds and licked his parched lips.

"All right," Mr. Morgan said. "Who's going to help put these poles back in place?" No one moved. "Well, come on! You knocked them down."

Pastor Cobbett shrieked, "If anyone dares aid the infidel, God will strike him dead!"

"Please!" Mr. Morgan cried. "Shut up! Now you, Teofilo. Grab the pole." There was a deep silence. Many men must have wanted to aid the stranger, but they knew that when he left Matareva, Pastor Cobbett and the wardens would remain behind. No one would help.

"God be praised!" the pastor exulted.

Then a most memorable thing happened. In Matareva there was a girl named Maeva. Even on our island of beautiful girls she was handsome. She had very long hair that was envied by our women, strong arms and good teeth, but although she was already past twenty no man had married her because Pastor Cobbett said she was cursed of the devil because she refused to carry a lighted lantern at night.

Now she left the huddled crowd and crossed to where Mr. Morgan was waiting. "I will help you," she said.

"Wardens!" shouted the pastor. "Take that evil girl!"

"Reverend," the stranger said patiently. "For the last time, go home."

"Wardens! Wardens! Seize her!"

Mr. Morgan waved the empty shotgun at the crowd and said, "If you don't want to work, get out!"

Slowly the wardens withdrew. Now Pastor Cobbett stood alone, facing Mr. Morgan and the girl. "Maeva!" he cried in an ashen voice, both commanding and pleading. "Your soul will rest in hell."

Mr. Morgan turned his back on the lonely, apocalyptic figure and said to the girl, "You? What's your name?"

"Maeva," she said.

"That's an odd name. Bring me the hammer."

That night in my father's kitchen a group of Matareva men assembled secretly. They said, "The wardens are afraid of this man. Even the pastor can do nothing. It's time for us to drive our persecutors from the island."

My father said, "It would be fatal to start a rebellion that didn't succeed."

"With Mr. Morgan it will have to succeed," another whispered.

A warden came to the door and the men hid under the porch. "Everybody here?" the warden asked.

"Yes," my father replied. Then he crept across the yard where my mother plants the crotons and hibiscus and in a few minutes he was back with Mr. Morgan.

"Morgan Tane," our oldest man said, "you are at war with the pastor. Good! May we join you?"

"Look, old man!" Mr. Morgan replied. "I'm at war with nobody. Now don't bother me any more."

He left us, but on Saturday he discovered that he had been wrong. He was at war. It began this way. Maeva, who had been working with Mr. Morgan, had slept each night at her brother's, but on Friday the wardens waited for her and had beaten her severely.

Next morning she limped up to the new house and sat upon the porch, her nose dripping blood. Some old women who hated the pastor gathered in bitter groups along the road. No one spoke. A warden went past and took the names of all who were watching.

Mr. Morgan rose late that day, for he had been working hard all week. The old women saw him stretch, sluice his head with a bucket of cold water and look at his tongue in the mirror. Then he came onto the front porch.

He looked with cold fury at Maeva's handsome face, all smeared with blood. Next he looked at the crowd of old women. It was a long time before he did anything. Then he fetched a basin of water and there on the front porch fixed Maeva's nose. It had been broken. After that he took her inside.

All that day there was whispered bitterness across Matareva. Word passed that any plans for rebellion must be stopped, for again the wardens had triumphed. It was said that what had happened to Maeva had finally convinced Mr. Morgan that resistance was useless.

On Saturday night, therefore, the wardens raided my father's home with new brutality and beat him for some minutes, adding, "We know you were talking with the white man. We know everything."

On Sunday we gathered as usual at the lagoon and lined up as the wardens directed. The bell rang strangely through the shattered windows and our procession started toward the imposing door.

At this moment Mr. Morgan appeared barefooted on the porch of his new house. Behind him stood the girl Maeva, her face bandaged. With long, careless steps, his toes kicking dust, the stranger walked along the dusty road and right up to the line of wardens. "Which one of them was it, Maeva?"

The handsome girl, her hair down to her waist, stepped from behind Mr. Morgan and pointed fearlessly at one of the worst wardens. "That one," she said.

The white man lifted his shotgun and there was a terrified gasp from the crowd, but he handed it to the girl and said, "I showed you how to use this. If anyone—a warden, the pastor, anyone comes at me, kill him."

Then slowly, like a wave about to crash upon the reef, he went to the warden who had beaten Maeva and with a sudden grab pulled the hulking man out of line. In silence, and in fearful efficiency, he beat the man until it seemed as if his small right hand could drive no more. The warden was fat, cowardly. Twice Mr. Morgan hauled him to his feet and waited until the bully got set. Then with merciless blows he knocked him down again. Blood was spattered across the white uniform.

So awesome was this cruel scene that no one in the procession moved, but we could see the beating from where we stood, and when it became apparent that Mr. Morgan was willing to fight the entire force of wardens, one after the other, a murmuring restlessness agitated the crowd and it appeared there might be a general uprising, but this was forestalled by the appearance of Pastor Cobbett.

"No one must move!" he cried in his great prophetic voice, but when he saw the ruined face of his leading warden he turned pale. Mr. Morgan, tired and breathless, stood back on his heels, blood across his dirty, sagging pants.

He spoke first. "The wardens told you I'd run away. Well, I like it here. I'll probably stay the rest of my life." He grabbed the shotgun from Maeva and walked slowly back to his house alone, and as we watched him go, barefooted and bent forward, we knew that even though he would not lead our rebellion, he was from that day on an atoll man.

We never called him by any name but Mr. Morgan. He received twelve letters a year, no more no less, each from the United States Government. Once when he cashed a batch of his pension checks with a passing trader he said, "It's good money. I earned it. Got shot up in France while the rich kids in our block stayed home." His only other reference to America came one night when the ocean hammered the reef in great violence, making thunder. "Sounds like the Third Avenue El," he said.

We were much surprised that after the fight he did not take the girl Maeva home with him. It was obvious that he could have any girl he wanted. He was brave and he had a regular income. At night pretty wahines began to drift by his house, but he took no notice of them. When curfew rang he usually went right to bed and twice when girls braver than the rest snuffed out their lanterns and hid upon his porch, he put on his sagging pants and led them boldly to their homes, where he delivered them to their mothers.

It may seem strange to people not of the islands, but we were all offended, men and women alike, that a stranger should have come amongst us and found our girls undesir-

31

able. My mother was commissioned to talk this over with Mr. Morgan, and she asked, "Are they not beautiful?"

"They're all right," Mr. Morgan said, his hands in his pockets.

"Then why don't you take one into your house? To mend you clothes? To cook?"

"Look," said the man gruffly. "I don't want any women around."

Yet it was he who finally ended the foolishness of the lanterns. It happened this way. My mother is not easily put off. She knew that every man needs a woman for cleaning up, if for nothing more. So she went to see Maeva, whose nose had now healed. She said, "Maeva, you must not let Morgan Tane live alone. It is no good." But Maeva replied that when she looked in the mirror she was ashamed. The wardens had beaten her so that she thought herself no longer pretty. But Mother knows well how love works and she said, "He will look at the hurts you received for him and he will let you stay."

So Maeva combed her hair, made a wreath of frangipani for her head and washed her feet. Then she went to the new house with her bed mats. She arrived when Mr. Morgan was on the reef and by the time he returned at sunset a fine meal was ready.

"That looks good," he said, and they ate together. Maeva had a face that men enjoyed to look at, so they spent a long time eating and finally Mr. Morgan stood up and ran his finger along her nose. "It's not much of a nose," he apologized.

"You fixed it well," she insisted.

"It's all right," he said. "Now you must go home."

Maeva allowed tears to come into her eyes and said, "Morgan Tane, it is no good for you to live alone. See, I have brought my things." With her brown foot she pushed open the door to the small room and there on the floor beside his large bed lay her sleeping mats.

Mr. Morgan studied them for a while and then stooped down and rolled them into a heap. He tossed them over his shoulder and started out the door. "Please, Morgan Tane!" the girl cried. "Not while it is still light. The village will laugh at me."

He dropped the mats and sat with Maeva while darkness crept over the lagoon. "Have you a wife?" she whispered. "In America?"

"Me? No."

"I am sorry," she said. "I am sorry you do not know that

32

it is good for each man to have his wahine." She moved very close to him and that night he did not make her leave.

Of course the wardens noticed this and early next morning, when Mr. Morgan was out to buy some canned beef from the Chinaman, they descended on the house, and arrested her, being very careful not to hurt her in any way, for they wished this affair to be completely legal.

At the jail Pastor Cobbett listened to the evidence and promptly sentenced her to three weeks at hard labor. The jail doors were locked and Maeva went to work.

When Mr. Morgan returned with the meat, he assumed that Maeva had gone back to her own home for a while, but when noon passed he felt a little relieved that he was not going to be bothered with a woman about the house. He preferred not to be bothered, so at dusk he carried Maeva's bed mats back to her mother. Within a few minutes he learned what had happened.

In a blind rage he stormed up to the jail and demanded that Maeva be released. The jailer said Pastor Cobbett had the keys, so Mr. Morgan grabbed a chair and knocked the door down. Then he set Maeva free and when the girl stepped into the street she was surrounded by other girls, each with a lighted lantern. Angrily, Mr. Morgan took a big stick and broke every lantern. The wardens, seeing that he had no shotgun with him, started to close in on him all together, but he shouted for the men at Matareva, and at last the great rebellion was on.

We burned down the jail, ripped the handsome doors off the church and chased the wardens all across the island. Whenever we caught one we threw him back to the women who did many funny things to the fat men, I can tell you.

Under Mr. Morgan's direction all the wardens were finally herded together by the lagoon. Their uniforms were disgraced in the mud. Their heads were sore from women's fists. "You'll leave the island forever," Mr. Morgan said.

The men of Matareva then cried, "Where is the pastor?"

The mob rushed to his house, but he was waiting for us. He had been waiting since midnight, a small, watery-eyed man in a black suit. He appeared on the porch and slowly the rebellion stood at attention. Pastor Cobbett raised his eyes and moaned, "God will condemn the island of Matareva forever!" The men nearest the porch moved back.

Now Mr. Morgan came up and said, "Go on back to bed, Pastor."

"God will bring all the curses of Babylon upon you!" the prophetic voice cried.

"What do you know about God?" Mr. Morgan asked impatiently, jumping onto the porch and shoving the little missionary back into the safety of the house.

Then there was a shout at the lagoon, and Mr. Morgan had to hurry down there, for some women had got hold of the worst warden and were beating him up all over again. Mr. Morgan made my father's house the new jail and put three men to protect the wardens until a schooner could be sent to Tahiti.

The long night ended with everyone singing and shouting. Then suddenly there was a profound silence, for to the east, behind the church spire, the sun began to rise. It flooded Matareva with wonderful light, and it was a great majesty to all of us, for in my lifetime the people of my village had never before stayed up all night. An old woman began a few nimble steps, and soon the entire population was chanting the fine dirty songs of long ago. "Wahine! Tane!" The music grew louder and we danced.

In the soberness of daylight my father and the village leaders met with Mr. Morgan to discuss what must be done next. "Done?" he asked. "I guess we'll have to build a new jail."

"What we mean is, about the pastor?"

"Why do anything about him?" Mr. Morgan asked.

"We'll need a new government. We must report what has happened."

"We don't need a new government," Mr. Morgan said.

"But the pastor?"

"There's nothing wrong with him. You've just got to stand up to him, that's all."

"But Morgan Tane, now that you have led us ... We would like it if you agreed ..."

"Don't take things too seriously," he said sleepily. "It's just like in France. We had a rotten sergeant. We argued with him. Then we beat the living hell out of him. After that things were all right."

"You mean you're willing to have Pastor Cobbett stay here?" my father asked in astonishment.

"Why not?" the tired man asked, and with that he went off to bed.

The effect of these events on Pastor Cobbett was unbelievable. When the wardens were banished we expected him to flee also. Instead, he became more active than ever.

Shorn of his temporal power, he increased his spiritual dominion over us. We would see him night and day tirelessly tramping our atoll, exhorting people to mind the ways of God. He had no pride, no shame. He would burst upon unmarried lovers and stand there in the midst of their confusion, pleading with them to marry like decent Christians.

He was now in his sixties, a little man with a mass of white hair. He continued to wear black suits and his voice was more booming than ever. We were no longer required to attend church but most of us did, for he changed the service to make it more inviting. He introduced twice as many songs and even fitted his own religious words to robust island tunes. I think he knew that our women mumbled the original verses about love-making by the lagoon, but he seemed not to care so long as they came to church. And always there was that small figure, thinner now, probing into every corner of island life.

For example, he went boldly to Mr. Morgan's house and said, "Morgan, you and Maeva ought to get married."

"Have a chair," Mr. Morgan said gruffly.

"I don't suppose you've ever thought about it," Pastor Cobbett said, "but Maeva would like it."

"I don't think she'd care," Mr. Morgan replied.

"Why not let her decide?" the pastor suggested.

"Hasn't she had enough of your religion? Broken nose? Public shame?"

"Mr. Morgan," the pastor cried as if he were in church, "where God is concerned things like that don't matter."

"You'd better go, Pastor. Such talk makes me sick."

"I'll call Maeva." Without waiting for permission the little man went to the door and shouted for the girl to come in. She was pregnant at the time and seemed one great, placid ball of humanity.

"Pull up a chair," Mr. Morgan said.

"Maeva," Pastor Cobbett began, "I've come here to ask Morgan Tane to marry you. In the church. Would that please you?"

The black-haired native girl looked at the two men, the one who had broken her nose, the one who had mended it with his own hands, and although she knew that she was offending the latter she said quietly, "Yes."

Pastor Cobbett rose dramatically and said, "You're right, Maeva. Any decent Christian woman wants to be married." With that he left.

There was a long discussion between Maeva and Mr. Morgan, but he finally said, "I understand how you feel, but I don't think I'll get married."

Nor did Pastor Cobbett content himself merely with religious matters. He performed all his old governmental functions, aided now by a council of native men, including my father, and he evolved the new plan whereby we made a better grade of copra for sale direct to Belgium.

Once, after a long meeting about health rules, he excused himself and went back to see Mr. Morgan, who never attended any discussions.

"I'm not going to argue with you, Morgan," he said bluntly. "I just want to tell you that I've seen lots of white men in the tropics. They all face three inevitable tests. One, have they the courage to marry the girl? Two, are they proud of her when she is pregnant for the first time? Three, and when the boat arrives from their own country—it always arrives, Morgan—do they introduce the woman and her dark children to their countrymen?"

That was all he said, and he must have known a great deal about Mr. Morgan, for the white man failed each test. He never married Maeva. Furthermore, he was ashamed and perplexed while she was pregnant, indifferent when the girl was born. And when schooners put into the atoll, Maeva and the baby were forbidden to appear in the front part of the house.

Once an American yacht sought refuge in our lagoon, but Mr. Morgan avoided the crew. Finally three of them forced their society upon him with loud cries of, "They say you're a real Yankee beachcomber!" He did not invite them into his house, but they came anyway with three cases of beer. When they were brave with drink one asked, "Is it true you're married to a beautiful native girl?"

"That's right," Mr. Morgan replied, his shoulders bent forward and his hands in the pockets of his sagging white pants.

We never understood what he did with his time. He didn't write. He never read books. He didn't like to fish nor did he sit and yarn with people about the old times. He was a man who lived entirely within himself. He did not even take pleasure in his glowing wahine, who always walked five steps behind him when they went to the beach for a swim.

And yet we knew that here was a brave man, perhaps the bravest we had ever known. Because of this knowledge, our disappointment in him was trebled, for we had hoped that he might lead us to a better way of life, one with more purpose and happiness. He was not concerned with this, and painfully we discovered that he stood for nothing. He was a moral zero and we knew that such a man could never show us how to govern Matareva.

When I became the schoolteacher I understood why my father and the other old men returned at last to the pastor. He stood for something. Of course, when he ranted, "It's God's will!" we were no longer fooled. We knew that no man can say what God's will is, but we also knew it was important that we be led by someone who was at least concerned about what that will might be. We had hoped for a better man than the pastor to lead us, but failing that we had to make do with what was at hand.

The years passed and we forgot Mr. Morgan. Life passed him by and he walked the beach, a man of no consequence, a man loved by no one except perhaps Maeva. Then suddenly he was catapulted tragically back into the orbits of our village as he had been years before. Now the women of Matareva gathered before the white man's house and wept, saying to one another, "At least he's human, like the rest of us."

Maeva was deeply stricken with our most dreaded illness, tuberculosis. I am told that elsewhere this disease lingers in the patient's lungs for many years. It is not so with us. There is the racking cough, the pallor under our brown skins and the chest all caved away. There is nothing we can do against tuberculosis, nothing except die.

I often saw Maeva in the last stages of her illness. It was terrifying. Here was a strong woman who had fished off the reef in her own canoe, yet now she was thin as a ghost, her face fallen in. Here was a girl so beautiful that sailors from schooners would walk like schoolboys to her house, bringing gifts, yet now even her lovely lips were sunk into the gasping mouth. She lay on the floor where she had always slept, and no one could look at her without knowing that death must already be sailing his canoe at the reef's edge.

The effect on Mr. Morgan was something nobody could have predicted. He seemed to us never to have loved his wife, yet now he sat day after day with her, his unlighted pipe between his teeth. He had sent his daughter to a family down the beach while he sat in the silent house caring for the dying girl.

Once when Pastor Cobbett came to talk with Maeva, Mr. Morgan could bear no longer the sight of that vanished face and he burst from the house like a madman. He came rushing down to see my father and cried, "God! God! She just lies there!" My father took him for a walk along the lagoon but the pounding waves that roared upon the reef reminded the shivering man of Maeva fishing. The stars coming out were like the candles she had burned in his house. He walked mechanically until my father had to leave him, and all that night Pastor Cobbett stayed with Maeva. In the morning Mr. Morgan returned, apparently reconciled to what must happen. When the pastor had trudged off, the white man said, "The lagoon with stars upon it is beautiful, Maeva." So far as we knew, he had never before commented in any way about the atoll he had shared for many years. Now he walked endlessly among us, hurrying back to Maeva to tell her how we looked, what we were doing that day. Once he stopped me and grabbed me by the arm. "Have you ever seen heron crashing down on a fish?" It was a common sight, the great black bill snipping the water, but he stood there transfixed.

The next day Pastor Cobbett asked Mr. Morgan if Maeva would like to have a few prayers. Mr. Morgan said he didn't think so, but Pastor Cobbett said he would come in anyway. He was there when Maeva died, quietly as if not knowing that this sleep was different. For a moment Mr. Morgan would not believe that she was dead, and then he stood by the bed crying, "No! No!"

All night he stood there by the wasted figure on the mat. Our old women came to dress the body and they thought it improper that he should watch them, but he would not leave. When the village keeners came to wail their penetrating lament for the dead soul on its vast journey, he fell into a chair and kept his hands over his ears. The weird cry of the mourners drove him mad and he shouted that they must stop, but they could no more forsake the dead then they could stop the sun from climbing at last above the trees of Matareva.

At the funeral Pastor Cobbett stood by the grave and preached great moving words so that we all wept for this good woman who was dead, but before the pastor ended Mr. Morgan left the graveyard and returned to the lagoon beach, where he walked for many hours. Finally the pastor said to me, "You must talk with him. He would be offended if I did."

I followed him until he turned and saw me unexpectedly. Again he grabbed my arm imploringly and asked in a hushed voice, "Have you ever seen a star like that? Casting a shadow across the lagoon?"

I said that at Matareva we often saw that star and he

threw his hands across his face and cried, "There was so much Maeva could have shown me!" He walked off in agony and I watched him for a long time. Finally I went up to him and said, "Morgan Tane, I think we should go to the Chinaman's and have a beer."

"That's a good idea," he said.

We went to Ah Kim's and opened two bottles, but after drinking only part of his Mr. Morgan said, "I think I'll go to bed."

We expected this upheaval of his world to bring Mr. Morgan at last into the heart of our village, but instead it drove him further from us. He did not even bother to recover his daughter from the house along the beach, and the family living there were very happy to keep the girl as their own, for they prized a white man's child.

So once more we forgot Mr. Morgan. He caused no trouble, spent his money cautiously. Sometimes from my school window I would see him shuffling barefooted along the beach, his shirt open, his pants hanging low upon his hips. Often he did not shave and for days on end we might not see him. His daughter Turia was growing up, a bright, fine-limbed girl like her mother. Once Pastor Cobbett, now seventy-six, found her with a sailor off an Australian ship and punished her on the spot. Mr. Morgan, when he heard of this, said she probably deserved it.

That is how things were in 1941, and then one day a schooner called to say that Honolulu had been bombed. We had an old radio on Matareva and under Pastor Cobbett's excited urgings a man from the schooner got it working. For days on end the pastor sat transfixed before it, piecing together the news of war in our ocean. He borrowed a map from my school and called the head men of the village together. He proved it inevitable that Japan would invade Matareva and to prevent this organized a complete lookout system, a line of fighters for the beaches and a hiding place for the radio.

Early in his operations the frenzied little missionary approached Mr. Morgan, who said, "The Japs'll never bother with this dump."

"But in war we must be prepared!" the pastor argued.

"I fought my war," Mr. Morgan replied.

"But it's your nation that is threatened!" Cobbett cried angrily.

"They're tough. They can look out for themselves."

He would take no part in the wild plans evolved by the

pastor, but when the government destroyer put into our lagoon and reviewed what Cobbett had done the defense minister said, "Remarkable! Remarkable! All we need give you chaps is a radio for sending as well as receiving." Later the government had to impose strict rules about this radio, for Pastor Cobbett reported voluminously every four hours.

Yet it was this radio which finally brought Matareva full into the war. Pastor Cobbett was listening one rainy, windswept afternoon when he heard the lonely signal of an American plane, lost in a violent storm. He rushed into the road crying, "Plane trying to find Bora Bora!" We hurried to the radio and heard a plea for any kind of help.

I was handed the microphone, and for twenty minutes I repeated over and over, "C-47. C-47. This is Matareva. Bad storm outside the reef, but you can land in the lagoon." It was weird and haunting to be sending words that might never be heard. Then finally came the crackling whisper: "Matareva. Matareva. We cannot land on water. Have you level ground?" The men about me argued for a moment and I reported, "C-47. C-47. There is no land. Crash on calm water a hundred yards from shore. Our canoes will save you." I said this fifteen times and at last we heard the bewildered pilot: "I cannot get there before dark. Matareva. Matareva."

A tall figure stepped beside me, barefooted, stoop-shouldered, no shirt. Mr. Morgan said, "We'll put lights on the motus. Lights around the lagoon."

"C-47," I cried in the flat voice that betrays no hope, no fear. "We will light the lagoon as follows." I started to explain but the pilot broke in: "How will we know where the shore is?"

Mr. Morgan grabbed the microphone. "Come in, you damned fools," he snapped. "You've nowhere else to go. Head between the green lights. Land short of the red ones." And as I sat there, encouraging the pilot, Mr. Morgan dashed out into the rain and shouted for everyone on Matareva either to get into his canoe or take a light and stand along the reef. When the first lights blew out he cried above the storm, "Pastor! Didn't you have some extra lanterns in the church?" When a man near the lagoon cried, "No plane can land in this storm," Mr. Morgan snapped, "If we don't save them, they're too dumb to save themselves."

He took a motor boat and a dozen lanterns wrapped in whatever green cloth the women could provide. He called for volunteers and set out across the lagoon to where the great waves thundered on the reef. Night came, and about the entire lagoon you could see the thin ring of lights, green clusters to the west, a red cluster marking the landing course.

"C-47. C-47," I called. "Everything is ready. The canoes will be at your side within a minute after you land."

The pilot called back in an ashen voice, "The lights? All set?"

And then Pastor Cobbett took the microphone and said in a low powerful voice, "Pilot! God will bring your plane in. God is riding with you."

The wind howled but above it we heard the droning of a crippled motor. We had never seen an airplane at Matareva, and everyone along the lagoon, those with beacons and those who tensely clutched their paddles, stared into the sky. A wavering light appeared and an astonished cry rose from all Matareva. The plane was so big. It was so low.

It came roaring in between the green lights. Its wings dipped perilously toward the water, then straightened. There was a long hiss, a flash of spray and gas tanks exploding in the night.

Instantly our canoes dashed in among the flames and our pearl divers leaped into the crackling waters. Not one American was lost.

We had a night of wild celebration. Each man of Matareva thought himself a true hero. We spoke endlessly of what we had done, whose canoe had been first among the flames, which man had stood knee deep among the sharks, waving his green lantern.

There were six Americans and we were amazed at how young they were. Their navigator, no more than a boy, blubbered when he saw Mr. Morgan. "We had a million dollars' worth of medicine and radio in that plane. We lost it all."

"There's plenty more where that came from," Mr. Morgan said. He took the six men to his house and for the next three weeks Matareva knew such excitement as we had never experienced before. The talk was all of America, and slowly Mr. Morgan became involved. He said, "Forget Pearl Harbor. We lose lots of battles. But we win lots of wars." He stared pointedly at Pastor Cobbett and said, "We taught the British all about that."

Once the plane captain, Harry Faber, said, "It was almost a miracle! I was scared silly but when I got my last instructions from your radio I took off the headphones and said, 'Here we go!' Then I heard a voice as clear as I can hear yours saying, 'You are in God's care.' And even though the plane exploded, we all got out."

"What did the voice sound like?" Mr. Morgan asked.

"Deep. Powerful. Speaking right to me."

"It was a miracle all right," Mr. Morgan said disgustedly. But when the picket boat came to take the flyers on to Samoa, he followed them right to the tip end of the wharf and shouted, "Give those Japs hell!"

Now he was truly at war. The picket boat gave him a large map and some colored pins. He kept it at the Chinaman's, and there he and Pastor Cobbett would sit hour after hour marking out the radio reports. We called them Churchill and Roosevelt, and when portentous things happened like El Alamein or the entry into Paris, the entire island would celebrate.

When the war ended, an American warship came to Matareva to give the island a scroll thanking us for our part in saving an American crew. The pastor had a big day! He arranged formal ceremonies and appeared in his black suit to give a long invocation. At the end of the prayer an American flag was hoisted over the church and the American officials gave Mr. Morgan a medal "for improvising a landing strip under extreme difficulties." They also left the flag, which to our surprise Mr. Morgan nailed on the wall of his front room. When boys of our village came to talk with him about America, he served citronade and said, "Now there's one country you ought to see!"

He lived in this way until 1946, when a schooner from Australia dropped by and landed a young man in khaki shorts. Before he had left the wharf our girls were screaming, "Harry Faber! American pilot! He come back!"

He hurried right to Mr. Morgan's house and clapped the tall man on the shoulders. "I swore I'd get back here to say thanks." He brought us six crates of things contributed by members of the crew we had saved. There were radios, ice boxes, many jazz records, books and more than a dozen fine Army blankets. "All stolen," he said proudly.

We made a great festivity for Harry, and the record player was set up in Mr. Morgan's front room, beneath the flag, where we gathered many nights to hear Bing Crosby.

But before long we noticed that Harry Faber was rarely at these pleasant sessions, and my mother, who always hears these things first, said that he was spending his nights with Turia Vanaavoa, as Mr. Morgan's daughter was now called.

Soon everyone on the island knew about the love affair, except Mr. Morgan, whom no one told such things. Then one day an old woman said approvingly, "Wouldn't it be wonderful if the American married your daughter?"

It took about a minute for the implication of this question to reach his brain. He looked very puzzled and asked, "Turia ... Vanaavoa?" He seemed unable to remember that this girl whom he had rejected was his daughter. But next day he found a piece of paper and suddenly his life flamed into purposeful being, as if Turia, and dead Maeva, and lost America, and even the vanquished wardens had all thundered down upon him like stormy waves upon a reef.

He read the paper twice and said, "Damn such nonsense." Then he carried it straight to Pastor Cobbett and jammed it under his nose. "What do you make of that?" he growled.

The pastor lifted his spectacles, cleared his throat and read the following poem, which is now famous in Matareva:

SONG OF A TROPICAL TRAMP

I have wandered through the islands with hibiscus in my
    hair,
I've surrendered my ambitions for a life that laughs at
    care,
I have loved an island maiden when the nights were far
    and fair:
And I've seen the constellations upside down.

I have watched canoes go gliding on a fairytale lagoon,
I have heard the sun come raging up a day, a year too
    soon.
Then I've waited for Turia and the rising of the moon:
    And I've heard the wild sharks twisting near the
    shore.

When the schooner fled outside the reef to run before
    the gale,
When palm trees bowed their heads to hear the hurri-
    cane's wild wail,
Then her lips on mine were golden brown and mine on
    hers were pale:
    For I've seen the stars surrender to the storm.

Sometimes within the city streets I hear a curlew cry,
I see the reef spume leaping up to meet a cobalt sky.
Then the island fever has me and I think that I must die:
    For I've seen the atolls baking in the sun.

Pastor Cobbett finished reading and put down his spectacles. "What's it mean?" Morgan asked.

"The usual bad poetry a young man writes," the pastor explained. "I never wrote any, but I recognize the stuff."

"Is it anything serious?"

Cobbett rose and stood with his hands behind his back as if about to deliver a sermon. Then he saw his friend's agnostic face and changed his mind. "Two kinds of men come to the atolls," he said simply. "You came here and made a life. You were one of us, and our problems were your problems. You helped us, for better or worse. But other men come like birds of passage. They think it's part of growing up. To see strange places. To love strange women. Maybe they're right, but it's hard on the places. It's very hard on the women."

"That's what I thought it meant," Mr. Morgan said grimly. "But I never found much time for reading." Clutching the poem in his hand he strode back to his house, where he found Harry Faber reading a book. "You write this?" he asked.

Harry looked at the poem and said yes.

"It's time you left Matareva," Mr. Morgan said.

"What do you mean?"

The old man began to shout, the only time we ever heard him raise his voice. "Damn it all. I didn't save your life so you could come back and make a fool of my daughter." We were dumbfounded! We had even forgotten that Turia Vanaavoa was his child, and now after all the years he trembled with fatherly concern!

"Wait a minute, sir!" the flyer protested.

"I said it's time to go, Harry. You smart guys who come down here like birds of passage. There's a schooner out there. Get on it!" And that night Harry Faber was on his way to Tahiti.

The girl Turia was heartbroken. She had a copy of the poem and a guitar player set it to mournful music, which our wahines still sing with tears in their eyes. Mr. Morgan amazed us by insisting that Turia come back to live with him as his daughter. The Vanaavoas made no protest, for they had enjoyed the girl as she grew up and now it was time for her to have a life of her own. She started going with a young man of our village and when she became pregnant told her father that she wished to get married. "It's high time," he said.

The wedding was held in church, the last occasion on

which Mr. Morgan ever wore a tie. Later he gave a reception in his house, but we noticed that the American flag had been taken down. He gave an embarrassed speech about his daughter's happiness and then disappeared. When I went home I saw him sitting on the sea wall, the solitary man whom life had subtly surrounded as the coral polyps working on our reef once surrounded a portion of the vast sea and made it habitable. I was inspired to rush up to this man and say that we were proud he had made Matareva his home, but as I moved to do so, I saw that he was sitting with Pastor Cobbett. What they were talking about I do not know.

Polynesia

The prime minister of New Zealand was on the spot. The opposition cried, "Why hasn't the Governor provided social services for our Polynesian islands?"

Replied the minister in effect, "We have not provided old-age pensions because in Polynesia old people are cared for. We haven't built orphanages because no child is ever without a home. There is no need for mental hospitals because Polynesian life doesn't provoke nervous breakdowns. And there is no unemployment insurance because no islander would see his brother starve."

What kind of people built so gentle a civilization? They originated somewhere in Asia, perhaps in one of the valleys of India. Oppressed by more warlike tribes, they drifted eastward to the Malay peninsula. Even there competition was too keen, so they set forth on what have been termed "the most daring voyages the world has known." In their small canoes they made the Vikings seem like nervous homebodies.

In penetrating thrusts they touched at all the islands between Malaya and Peru, reaching north to Hawaii, south to New Zealand. When they encountered hostile natives (New Guinea, Solomons) they passed by and set up small holding stations on outskirt islands, so that even now in the midst of savage black areas you often find minute atolls containing fair-skinned Polynesians. In general, however, they pushed ever eastward until they reached the islands they now inhabit. (Scholars pooh-pooh recent theories about settlement by ancient Peruvians, drifting westward on ocean currents.)

Polynesia—many islands—is vast in extent, meager in land and population. Its thousand atolls reach from the Date Line to the 110th Meridian, 70 degrees compared to 55 for the United States, yet altogether it contains fewer square miles than Connecticut, fewer people than Oklahoma City.

Yet Polynesia's influence on world thought is far greater than its size would warrant. Musical names like Tahiti, Rarotonga, Bora Bora carry an emotional freight to all the cold countries of the world, and Polynesia, the dying civilization, haunts the minds of white men who destroyed it.

This provocative empire begins at Tonga, the independent kingdom with a parliament of its own. Farther east are the

Samoas, the western portion of which, governed by New Zealand on behalf of the United Nations, is probably the finest remaining center of Polynesian life. Nearby is American Samoa, a jovial little island three or four generations behind the rest of Polynesia in cultural advancement. Then come the heavenly and little-known Cooks, owned outright by New Zealand, followed by the world famous Establissements Français de l'Océanie containing immortal Tahiti, the tragic Marquesas and the myriad atolls to the east.

Far to the south lies lonely Pitcairn (British) to which the *Bounty* mutineers fled, the scene of debauched tragedies and stately aftermaths. Far to the east off the coast of Chile, which governs it, lies enigmatic Easter Island, once the center of an intricate civilization now so completely obliterated that even its prolific writings cannot be deciphered.

People from one group of islands usually do not understand languages used in other groups—about as related as Italian-French-Spanish—but strangers rapidly learn the new speech. For example, the basic Polynesian word for house is *whare*. In Samoa it becomes *fale;* in Tahiti *fare;* in Hawaii *hale*; in the Cooks *are*; in the Marquesas *hae*; in Mangareva *hare*; in Fiji *vale*.

Nor do the people look alike. In Tonga they are stocky and dark, in Samoa large and fair, in Tahiti somewhat stunted and darker than the Samoans.

There it is! Vast, insignificant Polynesia, ruled badly by many different nations, victimized by all kinds of robbers. It is not rich. Its people seem to have few causes to be happy. It is a backwash in the world's eddies, yet these trivial islands have imposed on history the most lasting vision of the earthly paradise. Why?

To find the answer one must visit Tahiti, the emotional capital of Polynesia. Surpassing even Bali and Capri in attracting gifted people from all over the world, Tahiti is the symbol of hedonism. It is a small island, with only 600 square miles, and may be likened to a sombrero touching a derby. The only good lands are around the rims of the two hats, the interiors being mountainous and inhospitable. Their is not enough land for everyone, not enough food to supply the population. (Most comes from Australia.) The natives are not noticeably attractive, since early in life they lose their teeth—a heritage from the decayed stumps of English sailors—and many are afflicted with elephantiasis, next to leprosy the most repulsive of diseases. In spite of all this the island is a paradise, and here is why.

Tahiti is beautiful. The mountains are like no others I have seen. Treeless, they are sometimes orange red, sometimes iridescent green. They are shot through with splendid valleys, sheer cliffs and catapulting waterfalls. From one casual spot no one has even named you can see nine superb falls, two of them hesitatingly delicate as they drift down in spray. The black beaches of Tahiti are unparalleled, composed of volcanic ash across which tumbling breakers glisten. At the feet of waterfalls are pools crisp with mountain shrubbery about their edges, cool and inviting to the swimmer. The road round the island is a changing panorama of magnificent scenery, but nothing on Tahiti is so majestic as what faces it across the bay, for there lies the island of Moorea. To describe it is impossible. It is a monument to the prodigal beauty of nature. Eons ago a monstrous volcano exploded and the northern half sank into the sea. The southern semicircle remained aloft, its jagged peaks looming thousands of feet into the air. From Tahiti, Moorea seems to have about forty separate summits: fat thumbs of basalt, spires tipped at impossible angles, brooding domes compelling to the eye. But the peaks which can never be forgotten are the jagged sawedges that look like the spines of some forgotten dinosaur. They stand together, the peaks of Moorea, forever varied, forever new. I once watched them for thirty days, at dawn, at sunset, in the heat of day, and they showed an infinite variety. They were only nine miles across the bay, but in a storm they would seem to be at the very edge of the horizon. At dawn the orange sunlight made them angry ghosts. At dusk lingering shadows made them quiver in the sky. They reached into the air and pulled down clouds; they dressed in gold and purple. If Tahiti boasted of nothing more than these faery silhouettes across the bay, it would still be one of the most fortunate of islands.

Tahiti encourages the wacky life. In a world grown exhaustingly serious, here you can observe the rich variety of life. In one day—that's less than sixteen hours—I witnessed the seven following incidents: (1) There was a small riot at the school, more noise than trouble, but a leading businessman who had no doubt often suffered there in his youth jammed on the brakes of his truck, leaped astride the hood and shouted fiercely, "Vengeance! Vengeance! Death to the teachers!" Having provided this vocal support, he got back into the truck and drove off. (2) A woman of forty appeared for dinner at the leading hotel dressed in sneakers, midriff bathing suit and sable overcoat. (3) In a crowd of girls I noticed one with an ugly complexion and a strange manner. Finally I asked about her and was told, "That's Jules from Moorea. He didn't want to be a man so everybody agreed that he could be a woman." (4) At the boxing matches a gigantic bruiser dashed to the middle of the ring and cried, "You have been very patient. All night you have waited for a real champion of box. Well, here I am!" At the bell he roared out, swinging like all the windmills of Holland. Four minutes and twelve seconds later he was colder than a dead squid. When brought to, he jumped up and bellowed, "I'll be lots better next week." Explained his manager: "We have to keep him likkered up to keep him brave. This time we overdid it." (5) A Frenchman with no money arrived in Tahiti and announced that he was the son of a viscount. Everyone knew he wasn't, but they humored him. "After all, if he wants to be the son of a viscount, why not? The funny thing is that after two years we began to think he was, too." (6) A wealthy man and woman were flying back to Honolulu. Two Tahitian girls said they'd never been up in an airplane and would like to go along. Three weeks later we received the news: "We enjoyed the trip so much we're going on to Paris." (7) The copra crop was bad in Paea and parents hadn't much money for Christmas, so the chief sent word to all children: "It is very sad. Père Noel just died."

Tahiti insists upon relaxation. When James Norman Hall, famous co-author of *Mutiny on the Bounty*, was worried about a novel that wouldn't come right, he developed stomach ulcers. "Nonsense!" said local doctors. "In Tahiti? It's impossible." Nevertheless Hall flew to Honolulu for expert advice. "Ridiculous," said the specialists. "Upset stomach, that's all." Citizens of Tahiti were much relieved because no one can get an ulcer on that island. In Tahiti you see more happy people per hundred than in any other part of the world. Here even the Chinese smile! Here even men are allowed to dress comfortably!

Tahiti has unique sex freedom. A bitter critic of the island has sneered that its charm is explainable solely in terms of the "erotic mist" that hangs over the island. It was, perhaps, prophetic that the first geographical feature named by white men was Point Venus! A foremost allurement has always been the frank affection native girls have for white men. Reported one missionary: "And out of pity to these girls, as we saw they would not return, we took them on board; but they were in a measure disappointed. . . . Nor did our mischievous goats suffer them to keep their green leaves, but as they turned to avoid them they were attacked on each side alternately, and completely stripped naked. . . . It was not a little affecting also to see our own men repairing the rigging, attended by a group of the most beautiful females. . . . No ship's company, without great restraints from God's grace should have resisted such temptations; and some would probably have offended, if they had not been overawed by the jealousy of the officers and by the good conduct of their messmates."

I remember as a boy poring over the accounts of early navigators and coming repeatedly upon that cryptic phrase "so we put into Tahiti to refresh the men." Or, as one captain added, "with limes and otherwise." Yet the fact is that women like Tahiti as much as men do. Those who enjoy it most are married couples, and surely the great visitors whose writings have made the island famous were not all in search of a sexual holiday. Yet the old reputation lingers, aided by the diligent efforts of roistering girls who come each year from outlying islands to have a last fling before settling down. The skipper of a visiting ship saw two such wahines climbing the ladder. The oldest asked, "Captain, you like to make love?" He was astounded and said, "You're very pretty but . . ." "Not me!" the girl cried. "I asked for my friend. She's very shy."

Tahiti is French. Much of the charm is due to the tolerant, democratic French. In Samoa all people are classified according to five rigid degrees of whiteness: all white, 75%, 50%, 25%, all black. The courts decide your classification, and once it is given, your education, ability to own land, type of medical service and social life are rigidly set! In Tahiti a man is a man. If he is white and a drunken bum, people ignore him. If he is pure Tahitian and a jovial spirit, he is an honored guest everywhere. Under British or American rule the great humane spirit of Tahiti would have been stifled. Under the more benevolent French it has magnified year by year.

But above all, Tahiti is Polynesian. Without these remarkable people, the island would be nothing. With them, it is a carnival. They are generous, courageous, and comic. They wake each morning to a fresh day that has forgiven the previous day's outrages. In pursuit of money they are irresponsible. In pursuit of happiness, dedicated. They are the perpetual adolescents of the ocean, the playboys of the Pacific.

Beyond these six attributes, Tahiti has another which

makes it doubly exotic: the town of Papeete, a rambling tropical center of 13,000. It is one of the world's great ports of call, comparing with nostalgic and wonderful names like Rangoon, Singapore, Shanghai, Valparaiso and Acapulco. Yet it is grander than any of these, for at Papeete the ships of many seas dock right along the main street. From the stern of a Hong Kong junk to the post office is twenty yards. From the bowlines of a San Pedro yacht to the bank is one city block. Without qualification I can say that the waterfront of Papeete, with Moorea in the background, is unequaled.

The daily pageant is more beautiful than a ballet: The *Orohena* is back from the Gambiers to discharge a load of copra. Huge half-naked Polynesians stride up and down the gangplanks, wreaths of flowers about their heads. The seasick *Hiro* is in from Bora Bora with a cargo of turtles that are flopped over on their backs and left kicking in the sunlight. The loveliest schooner in the South Pacific, both by name and sweep of line, *L'Oiseau des Iles,* is leaving for Makatea's phosphate mines, its trim white prow cutting the bay's green water. The *Mitiaro,* barely afloat, limps in with a cargo of retching Chinese from Moorea, the boat of which it was said, "When they tie it up at the wharf people half a mile inland start to heave." The Chinese stagger off, catch their bicycles as they are landed and pedal away to market. And everywhere are the small bonita boats, their roofs covered with palm fronds, their holds choked with iridescent tuna caught that morning.

In fact, the port of Papeete is so colorful that yachtsmen who have circled the globe say, "There's only one thing wrong. It should be located right off the tip of Sandy Hook, because the way it is now, you get there too early in the cruise. After Papeete, everything else is an anticlimax."

Yet many visitors despise Papeete. They have no words strong enough to describe its shanties, its poor water, crowded alleys, honky tonks, bootleg opium, wildcat gambling and rapacious prices. They say, "You hear about the glamorous beaches, but you can't find one where the average yokel is allowed to swim." Such critics leave in a hurry and complain endlessly to friends back home that "everyone who ever wrote about Tahiti from Pierre Loti to Frederick O'Brien is a liar." As a much-disappointed friend of mine said, "Papeete? What a bust! Tia Juana without tequilla."

There is much to the comparison, for Papeete does resemble a Mexican border town, not so dirty along the main streets, dirtier in the alleys. To those who insist that all picturesque towns look like Siena or Stratford-on-Avon, Papeete will be disappointing, but to others who love the world in all its variety, the town is fascinating. My own judgment: any town that wakes each morning to see Moorea is rich in beauty.

I like the cluttered streets and the neat parks, the narrow alleys and the wide verandahs, the jumbled stores each with some one unpredictable thing for sale: *"En Vente Ici. Dernier Arrivage.* Campbell Soup." I like the noisy poolrooms, the perfume shops, the policemen on rickety bicycles, the Chinese dress shops with sewing machines whirring like mad, the dreadful hotels, the worse ice-cream stands and the happy faces. It has been aptly said of Papeete, "It drives Englishmen, schoolteachers and efficiency experts crazy." There is something childishly delightful about every aspect of the place. One movie house advertises the *Hunchback of Notre Dame* as "Super-sensational, Archiformidable, Hyperprodigieux!!!!" Whereupon the competition states baldly of René Clair's *Le Million*: "The best motion picture in the world." At which the first springs a trap: "Le *Hunchback* avec Gene Autry!!! Pas de Conversation. Beaucoup de Cowboys!!!" In fact, so powerful is the lure of a cowboy picture that the leading popular song in Papeete goes:

> I'm a frustrated Tahitian cowboy
> A ridin' the range every night.
> The wahines are thick as cactus
> But there's never a dogie in sight.
> Oh I want to be just like Gene Autry
> With bright shiny saddle and spurs,
> But all I can find to round up
> Are bee—oo—ti—ful brown skin-ned girls.

To appreciate Papeete you must see it around the clock, for its mood changes with each hour. It's Christmas Eve, the end of a very hot day, and a cool breeze blows in from Moorea, whose golden peaks are slowly disappearing. There are many public celebrations, but the finest is at the Hospital, where all the children of town seem to have gathered: little French girls in crisp dresses, English boys in knee breeches, Tahitian children with eyes like embers, Chinese youngsters with their black hair pasted down. They all squeal at the spectacular fireworks.

After the fiesta older boys and girls go down to the waterfront, where a carnival, housed in grass shacks, is in progress. You get five rifle shots to knock over a clay target, five baseballs to knock down a pile of tin cans. Kiosks sell pineapples, drinking coconuts and chunks of pie. There's roulette, ring-tossing games, and a big black box into which you can't see but out of which you must fish the big prize. The game is called, in big letters, OU EST GUS? At one end of the carnival is the sailors' dive, Les Révoltés de la Bounty, boasting huge murals in the rawest colors ever mixed which show leading scenes of the tragedy with a gruesome Fletcher Christian leering from the shrubbery of a huge beard, surrounded by kegs clearly labeled RHUM.

Now the crowd converges on Quinn's, a mixture of dance hall and bar. It has no equal in the Pacific. Around a small floor are ranged postage-stamp tables behind which are booths with wooden benches. By the door, on a raised dais, sits the frenzied American pianist Eddie Lund, the Tahitian wonder boy. Small, underweight, bald-headed, he is a jovial tunesmith who produces one lilting song after another. He has written an island opera, dozens of popular ditties and hymns. He writes only Tahitian words, rare bouncy jobs, and is the second-best-loved American ever to have hit the island. He looks like Eddie Foy, eats huge meals, loves to gamble with Chinamen and starts every conversation with "Hey!"

Tonight he has a big crowd, and here is a chance to see once and for all whether there are any beautiful girls in the South Pacific. So you take a seat near immensely fat Lucy Drollet, who rides to every dance on a trembling bicycle, sporting an expensive evening gown. She never dances herself, but each of the couples stops by to say hello, for she is one of the island's grand old ladies.

Then suddenly your head begins to snap! That glorious creature, who was she? That willowy thing nearly six feet tall? Before you, dancing with American beachcombers, French officials, sailors and plain tourists are some of the most striking girls you've even seen. "Like Madison Avenue on the first warm day in spring, but with fewer clothes on." Where did they come from?

Most of them are half-castes. The real beauties are apt to be Chinese-Tahitian, the next most attractive French-Tahitian. You don't see them about the streets of Tahiti very much, but on big nights at Quinn's they bedazzle the eye.

Then you begin to chuckle. No matter how tired you are, you have to laugh, for there on the floor is a dumpy, dark girl with extraordinary hair that reaches to her waist. With a frangipani behind her right ear (looking for a fellow; left

53

ear, got one, not in the market) a leering look of joy across her flat face, she is in town for a big Christmas Eve. A friend whispers, "Just down from Bora Bora. Look at her stomp." And somehow she drives away your vision of the slim beauties, for she is the classic Tahitienne that the great navigators met years ago; the happy, shamelessly lewd, delightfully primitive island girl. If you smile at her once too often, she will bang her way to your table, push aside your wife or sweetheart and cry, "You like to dance with me?"

At eleven-thirty the crowd begins to desert Quinn's and move toward the main square, where a huge gathering presses against the cathedral doors. At this late hour there is no chance of getting into the midnight Mass, but loud-speakers will relay it to the congregation outside. Then comes a whisper: "It's Eddie!" and the frenetic little pianist, dressed soberly, hurries through the crowd and shortly the organ begins to peal forth the exquisite French hymn to Christmas, *Cantique de Noel*. Christmas, which had arrived in Fiji twenty-two hours ago, now comes to Tahiti at the very end of a long, happy day.

At one in the morning the Mass ends, and dancers hire taxis which whisk them out to the Lido, a dismal barn east of town, where a weary orchestra hammers out old tunes. The dancing is apathetic until a sailor smashes a beer mug on the floor and a riot ensues. When it ends, a livelier mood prevails and someone begins to chant a Tahitian stomp.

There is a breathless moment. Then everyone starts clapping hands. The band springs into hectic action, and from the crowd out dashes a kind of hurricane. It's the Bora Bora girl! She kicks off her tight shoes and you can feel her big feet saying, "Ah!" A slim, no-hipped boy leaps into the air and lands before her. "Wahine!" cries the crowd, and the Tahitian hula is in progress.

It is difficult to describe this dance without sounding inde-cent. An army chaplain once said, "If there weren't so much noise and good fun, that would be a very dirty dance." It combines the maximum sexual suggestion plus the violence of primitive joy plus the bellylaugh of a riotous Falstaff. It goes to the ultimate roots of life, man-ness and woman-ness without shame or smirk. I know two white women who felt sick after seeing their first Tahitian hula. Said one, "It's like watching people undress. But worse." I was with a naval of-ficer who watched with his lower jaw ajar. Finally he broke into an immense grin and cried, "Oh, boy! If they could see this in Richmond!"

And pretty soon those slim beauties who looked so coldly perfect at Quinn's kick off their shoes and start whooping it up with bank tellers who suddenly resemble long-repressed collies allowed to romp in the park. No one has ever come close to apprehending the spirit of Tahiti who has not seen a group of staid people mysteriously erupt into the frenzied gyration of this sexual pageant.

It is now toward four on Christmas morning and taxis begin wandering back to town. Then comes perhaps the most silent and inspiring moment in the South Pacific, for you drift into the quiet port where the majestic schooners ride peacefully and you see the sleeping forms! Under each verandah monumental bodies lie sleeping on the pavement, their heads on doorsteps, their massive hips pressed against the warm concrete. Perhaps they arrived on a late schooner. Or they are waiting for the market to open. Or they had a room but it was too stuffy. They are asleep, close to their earth, like majestic statues laid down to rest.

You watch in the darkness and realize with a shock that you have seen all this before! But where? Then you remember! Gauguin! He saw these massive forms, this somber beauty, the mysteriousness of this race. There is no single way to prepare yourself for Polynesia comparable to memorizing Gauguin. In Tahiti today, on this hot Christmas, you will see every color he used, every model he studied. The significant fact about Gauguin, who died in terror, hating life, is that in Polynesia he painted with infinite love. His brooding spirit crept into every canvas; his compassion rests with every painting.

You leave his sleeping people and walk along the noiseless alleys to the market, a sprawling concrete area protected by iron fence, and there you see the real Christmas gifts of Père Noel: the food, the flowers and the fish. You see long rows of tuna glistening in the pale light, whole sides of beef, legs of mutton, dressed pigs. Within the barred fence not a figure moves, but you see stacks of fruit, baskets of vegetables. The towers of food are so beautiful—golden, yellow, green, purple—that you wish they might never be disturbed.

Then slowly daylight begins to touch the upper peaks of Moorea and the sleeping sidewalk figures shake themselves and wander to the market. By five o'clock the watchmen allow stall keepers to slip inside. Then a pleading, pointing hullabaloo begins: "Save that bonita for me!"

"Those bread-fruit are mine." And at five-thirty the gates swing open. In rush the housewives of Tahiti.

The scene is magnificent, something Verdi would have staged had he composed an opera about Papeete. There is a wild dash, a haggling in four languages, a fine battle for the day's food. You plunge into the maelstrom and are swept along to where the flowers are: frangipani, hibiscus, croton, bougainvillea, bird-of-paradise, and everywhere the bunches of tiara tahiti, a gardenia-like flower with an irresistible odor.

The full riot lasts an hour and then a worse begins! The buses arrive! They back up to the gates, gaudily painted and with long benches providing seats for thirty. At seven o'clock eighty-one people are crammed inside. Outside hangs every conceivable kind of island produce, including an entire side of beef flapping in the dust. The top is a miniature market with bicycles, a baby carriage, three beds, two live pigs and a dozen vegetable gardens. The truck starts feebly. It rumbles along for two blocks and stops in front of a restaurant, out of which come eleven men who somehow climb aboard dragging three pigs whose squeals would wring the heart of Nero. The music of Papeete is the piercing scream of pigs, and never did such good food make such terrible protest about becoming so.

As you watch this riotous end of Christmas night there comes a final catch at your heart, for there in the bright sunlight is the Bora Bora girl! Her sailor is almost asleep on her shoulder. She is carrying her shoes in her left hand, munching a mango in her right. Her red dress with the big yellow pattern is pulled awry, but her big expressive face, wreathed in wilted flowers, is gleaming. She is very happy.

What kind of people live in Tahiti? Four kinds: Tahitians, Chinese, Frenchmen and other Europeans, mostly English and American. (There is no American consul for hundreds of Americans, but there is a Belgian and a Norwegian, for one national each!) It will be interesting to meet some of these people, for they prove that diverse races can live together in harmony.

For a real Tahitian family consider the Bambridges. "Notable," says a prominent member, "because we are probably the only natives not descended from a queen of some kind!" Old Thomas Bambridge was a fire-eating English missionary with a gift for carpentry and an eye for native girls. He had twenty-two children, of whom John Bambridge stayed in Tahiti. John married a handsome native girl, one of whose sons went to the United States, where he became well known as a musician. When his first wife died John came upon the English pirate Tapscott, a hell-raising renegade who had abducted a wife from the cannibal islands. The old free-booter had a beautiful daughter whom John married. They lived on into the twentieth century, rich and respected, famous for being the first Tahitians to own an automobile, a Model-T.

By the pirate's daughter Bambridge had nine children who were to make the name historic. George became mayor of Papeete and served for nine years. He built an important store, made a fortune in copra and was acknowledged head of the clan.

Richard was the terror of the family and was sent to New Zealand to study farming procedures which would help Tahiti. He stayed eighteen years and returned with the announcement that he was fed up with farming. Thomas had somewhat the same experience with mechanics in America. A family sleuth was sent to track him down. "They met by accident on the streets of Los Angeles but Thomas said to hell with Tahiti." He didn't return till many years later. In the meantime brother Lionel became the business genius, organizing several corporations and many sidelines, from plumbing to dressmaking.

Then William astonished the family by becoming a movie star! He played in many Hollywood productions, including *Tabu* and *Mutiny on the Bounty*. A relative says, "He usually played the native chief but he was also very good as village constable." At one period of film shortage the local movie played *Mutiny* two or three times a week. "We all kept going to see Roustabout Willie say to Captain Bligh, 'No, thanks. No rum. It makes me dizzy.'" He returned home rich and is still a famous figure about town.

Tony Bambridge, the youngest son, was impressed with Willie's career and decided to string along. He now owns an impressive chain of island theaters (13), is an importer, runs a hardware business, holds immense areas of land and serves as business head of the family. He has thirty-two nieces and nephews, several dozen in the next generation. He works on the principle, "Give them what they like," and has several pictures which he runs over and over. The choicest is *Aloma of the South Seas*, "the purest corn ever grown, and in Technicolor." It is so completely ridiculous that it packs them in, howling with delight at the blunders. Another sure-fire hit is *South of Tahiti*, which has a big scene with a tiger. Says a critic, "The house goes wild when that beast appears, because on most islands south of here there aren't even any mice."

The Bambridges exemplify much of Tahitian life. Closely knit, generous, pushovers for John Barleycorn, they have a gay life. Combining all bloods, they travel anywhere at the drop of a hat, feel at home across the world, are happiest in the islands. After they struck it rich they began to wonder about those English Bambridges from whom the old missionary had sprung, so they got in touch with a family-tracing outfit in London, and sure enough the original family was located. George Bambridge wrote a careful letter extolling the Tahitian branch's respectability. Back came a heartening letter which ended, "We assume that your family still represents full-blooded English stock." George wrote an effusive reply explaining about the pirate Tapscott, the cannibal's daughter, the many Tahitian beauties and the strain of American Indian. He never heard from the English line again.

The Chinese counterpart of the Bambridges is remarkable fifty-year-old Ah You, who looks about thirty-five. The father of thirteen children, this prosperous storekeeper is also leader of the Chinese community. As president of the Association Philanthropique Chinoise it is his job to collect money to keep local Chinese from becoming indigent. (Only 13 accept support). He is also a member of the school board and active in politics.

Ah You remains a citizen of China, as do all but ninety of his countrymen. After the war two boatloads of longtime residents were repatriated, it being the goal of most Chinese overseas to die in the homeland. (Local whites mourn: "Those damned Chinks took a million and a half dollars home with them, all picked up from American troops.") But many have come back to Tahiti "because they found China wasn't even fit for dying in."

Ah You and his countrymen constitute no problem in Tahiti. They intermarry with Tahitian and whites, behave themselves and do all the island baking and clothes manufacturing. They also run the laundries at prices which should make them millionaires the first year. (Clean a suit: $4.00. Do an ordinary 76¢ wash: $3.92.)

Ah You's thirteen children will all receive the best education their franc-sharp father can provide. The three oldest boys attended California universities, the first going on to Columbia for his master's. The oldest daughter studied dress-making with Maggie Rouff in Paris and is now the island's fashionable couturière. (Her first dozen dresses were flops: "Tahiti women don't need the padding required by the French.")

His other children attend Catholic school—the family attends no church, is strictly Confucianist—for which he pays 80¢ per month per pupil. He hopes his money holds out long enough to send them all to college. The boys insist upon America; the girls want Paris. In the meantime they troop off each week for private tutoring lessons in English at the home of Mrs. Smallens.

Ah You and his family typify the Chinese in Tahiti: hardworking, well-heeled, law-abiding, prolific, education-hungry. They all feel that the coming of Communism to China will not affect them, in which they are probably wrong, for in the South Pacific no matter how important men like Ah You become, the ultimate power in each community is the Chinese consul. Soon there will be a Communist consul in Papeete.

As for the white men in Tahiti, none is more colorful than handsome gray-haired, fortyish Lew Hirshon, whose business ventures have been the talk of Tahiti for the past fifteen years. The son of a well-to-do New York family, he was drifting about the world after college and stumbled into Papeete. So far he has stayed nineteen years. Early in his visit he met a fabulous Greek woman who taught him theosophy "and the purposeful goodness of daily living." He has put her principles into action and has spent his money freely to help Tahiti, and himself. He owns the most famous island schooner, *Hiro*, named after a great Maori navigator in the age of fable. He also runs a laundry, the ice plant, part of the main hotel, a copra plantation, a prosperous pig farm, a flock of sheep and numerous smaller enterprises. He's had the good luck to make spectacular flops of several ventures (tuna canned on the spot, wine from pineapples) so that people do not have to think of him as a superman. "Lew's just a guy who is trying."

He keeps well informed (*Saturday Evening Post, Time, Atlantic, New Yorker*) and will argue passionately about anything. Known as a "quick burn" he is specially infuriated by two questions often asked by tourists: "What's the matter with So-and-so? Why would a decent chap like that waste his life in a dump like Tahiti?" (Lew: "Maybe because he damn well likes it here.") "How many natives are there in Tahiti?" (Lew: "We're all natives. There's about 30,000 of us.")

To appreciate the wonder of island life, you must attend

59

one of Lew's *maa tahiti,* a Sunday feast in the old style. You sit in a large dining room that overlooks the Diadem, a circle of jagged spires that form a crown, but after a fleeting glance you forget the scenery. On banana leaves—when ironed they lie flat like linen—a mammoth feast has been spread. Large crocks of coconut milk will form the basic ingredient, for into its rich sweetness will be tossed raw fish, taro, breadfruit, baked bananas, lobster, shrimp, chopped onions and mussels. The smell is wonderful and you dip your hands in, for no spoons are allowed at a *maa.*

The trick is to eat everything with the maximum amount of intake so that your host can hear that you enjoy the feast, but you can't do so well because James Norman Hall, across from you, is in good form, while Bouzou, the great guitarist, can be heard in the next county. At your side slim Bill Stone, gifted writer of children's books and perhaps the sharpest mind in the island, shows you how to handle the roast pig when it comes by on a giant platter. There's a German count, a French banker, people of all bloods, all accomplishments. Conversation is in four languages, the most common single word being *fiu,* Tahitian for anything unpleasant: "I'm fiu on that dame." "I'd have some more pig but it would make me fiu."

But above all the chatter one voice is dominant, a very low, musical contralto belonging to Lew's breathtaking French-Tahitian wife Elianne. In a green-and-white pareu she is the perfect hostess, alternately listening to her husband or rocking the place with irrepressible tales about Paris and New York. She's the leading singer on the island, and her records—you'd swear it was Ezio Pinza—are famous in the Pacific. Elianne passes the four wines, after which Bouzou plays on his guitar and the guests watch island girls do the hula, and when you go home with the ring of good talk in your ears, the taste of rich wine on your lips, you swear never again to ask why good old So-and-so stayed in Tahiti. You know!

There are other white men who do not live so well as Lew Hirshon. One Frenchman spends less than a dollar a year, lives with the chickens under a native porch. An American makes it on $270 a year—one can of tinned meat a day, coffee on week-ends—but the days of free and easy beach-combing are past. It takes money now.

Consider the case of two good-looking young Americans from Los Angeles. Homer Morgan and Hank Clarke were two G.I.'s looking for something to do after the war. They stumbled upon an advertisement for shark fishermen willing to invest some money in a venture which was bound to clean up millions in Tahiti. The bait caught them but never the shark, and they wound up with a boat and a shack on the beach "facing the damnedest view of Moorea you ever saw."

They say Tahiti is twice as much fun as anyone ever told them, but they add, "You can't live on less than $140 a month." They figure their budget this way: $75 for lodging and food; $35 for having fun; $15 for emergencies (more fun); $10 for taxi fares (still more fun); $5 for odds and ends. A dance date at Quinn's with four drinks for yourself and girl comes to $4.00. If you can collect a gang—always simple in Tahiti—and hire a truck you can do Quinn's and the Lido for about $6.75. Their principal trouble is that they keep falling in love with girls who live a $3.00 taxi fare out in the country. "We thought of taking them home by bus, but when we got there we found 64 people in 19 seats."

One of these days they'll return to the States and take jobs, "which could prove catastrophic." They have several negative comments on the beachcombing life in Tahiti: Not much cultural life. No intellectual stimulus. No decent library. Restaurant food is disgraceful. (An average Texas 45¢ lunch: $1.40.) But I noticed that Saturday after Saturday they turned up at Quinn's with the most dazzling beauties on the island. When I reminded them of this they said, "Well that does compensate for the poor library!"

Tahiti has always attracted interesting people. My favorite is James Morrison, one of the *Bounty* mutineers whom terrible Captain Bligh described as follows in his list of criminals to be apprehended and hung: "Boatswain's Mate, aged 28 years, 5 feet 8 inches high, sallow complexion, long black hair, slender make, has lost the upper joint of his forefinger of the right hand, tattooed with a star under his left breast and a garter round his left leg with the motto, *Honi soit qui mal y pense*."

Morrison had a high old time on Tahiti, liked it so much he refused to accompany Christian to Pitcairn. He was captured by the *Pandora*, lived chained in the horrible Pandora's Box, survived the loss of that ship on the Barrier Reef of Australia, being the last man to have his shackles removed as the hell ship went down. (Several of the mutineers were not released and perished with the ship.) He stood naked for two days in the broiling sun, having been forbidden by his captors to stand in the shade, and lost much of his skin. In despair, he dug a grave in the sand and lay buried to his neck until a new ship was ready.

He stood trial in England and heard his defamers swear that during the mutiny: "James Morrison was looking over the taffrail and called out in a jeering manner, 'If my friends inquire after me, tell them I am somewhere in the South Pacific.'" His manner and courage were such, however, that the court acquitted him, whereupon he rejoined the Navy and served with honor as a gunner!

Captain David Porter was another worthy. In charge of American ships of war, he grew tired of chasing British vessels across the Pacific in 1813, so he varied his duties by setting up the colony of Madison in the Marquesas, which he formally annexed to America. War becoming again pressing, he abandoned the colony, which was promptly murdered.

Dorence Atwater, of Connecticut, won in Tahiti the distinction of the longest tombstone inscription on record. It happened in this way. At the earliest possible age he enlisted in the Union Army, was promptly captured and tossed into notorious Andersonville Prison, where at risk of his life he compiled a secret list of all Union soldiers who died. Back in civilian life, he tried to peddle the information to families of the bereaved and ran afoul of the law. After much wrangling he was rewarded for his bravery by the consulship at Papeete, where he sired an impressive family. His immense tombstone narrates, frontside, the salient facts of his life, backside the entire history of Andersonville, in fine print. It is a symbol of the abiding affection in which Tahitian families hold the old daredevils who came among them.

But Tahiti would never have become world famous if only hell-raisers had loved the islands. To this remote haven have wandered men of great genius, and it is their work which has broadcast the mysterious charm of Polynesia.

The French sent Paul Gauguin and Pierre Loti, who is now commemorated by a florid statue at the pool he made famous in his lush story of Tahiti. The statue is something of a disappointment to the local French. A fiery young novelist arrived some years ago with the cry, "It's a disgrace! In a French colony! No statue of the immortal Loti!" He took up a subscription, went back to Paris and had the statue made. When it was erected the local patriots received a shock: It didn't look at all like Loti. It looked exactly like the young novelist!

The English provided Robert Louis Stevenson, Rupert Brooke and the queen of gush, Beatrice Grimshaw; while the

Americans sent Herman Melville, Jack London, James Norman Hall and lurid Frederick O'Brien. It is provocative to remember that the greatest American novel was conceived in these waters, for without Melville's stay in Tahiti and the Marquesas there would never have been a *Moby Dick*. As for Hall, he is the most universally loved American ever to have lived in Tahiti, and one might safely include all Europeans in the comparison. His work is a kind of tribal accomplishment. Boys in Papeete will tell you sorrowfully, "Jimmy is bogged down on Chapter 18." A Chinese adds, "I hear Hall is going through hell on Chapter 18." Then a cable arrives from Honolulu: "Got past 18." The news is flashed about the island. At Quinn's Eddie Lund cries to passing dancers, "Hey! Hall says he's past 18." And everybody is happy that their Jimmy is back on the beam.

But there is another side to the French islands, tragic, lonely, terrible, and no one has perceived it so devastatingly as a thin, mystical Frenchman, one of the greatest navigators who sailed the Pacific, one of the most thoughtful men ever to have immersed himself in an alien civilization. Alain Gerbault was a world-famous tennis player, a gifted writer, a man passionately addicted to the sea. In a pitifully small boat he circumnavigated the globe, and that was his undoing, for he saw the Polynesians. Emotionally he remained a child, obsessed with the terrible tragedy of the French islands.

Listen to a Polynesian: "Alain searched the world over for peace of heart. He found only cruelty, the savagery of white men. He saw my people sitting glassy-eyed while their history and their grandeur dropped away. Alain told me of the wonderful woman who once had known all the chants. Now she got drunk every day. 'Hello, Alain. I am drunk because my fine son went away.' He was ten kilometers down the road. The next day, 'Hello, Alain. I am drunk because my son, he came home.' "

Gerbault despised the French policy of selling grog to natives simply because France made a lot of money on wine. (In 1946 returning native soldiers were denied civil service jobs, were paid off in licenses to sell liquor.) He was horrified when he found impoverished natives drinking clorox or worse. He compared their low estate with what Bligh had reported in 1788: "If at any time one of them has been induced by the European seamen to intoxicate himself, such unqualified contempt and disapprobation are manifested toward him by others, and he seems to feel so strongly the impropriety of his own conduct as never to be guilty a second time, even though earnestly entreated."

Gerbault excoriated Papeete with its cheap white civilization. He called it a "forlorn and disgusting town." When the French colony tried to lionize him, he ignored them with insults. When the government passed a decree forbidding natives to wear the old pareu, he bought himself a red one and went barefooted through the streets. He tried to waken France's conscience to the tragedy of Oceania, of the noble Marquesas where ninety-nine out of a hundred had died of disease and despair. He saw those majestic, spired islands when the valleys were empty of sound, when the great artists in wood were no longer even remembered.

"It was a tragedy that never left his mind. He could find no equal to such ruthless destruction by drink, venereal disease, murder and plague. Here was desolation complete, planned and cruel."

Alain Gerbault died in 1941, "a solitary of the oceans, the poet of the Pacific." He left behind a book, *A Paradise Is Dead*, a terrible indictment of all who have betrayed the islands: "the stupid and ferocious administrative machine, the reign of mediocrity, the sailors who debauch the girls, the tourists who bring only the gospel of gold." He was happy in only one part of Polynesia, and he always referred to that island as "Bora Bora above all." Where is this remarkable island, considered by most judges to be the most beautiful in the world?

I saw it first from an airplane. On the horizon there was a speck that became a tall, blunt mountain with cliffs dropping sheer into the sea. About the base of the mountain, narrow fingers of land shot out, forming magnificent bays, while about the whole was thrown a coral ring of absolute perfection, dotted with small motus on which palms grew. The lagoon thus subtended was a crystal blue, the beaches were dazzling white, and ever on the outer reef the spray leaped mountainously into the air. That was Bora Bora from aloft. When you stepped upon it the dream expanded.

On Bora Bora lived one of the proudest Polynesian peoples, the last to surrender to French rule. They were brawling, freedom-loving, rugged, good-looking islanders, relishing the old songs and dances. Many visitors other than Gerbault referred to this heavenly spot as "Bora Bora above all."

Then in the dark days following Pearl Harbor the American Government, as a result of secret negotiations with loyalist French forces, invaded the island with bulldozers, juke boxes, airplanes and lots of money. James Norman Hall has described the cataclysm in *Lost Island,* whose title betrays his Gerbault-like reaction to the invasion.

But was it a tragedy? I think not. In the last stages of war I was sent to Bora Bora to write the secret history of our occupation and I saw no tragedy. I saw a human comedy, as Balzac understood that poignant phrase. For example, we were governed, Navy-wise, from Samoa, and once a stuffy commander came over to give us a lot of trouble. At a dance where the local girls flourished, this tin-trying-to-become-brass made a series of disparaging remarks about the island skipper. Finally a local girl could stand it no longer. "Worthington!" she shouted. "Hold my teeth." Thus stripped for battle, she flung herself across the officers' club and butted the commander right in the belly. After that we had less interference from Samoa.

Traditionally Bora Bora was an island where girls loved to have babies which they could give to older couples who had no children, where fathers built their daughters separate cabins "so they could be alone for their courting." Imagine dropping several thousand young American men into such a society! The result, as one observer said, "was astonishing and prolific." The local missionary was able to keep some semblance of order until a lively Bora Bora girl produced a red-haired American son. After that the riot was on. Soldiers and sailors protested when they had to go back to the States, and the islanders protested even more when the last contingent was pulled out. They had found a type of society they liked, a body of men they loved. I probed into all the records of Bora Bora and can say that our men were not a disgrace to their country.

Listen to Homer Morgan and Hank Clarke reporting: "Bora Bora is the loveliest island we ever saw. Maybe that's because the people knew right away that we were Americans. Wherever we went families hauled out the handsomest kids you ever saw and said, 'American baby. Nice, eh?' We counted 103. Half an hour after we landed we were given a bicycle, a free meal and a tour of the island in a jeep. They treated us like visiting potentates and when we left they said with tears in their eyes that they hoped the Americans would all come back some day."

The nature of my work on Bora Bora drove me to a consideration of the moral problems involved in the submersion of Polynesia. I knew the tragedy of the Marquesas, the disintegration of Tahiti and the brutal annihilations of the Peruvian slavers. No one could even explain such barbarities, let alone condone them; yet I had to conclude that Polynesia could never have escaped the onrush of white civilization, such as it was. These islands were doomed before the white man arrived. The finest young people were associated in fantastic societies which made abortion obligatory. Even the languages were dying. Once-noble Tahitian does not use the following consonants: b, c, d, g, j, k, l, q, s, w, x, y, z— nearby Rurutu also drops f and h, thus having the most meager alphabet known—replacing them by glottal stops between vowels, so that the language sounds like a series of grunts. (In Tahitian *oe* has four different pronunciations, depending upon the glottal stops: 'oe was once koe—you; 'o'e was once koke—sword; o'e was once onge—famine; plain oe—bell.) And as for bemoaning the intrusion of white blood, Polynesians themselves are a mixed blood: Indian, Malayan, Javan, Fijian, I could see no more reason to lament the loss of strictly Polynesian characteristics than I do to bewail the submersion of Picts and Jutes into what later became England. A good people developed there. A very good people is developing in modern Polynesia. (In Aitutaki 76% of births, 1943–46, were half-American children, and the island is reported as never happier, the children never more healthy.)

Population is on the increase. Health services multiply each year, and clean youngsters play basketball and soccer. (In Bora Bora it's baseball; in Samoa, cricket. Educational facilities are being constantly improved, and the standard of living is being raised. Sentimentalists who moan against natives improving their diet with refrigerators and can openers—"Why, they live on Chinese bread, Australian beef and American pork and beans"—could complain with equal logic that dear old ladies in Boston no longer dip tallow candles because they prefer electricity.

Consider just one small improvement in native life. On the eastern end of Tahiti lives Paeara Tavaearai, a patient, handsome-faced man of sixty. He lives forever on a straw bed, for he has elephantiasis. His hands are like obscene hams, his forearms like the trunks of trees. His legs, stretched helplessly apart, are so big they cannot be moved. Their skin is hard and scaly, like diseased bark. He appears to have no toes and, worst of all, the same gross inflation has reached his scrotum. He has a disease for which there is no cure.

How did it happen? Years ago he was infected by a

mosquito which pumped into his blood a host of minute baby worms, called filaria. (The disease which causes elephantiasis is filariasis.) In his body these worms prospered until they became visible to the naked eye—four or five inches long, as thick as a thread—and dangerous to the lymph glands which they congested. Gradually the glands, especially those in the leg, became clogged, whether from the bodies of dead worms, or from their excretions, or because of scar tissue formed by constant irritation is not yet known. At any rate the glands stopped hauling away refuse which now began to collect in the leg.

The first sign of trouble was a crise (kreez), a long, painful red streak along an arm or leg. In time it went away, but inevitably it came back, and when enough years had passed, elephantiasis developed. No one bothered about it much, for it was not a killer. The legs did not become gangrenous because the circulation of blood was not affected. The sick merely hid in back rooms, lived off charity and had no hope.

That is, they had no hope until two spanking bright young Americans arrived from the University of Southern California to help a brilliant French doctor attack this incurable disease. Dr. Henry Beye, a Johns Hopkins graduate, is a gray-haired young specialist in tropical medicine. With the aid of a new drug, hetrazan, he is able to kill microfilaria in the human body. (Mysteriously, microfilaria, the offspring of adult worms, cannot develop into baby worms unless they pass through the body of a mosquito. Most Tahitians carry microfilaria in their blood, harmlessly.) What hetrazan does to the adult worms is not yet known, but Beye thinks it kills them, too. Of course, no drug will reduce the swollen limbs of advanced elephantiasis, but tight bandaging has brought the dried, calloused skin back to pliancy and has effected marked reductions.

Beye is aided by a bullet-headed Kansan, Dr. Allen Edgar, who is death on mosquitoes. He states flatly, "In five years we could lick elephantiasis on this island! All we have to do is kill the mosquitoes." With DDT, house inspections and clean-up campaigns he is making a big start. Pessimists say, "We've always had elephantiasis. When the Americans get tired and go home we'll have it again." But in a single year Edgar has effected an immense improvement. (Worst breeders of mosquitoes: rat-eaten coconuts, old automobile tires.)

Two experiences disturb his health program. House 33—he has a number for every house on the island—is set amongst some of the neatest mosquito-free residences in Tahiti. But when he reaches it on his weekly inspection, he shudders. It's a big, rambling affair with verandahs, long steps and flapping shutters. Six or seven men lounge about, no shoes, pandanus hats, sleeping in the sun. A variety of women live there, too, plus numerous children. There's a lot of singing, a lot of mosquitoes. In the back, under a tree, two pretty girls in skimpy pareus drowse while a third strums a guitar. When Dr. Edgar approaches with his mosquito trap the girls summon enough effort to shift their legs so that he can see if any mosquitoes have gathered. "Don't let me interrupt," he says as he studies the brown ankles. "You won't," they assure him drowsily.

Farther along he meets another defeat. Here he has set up a control area, "to be left just as dirty as it always was," the idea being that mosquito counts would be made here and then compared with the spic-and-span areas which his men had cleaned up. But the local chief, hearing about how fine the rest of the island was looking, organized his people at night to give the area a real brush up. The result: the horrible example has fewer mosquitoes than the DDT areas! Edgar has threatened the chief, but every night the land is swept clean. Says Edgar: "A ridiculous way to conduct an experiment."

Another American who has had an astonishing effect on Tahiti is dour, tall, competent Leland Carver of Ogden, Utah. An unpaid Mormon missionary, he arrived some years ago with a visionary plan for a great temple. He bought land near Papeete and pitched in. Now it's completed, a gleaming white, rambling one-story affair built of 60,000 cement blocks he himself poured. The temple, with its fine organ and rich woodwork, is probably the most striking building in the South Pacific. Say the natives proudly: "The only place in Tahiti with nine toilets!"

Tahiti has always had close ties with America. In whaling days it was a stopover point. During Prohibition it was a massive loading port for rum runners that supplied Mexico. But in recent years Americans have been extremely unpopular in Tahiti. Putting it bluntly, they weren't wanted. In fact, after Russia and Tibet, this island was the most difficult spot in the world for an American to visit. Only the wealthy could meet the financial requirements. (Large deposit refunded in monthly installments after you left the island.) Inflation was astronomical—$1,700 car: $9,000; 89¢ laundry bucket: $11.20—living quarters unavailable, and police surveillance objectionable: If you didn't spend enough money you were asked to leave.

A Frenchman has said apologetically of this period: "What we really wanted was a cinema in San Francisco called Tahiti. Rich Americans would go there, see a colored movie of Moorea, get a frangipani lei, and watch two Tahitians dance. As they left, they'd hand us $3,000. That way we'd have the money, they'd have seen Tahiti, and Papeete wouldn't be cluttered up with American tourists."

When I applied for a visa in New York I was told, "Forget it. We just don't want tourists down there." In San Francisco I was goaded into making a classic blunder: "But I've got to get there. I'm a writer." The woman in the consulate laughed derisively, "Writers we don't want. You all turn into beachcombers."

In desperation I went to Papeete without any visa at all, and the police were so astonished that I would risk a thousand-dollar plane ride when the chances were that I'd be tossed out, that they let me in. And when I landed I found once more that glorious Tahitian sunlight, the happiness, the friendliness. (In terms an American will appreciate: On the first day three strangers offered to lend me their cars. I took them, in turn.)

Moreover, I found that Governor Anziani, a well-trained economist, had come out from Paris determined to remove the insults under which Americans had suffered. The welcome is now wholehearted. There's even an official committee, with government funds, to make the American feel that he is an honored guest. A new hotel is planned, new swimming beaches, bright attractions. In the meantime, at Les Tropiques, you can rent a five-room bungalow ten feet from the lagoon and with a view of Moorea for $80 a month.

But for many years the cost of a trip to Tahiti will be great. By plane you can get to Australia for less ($640) than you can get to Tahiti ($650). By boat it's very difficult. Big liners no longer call. Small freighters are jammed months in advance. ("Sorry! We can't even put your name on the waiting list for the next eight months.") And when you reach Tahiti you ought to count on spending about $500 a month. You can get by on $300 if you skimp on taxis, but the businessmen say frankly, "We want the rich tourists, not cheapies who have a high time on five bucks a day." Says the earlier apologist, "We still want that $3,000, but we realize we have to take the tourist, too."

A primary cause of high prices is the inadequate money

system. The lowest practical unit is the five-franc note, equal to 8¢. (There are coins and notes of smaller denomination, but rarely used.) Therefore, everything that in another country would be a nickel is 8¢—ice cream, shoe strings, bananas—which is pretty bad, but dime articles are worse. They cost 16¢!

In addition, the money that is available is the filthiest, raggedest, most loathsome stuff that could be passed from hand to hand. I have just come from the bank and have fourteen notes before me. There are six different sizes, the largest suitable for a place mat at a bridge luncheon, the smallest about the size of a Liberian postage stamp.

Not one of the bills is untorn. The worst is indescribable, a tattered, sweaty smear with all corners missing. The best is mended with a chunk of brown butcher paper. Each is begrimed, sleazy, and repulsive.

I asked a Frenchman how a colony could tolerate such a currency. (No wallet can be devised to hold the fodder. Some women carry raffia bags a foot square.) He replied, "So much of it wears out while in use that the bank makes an automatic profit of 4%." The most ridiculous aspect is that even the Government quotes prices for which no change can possibly be made. (Eighty centimes for a letter.) Today in Tahiti's largest store I was given my change in matches! At the post office you get it in postage stamps, "which," adds the Frenchman, "get lost, so there's another ½% profit!"

Yet in spite of costs, Tahiti is worth every cent you spend. In one week I met eighteen couples who had "stopped by for a month or two." The average length of time they had lingered on was eleven years! Said Bill Stone, "I knew what I liked when I saw it."

The other islands of Polynesia are equally difficult to visit, equally rewarding. If I could vacation on only one Pacific island I would choose Rarotonga. It's as beautiful as Tahiti, much quieter, much stuffier and the food is even worse. But the climate is better and the natives are less deteriorated. But to get there you need special permission from the New Zealand Government.

For Tonga you cable the prime minister. If you have enough money, a return ticket, and a place to stay, you may get in for two weeks. Says the Government frankly, "We have no room for more people." For Western Samoa you can get a transit visa fairly easily, but if you want to stay any length of time you need personal permission from New Zealand. American Samoa was very difficult when I applied.

Only high Navy brass could grant permission: "If you can prove financial responsibility, tetanus shots and a legitimate purpose we can let you land for a short stay up to October 1. After that, impossible." All Pacific governments are afraid of a postwar, atom-scared flock of beachcombers. "Keep Out" signs are posted everywhere.

Yet these islands are enchanting to visit. On Tonga many years ago a devout English missionary heard the majestic native voices and devised a unique Arabic numeral system of musical notation. He reasoned, "With such talent why should they sing bang-bang hymns?" Now, in Tonga, you can hear a massed choir of five hundred sing *The Messiah* with local soloists. You refuse to believe that such sounds are possible from the human throat. I heard a choir of fifty do Brahms, and the effect was like the ocean hammering into the unequaled caverns on the south shore of the island. Here the sea is impounded in vast cups, and it spouts fifty feet into the air through blowholes. There is not one spout here, but a five-mile line of them, marching in the moonlight like some weirdly beautiful army off to a ghostly war.

Western Samoa is composed of two large islands and Upolu contains probably the finest remaining Polynesians. Its men and women walk like gods with unmatched dignity. Never will you see in London or Paris old men so handsome as these Samoans. They are politically alert, intellectually able. And their island is a masterpiece of quiet charm. For example, the road from Faleolo airport to the capital at Apia is a dreamy path of sun-speckled beauty.

On either side small villages crowd down upon the asphalt. Flowers of all description festoon the way. Each house is a work of art, a lozenge-shaped platform from which rise golden pillars of palm wood. Upon them is rested a thatched roof, perfectly proportioned, intricately designed with patterned sennit. There are no walls, simply bamboo slats which can be dropped as needed. Nor are there interior partitions, other bamboo slats being shifted about as needed. Stones about the houses are whitewashed. Grass is kept so immaculate that it forms an endless park. Sometimes to the north the ocean is visible, while to the south rise the big hills of Upolu.

No island, not even Bora Bora, had a more profound effect upon American troops. Along the main road are several shady pools where Samoans have always bathed. It was rather difficult to get Marine trucks past those pools when fifteen or twenty native girls were soaping down, their sarongs

71

stretched out upon the bank. It was equally tough to get aviators back to camp when all along the road, in houses with no walls or partitions, the same girls went to bed by lamplight.

And yet for all its sensuous charm—Samoa is very hot, very wet, at times tropically oppressive—this island causes any thoughtful American much heart searching. Here is why. The Germans held Samoa for less than a generation, yet in that time they did more to improve the island—they provided better health services, finer roads, better economic systems—than America provided her Samoa in forty years! Judging solely by material criteria plus the ability to keep order, the colonizing nations of the Pacific rate in this order: 1 Germany; 2 the Dutch; 3 Great Britain; 4 Japan; 5 United States; 6 New Zealand; 7 France; 8 Australia; 9 Chile.

But when you have made that ranking, you immediately think about the goals of human life. What is a good government? Perhaps the best is that which provides the greatest happiness for the greatest number, assuming certain fundamentals like a just police force, a money system and fair trials. By such standards the worst governing power ever to have hit the Pacific was Germany. Wherever she went there is cleanliness—and hatred. There is order—and undying lust for revenge. So forgetting the good roads and considering only the happiness of people, the order among nations becomes: 1 France; 2 United States; 3 The Dutch; 4 New Zealand; 5 Great Britain; 6 Japan; 7 Australia; 8 Chile; 9 Germany.

Furthermore, if you consider also Hawaii and the Philippines—and if you forget Puerto Rico—America's accomplishments are enviable. We have been decent and humane, one of the good colonizing agents. In Samoa we have been less than adequate—for example, Samoans are not citizens—but even so our fair play has impressed the natives. Recently they announced that although they hoped Western Samoa would gain her independence from New Zealand, they preferred to string along with the Americans. "We have been well treated," they said.

In any discussion of Polynesia the question always comes up: "Is it really a good place in which to escape the pressure of modern life?" Let's look at some cases!

Are you a businessman fed up with labor troubles? In the Cooks you'll be plunged right into the middle of a jurisdictional wrangle between two labor unions, one of which is probably Communist.

Are you worried about Communism? In Tahiti you'll find that a clever French Communist flew out to dominate the last election. Everyone is worried lest their new deputy, a native for the first time in history, vote the party line when he gets to Paris.

Do you dream of playing pirate and hunting buried treasure? You can if you conform to the requirements of the local ordinance, "Treasure Hunters, Governance of," Section C-2° of which reads: "If the treasure is found on private property, 50% to the discoverer, 25% to the owner of the land, 25% to the territorial government."

Are you tired of screwball politics? In Tahiti the most powerful party is organizing an election campaign on three promises: "For each family—more land. Free legal service. Two hundred feet of sewer pipe."

Do you want release from the cost of living? You can get by in almost any part of Polynesia for only 50% more than you pay in Illinois. In Tahiti, of course, the cost is twice as much.

Are you seeking a refuge from the atomic bomb? Here at last is a legitimate reason. Polynesia presents, because of its isolated geographical location, one of the least likely targets on earth. "But," says a cynic, "I'll bet they thought the same about Guadalcanal in 1937."

There is only one good way to decide whether or not you really want to knock about Polynesia. Would you travel five thousand miles for a chance at a trip like this?

At dawn you climb aboard the schooner *Orohena* lying at the dock in Papeete. The cook shows you to your bunk and you find to your amazement that you will share postage-stamp accommodations with four men and women you've never seen before, and who don't know one another! You will sleep with your face five feet from the man above you, and the steward explains that women usually agree to undress first, while the men wait on deck. You'll live that way for thirty days.

The *Orohena* casts loose and stands out in the channel for Moorea, heading northeast toward the atolls. Each morning you will waken to find some new coral island off the bow, some enchanting lagoon, "and," adds the supercargo, "some godforsaken place where flies are as thick as regrets in hell."

At Rangiroa you pick up a hundred natives with pigs, guitars, breadfruit and babies. They sleep on deck, right outside your bunk, and some of them sing all night. They are going south to build a Catholic church.

At Hikueru, made famous by Jack London's description of the terrible hurricane that devastated the island, you watch copra being loaded and for the first time smell the sickening odor that will haunt you for the next three weeks. At Tatakoto the copra bugs come aboard, and from then on you scratch your hair continuously.

The food is good, clean Navy fare prepared French fashion. You've grown to like your bunkmates and the cook assures a lady passenger, "After you've slept with a man for thirty days you know the best and the worst."

Now the lazy days begin. You drift from island to island, sometimes going ashore to barter for pearls, sometimes swimming in the lagoon. Then you drop far south toward Pitcairn and put in at tragic Mangareva, a superb and broken lagoon which used to house many thousands of natives but which now holds a few hundred. Here you see the massive church whose Christian doctrine could not save the lives destroyed by unchristian practices.

Then for several days the sunlit beauty is shattered. You see the yachts *Denise* and *Hotu* cracked up on the ever-dangerous reefs which year by year destroy unwary ships. At Vahitahi tragedy strikes your own schooner. The reef is engulfed by a stormy surf. The longboats try to reach it, but the sea lifts one high into the air. A seaman falls out and the boat crashes down on him. You see him perish in the sea he always feared yet blindly followed.

Now the captain picks up a hundred and fifty deck passengers, bound for the consecration of the new Mormon temple in Tahiti. They sleep everywhere, in the holds, on deck, in life boats. Two huge fellows lie on the railing itself, their legs wrapped about spars. Water gives out and you get one quart a day for everything: drinking, washing, laundry. Food runs low and you watch the cook open one tin of bully beef after another. The man in the bunk opposite you is completely fed up and begins to leave his underwear on your bed. It is steaming hot whenever the schooner lies to for more copra.

So one night you sleep on deck, and the vast sky looms above you in shattering majesty. You get to meet some of the deck passengers—they pay 80¢ a day—and you begin to learn their songs. In the darkness they point out misty islands and narrate old tragedies. You find that you are surrounded by people you like, the calmest, kindest, most generous you have ever known.

Regretfully one day you see the jagged peaks of Moorea.

"Ah!" the island wahines cry from the prow. "*Voilà!* Papeete!" Slowly the *Orohena* warps her way to the dock. Three women rush up with leis of frangipani. You step ashore and your knees won't work and you even kiss on both cheeks the man who left his socks on your pillow. You've had a schooner holiday for $165, and then comes the test!

As you lurch along the streets of Papeete you see a blackboard sign in a Chinaman's shop: "*Vendredi. Le Navire Monotui pour les Iles Marquises.*" And if you're the kind of person whose heart skips a beat and you cry, "The Marquesas! That's for me!" then you'll like Polynesia.

Let me try to compress the wonder of this perverse, hilarious world into one incident. When missionaries came to the Cooks they arrived so intent upon saving souls that they forgot to turn the calendar back a day. For a generation they drove ship captains crazy. On Sunday in the Cooks no one ashore would work. The next day would be Sunday aboard ship and the crew took off. Sometimes when a holiday followed Sunday the situation became chaotic.

Everyone tried to make the islanders hold their calendar back a day. "Have two Saturdays in a row," the Government begged, but they said that would be foolish. They liked their calendar the way it was. Then somebody had a solution so perfect for Polynesians that it was accepted at once. They had two Christmases in a row! As the first one ended, everyone launched right into a second Christmas Eve, and for two days the islands were a festive madhouse. After that the Cook calendar was back in line. Asked the islanders, "Why didn't they think of that in the first place?"

Povenaaa's Daughter

*He saw these massive forms, this somber beauty,
the mysteriousness of this race.*

North of Tahiti the *Hiro* began to roll, and before long all
passengers were seasick. That is, they were all sick except a
remarkable Polynesian woman of fifty who sat on one of the
forward hatches munching something she had pulled from a
paper bag.

She was ridiculously fat. Her jowls seemed to run down
onto her shoulders and her body, from neck to knee, was one
unbroken ball of suet, covered by a blue-and-red Mother
Hubbard which swayed solemnly about her ankles with each
motion of the wallowing ship.

The bag from which she selected her dainties was quite
greasy, and two men, long hovering at the vomit point, were
thrust over when they saw what this large woman was eating.
For Maggi—that was her only name—was eating fish heads.
She would lift one from the bag, inspect it, then crack it with
her teeth. There would follow a sucking sound, a smacking of
lips and then more cracking, as if a dog were worrying a
marrow bone. When she had quite drawn out all the
goodness from the fish head she would toss the skeleton in an
arc over the rail and into the sea. Then she would loudly
suck each of her eight fingers before probing once more
among her inexhaustible supply of delicacies.

At the ship's rail hung a limp Chinaman, so sick he
thought he must die. Four times, just as he hoped he was
becoming accustomed to the wicked roll of the *Hiro*, a fish
head would go whirling past his face and he would collapse
with retching. As the fifth head passed an inch from his nose
he stormed in outraged protest, "For the love of God, fat
woman! Stop eating those fish heads!"

The woman in the Mother Hubbard put down her paper
bag, wiped the grease off her huge cheeks, and looked at the
miserable Chinaman. Placing her hands at spots where her
hips had once been she taunted, "You've thrown over more
than half of yourself. Jump after it!" Then, with ponderous
grace, she rose and lurched over to the rail, where she
swatted the sick man on the back. "Throw it up, Kim Sing!"
she cried. She drew a greasy fish head from her sack and
rubbed it under the Chinaman's nose, holding him by the

76

waist as he heaved in agony. "That wasn't so bad, was it?" she asked like a mother.

Affectionately she dragged the near-dead Oriental to her hatch. After consuming two more heads she tossed the bag into the ocean and wiped her hands on the ample hem of her dress. Then, belching twice, she adjusted her huge bulk to the ridges on which she sat and asked, "Did you accomplish anything in Papeete?"

For a moment the sick man was unable to reply, but somehow the vast amplitude of the woman encouraged him and he said, "I made a contract for all my vanilla."

"Good!" she said with a crisp finality that meant she was saying nothing about her own mission to the capital.

But toward morning the Chinaman saw her smiling to herself in considerable satisfaction and he asked, "What did you find in Papeete that makes you smile, Maggi?"

She was not to be tricked. She laughed to herself for a moment, then rose and hurried to the rail. She peered into the stormy night and caught, along the horizon to the east, the first faint glow of dawn. It was a mere thread of pale light, yet as it played upon the tempestuous waters she could see, past the prow of the ship, waves breaking upon a reef. She studied the scene for some moments until she was satisfied that it was indeed her reef. Then she returned to the hatch and cried in a loud voice, "We'll soon be there!"

This caused a great commotion among the restless steerage passengers and they crowded the rail to catch the first sight of Raiatea, the ancient island from which all of Polynesia had been settled in the old days. In the dark mistiness of dawn they saw the island mysteriously appear out of the ocean, the spray high upon the reefs, the rain clouds low upon the historic hills.

Then suddenly, like the shifting mood of a wind that scurries across the surface of the sea, the passengers stopped mumbling to themselves, and Maggi, forgetting the Chinaman, elbowed her way forward to the prow of the ship, where she stood in the morning rain. She stood with her head cocked as if she were listening for a sound. But she was not, for on one of the off-shore breezes came the most puissant of all island smells: the sweet, rich, perfumed, heavy, unforgettable odor of vanilla, ripening after harvest. The alluring sweetness filled the ocean. It was like the fragrance of many flowers, the richness of fine food, the sweetness of tropic sunshine. It was the smell of dawn. It rolled in blankets from the shores of Raiatea, the symbol of wealth, the reward of labor.

Fat Maggi breathed heavily and thought, "I would give everything I smelled in Papeete for this. They speak of Paris! Pouf!"

As the *Hiro* warped its way to the creaking wharf, Maggi waited impatiently at the gangplank and even before it was secured started to let herself down onto the dock. A group of cheering young men helped her, yanking her red-and-blue dress awry, but as soon as she felt the earth under her feet, she shook herself loose and plopped onto her head a pandanus hat, which she secured with one hand while running as fast as her bulk would permit through the copra sheds and down the main streets of Raiatea.

As she hurried along many villagers called to her, seeking news of Tahiti. But on this day Maggi had no gossip to spare. She hurried on and at last half-galloped through the open doors of the island's only hotel.

"Povenaaa!" she bellowed. "Oh, Povenaaa!"

The hotel into which she had thus burst—Le Croix du Sud—was such a place as would have captured the imagination of Joseph Conrad had he voyaged to Raiatea. It was a two-story affair with an interior balcony off which opened several dismal rooms. The ground level was crammed with small, square tables, each attended by four chairs. An open kitchen, with many battered pots and pans, led to the rear and a dirty bar edged one side. A Japanese octagonal clock had run down some years before and now showed three-twenty, while a fly-specked portrait of Clemenceau surveyed the bar. And in one corner, bare-footed and with torn shirt, huddled a thin, unshaved Polynesian man, sleeping off his drunk. This was her neighbor, Povenaaa.

Maggi's cries having had no effect upon the sleeper, she let fly with a solid kick and shouted, "Povenaaa! What a morning to sleep!"

The drowsy man twisted on his numbed hip, punched two dirty fists into his eyes and looked up protestingly. When he recognized Maggi he scrambled to his feet, using her solid body as a post by which to haul himself to attention.

"Maggi!" he cried, embracing her warmly. "I didn't expect you!"

"Oh, Povenaaa! What news?"

He became all attention. He took off her hat and placed it carefully on a hook. He held a chair for her and banged furiously on the table for service. "Hey, there! Two breakfasts!"

A misanthropic servant stuck his head out from among the

78

pots and asked dolefully, "Who's going to pay for two breakfasts?" Then he saw Maggi and smiled wanly. "For you, two breakfasts."

He produced coffee cups which weighed a pound each, great brutal things, cold brioches and rancid Australian butter, served in a tin with a jagged edge. As Maggi sipped the chicory-laden brew, Povenaaa twisted his toes around the rung of the chair and asked impatiently, "What's the news, Maggi? Money?"

The big woman tried to play coy and savored her coffee down to the sticky sugar. Then she straightened her Mother Hubbard and said with tremendous import, "What we've waited for, Povenaaa. The Americans are back!"

The effect of this news on Povenaaa was electric. He rubbed his unwashed face, pressed down the front of his dirty shirt and cried ecstatically, "Ah! *Les Américains!*"

"Yes. The yachts have begun to arrive."

"Lots of men?" Povenaaa drooled. "Lots of money?"

"Like the old days," Maggi replied, and the two neighbors sighed nostalgically. Then abruptly, as if a deal had been concluded, Maggi slapped the table and cried, "Well! Why do we wait? Get Teuru!"

Povenaaa rose creakingly, shook the hangover out of his joints and went uncertainly to the door, bellowing, "Teuru! Teuru!"

From a clapboard house down the road a young girl appeared. She had been interrupted at her toilet, for she carried a brush with which she tugged at her long black hair which fell to her waist. She was barefooted and wore a cotton skirt with a skimpy bandanna halter. She was not a girl of extraordinary beauty, but she was handsomely proportioned and majestically straight in the Polynesian fashion. But her most memorable gift was a gamin smile and flashing black eyes that brimmed with an inner merriment.

She stood in the dust of the road, looking for her father, and when she saw him stumbling out from Le Croix du Sud she laughed affectionately and said, "Father! Stop the noise! You're drunk again."

"No, Teuru! Such news!"

His daughter remained in the road, brushing her hair, until Povenaaa shook her by the shoulders. "Maggi's back!" he cried like a little boy relaying Christmas news.

"So soon?"

"And with such glorious news!"

With much nervous excitement Povenaaa led his daughter

79

into the hotel and arranged a seat beside Maggi, who pinched her on the chin and cried, "I'm so happy for you!"

Before Teuru could ask why, some tourists from the *Hiro* entered the hotel and the men could not keep their eyes off the young girl, for it was deliciously apparent that she wore nothing beneath her cotton skirt, since Povenaaa had forced his daughter into her chair in such a way as to expose a splendid leg.

The men's eyes popping at the bar gave Maggi intense pleasure but after the peep show had continued for some minutes, unknown to Teuru, the fat woman leaned over and with ostentatious prudery pulled down the offending dress. "Never show that much," she whispered, "except on purpose."

Povenaaa clasped his hands and giggled, "Teuru! You're going to Tahiti!"

At this Maggi clasped her young friend's hands and cried, "Oh, what I could do in Papeete these days if I was seventeen, like you."

"What's happened?" Teuru asked, caught up in the excitement.

Povenaaa giggled again. "The Americans! They've come back!"

"Yes, thank God!" Maggi drooled. "And you're going down to live on the best things dollars can buy."

"But I've never been to Tahiti," Teuru protested.

Maggi pulled her chair away from the bar and whispered, "You'll go, Teuru, and on the first day you'll meet a rich American on his yacht. All across the Pacific he'll have been dreaming of you."

"But I've never seen an American," Teuru pointed out.

Maggi ignored the interruption and said, "He'll let you live in his cabin. You'll eat your meals at the Yacht Club. Chinese girls will sew your dresses."

"You'll wear shoes, of course," Povenaaa interrupted. "White men like their girls to wear shoes."

"And if you find a handsome young lover," Maggi continued, "you'll have enough American money to pay his rent at the Hotel Montparnasse, where you can meet him at night."

"When the rich American is asleep," Povenaaa explained.

"And when the yacht sails there'll be another one coming in," Maggi said, recalling her boisterous youth in Papeete. "And who knows? Maybe later you will even get married."

Teuru listened to this recital with close attention. Povenaaa had always told her that some day the rich Americans would be coming back and it would be heaven for pretty girls. "And you'll be pretty!" he had assured her.

"But I wouldn't know what to do," she blushed.

"Do!" Maggi roared. "You don't do anything!" Then she dropped her voice and said, "With American men it's very simple. Look at that fellow at the bar. He's French, but all men are more or less the same. Povenaaa and I will leave. I'll manage to pull your dress up the way it was before. Watch what happens!"

As the big woman led Povenaaa from the hotel she hiked Teuru's dress accidentally, and all the men at the bar snapped to attention. A wife complained, "You haven't stared at me like that for ten years, Henri." To which he replied, "Ah, yes! But you haven't looked like that for fifteen."

Then one of them reacted as Maggi had prophesied. In three minutes he was trying to buy Teuru a drink. "I don't drink," she laughed. "My father does enough for both of us."

"Was that your father leaving here a moment ago?"

"Yes."

"Remarkably handsome fellow," the tourist said.

"You sound very silly," Teuru replied, whereupon the man coughed. At this poing Maggi and Povenaaa returned. The Frenchman was completely confused and became more so when Povenaaa said, "Thanks, I'll have a cognac."

When the tourist had been eased away, after paying for the drinks, Maggi said, "See! It's simple! And with an American—much easier." Dramatically she fumbled in her bag and produced a slip of paper. "Voilà! M'mzelle Teuru! Her ticket to Tahiti!"

The excitement of an actual ticket on the Hiro and the lure of Papeete were powerful, and Teuru's dark eyes bubbled with merry anticipation, but suddenly they sobered and she said, "I can't go."

"Why not?" Maggi snorted.

"I promised . . . Kim Sing . . . to work his vanilla vines again."

Povenaaa exploded. "The Chinaman's vanilla! You compare that to a rich American!"

Maggi said quietly, "You were too young during the war, Teuru. We never smuggled you across to Bora Bora. But the lucky girls who did reach the American camp—they lived in paradise."

"A true paradise," Povenaaa cried. "Canned food. Jeep rides. Trips in the airplane. Whole cartons of cigarettes."

Maggi explained, "There's no reason to be afraid of Americans. I remember when they had a certain major who was what the men called an old bitch. Nobody could do anything with him. So I sent Hedy over and half an hour later she had his pants off."

Inspired, Povenaaa went to the door and roared, "Hedy! Come here!"

In a moment the heads at the bar almost snapped off, for into the doorway came a slim Polynesian girl of twenty-four. She held a very blonde child by the hand, and these two created a sensation of perfect beauty. Hedy—she had been so designated by the Americans—had the delicate quality of the actress from whom she had been named, but the frangipani flowers in her hair were her own device. When she spoke her voice was childish and musical. She did not want her daughter to enter the bar, so she said, "Major, you go back home." Then she saw Maggi and cried in her tinkling voice, "Good return, Maggi!"

"For you it's good," Maggi chuckled.

"You bring a message?" Hedy asked, keeping her eyes shyly upon the floor so that she would not have to look at the strange men along the bar.

"Such a message!" Povenaaa beamed.

"The Americans!" Maggi whispered, "They're back."

Unlike Teuru, Hedy knew how to appreciate this luxurious news. She smiled with delicate satisfaction, moved a little nearer Maggi, and sighed, "During the war they used to say, 'Come peace, Baby, you'll see me back here with a fist full of dough.'"

"She talks just like an American," Povenaaa said proudly.

Hedy sighed again and sort of hugged herself. "I should like to be in Papeete now!"

"And here's your ticket!" Maggi cried, producing another strip of paper.

"Oh, Maggi!" Hedy cried, embracing the fat woman. Then she pouted, "But what about Major?"

"I was thinking about Major," Maggi said softly.

There was a long moment while Hedy and Maggi stared at each other. Then, impulsively, the younger woman kissed the older and laughed, "You've always wanted Major, haven't you? Well, she's yours."

Povenaaa was sent to find Major and returned shortly with the fair-haired little girl, who ran promptly to her mother, but Hedy lifted the child deftly into Maggi's voluminous lap. "Maggi's your mother now," Hedy said gently.

The little girl looked first at her mother, then at her new mother. Both women winked at her and before the winks had rustled to rest, little Major—named after an American officer long since forgotten—accepted the new order. Hedy patted her approvingly and whispered, "You be good. Hedy's going to Tahiti."

Then Povenaaa spoke, officially, "You girls will love Papeete. I want you to behave yourselves. No drinking. Don't become bums like me. And remember that Americans do not shoot pistols all the time like the movies. I've known some very decent men." Then he stopped. He saw tears in his daughter's eyes. "What's the matter, Teuru?" he snapped.

"I want to see Papeete," she said haltingly. "I think I would like Americans but . . ."

"Poor little Teuru!" Povenaaa whispered. But her indecision frightened him and he realized he must tell her the whole truth. "You must go," he pleaded. "For my sake if for nothing else. For if you could save only three hundred American dollars . . . Well, I could buy that surplus jeep on Bora Bora." He looked at Teuru in triumph, as if the coveted vehicle were already his. "And with a jeep! Why, I could be a very important man in Raiatea. With a jeep, that is."

The *Hiro* blew its whistle once. "I must pack!" Hedy cried. "Maggi! You must help me."

The two women bustled out of Le Croix du Sud and one of the men at the bar came to Povenaaa's table. "Your pardon, sir. Who was that remarkable girl?"

"The big one or the little one?" Povenaaa asked.

"The . . . younger one."

"Name's Hedy. She's going to Tahiti." Then he grabbed Teuru's hand and started for the door, where he turned and added proudly, "And my daughter's going, too."

The *Hiro* blew its whistle twice, and then followed an amazing pageant of Polynesian life. Everybody on the dock began to weep. Maggi lowed and whimpered like a grief-stricken heifer. Povenaaa blubbered helplessly, repeating over and over again, "My daughter! My daughter!" Stragglers who had drifted down merely to watch the *Hiro* were caught in the lamenting and they too wept in an abandonment of sorrow. Tahiti lay less than a hundred miles away, and the ship sailed each week, but the sorrow in Raiatea could have been no greater had the passengers this day been destined for the Arctic wastes.

In a final debauchery of despair Maggi shrieked, "Hedy, look after Teuru!"

Hedy burst into passionate tears and screamed, "Povenaaa, I'll show Teuru what to do."

The *Hiro* blew its whistle the last time and stood out into the channel, and as it did so a transformation came over Hedy. She stopped weeping instantly, lifted her lovely head into the breeze and looked southward. "Oh, Teuru," she whispered happily. "Tomorrow night we shall sleep in Papeete!" Then a frown puckered her forehead and she added, "But I wonder with who?"

Teuru blushed. A delicate color came to her cheeks, shining for a moment under the soft brown skin. "It's all very well to joke about such things, but . . ."

"Sssh!" Hedy warned. "Those gentlemen are looking at us. I'll bet they want to buy us some beer." But when she turned she saw that Teuru was weeping. "Why are you crying now?" she asked sharply. "The boat's sailed."

And Teuru sniffled, "You've been away from home before. I haven't."

But by the following evening, when the *Hiro* like an exhausted porpoise rolled on toward Tahiti, Teuru's bubbling good humor returned and she shared in the general excitement as the glorious climax of their journey unfolded. To the west sprang the peaks of Moorea, crimson in sunlight. Ahead loomed the stumpy, cloud-wreathed hills of Tahiti. Seagulls dipped majestically about the ship, welcoming it as if it were a rich caravel, and even the seasick cattle revived as they caught the scent of land.

"Hedy!" Teuru cried, "look at those beautiful ships!"

"They must be the yachts," Hedy said, straightening her dress.

"And the white spires."

"Churches," Hedy guessed, keeping her attention focused on the yachts.

"But what's that?" Teuru cried.

To starboard, tied up to the quay that ran along the waterfront, stood a huge ship painted white. Along its deck moved sailors, also in white, each with a red pompom on his hat. "It's a French ship," Hedy sniffed scornfully. "You stay away from the French."

"It's lovely," Teuru said happily. "Even if it is French." Like most residents of the northern islands, she had inherited a revolutionary hatred of the French who had subdued her islands last and with force.

"Ah!" Hedy cried. "Those yachts are American!"

But Teuru was fascinated by the warship, and as the tired old *Hiro* limped into port she stood at the railing and stared at the cruiser *Jean Delacroix* as long as it remained visible. Then, perforce, she had to look elsewhere, and for the first time she saw the rich panorama of Papeete.

Along the quay important Frenchmen bustled in coats that seemed too tight. Chinamen rode bicycles that teetered perilously, while handsome native men from the fishing boats hauled bonita onto the cobbled stones. Girls in Paris frocks walked slowly back and forth in twos and threes as officials in uniform bustled about giving orders and a nest of tourists lolled in a rented sports car blowing their horn at everyone. Three nuns waited on the dock for a sister reporting in from an out station, and innumerable black and white and yellow boys ran screaming into alleys.

There was a color about Papeete that night that Teuru never would forget. The white clouds turning to purple. The silvery flash of bonita as they scintillated in the sun. The golden yellow towers of the Douane. The majestic motion of many people as their various colors blended, and everywhere the glorious flowers of Tahiti.

That was how Povenaaa's daughter arrived in Papeete. She stepped upon the dock barefooted, in a close fitting green-and-white pareu, her long black hair reaching her waist, a frangipani behind her left ear, a little wicker suitcase in her hand, and on the back of her head, a straw hat. She took a deep breath of the new air and whispered, "We're here, Hedy."

The older girl presented a much different appearance. She wore shoes, very high in the heel, and a dress drawn tightly about her small waist. Her hair was done in plaited strands wound into a crown. For lips she had two scarlet dabs, but against the white flowers in her hair they seemed appropriate. She handed Teuru her suitcase, explaining, "American men don't like to see pretty girls lugging things."

As if she had lived in Papeete all her life, she led Teuru off the dock and westward to where the yachts were anchored. She knew she had little time, for the sun already had the peaks of Moorea aflame. Then abruptly she stopped. Suddenly she was no longer in a hurry. Motioning Teuru to stay behind, she sidled along the waterfront to where a yacht was tied stern to. A man of fifty was leaning over a board, cleaning fish. Hedy laughed musically and the yachtsman looked up.

"Watcha laughin' at?" he demanded.

"That's no way to clean a fish!" Hedy taunted.

"Whatsa matter with my way?"

"You'll cut yourself." She leaned slightly on the ropes, swaying with the motion of the ship. Then she laughed again.

"You think you could do it any better?" the yachtsman asked.

"Sure!" Hedy cried, using a French accent she had found irresistible during the war.

"If you're so smart, let's see." The man reached aft with a boat hook and steadied Hedy as she swung herself aboard. "What's your name?" he asked.

"Fish-cleaner," she teased.

"No. Your real name."

"Hedy," she replied.

"Like Hedy Lamarr?"

"Yes. An American major said I looked like her." The petite girl leaned over to survey the mutilated fish, but she was careful to keep her lovely profile steady for several seconds.

"Say!" the yachtsman cried. "You do, at that!" He moved toward her, attracted by her extravagant charm, but as he did so she lifted the fish and laughed at him with tinkling music.

"You've ruined the fish," she said.

"Where'd'joo learn to speak English so good?"

"Oh!" she cried. "My bag!" She ran to the stern and started to shinny down the ropes.

"Don't go!" the American cried.

"I'll be back," she reassured him.

"What are you going to do?" Teuru whispered.

"Stop here for a while," Hedy said.

"What am I to do?" Teuru pleaded.

"Well," said the self-assured little beauty with a flip of her head, "there's a lot more yachts."

"I couldn't do that."

Suddenly Hedy was all tender affection. "You're right! You've got to take these things very slowly. I remember when Maggi smuggled me ashore at Bora Bora. I was scared to death. I knew I'd never be able to talk with a major. An American, too."

"Were you?"

"Oh, yes," Hedy replied. She kissed Teuru good-bye and the girls began to cry.

"Whatsamatter down there?" the yachtsman shouted.

"My friend," Hedy blubbered.

"Whatsamatter with your friend?"

"She's never been away from home before!"

"Well, bring her along."

There was fresh sobbing, rising to a wail of remorse and lonely anguish. The American was totally bewildered as he watched his girl open her purse and hand the barefooted stranger a fistful of francs. He was even more surprised when Hedy wiped her eyes, flashed him a wonderful smile, pitched her bag aboard and shinnied up the ropes with the friendly cry, "All right! Where's that fish?"

Teuru was now alone in Papeete. Stuffing Hedy's benevolent francs into her suitcase, she pulled out a slim scrap of paper on which Maggi had scrawled two words: HOTEL MONTPARNASSE. She was about to seek a policeman when she beheld a sight that would have made the heart of any young girl dance with pleasure. Down the quay came three French sailors in dazzling white uniforms and red pompoms. Their shorts stopped crisply at the knee and they wore hard-ribbed white socks and highly polished shoes. They were laughing. They were laughing and making a great fuss, so that Teuru had to laugh, too.

They saw her hesitating at the edge of the road and quickly surrounded her. In French the tallest cried, "Ah, the village maiden comes to the city!" Then they offered her a cigarette.

"Ah! Virtuous maiden! She doesn't smoke!"

"I'm looking for a hotel," Teuru explained.

"*Voilà!*" the sailors shouted.

"What happens here?" a policeman asked, patting himself on the belly.

"We're showing m'mzelle to her hotel!" the tall sailor announced, making a little rhyme which his friends mimicked in mincing style.

They grabbed her by the waist and swung her down the street, so that she had to dance with them. Then they lifted her high into the air and planted her bare feet on the sidewalk. "The hotel of m'mzelle!" they cried, and then the leader said very seriously, "Let it never be remarked that the men of *Jean Delacroix* were not gallant. Your official welcome to Papeete." And he kissed her firmly on the lips.

"So too the engine-room crew!" cried the next sailor, holding her face to attention and wiping off his lips with his shirt sleeve.

But the third sailor stood back. He blushed considerably

and indicated that he would not force his attentions on Teuru. His companions mocked him and the leader cried, "M'mzelle! Our good friend Victor, he does not like girls! Therefore, on behalf of Victor, I salute you again." He lifted her into his arms, but this time Teuru did not feel his lips, for over his shoulder she saw the confused, scarlet face of Victor.

When the sailors left, their six handsome white-ribbed legs making rare patterns in the dusk, Teuru watched them for a moment, then laughed and hoisted her suitcase, turned on her bare feet and marched into the Hotel Montparnasse. This establishment, so inappropriately named, faced the peaks of Moorea, but otherwise its facilities were unspeakable. It had served wastrels and wanderers for almost a hundred years and in that time Rupert Brooke, Stevenson, Henry Adams, and Gauguin had lounged upon its dirty verandah, staring at the pantomime of Papeete. Now it was run by a German woman who wore stiff black lace collars, as if to bring to the hotel a respectability it had never owned.

"What do you want?" Frau Henslick snapped.

Teuru thrust the piece of paper onto the counter and Frau Henslick shouted, "What am I supposed to do? This says nothing."

"Maggi sent me."

"You mean the fat woman?"

"Yes!" Teuru beamed. "She said you might need help."

"I do," Frau Henslick cried. "I always do." She came from behind the counter and examined Teuru as if she were a horse. "Got your teeth?" Teuru opened her mouth and the woman nodded approvingly. "Can you work?"

"Yes," Teuru said. "I'm a good worker."

Suddenly the German woman screamed, "When you work here I want you to sleep in your own bed."

"What do you mean?" Teuru asked.

The German woman screamed even more loudly, "You island girls!"

That ended the conversation. Frau Henslick led Teuru to a dingy room, kicked the door open and said, "You start work at six in the morning." Before the girl could reply, the angular woman had disappeared.

It was then seven, and Teuru was hungry, but before she could ask about food she heard the heavy shouting of a man: "Damn it! I want some hot water!"

There was some scuffling and Frau Henslick banged open

Teuru's door. "You!" she shouted. "Take this upstairs to Mr. Roe."

Teuru lugged the pitcher to the upper hall and then wondered where she should deliver it. Reasoning that if she waited the man would shout again, she heard an irritated bellow issue from Room 16: "You old sow! Where's the water?"

Cautiously she pushed open the door and faced a young man standing in his shorts. He was red headed and had a week's growth of beard. "Thanks," he said, turning his back on her.

At the door she asked, "Are you an American?"

"Yes," he said, swabbing his face.

"I've never seen an American before."

"We're pretty sturdy stuff," he said, lathering his beard.

She started downstairs, but he came to the door and called, "You eaten yet? Good. I'm just getting over a four-day drunk. How's about holding me up till I get to the restaurant?"

"I'll put my shoes on," she said.

"Don't bother. I never wear any."

He made her sit down while he shaved, cursing the blade. Finally he asked, "Do I look pretty awful?"

"You look pale," she replied.

He studied the mirror and shuddered: "Let's get out of here!"

He took her to the Yacht Club and insisted that she order the best of everything. He himself took poached eggs but couldn't manage them. Instead he sat back and admired the way she stuffed down the meat and vegetables. "I was hungry," she said.

"I feel nourished, just watching you," he laughed, but she made him eat some of her meat and he said it tasted pretty good, so he ordered some more, and while he pecked at it, she told him of Hedy.

"Which yacht was it?" he asked. When she described it he said, "She'll be a wizard if she gets a nickel out of that old bastard."

"Do you know him?"

"I came down here with him," Mr. Roe said.

"You will go back with him, too?"

"I'd sooner be dead." From the street came the sound of music and he said, "Would you like to dance?"

"I have no shoes."

"You forget, neither do I." He led her to Quinn's, a place

Maggi had often mentioned, and there Teuru saw the gaiety of this island. As soon as Mr. Roe entered, everybody shouted to him and couples stopped by his table to ask what was new. He made no move to dance and she was not surprised when a very beautiful girl in shoes took him completely away. He did not return to Teuru at all but sat across the floor drinking gin and growing more glazed each hour.

In her embarrassment Teuru was about to leave when there was commotion at the door and the three French sailors roared in. The leader saw Teuru at once and swung her onto the floor. He was good at native dances and flourished his hips as well as an island man. Soon Teuru felt her hair swinging about her shoulders, and then, as earlier that night, she saw across the room the penetrating stare of thin-faced Victor.

When she joined the sailors at their table, the young man rose properly, bowed and said, "My name is Victor de la Foret," and in those brief words he opened for Teuru a completely new vision of life, because when she said that she was from Raiatea, he replied, "I was born there."

"You were?" she asked. "I never heard of you."

"In spirit," he explained. "I had an uncle who served in these islands, and from the time I was a boy . . ." Nervously at first and then with a rush of golden words he told Teuru the history of her island: the hills that contained the sacred marae, the straits from which the canoes set out to populate the Pacific, the forgotten groves where the lewd ritual dances were held. He was only twenty-one and he had never seen Raiatea, but he knew the island better than Teuru, who had left it only yesterday.

When Quinn's closed the young couple walked along the quay until they found a bench, and then he told her of the map he had drawn of Raiatea, many years ago. "It was marked with a star," he said.

"What for?" she asked.

"Raiatea was the source. Women like you bore brave sons and they risked all the dangers of the sea."

For a moment these new ideas cast a spell over Teuru and she was back in the age when men of Raiatea ruled the oceans. Not until that night had she known that she carried such blood. Better than she could have liked any American, she liked this young sailor, and impulsively she reached out her brown hand and touched the red pompom. "It dances," she said, "on your white hat."

Victor drew back and even in the faltering light she could

90

detect his blush. "You shouldn't have done that," he said nervously.

"Why not?" she asked perplexed.

"It's a rule," he said. "A silly rule."

"What is?"

"A girl ... who touches a pompom ... a sailor's red pompom, that is ..."

"I'm very sorry," Teuru apologized.

"It's nothing," he assured her. "A stupid rule. But she must kiss him."

This was not play-kissing and Teuru rose in embarrassment and started to leave, but Victor caught her by the hand and said quietly, "Tonight ... when the others were kissing you ... I was afraid."

In stately grace the barefooted girl bent down and placed her lips on his. Her long hair fell about his shoulders and across his eyes. At first he did not move. Then, in an excess of joy, he flung his arms about her and pulled her down upon his knees. "You are like the queen of my island," he whispered.

These words were very sweet to Teuru, but she was somewhat perplexed—recalling all that Maggi had told her about how men behave—when Victor made no move to kiss her again but spent the night asking her detailed questions about Raiatea. Toward morning, when pale light was quivering upon the tips of Moorea, a bugle sounded on the *Jean Delacroix* and Victor said he must leave.

"I must see you each day," he whispered. Then, staring at his shoes, he confided his secret. "I joined the *Jean Delacroix* to see these islands. Because, you understand, I am going to write a great poem about Raiatea. In the ancient days, of course."

A policeman stopped by the bench and said, "You'd better get back to your ship, vice-admiral."

"Will you talk with me again tonight?" Victor begged, and Teuru said that she would. She reached the Montparnasse at five minutes to six and Frau Henslick screamed, "Come in, you baggage. Are you sober enough to work?"

"I'm all right," Teuru replied. Indeed, she thought the words had never really applied to her before that moment. She felt all right.

"Then go up and see what Mr. Roe's making such a noise about."

There was a wild clatter at the head of the stairs, followed by a bucket bouncing down, step by step. "I said I wanted some ice!" Mr. Roe stormed.

"Get him some," Frau Henslick ordered.

Teuru hauled some up to Room 16 and Mr. Roe shouted, "Bring it in!"

Gingerly Teuru pushed open the door, keeping her eyes down, for Mr. Roe was wearing almost nothing and in his bed slept the pretty girl, who now did not have her shoes on. By no gesture did Mr. Roe acknowledge that he had ever seen Teuru, and it was apparent that he knew nothing of the evening before.

All that morning Frau Henslick kept Teuru hopping so that when siesta time came the girl did not even bother with food but fell into a death-like sleep for two hours, awakening only when the German woman shook her. "Mr. Roe wants you again," Frau Henslick said.

"He makes a lot of trouble," Teuru said sleepily.

"He pays his bills," the landlady said simply, and thus Teuru was introduced to the rules of Hotel Montparnasse. People who paid were let alone. Teuru learned never to enter any room unless invited. Each night after eleven stray girls from all the outlying islands wandered through the hotel, checking up to see if all the men were sleeping well. It was not uncommon for two or sometimes three girls to spend the night in one visitor's room: one in bed and two on the floor. If no other place was available, they crowded into Mr. Roe's room, for he never bothered them, and if, as was often the case, he found them in his bed when he got back, he would curl up in a chair on the verandah, unless he was very drunk, when he would roar, "Get the hell out of here. I've got to get some sleep." And there would be a scurry of bare feet down the corridors.

Teuru was not bothered by the Montparnasse because she herself lived in a kind of dream world. During almost every free moment she was with Victor de la Foret. On rented bicycles they rode and then clambered up to the pool of Pierre Loti where, generations before, the romantic novelist had wooed his island girl. They danced, went to boxing shows and sat in the movies. But most of all they talked: Teuru, who had been a quiet girl—Povenaaa's chin was always bobbing—now found herself able to speak for minutes at a time, relating her memories of Raiatea. True, she sometimes wondered when they were going to get around to those things that Maggi had said "were all that men wanted, anyway!"

When Victor finally did, Teuru was completely shocked. It

happened one night while they were sitting on the bench. The young sailor caught Teuru by the waist and cried, "We are going to get married!"

"Married!" Teuru repeated. She was astounded at the idea. After all, she was only seventeen, not nearly of an age to marry. She had not yet lived with a man, she had borne no children, knew nothing of life. She suspected that it was both unfair and ungallant of Victor to propose such a thing and in extreme perplexity she told him he had better go back to his ship.

"But will you marry me?" he begged.

"Not right away," she parried, and as soon as he had left she scurried across the quay to Hedy's yacht and scrambled aboard. In the darkness she upset a bucket and heard a gruff voice cry, "Get off'n this boat, you crooks!"

"Hedy!" she whispered. "It's Teuru!"

There were muffled protests but soon the Polynesian girl appeared. She embraced her friend and said, "The skipper complains a lot, but he bought me this robe."

They sat on the deck and Hedy listened carefully while Teuru explained about the wedding proposal. "I warned you!" Hedy cried indignantly. "I told you Frenchmen were no good. To expect you to marry him. So young! And no money!"

"What shall I do?" Teuru begged.

"You go back to Raiatea. Maggi and Povenaaa will tell you I'm right."

"Will you ever get married, Hedy?"

"Of course. In two or three years."

"Then why can't I?"

"At your age! You haven't even had a baby yet. You go home."

So next morning Teuru informed Frau Henslick that she'd be sailing on the Tuesday *Hiro*. The German woman bawled at her for being an ingrate, but Teuru was determined. Nevertheless, as the day ended she nervously watched the *Jean Delacroix*, waiting for the white suit and red pompom she had grown to love.

She was surprised, therefore, when Victor did not appear at the accustomed hour, and she was wandering idly along the quay when a young man in civilian clothes . . .

"Victor!" she cried. "I hardly knew you!"

"I was keeping it as a surprise. My enlistment's up and I cabled Paris for special permission to stay out here." He dropped his voice and added, "So that we could get married."

"But we can't!" Teuru objected. "I'm going home next *Hiro*."

"That's what I planned, too," he said eagerly.

"What did you plan?" Teuru asked, half in tears.

"To go with you ... to Raiatea. Our first home! We'll get married on Monday."

"But Povenaaa would never let us!" Teuru protested.

"We'll talk with M'sieur Povenaaa," Victor insisted, and on Tuesday they were aboard the *Hiro*. There was a fine cry as Hedy and her American saw them off, with many flowers. Frau Henslick was there, too, with more flowers, and an old woman from Raiatea who just came down for the general lament. Victor said, "I am sure it must have been like this when the canoes set out for Hawaii. But Raiatea's only a few miles."

Teuru said, between tears, "It's always so sad to part."

That night they sat upon a crate of knitting yarn and watched the timeless race of the moon across the tropical heavens. As new constellations appeared, Victor named them, and all around was the music of a small ship plowing through starry night: the lowing of cattle, the whispers of women talking, the patient throb of the reluctant engines, the cry of a night bird, the echo of waves against wood.

Teuru sat close to Victor and in spite of Hedy's warnings, in spite of what she knew Povenaaa and Maggi would say, she wanted to marry this Frenchman. She was about to tell him so when a mysterious sound came from the port quarter and Victor rose. He peered into the darkness and asked, "What is that noise?"

Teuru stood beside him, her face pressed into the wind, and before she could speak the first probing dagger of light cut across the waves and poised above the hills of Raiatea.

"My island!" de la Foret cried, and there was something in his passionate recognition of a land he had never seen that bewildered Teuru, yet at the same time she felt that she had found the one man with whom she could live forever happily. They stood like enchanted voyagers from another age as the pitching *Hiro* approached the island. These were the hills that had bred the bravest navigators the world has ever known. These were the valleys of the most lewd pagan rites, the sacred altars where human sacrifices had been dragged by the hair, the living monuments of a towering civilization—lost.

But their reverie was broken by shouts coming from the wharf. Some children had caught sight of the lovers and were screaming, "Povenaaa! Teuru has her American!"

The happy message sped through the crowd, for all the island knew of Teuru's mission, and all the villagers beamed approval of the handsome young American. Then, as the *Hiro* docked, there came a fresh commotion and the crowd fell back to make a pathway for Maggi, puffing and on fire. She took one look at the young people and shouted, "By God, girl! You've done it?" Then she turned and shouted, "Get Povenaaa!"

In a moment half the children on the quay were paging the town bum, and soon he appeared, barefooted, his pants falling away from his hips, his face a thicket of whiskers. Then, as his bleary eyes focused, he saw de la Foret and he cried in Polynesian, "I knew my daughter could catch herself a rich American!"

The gangway was lowered and Povenaaa received his first shock of the day, for when Teuru led Victor ashore, the first thing the young poet did was to stoop down and kiss the earth of Raiatea. "My God!" Povenaaa cried. "Is he sick?"

Maggi shook her fist at the *Hiro* and swore, "You'd give Jonah the seasickness."

Povenaaa led the procession to Le Croix du Sud and when the rancid butter appeared with the sour brioches he asked expansively, "And what part of America do you come from?"

Victor smiled and said, "I am a Frenchman."

There was a horrible silence while Maggi stared dumbly at Povenaaa's gaping jaw. Teuru tried to help things out by saying that Victor was really a French sailor, but that he'd been discharged on Saturday.

"Oh, my God!" Maggi groaned.

Now Victor tried to soothe things. "I've come here to marry your daughter."

"No!" Povenaaa exploded. "No French pig shall . . ."

"Father," Teuru pleaded. "Let's go home."

"I think we better," Maggi said limply. With anguish she paid Povenaaa's bill—what a hollow celebration this had been—and then started for the weatherbeaten house. Once inside Povenaaa miraculously produced four rickety chairs and demanded, "Now what's all this about?"

"I want to marry your daughter," de la Foret said forcefully.

"No! She's too young!"

"And besides," Maggi added. "Frenchmen are not welcome here."

"She's right!" Povenaaa stormed. "No Frenchman will marry my daughter."

Now Teuru spoke. "But I love him. He's very gentle. He's a poet."

This caught Povenaaa off guard. He stopped blustering and leaned forward. "Poets are very famous. Do they make a lot of money?"

"No," Teuru interrupted. "Not yet. But some day he will. He's writing a long poem. About Raiatea."

"Son of a pig, it's strange!" Povenaaa mused. "The world full of rich Americans and my daughter picks a poor French poet."

Ignoring de la Foret completely, Maggi took Teuru's hand and said, "I understand Hedy got herself a beautiful yacht. How did she get a yacht and you a poet?"

Teuru blushed and explained, "She didn't fall in love. I did."

This was enough for Povenaaa. He rose to his full height and announced dramatically, "There will be no marriage! Not between a poet and a girl only seventeen."

"What shall I do?" de la Foret cried, anguished that he must lose Teuru.

"You stay here, of course," Teuru replied.

"Here?" he repeated.

She lifted his bag and carried it into her small room. Next she fetched hers and placed it beside his. Then she stood in the doorway and motioned to him.

"You mean . . . I'm to stop here? With you?"

"But there's to be no marriage!" Povenaaa warned, defending his daughter from the unwelcome intruder. When de la Foret remained rooted in bewilderment, Povenaaa reached out and pushed him into Teuru's room. "You can stay here for the time being," he said grudgingly. "But no marriage!"

Disappointed and disgusted, Povenaaa slammed the door on the young lovers and slumped down beside Maggi. "A dog's luck," he mused bitterly.

"It's too bad," Maggi consoled. "But it'll work out . . . in time. The important thing is, be firm! Don't let them get married. He'll leave one of these days."

Povenaaa scratched his bewhiskered face and asked, "A poet? Do you suppose that's much better than a sailor?"

The disillusionment of young Victor de la Foret was catastrophic. It was not the disillusionment of love, for never had he been so happy. In the morning Teuru rose from their bed and polished the thin bamboo wafer she used on the vanilla flowers. Then she threw around herself a blue-and-white pareu and combed her radiant hair. Sometimes she would bring in pawpaw, some limes, a mango or a pot of black coffee. They would eat together while the morning birds made a symphony among the trees. Then she would kiss him good-bye and walk like some ancient goddess toward the vanilla plantations.

Nor was it the disillusionment of life with Povenaaa, who worked each night to bring America into the conversation. The disappointed father made it emphatic that a Frenchman was a pretty poor substitute for a Yank. He also delighted in dandling Major on his knee, adding that he guessed no babies in the world were as pretty as American babies. He said—staring boldly at Teuru—that he guessed any girl in the world would be mighty happy to have a child as intelligent as Major. He taught the child to sing an amazing version of "Yankee Doodle." Worst of all, in an old copy of *Life* he found a full-page color shot of a jeep. This he posted right where Victor and Teuru had to face it as they ate. But for the most part Povenaaa proved a decent sort, even though he used to ask Maggi almost every night, in a voice so loud that Victor had to hear, "I wonder when he's leaving."

No, the tragic disillusionment that overtook Victor de la Foret was that of Raiatea itself. Where had the once great civilization fled? How could the godlike subduers of the vast Pacific have degenerated into Povenaaa? Why, only last week sailors of Raiatea had fled back to port when a trivial storm overtook them at sea. He studied the relics of the island, hoping to find an answer, but in no stone could he detect a trace of the grandeur that had once inhabited this land.

Strangely, he found his only solace in Maggi, who often sat with Major on her lap, droning about the old days. She could recite the names of all the canoes that had penetrated the oceans even to Peru.

"But what happened, Maggi?"

"Now we stay home."

"But where did the grandeur vanish?"

"It's still here. You ever see Major's mother? Very grandeur, Hedy!"

"I mean the spirit of life."

"It's here. Some time Teuru will take you to a real island dance."

Word arrived that there was to be one on nearby Bora Bora and Victor arranged for a long boat to make the trip.

He rode aft with Teuru and for a breathless moment he could believe that he was sailing with the immortal canoes. Ahead rose the fantastic cliffs of Bora Bora, radiant in the sunlight. About him the birds wheeled as they had generations ago during the hegira. In counterpoint to the throbbing of the engine he could hear the men of Raiatea chanting songs whose very meaning had been lost in the dust of years. This was the historic grandeur of Polynesia: brown bodies thrusting forward into the unknown sea, frail boats riding to the sunrise. Ahead the sure knowledge that somewhere there must be an island. Behind the security of a beautiful homeland.

He had a further sensation of historic reality when he decamped onto the shore of Bora Bora where the cliffs dropped into the fairytale lagoon. As dusk came on, lovers from all over the island gathered and a tomtom beat out traditional rhythms. Men leaped into the ring and began furious gyrations. Soon they were joined by handsome girls. They danced, as if demented, a sexual ritual that probed far back into the past, until with furious cries the men caught the girls by the waist and threw them toward the jungle's edge. There was a timeless moment when the men leaped beside the girls as lovers ages ago had done before dragging the women into the bush. But now came a nervous giggle and the girls rejoined their friends.

The spell broken, de la Foret had to recognize not some dim memory of the past but the harsher actualities of now. This once godlike people! Look at them! Their teeth falling out from white man's food. Their health ruined with white man's diseases. Even the flaming moon that had once risen above the volcano to shine down on rare, savage bodies now limped up from a dead volcano and shed a pallid light upon a doomed and dying race.

"Teuru," he whispered, "let's go back." She understood his disillusionment and tried to round up the Raiatea sailors, but they were afraid to set forth in the darkness.

That was the beginning of de la Foret's illness. He had no fever, no disease. He was sick of that almost incurable malady: today. When he watched Povenaaa trying to sell his daughter to some rich American, he was sick. When he dissected the trivial life of modern Raiatea, he was sick. There had once been a glory, but today it was vanished. Therefore he was ill with today's illness.

His poem never got beyond the first canto. True, that fragment was superb and was published with distinction. It dealt
98

with Polynesia as a physical world: the sky, the stars, the lonely islands. It was when people were introduced that the poem turned to rot. Victor was aware of this and stopped writing. "I am sick," he repeated.

"You must come with me while I work the vines," Teuru laughed, and it was there that de la Foret rebuilt himself. Day after day he watched Teuru move among the vines, grasping in her firm left fingers the flowers that looked like orchids. In her right hand she carried the bamboo wafer, which she deftly stroked along the stamen, collecting pollen. Then, with a twist of her left thumb, she snapped open the flap that protected the pistil and deposited upon it the pollen from her bamboo. Then she allowed the flap to snap back in place, whereupon she squeezed the pistil to be sure the pollen penetrated it.

"It's so tedious," Victor complained.

"Vanilla's too important to trust to luck," she explained. She said that every flower impregnated by her gentle method would produce a vanilla bean. Those she missed would die that night. "I do the work of bees and flies," she said.

Since the flowers opened at eight and closed at four, Teuru and Victor spent most of each day in the sunny fields, re-working the same vines daily to pollinate each new flower. "Povenaaa must be a rich man with so much vanilla," de la Foret observed as he watched the long beans ripening in the sun.

"They're not Povenaaa's!" Teuru laughed. "They belong to Kim Sing."

Then the sickness returned. The sunny islands of Polynesia were now owned by Chinese and Frenchmen and Germans. Everyone prospered. Only the Polynesians withered. "You spend so much care on a Chinaman's vines," Victor protested. "Who cares for you?"

Teuru blushed. "Yes. Povenaaa was asking that last night."

"What do you mean?"

She would not reply but that evening Povenaaa was most blunt. He had Major on his lap and asked, "When will you have a white baby, Teuru?" His daughter blushed and made no reply. "Well!" Povenaaa continued. "You have a man for eight months now. What's the matter?"

Victor was outraged. "You shouldn't talk like that," he protested.

Maggi looked at him and sniffed. "Poets, hmmmm. I'll bet Hedy isn't fooling around with poets." She sucked at a bone

99

and then called for Major. Swinging the child onto her lap she counseled, "Don't you ever bother with poets, Major."

Humiliated, young de la Foret left the table. Teuru found him along the shore. "What kind of father is Povenaaa?" the poet cried.

"He knows I ought to have a baby pretty soon," Teuru replied.

"Stop it! Are you trying to drive me mad?" He pushed her away and stormed along the beach. When Teuru tried to keep up with him he shouted at her in a high, tormented voice and told her to go home. She sought out Maggi and reported the strange behavior.

"Was he crying?" Maggi asked.

"Yes," the perplexed girl replied.

"Good!" Maggi said, straightening her Mother Hubbard. "When a white man cries it means that pretty soon he's going home."

"Why?"

"I can't explain it," Maggi said. "Every time you think you understand a white man, something like this happens. But I noticed that whenever one of my men cried I could start packing his things."

"Why are white men so hard to understand?" Teuru asked.

"Because they're all fools," Maggi explained.

"But you yourself said there were some wonderful white men on Bora Bora."

"Yes, but they were Americans."

"But Hedy told me that when the major found she was going to have a baby, he cried."

"What about?" Maggi asked suspiciously.

"About his wife in America."

Maggi shrugged her shoulders. "It's as I said. White men are very strange."

Victor returned late that night. Lighting a small lamp by Teuru's bed, he scanned the poetry he had tried to write. It was apparently very bad, for one by one the sheets were burned. Teuru feigned sleep and watched him. Then finally she asked, "Have you nothing you want to keep?"

Startled, he dropped a flaming page and had to extinguish it with his foot. When he had done so he sat on Teuru's bed and held her dark head close to his. "Yes," he muttered. "I have one thing to keep."

"What?" she inquired prosaically.

"My memory of you." Then, as if he wished to explain exactly the meaning of this day, he launched into a long apostrophe to the fact that in the midst of a dying and degenerate world he had found one clean, pure symbol of the ancient grandeur: Teuru's placid beauty.

"What's 'placid' mean?" she asked.

He realized that she had not understood anything of what he was trying to say, and she, realizing that he did not intend making love, sighed and pulled away. "I've got to sleep," she said. "I must be up early."

When she rose, he had gone. He did not return and she heard that he had slept on the hotel floor like an ordinary tramp. When the *Hiro* arrived Major came running in with her childish news: "Victor go away!"

At first Teuru felt nothing. Victor was going back to France. Good. She went about her work, but as she did so she saw a vision of the young sailor in crisp whites, with a forbidden red pompom on his hat, and she burst from the house and dashed along the dusty road to the dock.

The *Hiro* was standing out into the channel, but she could see Victor against the railing. She was disposed to call out to him, but instead she stayed among the shadows and watched the boat recede into the distance. It was strange. As a girl she had often come to see the *Hiro* sail and aboard there might be some girl she had never really liked, but at the moment of departure she would break her heart with weeping over the loss of this unimportant girl. Now Victor was leaving and she felt nothing. But then he put his hand over his eyes, as if he were shielding them from the morning sun in order to locate someone on the quay. She started to wave her hand and cry "Victor!" but she realized that the *Hiro* was already too far from shore.

At last she turned to resume her work in the vanilla fields, only to find Maggi and Povenaaa weeping bitterly, consoling each other. "He was a fine young man," Maggi said.

"For a Frenchman," Povenaaa said, "he was all right."

Then Maggi with fortitude wiped her eyes and announced, "But we must forget him. Look!" And she produced a ticket for Teuru on the next *Hiro*.

"Only this time," Povenaaa begged. "An American. Please."

There was a somber quality in Teuru's return to Papeete. The day was overcast and the brooding hills were enveloped in fog. Along the beautiful quay there was a gaping wound: the *Jean Delacroix* was missing. There were no sailors with red pompoms, and the waterfront looked as if it had been betrayed. Even Hedy's yacht was gone.

But Hedy herself was waiting at the gangplank. The slim girl had a scar across her right cheek. After she had fallen into Teuru's strong arms she said, "He hit me with a dish. Night before he sailed."

"Was he a good man?" Teuru asked.

"Pretty good," Hedy said reflectively. "I managed a lot of presents and some money."

"What are you doing now?" Teuru asked as she trudged back to her old job at Montparnasse.

"I have another American," Hedy reported.

"You're lucky," Teuru said.

At the hotel Frau Henslick screamed, "So you've come back! Put your things in your old room. There's a Hikeroa girl in there now. Kick her out. She's no good."

Teuru was unpacking when the German landlady returned and announced, "Under no circumstances are you to give any food to that bastard Johnny Roe." This, Teuru figured, meant that Mr. Roe had stopped paying his bills. She was alarmed, therefore, when the American shouted for some ice. She filled the bucket and started upstairs.

"Remember!" Frau Henslick warned. "No food!"

Teuru was quite unprepared for what she saw. In bed lay the young American, very drunk. That was normal, but the once neat room was a shambles. Clothes were scattered everywhere, men's and women's, and as she picked her way among them she saw that Hedy was perched in the armchair, peeling an orange.

"Surprise!" Hedy cried. "I live here now!"

"Let's have the ice," Mr. Roe moaned.

"Don't worry about him!" Hedy laughed. "This is no yacht, but Johnny's a lot more fun."

"You ought to keep the room cleaned up."

"Johnny don't care. And besides, I can see where things are."

Mr. Roe was in as bad a condition as his room. His face was a pallid white and his hair needed cutting. "I think he ought to have a doctor," Teuru said.

"He's drunk."

"How does he live?"

"Traveler's checks. They're wonderful. I sign his name here, and a Chinaman cashes them."

"Then why don't you pay his bills? So I can bring him food?"

"We go out to eat now and then," Hedy assured her, but it

102

was obvious that most of the money went for her clothes and his gin.

So from time to time Teuru spent her own money to provide Mr. Roe a decent meal. She delivered it secretly so that neither Hedy nor Frau Henslick could berate her. One day she was sure that Mr. Roe was dying, but that very evening he and Hedy appeared at Quinn's. He was handsome in pressed whites. Hedy was breathless in a halter bra, a sweeping dirndl and gold slippers. Mr. Roe recognized Teuru and asked her to dance.

"I must owe you a lot of money," he apologized.

"You ought to stay sober and eat more," she advised.

She hoped that he would invite her to dance again, but he soon became staggeringly drunk and danced no more. There were moments, these days, when Teuru was almost unhappy. She would step out of the hotel and see that gaping empty space where the *Jean Delacroix* had anchored and she would recall Victor and his flashing white uniform. At such moments she would wish that somehow they could have married.

But it was difficult for Teuru to remain melancholy for long. Her happy, bubbling nature would assert itself and she would be swept once more into the rich pattern of Papeete life. In the evenings she would walk through the colorful streets, her head high, and she would find a dozen things to laugh at: tourists avoiding Chinamen as if they were killers, little girls acting like big girls and whistling at sailors, a Paumotu fisherman wrestling with a turtle. One night she stood for some time chuckling at a tiny Chinese seamstress trying to fit a very sour white woman with a white dress. Teuru's eyes bubbled with merriment as she watched the white woman trying to look important. Then she heard a rasping voice cry, "Don't move. Keep the light on your face."

She turned and saw a wretched little man of more than forty, pencil in hand, sitting in a doorway. His head was large and dirty. His clothes were borrowed and also dirty. He did not have good teeth and he was sketching Teuru's head.

"I must go now," she laughed.

"No!" he pleaded, and there was something in his voice that commanded her to stay. So she continued to laugh at the Chinese seamstress and the white woman, while the little man made hurried scratches on his pad.

"What are you doing?" she asked.

He showed her the sketch. "That's you," he said.

On that first night she talked a long time with Earl

Weebles, even bought him some beer, which they shared in a grubby cantina while he explained what sculpture was. "I can take a piece of marble," he began. Then he laughed nervously and said, "Damned little marble I see these days. But I can take mud or cement or even butter. And a human being grows right out of it."

"I don't believe you," Teuru laughed.

So he took her to his small room and for five successive evenings she returned and posed for him while he hacked away at a chunk of tree he had somehow lugged into the room. "You understand," he said in his rasping voice, "that I can't pay you."

But she was so convinced that this little man loved what he was doing that she sat willingly, amused by his earnest comment. "England's a rotten place to live," he said. "Too cold. I almost died there. Tuberculosis. But I always dreamed of Tahiti."

"How did you get here?" she asked.

"Damned near didn't. Got caught passing bad checks."

"Where did you learn to carve?"

"Never learned. Just started one day. Used to spend my last thruppence on museums. Went to Paris, too. Fine museums there. You ever been to Paris?"

"I've only been here twice," she laughed.

"You are very beautiful," he said. "Now! Would you like to see yourself?"

He stepped aside and allowed Teuru to see her portrait. She was astonished that wood could be hacked away until it looked like a human head: "My face isn't as lumpy as that!"

He explained, "I didn't try to make your face exactly as it is. I wanted to show it springing from the deep heart of Polynesia."

"What do you mean?" she asked.

"Your people," he said earnestly. "They are the most beautiful human beings I've seen. You are intended to represent them all." Then he tied a rope around the head and started lugging it into the street. "We'll see if we can sell it."

He hawked it through Quinn's, but nobody wanted it. He tried the Col Bleu with no more luck. There was a steamer in from Sydney and he offered it for two hundred francs, five dollars, thirty bob, any sum at all. He asked Teuru to stand beside it so the passengers could see the likeness.

"Don't look much like 'er," an Australian fireman growled, but he bought it for ten shillings. With the money Weebles took Teuru to Quinn's and ordered drinks. He danced, too, coming not quite as high as her forehead. Later, in his studio, he uncovered a three-foot piece of marble and said, "I've been saving it for something worthy. Would you pose for me?"

"Sure," she laughed, resuming the chair.

"I mean . . . undressed?"

She slipped off her clothes and stood in the wavering light, unconsciously assuming a pose that illustrated her strong peasant blood. "It is perfect!" Weebles said, but on that festive night when Teuru first stood in his room, he did not start to work upon the statue.

Teuru now entered upon a complicated life. During the day she listened to Frau Henslick's ranting. Occasionally she slipped out to get Mr. Roe some food, and in the evenings she posed for Earl Weebles as he carved out the series of heads and torsos that he peddled hopelessly through the streets of Papeete. But once after midnight, as she was preparing her bed in the studio, where she now slept, Weebles started to cough and blood came.

Often Teuru had seen this blood-cough in the islands and she knew its meaning. She tried to stifle her cry of pain, but it escaped, and Weebles, with his death sentence smeared redly upon his fingers, said, "That's why I stole money to get out here."

"But you mustn't stay in this tiny room."

"I can work here. That's what matters."

"No!" she protested. "You are killing yourself."

"What else can I do?" the pathetic little man asked, chopping away at his work.

"You can come home with me," she said simply.

She would accept no argument. Earl Weebles was dying, that was plain, and if he remained in this narrow, choked Papeete hovel he would die very soon. But in Povenaaa's big house in Raiatea he might live for many years. Accordingly, she took her savings to the shipping office near the cathedral and said, "I want two tickets to Raiatea. There'll be a lot of baggage." She spent three days trying to sell Earl's accumulated statuary but in the end she had to give it away. His tools she packed and sent aboard the *Hiro*.

As the little ship rolled northward to the rich vanilla lands it would have been natural for the eighteen-year-old girl to contemplate on why she, a girl of bubbling vitality, should be dragging along with her a consumptive and dying Englishman, old and ugly; but she did not engage in such speculation because what she was doing had been done in Polynesia since

105

the first day Captain Cook discovered the islands. The natives, rich and happy in their relaxed life, had instinctively reached out to protect the embittered or confused or deteriorated white man. It was a rare Polynesian family that did not have a record of some outcast cured of despair. The easygoing, sun-drenched natives kept white men as families near London or New York might keep beloved puppies. The wastrels were welcome to hang around the cool porches. They were welcome to sleep with the unmarried daughters. And if the time ever came when they were able to return to what they called civilization, there was a pang of regret in the bosom of the Polynesian family that had—perhaps only for a brief period—protected them as treasured pets. So on the northward journey Teuru stood barefooted, her fine head and chest forward to shield little Earl Weebles from the rain.

The arrival in Raiatea was not gala. Maggi took one look at the little shrimp and washed her hands of the whole affair. "Another passage wasted," she snorted, adding in a loud voice so that all on the dock could hear, "They tell me, however, that Hedy caught herself another rich American."

To Povenaaa an Englishman was no better than a Frenchman. He made it a point to stumble over chunks of statuary and then moan as if his shin had been fractured. At night he would sit on his porch and shout across to Maggi, "I wanted a jeep and look what I got. A stonemason that don't even know how to build a house."

But Povenaaa's troubles were only beginning. Teuru made him haul clay to Weebles' room and big rocks and stumps of trees. She bought him not a jeep but a broken-down old mare and it became a common sight to see sweating Povenaaa, his pants slipping down, straining along the roads, cursing bitterly while he dragged behind some huge object that raised a storm of dust and flies.

For the closer Earl Weebles came to death, the grander became his designs. His largest group showed Povenaaa, Maggi and Teuru standing by the prow of a ship at the critical moment when it hesitates at the edge of the ocean. Povenaaa was transmuted into a fearless navigator. Maggi was the symbolic matriarch bearing food and determination into the canoe. Teuru was pregnant, carrying the seed of Polynesia to a new part of the world. In this majestic group there were no fragments of a dying race, no wormy, whining Povenaaa. Here was depicted the dayspring of Polynesia.

It was this way with every statue Weebles carved. He did not record the death about him in Raiatea, for in the midst

of his own death he saw life. He witnessed the eternal on-
springing of humanity, and in his Raiatea pieces he created a
testament of life. Consider only his figure of the fisherman.
He wanted to use Povenaaa for this, but Teuru's father said
he'd be damned if he'd take off his clothes again for that
shriveled-up Englishman. So Weebles found an old man,
useless for anything, and handed him a spear. What evolved
was the figure of a man rich in years, poised for one last try
at the reef bonita. There was grandeur in the sagging belly
lines, compassion in the old head.

Earl Weebles saw these things. He said, "Raiatea is the
most beautiful spot on earth." It was also apparent that he
considered Teuru the most beautiful woman he had ever
seen. Endlessly he copied her placid beauty. She would come
home from working the vanilla vines, laughing, her hair
about her waist, barefooted and strong, and he would insist
that she stop just as she was, and he would prepare the
sketch upon which he would work that night.

It was curious that she never thought of him as an artist.
He was merely an unfortunate man who needed a last home.
She worked for him, posed for him, slept with him and com-
forted him when coughing spells attacked. She even enlisted
the aid of her cautious employer, Kim Sing.

This happened when she found that Weebles needed new
tools, a sketch book and some medicine. Her own money had
been used up and Povenaaa had none. So she went to Kim
Sing. "Why do you need so much money?" he asked.

"To buy rocks with."

"Rocks!"

"Please, M'sieur Kim. My friend needs many things."

"Can he pay back the loan?"

"He could give you a piece of sculpture, perhaps?"

The canny businessman laughed. "None of that stuff!"

"Then I'll pay it back," Teuru said.

"How?"

"You yourself said I was your best workman."

"It would take a long time."

"I'll be here a long time," Teuru insisted.

"But why should you do such a thing?"

"Because Weebles needs the money. Now."

"Are you in love with this man?"

"Of course not."

"Then why do you seek the money?"

"Because he's very sick," she said.

By such persistence Teuru mustered the help of many

people in behalf of Earl Weebles. In time she even wore down fat Maggi's contempt, whereupon she arranged for the sculptor to take his lunch at Maggi's, so that he could have hot food.

"I don't object to feeding you," Maggi puffed. "Most island families have some no-good bum eating their food sooner or later."

"Why do you tolerate it?" Weebles asked humbly.

"When I was young I liked to have a white man around. It was fashionable."

Weebles wiped his chin and said, "I could never express in words . . ."

"I know," Maggi broke in. "I must say that for you. You're grateful. You take the French poet that lived with Teuru last year. What a simpleton! Used to ask me, 'Maggi? Where has the grandeur gone?' I told him if he ever got a good hold on Hedy he'd have more grandeur than he could handle."

"The grandeur gone?" Weebles repeated incredulously. "I've never seen such grandeur before. The hills quiver with meaning."

"And you haven't seen Hedy yet!" Maggi added. In time she grew to like the wizened Englishman. "Weebles!" she cried one day. "Why don't you move over here with me?"

The little man looked up in amazement at the woman who weighed more than twice as much as he. "Not that," she roared, banging the table until the plate of fried fish clattered. "I was thinking that if you left Povenaaa's . . . If I took care of you . . . Then Teuru could go back to Papeete."

"Does she want to go?" Weebles asked quietly.

"Of course she does. She's got to catch herself a rich American."

There was a long silence, one of those hazy, fly-buzzing pauses during which the bedraggled Englishman stared at the fat woman. Finally he muttered, "I won't be there much longer."

"The sickness?" Maggi asked, banging her chest. "It's bad, eh?" Weebles nodded and Maggi changed the subject abruptly, "But you've got to do something with all that junk."

"What junk?"

"Those heads. Those things you carve."

"What do you mean?"

"I mean," she said, banging the table, "that pretty soon it's going to cave in Povenaaa's floor." That was when she started hauling one piece after another down to the *Hiro,* peddling them among the passengers. She sold by weight, asking a dollar a pound, but she was usually so sweaty and puffing when she lugged the stuff aboard that she would accept any reasonable offer.

Weebles was delighted. He had, in his lifetime, sold very few pieces and he glowed with satisfaction when Maggi reported good luck. "Remember that head of Teuru that looked like a cow? This morning I stuck a Swiss woman with it."

Weebles loved beer and in the evening when a sale had been made he would stand treat at Le Croix du Sud. Once, as Teuru raised the amber glass to her amber lips, the sculptor stopped, enraptured. He put down his glass, deeply affected, and begged to be excused. They heard him coughing outside and he waited in the road until Teuru left the bar. They walked through the deserted streets, down to the wharf where the sweet vanilla beans were waiting shipment.

"I've never been able to talk well," he said.

They had never said much, Teuru and Weebles, but this night great agitation gnawed him and he said, "You're very young . . ." but the precise words would not come, and he stood there by the straits from which the great navigators had set forth. His hands reached for hers and he felt the subtle structure of her bone and flesh. Finally he blurted out, all at once, "You have wasted these months on me."

There was a world more he wanted to say, but he was silent, an inchoate chunk of confusion which no chisel like his own had ever quite polished to completion. When they got home he begged her to pose for him once again, and Teuru stood there naked in her father's room. The statue was never completed, of course, for that night he died.

He was buried, as he would have wished, near the straits of Raiatea. When the funeral was over Povenaaa said, "Now we can get some of this junk out of here." He ordered the whole collection to be hauled away, but this was a silly command because he had to do the hauling. The smaller pieces he gave to people about the island who had posed for Weebles at one time or another. But he was stuck with the big ones. He tried to make Maggi take some, but she would have none of them.

"If I look like a blown-up whale," she snorted, "I at least don't want a picture of me around the house."

It was she who finally talked some sense into Teuru's head. She said, "It's all very well to be nice to men. A girl ought to be. Lord knows, I was in my day. But it's also necessary to

109

look out for yourself. How do you suppose I bought this house? A rich American, that's how. Now you get on back to Tahiti and find yourself a real man."

She bought Teuru her third ticket to Papeete and whispered consolingly as the *Hiro* blew its whistle, "You've had a no-good Frenchman and a half-dead Englishman. Get yourself a strong American and start having babies."

This time Hedy did not meet Teuru at the Papeete quay. Alone, the nineteen-year-old girl trudged back to the Hotel Montparnasse, where to her surprise Frau Henslick greeted her with an embrace. "You're the only girl I've ever been able to trust," she shouted. "That Hikeroa girl has your room again. Throw the tramp out."

Cautiously Teuru motioned up the stairs with her thumb. "Hedy still there?"

Frau Henslick put down her pencil and beamed. "She's the smart one. She's married."

"To the American?"

"That good-for-nothing drunk?" And although Teuru could hear no disturbance, Frau Henslick suddenly screamed, "Shut up, you lazy bastard."

"What's the matter with him?" Teuru asked.

"Nothing. Hedy stayed around till the traveler's checks were used up. Then she married this rich Austrian refugee. He runs the new curio shop."

Frau Henslick directed Teuru along the quay to a bright new store. Inside, a nervous Austrian tended shop, hovering like a frightened hummingbird above trays of exquisite jewelry. "Is Hedy here?" Teuru asked.

The Austrian fluttered to the back of the shop and with obvious uxoriousness called for his wife. In a moment she appeared, gloriously pregnant. She posed for a moment beside her birdlike mate and then said, "M'sieur Kraushoffer—you must never call him Herr Kraushoffer. He wants no more of that. He's a real sculptor, not like that dirty Englishman." She pointed out the delicate filigree work M'sieur did. "It sells very well."

In proof she led barefooted Teuru onto the sidewalk and pointed to a spanking new Renault. "Ours," she said simply. She made Teuru climb in, and they took turns blowing the horn. Then she kissed her friend and whispered, "M'sieur Kraushoffer has a rich friend. Tonight put on your best dress and eat with us."

The dinner was excellent, and Hedy was quite the grandest lady Teuru had ever seen. She commanded the servants what

110

they must do, served the wine with a dazzling smile and continually referred to how clever her husband was. The other guest was a moody Bavarian, Herr Brandt. He was, he announced, considering a business in Tahiti. He used many words that Teuru did not understand and wound up by trying to rip off all her clothes. She was not averse to love making, for Maggi had long ago instructed that this was natural for a girl after she was fifteen and that men seemed to enjoy it greatly. But Teuru compared rough, cold Herr Brandt with kind, gentle Earl Weebles and as a logical conclusion she smashed the German across the nose and ran back to the hotel.

In the morning Hedy appeared. She was furious, said that Teuru had insulted her husband's friend and that she must never come back to the shop again. Never. Tears followed with Hedy admitting that Herr Brandt had tried to do the same with her once, and that she had struck him too. She gave Teuru a wristwatch and said, "Take it up to Johnny. We broke up in a terrible row, and I stole most of his things. But I'm not mad at him any more." She fluffed out her pretty dress, said good-bye and walked down the quay, calling *"Bon jour"* to all the other respectable married women of the town.

It was some time before Teuru found occasion to deliver the stolen watch, but when she did she was dismayed at what she found. In a dark room, surrounded by filthy confusion, red-headed Johnny Roe lay sprawled on a bed he had not left for four days. He had not shaved. He had not washed. He had not eaten. He was a horrible cartoon of a man, so that even the stray island girls now let him alone at night.

"Mr. Roe!" Teuru called gently. In a month-old stupor he rolled his head slightly and stared at her.

"Who's there?" he mumbled.

"I've brought your watch back You must get up." She threw him a pair of shorts and insisted that he crawl into them, but when he tried to lead him along the hallway to the bathroom he collapsed. Teuru called for Frau Henslick, who hurried to the top of the stairs. When she saw it was Roe again she became raucous.

"I'll never touch that drunken swine again. I've hauled him back to his room for the last time." She stood over the crumpled body—the most recent in a distinguished line of men who had tried to drink themselves to death in the Montparnasse—and reviled the American while Teuru ran along the quay searching for someone to help her lift the inert form. Finally she got Johnny spread-eagled on the sheets. Then she washed and shaved him, holding his face tightly when the dull razor grabbed. He was bleeding when she finished, but he was beginning to look like a human being.

It was three days before he could walk to a meal. In that time Teuru had actually to chew small portions of meat and place them between his lips. She had also to buy him the gin he whimpered for, giving him a little less each day until she had weaned him back to strength.

Frau Henslick was outraged. She said that Johnny Roe should be tossed into the bay. "Shark's meat! That's what he is!" She said that as soon as he could move she was going to have him tossed in jail. And as for that room! Out he must go!

Teuru solved this by moving him down to her room, and it was there, in a grubby back hallway of the Montparnasse, that she finally learned how truly sweet it was to be in love. It was as Maggi had said, "Quiet bits of heaven." For Johnny Roe had come so close to wrecking himself that he could appreciate what Teuru had done for him.

"See what the Chinaman will give us for the watch," he suggested. She became adept in haggling over prices with the pawnbrokers and she hoarded both her salary and the loans on his jewelry. Like a French housewife she husbanded their wealth and spent it on things that would be food for Johnny. It was very good to watch him come alive.

"What happened to you?" she asked.

"I'd always heard about these islands. After the war I wanted to see them."

"Were you in the war?"

"Like everyone else."

"Why is it so many white men want to come to Tahiti?"

"You've got to have somewhere you want to go," he replied.

"What did you want to find?"

"You, I guess."

"We're out of money," she replied, changing the subject. "I'll have to get a job—somewhere."

"What can you do?" she asked.

"Best thing I ever did was fly a plane."

"Maybe I can figure out something," she said.

And that was how Teuru, Povenaaa's daughter, finally arrived one day in Raiatea with an honest-to-God American. As the *Hiro* docked Maggi and Povenaaa waited ecstatically.

112

They studied the clean-shaven, good-looking young man and Maggi cried in Polynesian, "I knew you could do it!"

It was a much different story, however, when the four of them faced the rancid butter of Le Croix du Sud. Povenaaa got right to the point. "I better hurry over to Bora Bora, because there's only one jeep left."

"You buying a jeep?" Johnny inquired.

Povenaaa winked broadly and patted Johnny on the arm. "It's good to see you here, son. How long you intend to stay?"

"As long as Kim Sing . . . that's his name, isn't it?"

"You know our leading merchant?" Povenaaa asked expansively.

"Not exactly. I hope to work for him, though."

"Work?" Maggi gulped.

"Did you say work?" Povenaaa gaped.

"Yes. Teuru told me . . ."

Now Povenaaa became all diplomacy. "Do you mean," he probed, "that you have to work?"

"Yes."

"You mean . . . you're broke?"

"That's right. If it hadn't been for Teuru . . ."

This was more than man could bear. Povenaaa became choleric and then spluttered, "Pigs! Dogs! Chickens!" What this meant he did not stop to explain. In majestic outrage he stamped from the hotel and did not show his face in the bar for three days. As for Maggi, she sank back in her chair and studied Teuru. Three times she started to ask questions but each time she shuddered and ended by ordering herself more beer.

By this time Kim Sing had opened his vanilla sheds and the rich smell permeated the bar, so Teuru said, "You'll get used to that smell. We'll go now."

She led Johnny across the road and presented him to the merchant. "An American?" Kim replied. "I couldn't pay an American decent wages."

"Any wages would be decent," Johnny confessed.

So each sunny morning Johnny Roe hauled out into the hot sunlight huge tarpaulins bearing the harvested beans, now five to seven inches long, laden with essence which the heat would tease into condition, so that in time the patiently tended beans became pliable and wonderfully odorous. At night he hauled the tarps in out of the dew, and when the beans were cured, he arranged them upright on big tables.

Then Teuru went to work. Sitting with her eyes at the

level of the bean tops, she bundled the licorice-colored beans into the quarter-kilo packages which were shipped to Paris. Forming her left hand in a circle, she would cull from the large assortment a few choice beans to make the outside of the bundle attractive. For the middle she saved the scrubs, being attentive to select each bean so that when the longer outside ones were pulled into position all beans would appear to be of the same length. Kim Sing said that Teuru's deft bundling earned him an extra 20 per cent.

These were happy days for Teuru. She watched Johnny thriving under the new regime and saw that he was growing brown and strong. It was fun, too, to have him working with her and she enjoyed watching him spend the money she allowed him at the bar. He drank only beer himself, but he was a great favorite with the young men of Raiatea, standing them whiskey and gin, beating them at darts. Sometimes Teuru told herself that she had been luckier than most girls, and the more she grew to love Johnny the more clearly she remembered frightened Victor and triumphant Earl Weebles. One night she told Maggi, "I've been lucky."

Maggi leaned back to count up the score. "By and large you have been," she agreed.

Only Povenaaa held out. Each time he saw Johnny he was humiliated anew. Pushing his forlorn mare along the roads, the cruelly betrayed man would dream of that last jeep in Bora Bora. Then he would hammer the mare and imagine it was Johnny Roe.

But when Povenaaa did finally accept Johnny it was completely, said he was the finest American he had ever known. The two men got roaring tight and stopped every stranger on the road to tell them the news. Teuru was going to have a baby!

Yes, Teuru was pregnant. Maggi, of course, had been the first to detect the happy secret and she commissioned Major to dash through the streets informing everyone. When Povenaaa heard, he left the mule right in the vanilla fields and came storming into the shed and informed Kim Sing, "We're going to the bar and get drunk." Then he had a better idea. He whispered to Johnny, "We'll stick the Chinaman for the drinks." Unctuously he said to Kim, "It wouldn't be a celebration without you." So the merchant paid for the bottles and Povenaaa giggled at having made the Chinaman a fool. But Kim Sing had plans of his own and when they were discovered they almost drove Johnny Roe crazy.

It happened one morning when Johnny came to work and

114

found Maggi, Kim Sing, Povenaaa and three other men rolling dice. Teuru stood nearby, watching the game with interest, advising Maggi, "You better try harder! You need three more sixes!"

"What's the game?" Johnny asked.

"Dice," Teuru said.

"I can see that. What's it about?"

Teuru blushed and looked away, so Johnny asked Povenaaa. "Don't bother me now," the excited man cried. Suddenly there were shouts of triumph and Maggi swore the Chinaman had cheated, but Kim Sing grinned happily and picked up the dice.

"The damned Chinaman gets the baby," Povenaaa spat.

"Gets what?" Johnny asked.

"The baby."

"Whose baby?"

"Teuru's."

"I didn't know Teuru had a baby."

"She doesn't . . . yet."

"You mean . . . my baby?" Johnny fell back with mouth gaping. Then he yelled, "Hey! What's this about my baby?"

"He won it," Maggi said disconsolately.

Grabbing Teuru the American cried, "What are they talking about?"

"When it's born," Teuru said. "All the people in Raiatea would like to have it. So we rolled dice."

"But it's your own baby!" he stormed.

"Sure," she said. "But I can't keep it. I'm not married."

"Your own flesh and blood!"

"What's he mean?" Teuru asked Maggi.

Johnny Roe looked beseechingly at the fat woman and asked, "Would you give away your own baby? Would you give away Major?"

The crowd in the vanilla shed burst into laughter and Johnny demanded to know the joke. "It's Major!" Povenaaa roared, punching Johnny in the ribs. "Major's not her baby. She's Hedy's."

"You mean that Hedy. . . ."

"Of course," Maggi explained. "Hedy had to go to Tahiti for a good time before settling down. So she gave me Major."

Johnny Roe had heard enough. He stormed off and bought two bottles of gin, and when Teuru found him he had returned to his Montparnasse days except that now he blubbered, "Our baby! You raffled off our baby with a pair of dice!"

He kept this up for a whole day and Teuru became afraid that it was the start of another epic binge, so she broke the gin bottles and said, "All girls give away their first babies. How else could they get married?"

Johnny sat upright, suddenly sobered. "What do you mean, married?"

"What man in Raiatea would want a girl who couldn't have babies?"

"You mean . . . the men don't care?"

"Very much! Since people find I'm to have a baby several men who never noticed me before have asked when you were going away."

"What happens then?" Johnny asked suspiciously.

"Then I get married."

Johnny fell back on his pillow and moaned, "It's indecent. By God, it's indecent."

So Teuru consulted Maggi who said, "I'll talk to him." She puffed into the bedroom and asked, "What are you moaning about?"

"This whole affair. It's indecent."

"What's wrong about it? Tell me, why did you come out here?"

"I was a drunken Papeete wreck, so Teuru brought me here."

"I mean why did you come to Tahiti?"

"Well, in California I was even a worse wreck."

"Why?"

"The war, I guess."

"We had a war, too."

"Mine was different."

"Oh, no. Eighty men from Raiatea volunteered and went into the desert with the Foreign Legion. We lost many men from Raiatea."

"They have a statue in Canada which says something about the ones who didn't come back being the lucky ones."

"Don't ever believe it! Is that what you thought, Johnny?"

"Something like that. I got all mixed up."

Maggi started to laugh. "I'll never understand white men."

"How do you mean?" Johnny asked.

"Like you," she said, puffing heavily. "You get sick at heart about something, so you come out here to cure the disease, and when you're cured you despise us for how we manage it. That seems ridiculous to me."

"It's even more ridiculous, how a girl's own father—how Povenaaa can send Teuru to Papeete."

Maggi exploded with laughter. "Povenaaa? Did you say Povenaaa?" She held her fat sides and shook her head hilariously. "Didn't anybody tell you? Povenaaa could have no children. That poor skinny man. We felt sorry for him in Raiatea so somebody gave him a baby to bring up."

"Who did?"

"I did."

Johnny Roe was stopped dead cold. They were pitching curves at him now and he was stopped cold. He started to laugh and finally kissed fat Maggi on the cheek. Seeing her chance, she grabbed him by the hair and kissed him back.

"You're a smart woman," he cried. "You're about the smartest woman I've ever known."

"I been around," she joked, talking like an American movie.

Johnny finally sat on the bed and asked, "How come you gave up Teuru?"

"I heard the rich Americans were coming to Papeete ... about the time of Zane Grey. I wanted to see things before I married."

"Did you marry?"

"Oh, yes."

"Where's your husband?"

"He was killed in the war. In the desert."

That was that. Johnny had no more to say, but as she left, Maggi added, "When you get back home ... Well, if you should ever make any money, send Povenaaa a jeep."

But Povenaaa did not have to wait upon such a miracle, for a more astonishing one took place right on Raiatea. One morning, about seven, a yacht put into the straits and an expensive launch, manned by men in white, hurried ashore. An elderly gentlemen with white moustaches asked many questions at Le Croix du Sud and ended by going to Kim Sing's vanilla shed. He stood in the doorway for a moment until his eyes became accustomed to the shadows. Then he saw what he was seeking.

"Hello, Johnny," he said.

The young American turned, clean, bronzed, solid-looking: "Hello, Mr. Winchester."

"I told your father I'd look you up."

"How is Dad?"

"Fine, fine. I think he'd like to have you back."

That night on the polished yacht Povenaaa and Maggi ate

117

off silver plates, but Teuru was not there. "I'm too fat," she told Johnny, insisting that he go. After brandy Mr. Winchester said he thought it was about time for Johnny Roehampton to be heading home. Johnny blushed nervously and agreed it was about time.

"He's been here long enough," Maggi said expansively.

"Too long," Povenaaa observed.

Johnny had much to do before shoving off. He thanked Kim Sing for the job. He gave presents to each of the gang at the bar. He bought Maggi a shawl and even promised to send Povenaaa a jeep.

But Povenaaa had been disappointed many times in his life and he was not to be taken in by any more tricks, so while Johnny was packing he rowed out to the yacht and consulted Mrs. Winchester. "I don't ask much," he said. "I'm reasonable, but I've had dreadful bad luck with Teuru."

"Who's Teuru?"

"My daughter."

"Is she sick?"

"No, she's pregnant."

Mrs. Winchester gulped. "You mean ... she isn't ... married?"

"Certainly not!" Povenaaa snapped. "It's my bad luck with her men I'm speaking of."

"What do you mean, her men?"

"I don't think she has good sense," Povenaaa explained. "First she brings home a Frenchman. He lives with us eight months and I don't get a sou. Then she brings home an Englishman. Not a sou. Now it's Johnny Roe. Still no money."

Mrs. Winchester grew pale. "You mean .. you would take money ... for your daughter?"

"Well, seeing that Johnny is leaving behind a baby that I'll have to feed ..."

Weakly Mrs. Winchester cried, "Griswold! Griswold!" When her husband appeared she whispered, "Get this creature out of here."

"What's going on?" Mr. Winchester blustered.

"It's unspeakable! This wretched man's daughter has had three lovers. Now she's going to have a baby and her father"—she shuddered—"wants to be paid off."

Mr. Winchester took out his wallet and said, "My dear, I warned you that Tahiti ..."

"Don't give it to him! Give it to the girl, if she's not some cheap. ..."

118

"I've seen the girl," Mr. Winchester said. "She's very decent."

He took his wife ashore and led her to the vanilla shed, where she gasped when she saw how lovely Teuru was.

"You're very pretty," Mrs. Winchester said.

"Johnny told me you were an old friend."

"Yes, we've known his family for years."

"What will Johnny do . . . when he gets home, I mean?"

Mrs. Winchester perceived that she had stumbled upon the classic island tragedy: the deserted native girl and the handsome white man. So she said gently, "He'll probably go back to college."

"And get married?" Teuru asked, smiling warmly as she whipped cords about her bundle of beans.

Mrs. Winchester knew that the brave smile masked the heartbreak of betrayal, so she said consolingly, "And you? What will you do?"

Teuru started a new bundle in her left hand and said thoughtfully, "I guess I'll get married, too. After I get rid of the baby."

Mrs. Winchester swallowed. "What do you mean? Get rid of the baby?"

"Kim Sing won it. After a few weeks I'll give it to Kim Sing."

"He . . . won . . . it?" the American woman asked weakly.

"Yes. He threw eleven sixes."

Mrs. Winchester retreated in a flood of nausea. At the door she bumped into Povenaaa and said to her husband between clenched teeth, "Give this despicable creature some money." Then she stared at Povenaaa and said bitterly, "You had to take care of the baby!"

Yet it was Mr. Winchester's money that finally settled many problems for Teuru. After the yacht left, with redheaded Johnny Roehampton staring at the dock until the headland had been breasted, Povenaaa slipped over to Bora Bora and came home with the last jeep. It was badly battered and carried a garish sign across the front: SHORE PATROL. But it ran and it had a horn. Povenaaa's first use of it was to drive up to Kim Sing's establishment and blow the horn like mad. When the Chinaman appeared Povenaaa stood up and announced to his former employer, "You, M'sieur Kim Sing can go to hell." Then he drove off down the middle of the road.

Teuru immediately came to apologize. She told Kim he had

119

always been kind to her family and that she appreciated this. "And now what will you do?" Kim asked.

Teuru looked at the bundles she had tied and said, "After the child is born, Maggi wants me to go back to Papeete."

"Papeete is very fine," Kim said.

"But the rooms are so small and dark. I don't want to leave Raiatea any more."

Kim Sing thought a long time and said, "You should tell your father."

So Teuru sought out Povenaaa at the new pier where he was hauling rock. "I'm not going back to Tahiti," she announced.

To her surprise Povenaaa said, "Good! We're people of importance now. We still have lots of money left from the yacht." Then, seeing Kim Sing approaching, he shouted, "And no daughter of mine is going to work for a damned Chinaman, either!"

Kim Sing came to the pile of rocks and said haltingly, "I did not come to ask Teuru to work for me again."

"Then get out of the way. Can't you see I'm a busy man?"

"I came to ask . . . since Teuru does not wish to leave . . . since I'm to have the baby anyway . . ."

When the meaning dawned on Povenaaa he slammed the jeep into low gear and tried to murder the Chinaman with it. "My daughter!" he bellowed. "Living with a Chinaman!"

From behind the rocks the merchant said quietly, "I am not asking her to live with me. I am asking her to marry me."

Then Teuru stepped boldly beside Kim Sing and said, "Yes, Povenaaa, we are going to get married." Povenaaa let his hands fall from the steering wheel and started to gulp, but Teuru said softly, "I went to Papeete three times for you. Now I shall stop in Raiatea."

Povenaaa washed his hands of the whole affair. He announced, at Le Croix du Sud, that if a daughter of his insisted upon such a thing he wished to hear no more about it. Maggi arranged the wedding and exacted from Kim a written pledge that he would not beat Teuru as some of his countrymen did their wives and that he would allow her spending money so long as she continued to wrap bundles of vanilla. But on one point he was adamant. Povenaaa came sniveling around and said that since his only daughter was leaving home he might as well sell the house, but Earl Weebles' big sculptures still cluttered up the place. "Why not move them into the vanilla shed?"

But Kim Sing—even though he had sworn not to beat his wife—was not a complete fool. So years later when hungry collectors from London and Paris reached Raiatea they uncovered the precious masterpieces in the most unlikely places. The classic bust of Maggi, for example—the one now in the Louvre—it was found propping open the door to the barn where Povenaaa kept his jeep.

Fiji

Imagine a group of islands blessed by heaven, rich in all things needed to build a good life, plus gold mines and a good climate. Picture a native population carefree, delightful and happy. Add a white government that works overtime to give honest service. Top it all off with a democracy that enables dozens of different levels of society—from Oxford graduates to bush dwellers—to have a fine time. That makes a pretty wonderful colony, doesn't it?

There's only one thing wrong with that picture of Fiji. The Indians. Nobody can stand the Indians. When threepenny bits were recently issued in an unconventional form, bankers experienced a phenomenal run. They discovered that Indian sharpsters were buying in quantity and scurrying to remote regions where the new coins were sold to gullible natives as sovereigns. The Indians made a profit of 7700% on each sale.

Of 7000 criminal cases tried in one year, 5000 had Indian defendants, although they represented only 50% of the population. In the same year they accounted for 80% of the income-tax penalties. Christian church schools are overrun with Indians who, when they are graduated, ignore the religion. Hospitals are jammed with Indians but boycotted by Indian nurses who say such work is fit only for natives.

When the Japanese threatened the islands—they were less than 900 miles away—no Indians volunteered for military service, and those finally forced into uniform were, with few exceptions, useless. Some Indian leaders indulged in near treason and many hoped for a Japanese triumph.

It is almost impossible to like the Indians of Fiji. They are suspicious, vengeful, whining, unassimilated, provocative aliens in a land where they have lived for more than seventy years. They hate everyone: black natives, white Englishmen, brown Polynesians and friendly Americans. They will not marry with Fijians, whom they despise. They avoid English ways, which they abhor. They cannot be depended upon to support necessary government policies. Above all, they are surly and unpleasant. It is possible for a traveler to spend a week in Fiji without ever seeing an Indian smile.

People from many lands have come to Fiji with sentimental sympathy for Gandhi's brave fight against British imperialism. They have been predisposed to like the Indians and to distrust the British. But one week in Fiji and they say, as one woman did, "I would like to eat every word I ever uttered in favor of Indians. If America had to put up with Fiji for a year, we'd all go crazy."

The question of what to do with these clever Indians of Fiji is the most acute problem in the Pacific today. Within ten years it will become a world concern. They were brought to the islands by grasping capitalists who needed a docile labor supply for the sugar-cane fields, just as American landowners needed Negro slave and Mexican labor for our cotton industries. But the Indians have stayed and raised large families until now they outnumber the native Fijians. Soon they will outnumber all the other races combined, and it seems inevitable that Fiji must one day become a colony owned, populated and governed by Indians.

Ramat Singh, from a sugar plantation, illustrates why the Indians are the way they are. He is twenty-nine years old, stands five-feet-nine and weighs only 138 pounds. He is very black and was married at twenty when his wife was sixteen. They have seven children.

Ramat Singh has a lease on some good land, but it belongs to Fijian natives, and after eleven more years he must turn it back to them. What he will do then he doesn't know. There is little land that can be bought by Indians. For the present he has a contract to sell his cane to the Colonial Sugar Refining Company, the second largest corporation in Australia.

Ramat hates the C.S.R., as do many of his silent friends. In 1888 his grandmother was brought over from India as an indentured worker, but she died in the fields after having been beaten by a white overseer. Ramat's mother was seven at the time, and against the law she was forced to work in the fields until her dead mother's period of indenture was ended. From his birth Ramat has hated Europeans and waits only until India, which is now free, expels them from Fiji.

He has studied sugar production until his fields are the finest in the region. His wife and children work the cane and he makes a fair living. He has saved £81 and has hoarded $300 he made off the Americans by selling rotgut whiskey and the address of a girl in Lautoka. He dreams of owning a small store some day.

His home is a two-room corrugated shack that is incredibly dirty. He hates this, especially when the children are sick, and if his store makes money, he is determined to build himself a real house, say twenty years from now. His wife is pregnant

123

again, a fact which pleases him, for he has discovered that big families hold together. Already his oldest son, nine years old and born at the time of his marriage, has saved £2 and $11. His daughter, almost nine, is attractive and may one day marry a store-keeping Indian.

He stays away from natives and white men. He keeps three goats, owns some chickens. He pays what taxes he must, rides buses with a mania, discusses politics with friends and is polite to the C.S.R. field men. He is sure that the Indian leaders in Fiji will force the British to build more schools—neither he nor any of his children has been to school—and he is equally certain that when the schools are built, Indian will be the language used for instruction. Meanwhile he saves every penny he can get and thinks of that store.

Ramat Singh does not think of himself as a revolutionist, but he is. He has only to wait, and one day he will own Fiji. He is one of the millions in many parts of the world who are proving that the cradle is more powerful than legislatures. If he has enough children, they will be able to buy Fijian land. In fact, they will own Fiji.

The land which he is determined to inherit has a vivid history. Less than a hundred years ago these islands of Fiji were the most cruel and barbarous on earth. Cannibalism had become a mania, with rules governing the murder and baking of enemies. Religion required that shipwrecked sailors be cooked and eaten the day caught. "If the mighty sea had not intended these men for you, it would not have sent them." In the worst areas compounds were built where prisoners were fattened, tied into compact living bundles, and roasted. In many parts of the islands choice bodies were salted away and dragged out for princely feasts.

The islands were in perpetual warfare. Villages were plundered. Huts were burned. Everyone captured was eaten. From one small island less than a mile square a band of ruthless predators subdued surrounding lands and exacted intolerable penalties.

And when the native fury seemed about to spend itself, beachcombers from many nations fought their way ashore, defied the priests who ordered them killed, and set up reigns of horror which included massacres, cannibal feasts and total degeneracy. The white savages excelled the black.

One of the worst was a Swede who called himself Charlie Savage. He was found by a British ship on a remote island, and no one ever knew how he got there. He was taken to

Fiji, where he jumped ship and became military adviser to murdering chiefs. He used firearms and shot hundreds of natives for the sport. He instigated cannibal feasts, debauched as many women as he could catch, had 150 known children, and gradually gathered about him a gang of European and Chinese killers equally depraved.

By 1813 he had so outraged the natives that he had to seek protection from a passing British ship, whose crew he inveigled into disgraceful wars of retaliation, in which corpses were carefully harvested for evening feasts.

But this time the natives outguessed their tormentors and massacred the lot, except six who fortified themselves on a hilltop. Charlie Savage and a Chinaman felt certain they could fancy-talk the natives into a truce and set off to do so. An eye-witness reports: "At that moment Charlie Savage was seized by the legs, and held in that state by six men, with his head placed in a well of fresh water until he was suffocated; whilst at the same instant a powerful savage got behind the Chinaman, and with his huge club knocked the upper part of the skull to pieces. These wretched men were scarcely lifeless when they were cut up and put into ovens ready prepared for the purpose."

Not all white murderers came to such an appropriate end. Others lived on to inflame the islands until Fiji became celebrated as hell on earth. It is doubtful if there has ever been a worse in the Pacific.

And then, within a comparatively brief time, the islanders foreswore their brutal practices, accepted Christianity, begged three different white countries to govern them and developed into what judicious travelers consider the most completely lovable people on earth.

It is doubtful if anyone but an Indian can dislike Fijians. They are immense Negroes modified by Polynesian blood. They wear their hair frizzled straight out from the head, so that the effect is one of a huge head set upon a rugged torso. They are one of the happiest peoples on earth and laugh constantly. Their joy in things is infectious; they love practical jokes, and in warfare they are without fear.

If encouraged, they will sing all night and sleep all day. Late visitors to their churches, where they sing *a capella,* are convinced there is an organ inside, so resonant are their voices. A hundred years of prodding by the British have failed to make the Fijians see why they should work for money. They love children and make wonderful nurses. A completely spoiled English boy of seven was turned over to a

125

huge Fijian woman. She stood him as long as she could, then dropped to her knees so that she was his height, sparred off with him and knocked him silly. When he cried, she yelled, "Get up and fight like a man." In three days he was cured and loved his huge tormentor.

They are so gentle that white women could cross the islands on foot without molestation. They are so tough that on Guadalcanal Japs looked for American Marines to surrender to because of what Fijians might do to them. They are so uproarious in their games—at which they are most skilled—that certain teams won't play them in football; they massacre the opposition just for the hell of it.

How was it possible for the descendants of ruthless savages to change so vividly in a few generations?

First, it is doubtful if their cannibalism was a permanent addiction. It seems to have been on the way out when whites like Charlie Savage introduced firearms and made it easy even for cowards to collect a meal. There were numerous instances in which a chief setting out to extirpate a neighboring community sent messengers ahead to warn them. Then, having arrived at the vacated community, he merely burned down the houses, stole some food and went home pleased with himself. Many of the most brutal massacres developed accidentally when horse play backfired into a hundred murders. Priests kept cannibalism alive, but the Fijians were never very successful warriors. When the really tough Tongans from the south invaded Fiji they met little opposition. The savagery into which the Fijians degenerated was a cultural accident—like the savagery into which Germans descended—and their recovery from it uncovered the real behavior pattern of this singular people.

Second, Fiji was saved by missionaries. These brave souls, who wrecked other islands, resurrected Fiji. It is true that by insisting upon clothes and European habits they also encouraged a fatal incidence of tuberculosis; but the spiritual salvation of Fiji is one of religion's most notable accomplishments.

Many of the missionaries were eaten, leading an irreverent planter to suggest that they triumphed by infiltration. But an endless supply of devout spirits took their places and argued the de-facto king into becoming a Christian. They warned him of the perquisites he must surrender—his many wives, his passion for human flesh, his predilection for treachery—and they argued so well that the old savage saw the merit of

126

their reasoning and Christianized Fiji by fiat. His soldiers murdered those who objected.

Third, although the conversion from cannibalism was dramatic, it was slow. In the 1870's, a planter's wife, going into her kitchen, saw a pair of human hands protruding from the pot in which the Fijian cook was preparing dinner. "Very good!" the cook said. "The best part!" Says the chronicler, "Her mistress got the pot down and sent the surprised woman packing with it, telling her never to come near the place again."

The early settlers gave Fiji one of the oddest alphabets in English. Since Fijians insert a vowel between any two consonants, it was difficult to devise a system of spelling that avoided juxtaposed consonants. For example, *Christ,* in Fijian becomes the inexpressibly lovely *Karisito. Britain* is *Beretani.* So in the Fijian alphabet *d* is pronounced *nd.* (The airport of Nandi is spelled Nadi.) *Q* is *ng.* (The great native drink is yaqona, pronounced yangona.) *B* is *mb,* and *C* is *th.* Thus the king who Christianized Fiji is Cakobau, pronounced Thakombau.

This Cakobau was a remarkable fellow. His family, especially his father, relished brutalities that make modern stomachs retch. His brother tried five times to murder Cakobau, after which unfraternal behavior their father ordered the brother's brains beaten out. Yet as a mature man, Cakobau had the intellectual power to weigh alternatives, to see what was best for his islands, and to decide that only by cession of his power to some white government could he hope to lead his Fijians into any kind of order.

Like several rulers of his age, Cakobau offered his lands to Queen Victoria. And as in many similar cases, the so-called rapacious British declined to accept the gift. So a group of thoughtful Fijians, spurred on by interested whites, offered the islands to the United States. Our Congress did not even acknowledge the offer.

Here were islands strategically situated, rich in copra, in fruit, in commercial possibilities. Ultimately, they were to become fabulously productive in sugar and gold. They were lands which permitted endless exploitation, lands destined to become the key of the South Pacific. And their king could not give them away.

He next tried Germany, but Bismarck refused the offer. Finally, in 1874, Cakobau succeeded in forcing his islands upon Queen Victoria, who was accordingly sent the king's war club, with which he must have dispatched hundreds of enemies before eating them. In 1931, the club was returned to Fiji, where it has become the mace of office whereby Christian law is dispensed to a very well-governed land.

Fiji is the land of tomorrow. The International Date Line cuts through the islands, and here each new day begins. The visitor who flies from Honolulu on Sunday morning arrives in Fiji on the afternoon of the same day, Monday.

During the war, the Navy tried to explain this to its officers, but after a few attempts, it was found that only the elite could comprehend the intricacies. The simplest explanation is this. The sun rises earlier in New York than in San Francisco; earlier in San Francisco than in Honolulu; earlier there than in Tokyo; earlier in Tokyo than in Bombay; earlier there than in Cairo; and earlier in Cairo than in London. It is obvious, therefore, that the sun must rise earlier in New York than in London. But everybody knows that it rises first in London and then in New York.

So to end this absurdity, an arbitrary median had to be selected where a new day could begin. Fortunately, the 180th Meridian, halfway around the world from the Prime Meridian at Greenwich, cuts through the empty Pacific. So each new days starts in Fiji—actually on an island 8 degrees to the east—where the sun first rises on the British Empire.

But the days that begin in Fiji now are not happy ones. Old promises are coming home to roost, and they are in conflict with one another, so that all groups in Fiji seem to be opposed to all other groups.

In 1874 Lord Salisbury gave assurance that any Indian who consented to indentures for work in the cane fields of Fiji would be granted political citizenship there when the indentures were discharged. Thousands of Indians volunteered. There were Sikhs from the highlands, Madrassis from the lowlands, high- and low-caste Hindus, and even some Muslims. They were very poor, uneducated, starving, unhappy people. The good food of the cane fields made them prosper. When their servitude ended, they preferred to remain in Fiji. Some of them had been of low caste in India, even untouchable, and in Fiji caste was pretty much disregarded. Others had surrendered high caste by fleeing India and would have to undergo a long course of reinstitution if they returned. But most important, in Fiji, they had enough to eat, they had freedom, and if they were frugal, they might some day own a store.

Indian families were tremendous. Girls married young, and if a child showed promise, it was common practice for all members of the family to sacrifice to put that one forward—as Scottish and Italian families do. Soon the Indian population leaped from one half of one per cent of the island population to more than fifty per cent. These black, aloof, suspicious, grasping, terribly capable Aryans had become the most important single element in the political, social and economic life of Fiji.

Year	Fijians	Indians
1891	105,800	7,468
1901	94,937	17,105
1921	84,475	60,634
1936	97,651	85,002
1948 est	120,000	127,000
1980 est	140,000	205,000

The impartial observer must admit that the Indians have earned the citizenship Lord Salisbury promised them. They have built Fiji. They made fortunes for the C.S.R. They helped start the gold fields. They swept the streets, ran the stores, made the clothes and waited the tables. In a typical year, 74% of new building was for Indian enterprises. None was for Fijian business. If Western civilization is correct in placing work above godliness, the Indians are better Westerners than either the British or the Americans. And they have produced an endless supply of new citizens, whereas the Fijian population has remained stagnant. Granted that the Indians refused to defend Fiji in war, they have defended it ably in economics, and perhaps that is what counts. The American observer in particular is loath to judge the Fiji Indians if he knows them well; they have done in Fiji what Americans have done around the world. They have worked and made things grow.

The second promise made by the British is perhaps more embarrassing than the first. When they accepted Fiji from Cakobau, they said that they would hold the islands in trust for the Fijian owners. Certain lands—termed Crown Lands—were turned over to the Queen, but all the rest were retained by the natives. (There is argument as to when this promise of stewardship was made. Indians claim it was never made.)

The British could not foresee, of course, that no amount of persuasion would make a Fijian labor like a slave in sugarcane fields. "We will give you money!" the overseers said. "What for?" the Fijian asked. "So you can buy things," the

129

C.S.R. explained. "Don't want nothing," the Fijian grunted. "Ah, but when you have money, you begin to want things," the white man insisted.

But what could a man want that a Fijian didn't have in his communal village? Food? It grew on trees. Clothing? A lap-lap was sufficient. And so it went. The Fijian proved the most intractable workman in the Pacific. Much addicted to walka-bouts, he would disappear from the cane fields after the most solemn bargains. He was a hopeless lout, utterly uncivilized, who put pleasure and singing and drinking yaqona above ten hours of hard work a day!

He retired to his hills and let the Indians do the work. He grew his own food and let the Chinese run the stores. He be-haved himself in his own compound and let the English make a lot of laws. He wore heavy clothes, as the missionaries said, and contracted tuberculosis. He died off by the thousands from measles and small pox, and by default he turned his islands over to the Indians.

It is a cruel trick that one land should be the common home of the most likable people on earth and some of the least likable. It is even crueler that the latter have all the at-tributes necessary for survival in the modern world and that the happy-go-lucky, Hiya-Joe! Fijians have so few.

In this impasse, the British Government has unequivocally announced that they must support the Fijians. In one of the most remarkable speeches ever made by a colonial governor, Sir Brian Freeston said, "The only logical long-range solution to the basic problem of Fiji lies with the leaders of the Indian community themselves. It is for them to consider, and to educate their followers in, the existence of the inescapable dilemma. Either they will continue to multiply beyond availa-ble means of subsistence, with consequent poverty and distress; or they maintain and improve their present standard of living by a voluntary reduction in their natural rate of in-crease."

Then, lest the implication be obscure, he said, "I wish to make it perfectly clear beyond question that there can be no going back on history. There can be no departure from the pledges given to the Fijian people by Her Majesty's Govern-ment at the time of Cession, and subsequently reaffirmed on innumerable occasions. There can be no encroachment, by legislative or any other changes, on the principle that Fijian land belongs to the Fijians and will not be taken from them."

Those are blunt and brave words. They have echoed around the Pacific, and the betting is three to one they cannot be enforced. A geographer who has studied this problem since 1910 says that a solution must be found within the next five years. He gives these reasons. The recent establishment of a free Indian nation has electrified Fiji's Indians. They now have an autonomous homeland to which they can appeal. Their more fiery leaders see India as a champion of multiplying power, one that will some day surely call Britain to task for not having turned Fiji over to its major population group, the Indians.

Europeans in Fiji were therefore astounded when the London Colonial Office assented to India's request that a Commissioner be set up in Fiji to guard the rights of all Indians not permanent residents of the islands. As might be expected, all Indians have felt that this officer—a consul in American terms—was their official representative. His arrival was the first step in the recognition of India's paramount interest in Fiji.

Daily exacerbations are now the rule and will increase as tempers grow thin. A white resident protests in the newspaper about the growing custom of using the prefix Mr. before Indian names. Thereupon, an Indian builder plasters an immense sign on each of his projects: "This house is being built for Mr. K.K. Chandra." An Indian delivers a growing oration about Indian culture and claims that its masterpieces far excel Shakespeare and should be taught in Fijian schools. A young Indian graduate, burning for a white-collar job, cries, "I have only two alternatives, farming or suicide." A descendant of Cakobau terms it effrontery for Indian politicians to harrangue their people on Cession Day—Fiji's Fourth of July—in view of their contemptible war record. An Indian scholar states that instead of the Bible, schools could well teach the ideals of Satyam Shivam. A half-caste reports that as between the industrious Indians and the still savage Fijians who had recently rioted against some half-castes, he would take the Indians any day in the week. And underriding all of this ferment is the unquestioned fact that many Indians favor Communism and see in Russia's advance a substitute for the Japanese thrust against British Fiji that didn't quite come off.

A specialist in the problem has suggested four solutions and has himself disposed of each as impractical. (1) Allow the Indians to have as many children as they want, eliminate the Fijians, and establish an Indian territory in Fiji. ("This would be criminal.") (2) Award the Indian an equal political and educational share in the Colony and trust to his fair play not to victimize the less industrious and tenacious Fijian.

131

("Idealistic and wholly impractical.") (3) Move all Indians to one of the two main islands and evacuate all Fijians to the other. ("Plan has merits, but Indians would resist like wildcats.") (4) Repatriate the entire Indian community, with compensation to be borne as a fixed debt upon the Colony. ("Soundest solution, but would entail the complete collapse of rich Fiji's economic structure.")

In short, there is no solution.

And yet, in the days before the storm, there are few places more pleasant to visit than Fiji. It consists of some thirty main islands, of which two predominate. The largest is Viti Levu, which is about the size of Connecticut. The western half of this tropical island always surprises Americans, for it resembles Wyoming. Red hills, sweeping plateaus and outcropping mountains make it surprisingly handsome. Along the shoreline one gets a slight feeling of the tropics, for palms flourish here. This is where the sugar cane is grown, and the visitor to an island often described as primitive is astonished to find a railroad crossing and recrossing the highway. Along its small steel cradles move rich cane to the C.S.R. factories.

Then suddenly, almost mysteriously, at about the middle of Viti Levu the climate, rainfall, vegetation and terrain change abruptly and one is no longer in dry Wyoming but in a teeming tropical jungle. Rainclouds, driven by the trade winds from the east, drop their moisture as they hit the central mountains. Rivers that look like tired dishwater wind heavily laden to the sea. Jungle plants crowd the road. Mist and storm engulf the land for days on end, and the rainfall is sometimes prodigious.

Yet the jungle is beautiful, for flowers and strange trees abound. Most of the population lives in this rainy sector. Small fields are cleared and planted with dalo (called taro on other islands). Vegetables grow luxuriantly and there are huge banana plantations. The land is rich and productive. The only animal to cause worry is the mongoose, imported from India, which has overrun the island and which eats young chickens.

The English, with a mania for wrong decisions in Fiji, built their capital at Suva, smack in the middle of the heaviest rainfall. Some vacationists never see the sun at Suva, while fifty miles away in either direction, sunshine abounds.

Yet Suva is a superb tropical city. It is cleaner than Papeete, better policed, better built. It is much duller, of course, for Papeete is French, but it is superior in most services and in health. People of all races walk its streets. It has a canal that reminds one of Venice. It has brawling markets, stately banks, two movie houses, numerous churches and more taxicabs per capita—all owned by Indians—than any other city in the world.

It is a thriving seaport, a center for heavy industry and a strong commercial city. One of its firms—there may be three others that do as well—cleared $375,000 profits in a recent year and had accumulated funds of nearly a million dollars lying idle in banks because of no place to invest them.

Suva is also the administrative capital from which all of Britain's islands in the Western Pacific are governed. The Solomons, the New Hebrides, the Gilbert and Ellice groups, even lonely Pitcairn are ruled from here.

The government quarters are a pleasant surprise to most visitors. In space, appointments, landscaping and effect they excel many American state capitols. Perpetually green lawns edged with flowers and giant palms set off the buildings in which a colonial government of the poshest sort supervises an immense and watery domain.

But for most visitors two phenomena are pre-eminent. By a strange coincidence, both the Fijians and Indians contain sects that specialize in firewalking. What they accomplish is unbelievable, but they do it. Pits of stones are brought to a white-hot state by huge wood fires beneath and over them. Then the barefooted firewalkers move deliberately and slowly across the glowing coals. After being on the fiery stones for as long as half a minute, they step out with no trace of burns or blisters.

Skeptical whites who have stepped among the stones have been hospitalized. Several explanations have been hazarded. The one which seems most logical is that the stones are tufa, that porous volcanic rock which is sometimes seen floating on the Pacific. This tufa is so constructed that it cools incredibly rapidly, enough so that heavily calloused feet can stand the heat. The firewalkers, however, insist that they are protected by faith. Either Hinduism or Methodism suffices.

The other memorable institution is the Grand Pacific Hotel. Run at a reputed loss by a New Zealand steamship company, it is the ultimate in tropical hotels. For $3.03 a day, it provides antique living quarters—no baths in rooms—which are kept scrupulously clean, plus three meals a day that are difficult even to describe. Dinner customarily runs to seven courses, and the guest may order as many items from each course as he wishes. The G.P.H., as it is called, is the only inexpensive thing in the tropics today.

A white man living there and participating in the full social life of the colony would wear a dress suit three times as often as a comparable man in New York City would wear his. There is no part of Fiji which is not civilized, although bush natives prefer a more naked kind of life. It is amusing to read modern accounts of savage Fiji. If some of the things were to happen that writers describe, it is dead certain that someone would merely go to the chief's house, lift the phone and call the police. And as likely as not, they would arrive in an Indian taxi!

But many natives prefer to follow the old ways. On a rain-swept hillside near the center of Viti Levu is a small village in which Takala and his family have a hut. It was built years ago of coconut logs, palm matting and thatched roof. It is bound together by sennit, twisted coconut fiber strong as rope, which grows golden brown and patterned with age. The hut has three doors as required by the health ordinance and a legend that gives Takala some comfort on windy nights. In the old days, it was customary to dig the main post holes of a house very deep and then to place in each a living slave to hold the poles steady while the earth was packed in. This insured the house against hurricanes such as devastated one Fijian island recently.

The hard-packed floor of the hut is covered by beautifully woven mats, of which a specially handsome one is reserved as a table. There are no chairs, but beds with mosquito nettings are stacked in the corner. Takala himself has a carved log for a pillow.

He is a Methodist and sings at the mission. His wife, whom he married when he was twenty-eight, is a devout Christian and often contributes her last penny to help starving children in China or earthquake victims in Ecuador.

Takala has had two children. The first died with measles. The second lived for several years but contracted tuberculosis from her grandmother. This disease is almost always fatal unless cared for meticulously. Doctors and nurses have visited Takala's village to instruct people in ways of avoiding T.B. But the villagers wear heavy clothes, get soaked in the rains, sit around telling stores, and die.

Takala is glad he doesn't live in Guadalcanal, where he served with the Americans. Fiji has no malaria, little elephantiasis or dengue. He tells his neighbors they're lucky. He's seen some bad islands.

He does not like to work. When he joined the Army to help Beretani, he worked like a horse unloading ships; but

134

what he preferred was jungle fighting with the Yanks. That was fun.

Of course, he does the jobs assigned him by the chief, whose words are even more important than those of the white governor at Suva. It was funny, during the war. The white governor sent signs and speakers to the village saying that Beretani was in trouble. Fijians were needed for the Army. Nobody in Takala's village went, because it would have been wrong to leave the fields of dalo without the chief's permission.

This made the white men furious and they said, "The Fijians are no better than the Indians." Then someone explained that it was not right for the white governor to yell his head off. Ask the chiefs. So when it was made plain to the chiefs, they returned to their villages and said which men must go. It was funny, there weren't enough uniforms to dress all the men who came down from the hills.

The governor said later that there were never such fighters as the Fijians. Two of Takala's friends were decorated by the Americans, eight by the British, and one of them got the highest military honor in the world.

But Takala does not like fighting. A smart young Fijian who had been to college in New Zealand talked with him one night and told how the black people of Africa had been overrun by Indians, too, and of how they had started a riot about it, and of how lots of Indians were killed. Takala said that was foolishness. If the Indians want more land, give it to them. If the Chinese want to own stores, let them. What Takala wanted was a clean place to sleep, a good wife, a string of fish now and then. He also wanted some children, but his had died.

The Americans, during the war, made a favorable impression on men like Takala. He liked their beer—he is not allowed to drink in Fiji—and preferred their free and easy ways to the more sober ways of Englishmen. But by and large Americans made less impression on Fiji than on any of the other islands. Several plane loads of the islands' most beautiful white and half-caste girls were flown to New Caledonia to serve as secretaries to American officers, and some of them married their bosses. Others went to the States to work. But today, the Americans are remembered principally for the useful buildings they left behind. One hospital has become a sanitarium for treating tubercular patients. Another is a training school for native teachers. A group of supply sheds has become the poorhouse.

135

One reason the impact of America was so slight is that Fiji is an intensely British colony. Fijians gave their lands personally to Queen Victoria, and except for the introduction of Indians, the British have given the Fijians a remarkably good government. The ties between the two countries are powerful. When a slice of Princess Elizabeth's wedding cake reached Fiji, it was raffled off for $70, and the money given to charity. The cake was then cut up. A thimbleful went to a Fiji girl at school in New Zealand, where it was divided among sixteen classmates. A fragment went to Australia, where it was on display. A portion went to Pitcairn Island, and at Guadalcanal, the American and British officers at the airbase auctioned it off and bought presents for the local leper colony.

The most substantial memorial to the Americans is the massive airbase, at Nadi (pronounced Nandi). Improved and enlarged by the New Zealanders, it is now the crossroads of the South Pacific. French planes from New Caledonia cross here on their way to Tahiti. New Zealand planes use it as a base for flights eastward to Samoa. Pan-American, Canadian, Dutch, Indian, Australian, and powerful British Commonwealth Pacific Airlines planes stop here on flights to America from Australia. The importance of Fiji to aviation is only now being discovered.

Therefore, it's surprising to find that the British, in order to lure dollars into Suva, which is 150 miles from Nadi on a wretched road, have decided to abandon Nadi and build a fog-bound airport on the reefs near Suva. The new drome will bring planes right into Suva's front door, and also perilously near the lowering mountains that hide in fog nearby. As one commercial pilot said, "They can build their new strip, but they better keep the old one open, because that's where I'll land."

The fight for dollars is just as acute in Fiji as elsewhere. Tourists are welcomed. American cars are dreamed about as wonderful things that used to be seen in Fiji years ago. American currency is hoarded whenever possible. Police searched a Chinese joint for opium and found hidden dollars. The owner was fined more for the currency than he would have been had they found opium.

It's a magnificent land. It is appreciated by Englishmen as one of the jewels in the Commonwealth, and they strive to keep the old ways intact. When a proper British lady left the G.P.H., she asked, as travelers should, whom she must tip. She was told: the head waiter, her personal waiter, the boy who served coffee in the lounge, the boy who served tea in bed each morning at 6:30, the room boy who made the bed, the shoe boy, the sink boy, and—here it becomes ridiculous—the boy who brought drinking water and the boy who put the ice in, for they were two different servants.

Now it is night in Fiji. An immense moon shines above the islands and creates a fairyland within the coral reefs. Industrious Indians set fire to their cane fields to burn away the refuse, and flames dance among coconut trees like mysterious swamp fires. Relaxed Fijians sit cross-legged in their huts drinking yaqona, singing, haggling over tribal problems. Chinese merchants have gathered at Bau for a game of mah jong. Half-castes are attending a dance in Suva; and in the Fiji Club, dour Englishmen convince themselves that the present administration is no damned better than the last. But the island moon, indifferent to the petty contentions of these groups, makes the night a thing of heavenly beauty.

It is interesting, at such a time, to speculate on what might have happened had the American Government accepted Fiji's rump offer of cession. Would these islands have prospered under American guidance? In what respects would they be better or worse off?

Well, if we had accepted the islands, the Indians would probably never have got to Fiji. Not that we are wiser than the British. After all, we imported Chinese to build our railways, Mexicans to grow our sugar beets, and Japanese to tend Hawaiian pineapple; but we would not have had access to Indians. Therefore, life now would be better, for any laborers we might have dragged in would have been more digestible than the Indians. No matter what irresponsible mistakes we made in other fields, there would now be some solution to the race problem. Negroes and whites in America get along together better than do the Indians and Fijians in Fiji.

Under our rule, the natives would not be so well off as they are now. Americans do not colonize well and the glorious Fijian savage would not have impressed slave-conscious Americans as he did the British. It is probable that a figure of immense capacity like Oxford-trained Sir Lala Sakunu, the Fijian leader, would not have developed under Yankee squatterism. He would not have been allowed to leave the islands for Harvard.

The governors of Fiji would probably have been a dreary line of Navy officers who couldn't make the grade as admirals and who were accordingly given a two-year holiday in Suva for consolation. The accidental good governor would have been preceded by some good-time Charlie and followed by a man who drank so much he had to be kept off battleships. Disruptive changes of policy would have come with each administration.

There would now be no stately administration building, no railroad, no tradition of justice built upon local conditions. Suva might be larger than it is now—and dirtier—filled with Americans who damned the Fijian as the Briton now damns the Indian.

The big event in Fijian history would have been the discovery of gold. The islands would have been gutted in the ensuing years; the mines would now be defunct, and the fortunes would have been carried off to Minnesota or New York, instead of to Australia and London.

About 1935, American capital would have wakened up to the fact that in an air age, Fiji was about the hottest bet in the ocean. There would now be an airfield at Nadi so big that any plane in the world could land. There would be a fancy hotel with big refrigerators out of which would come just about the same food as is now served. But at three times the cost.

The moon drifts behind a cloud and rain falls on Suva. The islands assume a majestic melancholy, and it is fruitless to speculate further. Fiji exists as it is, a tantalizing problem.

The Mynah Birds

It is interesting to speculate upon what might have happened had the American Government accepted the offer of cession.

In 1949 the United States closed down its consulate in Fiji for lack of business. But two years later the inflamed Patel case threatened the civil peace of this colony, and a distinguished young American was hurried back as an official observer. Mr. Louis McGurn was then thirty-eight, unmarried, trained in the hard schools of Palestine, South Africa and India. He was reported to have a very bright future in the State Department.

Unobtrusively he set up quarters in the Grand Pacific Hotel and let it be known that he had arrived to take a long vacation. He hired taxi cabs and took trips to various parts of the island, stopping overnight at one or another of the good hotels. He waited for two things: the arrival in Suva of the well-known British judge, Sir Charles Jacquemart, and the report of the civil action he had recently started in the courts of Boston, whose outcome had not yet been determined when he left hurriedly for Fiji.

To McGurn, the green lands of Fiji were a dream come true. As a child he had sat with Grandmother Richardson and listened to horrible accounts of these Cannibal Isles. A Boston ancestor, one Luke Richardson, had wandered to Fiji with a shipload of trinkets. Exchanging them for a cargo of sandalwood, he set out to make his fortune in China. But as he was about to haul anchor, Fijian savages fell upon his ship.

"Then," said Grandmother Richardson, "the wild men dragged the crew ashore and tortured 'em. They were terrible cruel. They ripped the skin off their feet and jabbed 'em in the belly with torches to make 'em dance in misery."

Sometimes at night Louis could imagine his feet with no soles. He would sweat and recall what happened next. "These cannibals grabbed the tormented men and dashed their heads against a sacred altar. Then they cut 'em apart, baked 'em and ate 'em."

Captain Richardson had been saved by three foul-mouthed Australians, who proceeded to massacre forty-seven savages for sport. This made the captain feel better, and three years

139

later he was back with more trinkets. This time he won his fortune and in later years spoke well of Australians. He left the city of Sydney $20,000 when he died.

In his travels about the islands McGurn easily recognized the bloody scenes described by his ancestor in the latter's book: *Ten Years in the Waters of the South Seas, Including Pertinent Observations on the State of Our Trade with China and the East.* Such discoveries gave him a sense of identification with Fiji.

Yet at the same time, his duties in the Cannibal Isles occasioned a sense of bitterness, for they reminded him of the fact that in spite of his regrettable name he was essentially a Richardson, of Boston. It had been easy, during the latter years of the preceding century, for the Richardsons to forget old Cap'n Luke's near piracy and opium trade. On his hundreds of thousands of dollars—nursed into millions—a substantial Boston family had been built.

Then, in 1911, Emily Richardson had revolted against her family and had run off with a dreadful Irishman, Timmy McGurn. He had died in a Monte Carlo brawl, but not before siring a son Louis and fixing upon that child the guttural name of McGurn. As soon as he got into Harvard, young McGurn insisted that he be called Louis Richardson McGurn, and when he introduced himself he placed so much emphasis on the second name that strangers often had to ask him to repeat the last.

It was toward the end of February, in the rainy summer season, that Sir Charles Jacquemart and his family finally arrived by plane from the Kenya Colony in Africa. They took rooms at the G.P.H. and that afternoon McGurn reported to Washington. "Sir Charles has appeared on the scene. Both factions, Indians and Fijians, trust him without cavil and the trial should soon begin. I knew of him when I served in Africa and he is a man of absolute probity."

It pleased McGurn that Sir Charles was to have a room next his own. He liked titles. He was no snob, having seen Palestinian Jews and Australian wharfies knock the spots off snobs, but he did think it appropriate that governments recognize with appropriate titles those of its citizens who lived and worked in such a way as to bring honor upon a nation. In the war, he had known a French baron of incredible bravery, and he felt that the man's actions were inspired partly because he was of noble lineage. He himself had often dreamed of being Sir Louis. So even if titles were forbidden Americans, he intended living his life as Sir Louis. In the war

140

against Japan that determination had won him two decorations. It had also accounted for his rapid advancement in the State Department.

Therefore, when he had finished his confidential report, he selected a neatly pressed suit, shined his shoes once more, and put on a sedate tie. Then he sat primly on the verandah outside his room and waited.

He had been sipping gin and tonic for some minutes when the French doors nearby opened. A large woman of fifty-five appeared. She wore a lacy dress favored by British women in the tropics, and after adjusting it carefully, allowed her large bulk to sink into a rattan chair which creaked painfully as it conformed to the bulges of her body. She shifted twice and then sighed.

"We've been coming here for thirty years and those mountains across the bay are finer ..." She lapsed into a wheezing silence.

McGurn rose and made a little bow. "May I presume?" he began.

"Pshaw!" the plump lady interrupted. "No ceremony with me. I'm Lady Jacquemart. That gin and tonic you're drinkin'?"

McGurn was flustered for a moment and then said, "I'm Louis Richardson McGurn."

"Don't mumble," Lady Jacquemart snapped. "What's that last name?"

"McGurn."

"How'd ja spell it?"

Painfully, Louis spelled out the ugly name. "My father was born in England," he elaborated. "Surrey."

"Sounds like a boxer's name," Lady Jacquemart said approvingly.

"I used to box," McGurn replied.

"Three minutes ago I asked if that was gin and tonic," Lady Jacquemart laughed. The American blushed and poured her a drink. She produced a small lace handkerchief and wiped the perspiration off her upper lip. When she reached for the drink, McGurn bowed slightly.

"You've got demmed pretty manners for an American," she said. "Where'dja learn 'em?"

"Boston," he said proudly.

"Stuffy place," she snorted. "I prefer Carolina. I like hot lands with plenty of niggers."

McGurn winced and peeked about to see if any of the colored servants had heard, but Lady Jacquemart continued

141

sharply. "Don't cringe. They're niggers. In the Empire they are."

The American coughed and said, "We've been carefully taught not to say 'Empire' any longer."

"Empire?" Lady Jacquemart exploded. "What've they been tellin' you? It's a Commonwealth? Fiddle-de-cock! Fiji belongs personally to the King, bless 'im, and if we're not smack in the middle of the Empire right now, you can fry me for dinner."

Before he could answer she turned and yelled sharply, "Antonia!" There was no reply and she called again. Then she nudged McGurn in the arm. " 'Dja mind pokin' your head in that second door and callin' my daughter?"

McGurn rose, placed his gin carefully on the wicker table, and moved down the verandah to a pair of closely locked French doors. He tapped politely and then shrugged his shoulders at the Englishwoman.

"Give it a good bang," she directed, kicking out with her left foot.

McGurn obeyed and heard a sharp voice inside the room. "What's the row?" Before he could reply, the doors burst open and before him stood a bonny English girl of twenty-two. She had a mop of red hair, a smooth, highly colored face and broad shoulders like her mother. She was barefooted and wore only a slip. Seeing McGurn, she cried, "Hullo, wrong room?"

The American bowed and said with an amused smile, "Your mother."

The girl cried, "O.K., Mums. Be right with you."

"Get some clothes on," her mother commanded without even looking at the door.

"Roger wilco!" the girl laughed. As she pulled the French doors inward, she left her head sticking out so that she could smile at McGurn. "Thanks awfully," she said. "I'll look better in a moment."

Again McGurn smiled his amusement and bowed. When he returned to his chair, he said, "Attractive girl, your daughter."

"She'd go around naked if I didn't watch her," Lady Jacquemart snorted. "She grew up in hot lands."

"Not in England?"

"Heavens, no! We despise England, as a place to live. Too demmed cold. Sir Charles"—she called her husband S'Chalz—"has had a roving commission. Wherever there was trouble, they sent him. He's here now to clean up a notorious case."

"Yes. There's great discussion of it."

"Those wretched Injians!" Lady Jacquemart snapped. She uttered the last word with obvious distaste.

McGurn cleared his throat and said slowly, "If Sir Charles thinks that of the Indians, I'm surprised . . ."

Lady Jacquemart chuckled. "Never impute my thoughts to S'Chalz. I'm really an old gossip. S'Chalz, on the other hand, is the soul of rectitude."

She could have chosen no more fitting word to describe her husband, who now appeared on the verandah. Sir Charles was some six-feet-three and weighed less than a hundred and sixty. He had gray hair and a black moustache, which he dyed. He was rigidly erect and his face had the impersonal glaze of the complete judge.

" 'Lo Chalz," his wife said.

"Evenin', Maud," he grunted.

His wife began, "This is a young American . . ." but Sir Charles totally ignored McGurn. Then followed a long silence as the judge sat down. Lady Jacquemart winked at McGurn and shrugged her shoulders. She said nothing, for it was agreed between the judge and his wife that in company he would set the topics of conversation. In this way, he avoided embarrassment over the trials he might be conducting. Finally he said in a doleful voice, "It's quiet here by the bay."

The subject having been nominated, like trumps at whist, McGurn played one of his small cards. He said, "It's quiet now, but in the morning the birds make a fearful clatter."

At this, Sir Charles noticed the American. "Mynahs," he grunted.

"Those dreadful birds!" Lady Maud exploded.

"They certainly caught on in this land," Sir Charles said.

"Aren't they native?" McGurn asked.

"The Injians brought them along," Lady Maud explained with much contempt, "when they came here to work the sugar."

Sir Charles recalled other years. "When we first came here birds of all kinds clustered on that lawn."

Lady Maud added, "The frightful mynahs have driven them all away."

"Gresham's law of ornithology," the judge reflected. "Sparrows and mynahs drive out the better coin."

143

"Like everything else, they should have been kept in Injia," Lady Maud announced firmly.

Sir Charles turned crimson. "Really, my dear ..." he began.

But his wife was not looking at him and added, "The birds are as vicious as the Injians who brought them. Between them, they've ruined Fiji."

Sir Charles rose abruptly and in austere dignity stomped off the verandah. Lady Maud clapped a fat hand over her mouth and mumbled, "Goodness, I've done it again." She struggled to rise from her rattan chair and McGurn helped her. As she stepped through the French doors, the American could hear the acidulous judge protest, "One day you'll ruin me."

And to McGurn's surprise, Lady Maud poked her husband in the ribs and chuckled. "It'll only be because I'm so stupid," she said puckishly, whereupon they both laughed.

At this moment, the French doors farther down the verandah opened and Toni Jacquemart appeared. "Hullo," she said cheerily. "Where's the clan?"

"Inside," McGurn reported, jerking his thumb at the door behind him. "I'm Louis Richardson McGurn."

"What was the last name?" the pink-cheeked girl asked.

"McGurn."

"Oh, Irish!"

He was about to disclose his English ancestry, when he saw a merry twinkle in the girl's eye. He laughed and said, "As Irish as they come."

Toni Jacquemart gripped his hand firmly. "What ya drinking?"

"Gin and tonic," he replied.

"How frightfully British," she laughed. "Any coke?"

McGurn winced and said, "I never drink it."

"It's my favorite," Toni said.

"Where'd you meet up with it?"

"Here, during the war. Pops was stationed here and there were scads of Yanks about. You ever hear of the Duchess?"

"No." The servant appeared and, to McGurn's inner satisfaction, said there hadn't been any coke on Fiji for two years. "A lemon squash?" the black man asked.

"If that's all you have," Toni sighed. "This Duchess," she explained, "was an American DC-3. Stationed on the other side of the island."

"At Nadi?" McGurn asked.

"Good old Nadi!" the girl chuckled. "Each Friday, the

144

Yanks flew the Duchess over here to pick up a full cargo of pretty girls. Half-castes, Chinese, white girls! It was a lovely trip. The girls stayed overnight at the BOQ. Big dances. Fine food. There was necking galore."

McGurn shivered. "Did you go?"

"Nope. Mums said I was too young. But once when the major himself asked Mums to be a chaperone I tagged along and had a wonderful time. The Americans got Mums tight and there was a hell of a go!"

The doors behind them opened and Lady Maud appeared. Her daughter leaped up and grabbed her by the shoulders. "I was telling Mr. McGurn—it's Irish and very lilting—about the time the Americans got you spiffo."

Lady Maud laughed. "What a delightful time we had! The girls of this island wept when that plane was taken away."

"Mums volunteered to chaperone again," Toni said, "but Pops put his foot down."

"He takes a very dim view of white men mixing with colored girls," Lady Maud said sternly. "I must say I do, too."

"But you were the chaperone!" McGurn said.

"The men were Americans," Lady Maud laughed. "They don't have to run a thousand colonies."

From within the hotel a musical chime began to sound and Toni jumped to her feet. "Dinner at last!" she cried.

Up and down the interior balcony walked an Indian with his chimes, beating them as if to summon the spirits of all the notable feasters who had lived in Fiji. The lovely tones died, and from each room appeared the Britons who, by their own devious routes, had this night assembled in the Cannibal Isles.

They were a stately crew. The men were often old and feeble, but they dressed for evening meal. Their women occasionally gave evidence of pinching pennies, but in the lacy shawls of a generation past they appeared in formal minuet as they progressed to the spotless linen and shining silver of the dining hall.

The Jacquemarts were led to a corner table where Sir Charles could keep aloof from diners who might otherwise embarrass him by commenting on the trial. Lady Maud, with no such inhibitions, held court and nodded to all the old hands. Toni sat beside her and cried a cheery "Hullo" to everyone. "We won the hockey game," she announced.

"Seems to me," Lady Maud observed icily, "that at your age you'd be giving up hockey."

Toni jabbed a forefinger into her mother's soft arm, " 'Twould do you some good to have a go at it."

"Antonia!" her father interrupted snappishly.

"It would, Pops! You don't appreciate how boys study a girl's mother. They want to see how the girl is going to look in twenty years."

The judge snorted and withdrew into his shell. Lady Maud nodded graciously to friends who greeted her and said out of the corner of her mouth, "That Mr. McGurn seems a right decent sort, Antonia."

Toni screwed her mouth up into a gangster snarl and whispered, "Let me pick me own men, see?" Lady Maud, against her will, broke into a smile and said, "You don't seem to have done very well, so far." But she was pleased to see that Toni, out of the corner of her eye, was looking at the American.

McGurn, seated across the dining room in quarters reserved for Americans and other vagrants, was at the same time studying Toni. She was, he thought, not a beautiful girl. But she had that glowing English complexion which makes any woman attractive, even if she was inclined to plumpness. "She's not fat," he mused. "Not like her mother." Then he looked at Lady Maud sprawling over her chair, and he thought happily of the straight, frail women of his family, the Richardson women. They had been beautiful, his mother loveliest of all. She could have married any man in Boston, and she chose Timmy McGurn. Her son Louis could certainly have arranged her life for her better than that.

His regrets about his mother were interrupted by an Indian messenger, who tapped him respectfully on the shoulder.

"Meestair McGurrrrn? A man outside to see you."

Louis put down the forkful of food he was about to stuff into his mouth, English style, and said, "Tell him he must wait."

"He says very important," the Indian persisted.

McGurn had learned never to become impatient—or rather, never to betray that he had become impatient—and he said gently, "You can see I'm eating. Tell him that."

But the messenger said in a low whisper, "This man says it's to do with your mission."

McGurn masked his astonishment and said, "Perhaps I'll see him now." He rose unobtrusively, nodded when Lady Maud smiled, and followed the messenger.

At the curb outside the hotel, a thin and very black figure awaited him. "If you will be so generous as to pardon me,"

146

the cadaverous figure apologized unctuously. "Only a matter of gravest importance could justify . . . Permit me, my card."

The funereal face broke into a flashing smile and a tiny card was thrust into McGurn's hand. By the misty light of a street lamp he read: "Mr. Ramcheck Devidas Billimoria. Christian. Dealer in Souvenirs of All Kinds. Cats' Eyes. Tortoise Shell. Fine Indian Ivory."

McGurn had sometimes seen this man about the streets of Suva. The Hindu-turned-Christian carried a small cardboard suitcase, heavily stamped to make it resemble alligator. He appeared to eke out a mean living so that he could wear a threadbare European suit and pointed shoes. His skin was midnight black but he had mastered the trick of looking directly into the eyes of Europeans, whereas most of his countrymen looked away.

"And what did you wish?" McGurn asked cautiously.

"It concerns . . . your mission."

McGurn showed no surprise and asked, "Yes?"

Billimoria had not anticipated this, so he fumbled for a moment. "Your mission for the United States Government," he said.

"I have no mission," McGurn said coldly. "Anyway, I don't deal with informers, Mister . . ." He looked with studied insolence at the preposterous card.

The Indian did not flinch. "Neither do I, normally. After all, there's nothing much lower than an informer, is there, Mister . . ." Here Billimoria appeared to fumble for a name exactly as McGurn had done. "But your man Harvey . . ."

"Who?"

"Joe Harvey. At the airport."

McGurn had met Harvey, but he had no knowledge of his affairs other than that he came from Kansas City and was an airport engineer working on Pacific Air Transport's base at the new Suva field. "I see no reason why Harvey is any concern of mine."

He started to leave, but the Indian pressed a long index finger into his chest. In a deathly whisper Billimoria asked, "We don't want to see Harvey killed, do we? Not at this time?"

McGurn tried to appear very casual and asked, "Why should a young man like Harvey be killed?"

"Because he's what you Americans call 'running around with' an Indian girl." He paused, then whispered sinisterly, "Our Indian men don't like it."

McGurn smiled. "I understand, Mr. Billimoria. The

147

American has stolen your girl. Why don't you go home and forget about it?"

He turned his back upon the informer and took two steps toward the hotel, only to be caught by the arm and jerked about. "McGurn!" Billimiora threatened, insulting the white man by omitting the "mister," "You're a fool! If Harvey debauches an Indian girl, there will be grave trouble ... when you want it least." Almost mysteriously, the Indian slipped away into the shadows.

McGurn was disgusted. His food was cold, the Jacquemarts had left the dining room, and he was worried. It was quite probable that Harvey had struck up some kind of acquaintance with an Indian girl. There was a certain type of American man who could be counted on to shack up with absolutely any kind of woman. You couldn't designate the type of female who would be too low for some American to crawl into bed with.

McGurn ate a few spoonfuls of dessert and left the table. "Damn it," he muttered, as he climbed the stairs to his room. "If the young fool has to toy around with color, why does he do it now? Can't he wait till the trial's over?"

The pressure of this trial was on everyone that rainy summer. An Indian had accidentally killed a Fijian with a taxicab. Then he had fled from the scene and been reported by a Fijian woman who had subsequently been beaten up, whereupon some Fijians had caught the man's brother and thrashed him. Tempers were at an ugly pitch, and on the very day that Sir Charles Jacquemart arrived to try to straighten things out between two warring races who respected him, an irresponsible American was goading the Indians to new threats of violence.

His evening ruined, McGurn shifted into a sack coat and wandered down to the cinema, where a British comedy of great reputation was playing. But even the *Tawny Pipit* was ruined, because at intermission he saw in the center seats reserved for white people the blond head of Joe Harvey, and next to him the jet black hair of a slim Indian girl. McGurn gasped at the young man's public folly and noticed that English members of the audience were outraged. He overheard a woman whispering, "Trust an American! They'll wallow anywhere." He felt that the censure was merited.

He would have left the cinema in disgust, but Harvey had already spotted him as a fellow-American and strode boldly up the aisle with the girl on his arm. "Hey, Yank!" the young man called. "Don't duck! I want you to meet my girl."

English patrons nearby moved away in disgust. "This is Pata Cadi," the young man said.

The slight girl bowed in acknowledgment. She was twenty, golden skinned and dark-eyed. McGurn could do nothing but bow slightly and say, "It's been a good show so far, hasn't it?"

The next minutes were agony for Louis McGurn. He stood conspicuously by his seat while Harvey and the Indian girl blocked the aisle. He recalled the statement an English woman had made in Calcutta: "The Americans are like tomcats, forever on the prowl among the alleys of the world." And here was a prime tomcat hauling his catch into the middle of British society. He blushed and wondered if Americans would ever learn to behave when they were away from home.

As soon as intermission ended, he slipped out of the cinema. When he reached the G.P.H., he found Toni Jacquemart in the lounge surrounded by three young men. As he climbed the stairs, he heard her provocative cry, "Good dreams, Yank." She spoke with the mocking arrogance that English people use when referring to Americans or Australians. McGurn was ashamed of his nationality.

In the morning, his fitful sleep was broken by the mynah birds. They had found a swarm of flies in a tree near the hotel, and their chatter was unbelievable. Like a thousand children at a picnic they screamed and brawled. Back and forth they rioted until McGurn had to rise in desperation.

Wrapped in a conservative robe of dark-blue silk, he rubbed his sandy eyes and stepped onto the verandah to watch the mynahs. They strutted like cabinet ministers in a duck-like waddle. When they ran they placed one yellow foot in front and then brought the other up to match it, producing a grotesque and drunken lurch. They were always hungry, always fighting in scrannel screams. They possessed Fiji. It seemed only a matter of time until they evicted all other birds, as their Indian masters must force out all other races.

"Hang the clatter," McGurn muttered, but his attention was promptly diverted by Sir Charles, who appeared on the verandah fully dressed, combing his moustache with a bony forefinger.

Neither man spoke for at least five minutes; then abruptly the judge pointed to the remarkable trees where the birds were quarreling. "Weeping figs," he said sepulchrally. McGurn looked at the tangled brown parasites that hung from the branches like myriad snakes.

After five more minutes, he asked, "What parasite is that?"

Sir Charles thought for several moments and said, "Part of the tree. Aerial roots." He noticed a Fijian fisherman walking along the quay, carrying four fish and a spear. "Boy!" the judge cried sharply. He added a series of commands in Fijian and the fisherman grinned. Dropping his burdens, he leaped into the air and grasped a tangle of roots. Thus suspended, he jerked his entire weight against the thin wiry strands. They held like cables.

"Good-oh," the judge cried.

"Remarkable," McGurn said approvingly. The judge stood silent for some moments, grunted and went indoors.

In a moment, his wife appeared. She had the servant bring a pot of tea and offered McGurn a cup. "Well," she said slyly. "Hear you entertained an Injian girl at theatre last night."

McGurn sighed audibly. "Where did you hear that?"

"When you've become an old gossip, you hear everything."

"One would think an American might be especially careful right now . . ." McGurn began.

"Yes, an Injian girl, too," Lady Maud said, as she sipped her tea. "I imagine the Injian men are not pleased. You know there's a great shortage of women among the Injians, the beggars."

"She was," McGurn said ruefully, "rather pretty."

"The loveliest girls in the world are colored," Lady Maud said firmly. "That's why it's so difficult to raise sons abroad. If ever I meet God, I shall propose that all white girls of good family be beautiful. All others will be ugly. Unfortunately, it's the other way around. My own girls just escaped being ugly. My oldest was really quite repulsive for years. I couldn't stand her. Then she found she wanted a man, so she did what she could with herself and wound up fairly pretty."

"She took after her mother," McGurn said archly.

"My God," Lady Maud said. "That one creaked. Only the French can get away with a crack like that." She laughed and McGurn said, "I meant that you weren't completely repulsive."

Lady Jacquemart liked this and said, "I take pride in few things. But I am exceptionally pleased that my children escaped color. We were frightfully worried about Teddy. He formed an attachment for a brown girl in Malaya. I think he lived with her, but common sense prevailed. Actually, of
150

course, he married an Irish girl, which wasn't much better. Oh, dear!" she fluttered. "And you're Irish!"

"I'm English," he corrected. "Surrey."

"Of course. You told me before. Well, I'm sure the Irish and the half-castes will inherit the earth one day, but I shall be dead, thank heavens."

The musical gong heralded breakfast, and in the fig trees the mynah birds made new havoc. In that moment by the sea, with the rain just beginning and the Indian gong sounding, Louis McGurn had an overwhelming sensation of being in the tropics. What he had come to observe was a tropic storm fought out by races not his own. There were summer hurricanes afoot that he could not see. He felt quite alone in a strange world. Only the Jacquemarts were his kind. Even that foolish American from Kansas City was an alien. He wanted to cry out to Lady Maud not to leave the verandah.

But at this moment, a mynah bird flew onto the table and snatched up a piece of bread crumb. Lady Maud slapped at the insulting bird with her fan. "Dirty invaders," she cried, retreating to her room.

After a leisurely breakfast, Louis McGurn left the dining room and stood for a moment at the entrance to the G.P.H., rejoicing in a scene he had grown to love. Before him stretched a handsome sports field. To the left were the impressive government offices, to the right the high commissioner's mansion. Far to the east, beyond the tennis courts, were flower gardens, and all along the roads were royal palms and bright croton.

McGurn liked this splendid panorama, for it seemed to him to represent those values to whose cultivation he had dedicated his life. The British had ruled the world for some centuries and now it had come time for the Americans to assume the burden. This square of beauty indicated how to govern. Build well. The British could easily have governed a bunch of savage islands from mean shacks. But if you believed that one day all the world would know order, you built stately and pillared mansions, even at the edge of the jungle. To do so gave an earnest of your intentions.

Louis McGurn was willing that his life should be spent in building such edifices throughout the world. But right now he had to talk with young Joe Harvey and drum some sense into the boy's head. He called a cab and drove out to the airdrome.

Finding Harvey's office empty, he walked out into the

151

bright sunlight and looked around. He approached a group of Fijian laborers, giant barefooted blacks with kinky hair and glistening torsos, and asked for Harvey. At the mention of the name every man grinned, and one big chap waved toward a shack a hundred yards beyond. McGurn found Harvey there, alone.

"Those black boys seem to like you," McGurn said.

"They're my pals," Harvey replied.

"And Miss Cadi?"

Harvey seemed to miss the point of the question. "I met her down at the Galta Milk Bar. She works there. A beauty, eh?"

"Very attractive," McGurn said with forced enthusiasm. "But I thought there was a great shortage of Indian women. Don't the Indian men resent . . ."

"Annh!" Harvey sneered. "They don't scare me." He whipped out his wallet and showed McGurn a threatening note: *"You'll be sorry if you keep on seeing Pata Cadi."*

"That's doesn't worry you?" McGurn asked.

"Nah, those punks make me a little bit sick."

"I used to be stationed in India," McGurn said. "Sometimes those men are jolly tough."

He had used the wrong word. When he said *jolly*, young Harvey froze up. There was a moment of silence and then the youngster asked bluntly, "You come down here to warn me about seeing Pata?"

"What makes you . . ."

"Because last night in the movies you almost wet your pants," Harvey said. "Why in hell do you suppose I stood smack in the middle of the aisle? Because it was eating you so."

"Wait a minute," McGurn said quietly. "You're jumping at a lot of conclusions."

"No, I'm not," Harvey replied, grinning broadly. "Everybody in town's been trying to figure you out. You're here to sort of help out the British, we figure."

"Who is *we?*" McGurn asked patiently.

"Pata and me."

. "That was your opinion?"

"Yes. We are right, weren't we?"

"No. I'm dreadfully sorry, but you were totally wrong. I have nothing to do with the British."

"Then why do you try to be more English than they are?"

The conversation had turned into quite an unexpected channel and McGurn was distressed. He said, "I'm simply an

American citizen who has lived in India. You're heading for great trouble."

"In the war, I learned how to handle trouble. By the way, what did you do in the war?"

"Just Germany and New Guinea." McGurn replied evenly.

Joe stood back and said in frank approval, "I guess you can claim you saw the war."

A nebulous bond of brotherhood-in-arms thus established, McGurn took advantage of it to say, "I'll admit I came down here to raise the devil about the Indian girl. But what's really important is this trial. Tempers are very tough. The English would . . ."

Again, he had said the wrong word and the fellowship was destroyed. "Mr. McGurn," the young aviator said, "I owe you the respect you earned in the war. But I don't care for the English. You came down here to explain British ways to a dumb hick from Kansas City. You'd be surprised at how much I know. I served with the British in Cairo, and even if they did save the world, I don't want any part of their system."

"It's the best we have in Fiji," McGurn said quietly.

"Then I don't like even the best. I don't like white people in the saddle and everyone else in the gutter. You may get a thrill out of aping the English. I don't."

"Damn it!" McGurn snapped. "You're an arrogant young pup. If you only knew how young you are. All over the world civilizations are crumbling. India, Java, China. It's our duty to help sustain them."

"No," Harvey said abruptly. "Pata and I have talked this out . . ."

"What can she know?"

"In her own way, Mr. McGurn, she knows more than you do."

"I should like to meet this remarkable girl."

"It would do you a lot of good," Harvey said. "How about dinner with us? Tonight?"

"In public? The three of us? Well, hardly!" Instinctively, McGurn cringed.

Joe Harvey was disgusted. "You afraid the British might object? Okay, skip it. Go have a pot of tea and quit worrying. I'm shipping home next week. This job's done."

The diplomat tried not to show his relief. Aloud he reflected, "A week? A lot could happen in a week. I don't suppose you'd promise to stay away from Miss Cadi during that time?"

Harvey slammed open the door. "Why don't you get the hell out of here?" he snapped.

As he left, McGurn said with deep compassion, "I came out here, Joe, to warn you. Don't get hurt."

Harvey laughed. "I'm not the kind that gets hurt," he said.

At the airdrome gate, Louis McGurn rang for a taxi. In a few minutes, a mournful Indian arrived in a new Ford. "Nice car," McGurn said as he climbed in. The Indian said nothing. On the way into the Triangle, the American asked, "What do you think of the new wing to the government buildings?" There was no reply and he repeated the question.

Very cautiously, the Hindu slowed down and said, with no inflection, "Traffic court. Where they fine you for speeding." At the Triangle, McGurn tipped the man a bob. There was no acknowledgment.

The American left the main business streets of Suva and sought out the Galta Milk Bar. Behind the counter, stood slim, neat Pata Cadi.

"Miss Cadi," McGurn began.

"Yes, Mr. Harvey just called and said you'd be in to see me."

Louis McGurn smiled stiffly and nodded. "It would be good if we could talk," he said.

She shrugged her shoulders. "Would you be embarrassed if we talked by the canal?"

"Not at all," he said, waiting until she had gone around the counter and called to her assistant. A very black girl came forward and took command of the bar.

They walked slowly up the main commercial street of Suva, passing countless Indian shops where huddled men sat all day making suits or selling ghee. Finally, they came to where a small canal drained a swamp, and along the southern edge of this canal, they entered the green-pillared arcade that led into the Morris Hedstrom South Seas Store. They stood by the wall of this arcade and looked down at the opposite edge of the canal where Fijians and Indians and Chinese and half-castes conducted a noisy market.

"This has always reminded me of Venice," McGurn began.

"It reminds me of something much more precious," the Indian girl replied. "This is where Joe first kissed me." She paused and Louis McGurn studied her sharply. She had the wide forehead and thin nostrils that distinguished the patrician women of his own family. She also used the excellent diction that they had used. He had gone to Galta Milk Bar to

154

lecture a peasant, but this charming gentlewoman was disconcerting. Most disconcerting.

He leaned back against a pillar and stared at the dark canal waters, groping for his next words. Pata continued, "I must put your mind at rest, Mr. McGurn. This is not a casual island romance. I saw too many of them during the war. The white man never marries the colored girl."

"Then you really love this American?" McGurn asked.

"In a hopeless sort of way . . . yes. But not hopeless, either. All the men I've ever known have been tied up in knots. The English are the worst. The Australians are not so bad, but they are so pathologically afraid of anyone with color. Ashamed of owning that great empty continent with so many hungry colored people breathing down their necks. Once we thought the Americans were the world's free men, but you are frightened too, and we poor Indians are the prisoners of fear. Into this mess of futility Joe Harvey . . ." She stopped and blushed. "I don't know why I'm telling you this except that we consider you a very important person . . . I mean, you being a member of the State Department."

McGurn denied this. "I'm only a visitor."

Pata Cadi smiled frankly. "Every interested person in Fiji knows who you are, Mr. McGurn. After all, there are many people in India who respect you very much."

"Very well," McGurn said. "Since you know I served in India you will respect me when I say that your affair with Joe Harvey . . ."

"It is not an affair . . . yet."

"It can end only in tragedy."

"And your mission, Mr. McGurn. You know, of course, that it too can end only in tragedy."

"What do you mean?" McGurn asked abruptly, no longer the diplomat.

"What can happen to this island of Fiji?" the Indian girl asked. "Its tragedy is inevitable. Look! Over there in the shadows! Billimoria, watching us!"

McGurn made no movement except to step closer to the Indian girl, as if he were trying to date her rather than interrogate her. "Is Billimoria in love with you?" he asked bluntly.

"Him? He loves no one! He hates. He hates the British. He hates the Americans. He hates me because I love a white man." She stared into the canal. "Like Hitler he dwells a great deal on foreign men ravishing our women."

"What does he hope to get out of it?" McGurn asked. "Would Indians follow a Christian?"

"He's no Christian!" Pata cried scornfully. "He was a convert only to get a free education. Now he's a Hindu again and most Indians commend his duplicity."

McGurn whipped about and caught sight of Billimoria hiding by the Kuo Min Tang building. "A sinister man like that hates you, and you're not worried?"

"No!" she said firmly. "I will not allow a fanatic to tell me what I must do. I don't care about his dream of a great Indian Empire or the marching soul of Gandhi. I want merely a home where I can live in peace." Her face flushed. "These islands, here, could be the paradise we seek. Free Indians and happy natives and such white men as would work with us."

"Now you sound like Billimoria!"

"I'm willing to wait for time to accomplish these things. But Billimoria ... He reads wild magazines from India that actually call upon Indians to murder white men who do not stand at attention when the anthem is played! Can you imagine that?" She stamped her foot.

McGurn had to laugh at her tiny anger. "Joe told me I should talk with you. Now I understand why." Automatically he gave her his professional smile then immediately sensed that here was someone who merited more than conventional gestures. He perceived her as one of that inarticulate group who are always on the verge of making things work. They never do because tragedy—war or pestilence or a new election or death—intervenes. Yet they try.

"Miss Cadi," he said abruptly, "I come to you as a suppliant. If you have no fear of Billimoria, please at least help me. He wants to see something happen to you. He could start a riot. Wreck the trial. Make the British seem . . ."

"You are like a very old man," Pata said quietly. "You want to hold things together as they are ... a little longer ... just a little longer."

With intense fervor McGurn said, "I hope you find a better way. Until then, please don't see Joe again ... at least until the trial's over."

Pata smiled directly at the diplomat. "You're asking me to give up the last few days I have with Harvey?"

"And you refuse?"

"You may be a statesman," the girl said, "but you've a lot to learn about love."

Suddenly Louis McGurn of Boston acknowledged that he had come upon a fresh, hard, honest human being. He bowed before her as he would have done to Lady Jacquemart and said, "I wish that statesmen could put their trust in people like you."

"You don't?" the girl asked in surprise.

"There are not enough of you," McGurn replied.

"Then may God have mercy on you," Pata said.

"I was about to say that to you," McGurn replied, deeply moved.

They shook hands and Louis McGurn returned to the G.P.H. about as agitated as he had ever been. The chimes rang for dinner before he gained control of himself, but he had not finished ordering before he felt a familiar tug at his elbow. It was the mournful Indian messenger with news: "A man waits outside to see you."

"Oh, not again!" McGurn groaned. He had hoped to talk with Toni after dinner, but since he had never in his diplomatic life chosen pleasure before duty, he turned his back on the Jacquemart table and followed his dark guide.

In the shadows he found Billimoria, more forlorn and cadaverous than ever. "Good evening," McGurn said.

"Good evening, sir," the Indian said warmly. He reached for McGurn's hand and pumped it eagerly. "I was so relieved to hear that you went to see both Harvey and Miss Cadi. I appreciate your co-operation."

"That's hardly the word," McGurn said with extra suavity. He had sworn that no matter what Billimoria said tonight, he would not become ruffled.

"I'm sorry, sir, indeed I am," Billimoria apologized. "I am aware that like any public servant . . ."

"I'm on vacation," McGurn insisted, pleasantly.

"Ah, yes. Well, as the older friend, then, your mission was a failure. Mr. Harvey has taken Miss Cadi to a dance. I insist that such behavior is dangerous."

McGurn drew in his breath. "Is there anywhere we could speak for a moment?"

"Here," Billimoria said.

"You'll excuse me. This smacks of conspiracy, doesn't it?"

Billimoria smiled. "I have a cab."

"I'll be with you," McGurn said. "Just a moment." He hastened indoors and went boldly to Toni's table. "I had hoped we might have drinks . . . later," he began.

"Why don't we?" she asked disarmingly.

"I've a beastly meeting . . ." Toni laughed at his British affectation and waited. "But would you wait up for me? Please?"

She smiled with tomboy frankness and said, "Sure! I'll play draughts with the old gentlemen."

McGurn bounded back to the cab with unprofessional exuberance, which was dampened when he saw that the driver was the same one he had traveled with that morning. "One of your men?" he asked.

"I have no men," Billimoria reassured him. He spoke to the driver in Hindustani and soon the cab wheeled up in front of a Suva tailor's establishment. A single unshaded light suspended from the ceiling cast an eerie glow upon the bolts of expensive cloth. Four men sat in semi-darkness stitching garments for Europeans.

McGurn's wraithlike guide led the way through swinging doors at the rear of the shop. Behind him, the American entered a small room. It was barren. A single chair, a small table, a polychrome portrait of Gandhi and some reading matter in a corner constituted the room's equipment. "You have the chair," Billimoria said unctuously.

"Thank you," McGurn said with a great show of politeness. "Now what are we to talk about?"

"Harvey," Billimoria said menacingly.

"Good!" McGurn said eagerly. "I have very good news to report to you. I spoke with both Harvey and Miss Cadi and they see the reasonableness of your demands." He sat back to see what effect this irony would have on the Indian. To his surprise, Billimoria nodded his head sagely.

"But they're dancing tonight!" the Indian said.

"Ah, I know. But my friend, we must be patient. Harvey told me he was leaving within the week."

The news was unexpected and Billimoria seemed disappointed. "In that time, much could happen," he whispered hopefully.

"In that time, nothing must happen," McGurn said earnestly. "My friend, the trial starts tomorrow. Tempers will be sharpened. Please let's you and me do nothing to disturb the equilibrium until the trial is ended."

"It depends on what happens in the next fifteen days," Billimoria threatened. "We Indians have watched many white men ogle our girls. And we haven't liked what followed. We are determined that our race shall not be sullied."

"God!" McGurn thought. "Where have I heard that before?" Aloud, he said, "I beg you to be patient, Mr. Billimoria."

"We shall be, up to a point."

"And then?" McGurn asked calmly. He was determined above all not to get angry with this fool.

"England is in retreat all over the world," Billimoria said, standing quiveringly straight. "We threw them out of India. The Boers will throw them out of Africa."

"Aren't you terribly afraid of what the Boers will do to your people . . . then?"

"You started it," Billimoria cried, ignoring the question. "You threw them out of America."

"They throw very hard," McGurn said firmly. It was then that he conceived the idea that Billimoria was really mad. The thin fanatic's apocalyptic figure in the murky light was one never to be forgotten. McGurn thought, "He is the mad devil whom we all fight."

"And so we do not worry," Billimoria continued softly, "about upsetting one small trial."

McGurn thought, "This is completely crazy! My arguing with a maniac like this! I'm not involved in this madness." He shook his head briefly, as if to cast out evil and proposed, "Let's promise this, Mr. Billimoria: I'll speak to Harvey again. And you will promise not to . . . well, not to disrupt things?"

"A sacred promise," Billimoria said dramatically. "On my word as a Christian."

McGurn let this pass and shook hands solemnly with the madman. When he left the barren and foreboding room, the same taxi was waiting for him. On the desolate ride back through the rain, he spoke twice to the driver and got no reply. Finally, he said, "Your Mr. Billimoria is very brilliant."

Immediately, the driver burst into voluble approval. "He's a wonderful leader. No one puts anything over on him." He said much more, but McGurn had heard enough.

At the hotel, McGurn felt that he had burst from out the darkness of Billimoria's turgid mind into the bright clarity of Toni's. She had drinks waiting on the lower verandah and sat handsomely against the backdrop of rain that strung a hazy veil across the harbor. A ship putting out to Levuka showed fairy lights, and its last crying echoes made the night beautiful.

"Toni!" the American cried with real delight. "You look so . . . refreshing."

"I've always liked talking with Americans," she said bluntly. She was so clean and appealing that McGurn could not possibly hide his feelings.

"I was afraid you might have gone to bed."

"I should have waited considerably longer," she said, and his head throbbed with happiness.

He could not know that Toni wished to talk with him because she remembered Yanks of quite a different sort. Once during the war, she had deceived her mother and flown across the island to the American airbase, where she had met a rollicking fighter pilot. They had, as she expressed it, "necked up a storm," and he had named her his Little Duchess. When he left for Guadal, he informed her that he was married. She still carried an angriness about her heart; but at the same time, she thought that she could have been happy with that Yank. She had enjoyed his clean laugh, his sense of freedom.

In her travels with Sir Charles, she had met many homesick men who had wanted to marry her. This had not turned her head. As Lady Maud said, "If a woman can't marry off her daughters in the tropics, she must have reared a nest of gorgons." But Toni was tired of empire builders. She was tired of the white man's world and the white man's law, administered in mock justice by her austere father. For that very reason McGurn disturbed her. At the precise time, when England was laying down some of the burdens of empire, America was picking hers up; and the type of man to do this work was the same whether English or American. "Mr. McGurn is very tedious," she was thinking. And yet he was not a man to dismiss easily.

"Your family has a fine liberal spirit," he was saying.

"Due mostly to Mums," she replied. "Mums works on the principle that human beings are primarily animals. That sure keeps down neuroses."

"And your father?"

"For him, people are totally damned and always breaking laws established by right-thinking Englishmen."

"And you?" he asked, lighting his pipe.

"I partake of both. Men are animals who must be kept in line."

"You really think that?" he asked, nervously puttering with his pipe so as to keep from reaching for her hand.

"Of course I do!" she said lightly.

"What about man as a divine, aspiring creation?"

"Where have you seen the divinity? What aspiration?"

It was then that he began to realize that he bored her. It was a frightening sensation. Here was a girl he could love. He knew it. Yet he knew that she thought him uninteresting. "What kind of people do you like?" he asked abruptly.

160

Now it was her turn to feel that this rain-swept evening in Suva was heavy with importance. Here was a man who was cautiously feeling his ground so that he could determine whether she was the kind of girl he wanted to marry. "Oh," she said casually, "in spite of my theory I tend to like men . . ." She stopped. She realized that he had not asked her what kind of men she liked. But she added, "Well, like you. Enough brains to get by on. Maybe a little more daring." She paused and then added with a laugh, "Like most girls. A beast with brains."

"I don't know about the brains," he laughed, "but as for the beast . . ." Suddenly he took her in his arms and kissed her. Finally, when the hotel lights had been extinguished, when the tropical rain had settled into a throbbing fall, he walked her to her door.

Next morning the mynah birds wakened him long before his usual hour. Reluctantly he pulled himself together and went out on the verandah. Lady Maud was waiting.

"Tea?" she offered brightly.

"Yes," McGurn replied with no enthusiasm.

Lady Maud twisted her head and leered at him. "It'll rain for two more weeks," she said ghoulishly. He sat down with her and started to offer some commonplace about the weather when she stopped him with a bombshell. "I hear you were necking with my daughter last night." Before he could recover she added, "I've got to speak frankly. You won't like this but here goes. If you want to marry Toni, you've got to be less stuffy."

McGurn coughed. He was completely set back; then, as if he were at a disadvantage in a chancellery, he said slowly, "I'll have some more tea, if you please."

"I don't understand it," Lady Maud continued, "but Toni has an affinity for Yanks. She'd like to live in America."

McGurn swallowed very hard. "Is there any chance . . ."

Lady Maud studied him carefully. "You're very tedious. But you would also make a good husband."

The American kept his lips to his teacup for a long time. Then he said carefully, "By those standards I should think Sir Charles a bit—forgive me—stuffy, shall we say?"

"S'Chalz!" Lady Maud exploded hilariously. "My God, he's so stuffy taxidermists look at him with pride. Oh, my dear young man, if you think that by patterning yourself after S'Chalz you'll win Toni . . . Oh, what a dreadful error!" She laughed merrily and added, "Find a model as far removed from S'Chalz as possible."

At breakfast he was considerably bucked up when Toni went out of her way to smile at him. His fears returned, however, when he arrived at the airdrome to see Harvey. The young man began by being ultrapolite, but when McGurn finished his warnings, Harvey said, "Too late, chum. If Billimoria wants to start trouble, now he's got a reason."

"What do you mean?" McGurn asked nervously.

"Last night Pata and I decided that since we have so few days ... Well, she moved in."

McGurn actually fell into a chair. "What utter folly!" he said in a low, impassioned voice.

"I'll be leaving in a few days," Harvey reassured him.

"A few days may be all they need. Joe, you're asking for trouble."

"Sometimes a fellow doesn't care," Harvey replied.

Then McGurn became fighting mad. "Listen!" he commanded. "Less than a hundred years ago one of my ancestors lost an entire crew on these islands. Roasted and eaten. People of good will came here and changed all that through self-sacrifice and devotion. Don't ruin their work, Joe."

"I'm to give up the one powerful happiness I've known? For what?"

"To help an island through a time of crisis."

"And when it passes, another crisis comes along."

"All right! Then you try to heal that rupture, too," McGurn pleaded. "Life is a series of crises. Only cowards throw in the sponge."

"Very noble," Harvey sneered. "Very Sunday school. Maybe what you ought to do is let the whole rotten edifice crumble. Start over new."

"You're wrong to throw in the sponge that way, Joe. This mess is no worse than others in the world. You pitch in here and see what can be done. You don't wreck a civilization with irresponsible actions."

"Our actions are terribly responsible, McGurn. Pata and I worked this out last night."

"So you'd ruin her life ..."

"Ruin? What's your definition of life? The protection of virginity till you're eighty? Wearing stiff white shirts like yours? You be careful, McGurn, that you don't ruin your life!"

There was nothing more to say. For McGurn, Joe Harvey was the new barbarian who would one day desolate the world. Back in his room the diplomat lay down and thought, "It would be so easy to forget the whole mess, as he called it.

But you've got to try to hold things together." He was brooding upon the agitated world when he heard Toni's clear voice outside his door.

"Want to go for a boat trip, even if it is raining?"

In the days that followed Louis McGurn lived in a kind of dream. Wherever he went through the wet streets of Suva he saw Indians who resented his presence. He saw Fijians who laughed as if there were no day but now. And he saw thoughtful white men deeply disturbed by the trial. Most of all, he saw Toni.

Wherever they went—these two self-analyzing, debating creatures—they seemed to see Pata Cadi and her white lover. Once Toni noticed them in the cinema and she whispered to McGurn, "I'd like to be in love like that. Just once." To his astonishment he impulsively grasped her hands right there in public and exclaimed, "I am."

Nothing happened to upset the trial, and with great relief McGurn greeted the last day of Harvey's residence in Fiji, but his spirits fell when the young American appeared in the G.P.H. shouting across the lobby, "Well, chum. I'm shoving off tomorrow."

"Considerate of you to stop by," McGurn said icily. "I trust nothing will happen before you get away."

Harvey grinned. "Still the old worry-wart, hey?" McGurn managed a stiff smile and Harvey continued. "My Fijian pals at the airport are throwing me a farewell feast. Pata's coming and I thought you might like to join us and bury the hatchet."

McGurn visibly withdrew into his shell of conventionalism. He was about to refuse the invitation when he saw Toni Jacquemart running down the stairs to join him. "You're Joe Harvey!" she cried, extending her hand.

"I stopped by to invite Mr. McGurn to a native feast," Joe explained.

"Sounds wonderful," Toni exclaimed. "And I'll bet your Indian girl is going, too. Oh, Louis! Can I tag along?"

"I'm not going," McGurn said flatly.

"Oh!" Toni's mouth drooped. "Can't you cancel . . ."

"It's not another engagement," McGurn explained honestly. "It's just that . . . well . . . it isn't the thing to do. Not now."

Toni flushed and turned away in anger. "Tell me, Mr. Harvey. Would you and your pretty girl take me? Even if Mr. McGurn can't make it?"

"Sure!" Harvey agreed, shaking her hand vigorously. "But you know, this isn't exactly full dress."

"That's why I want to go." Toni laughed.

"But it would be more fun," Harvey said, "if Mr. McGurn came, too."

The diplomat felt cornered. He knew how dangerous the murky hills of Fiji were, with the winds of hate tearing across them. He knew that as an official observer he had no business getting mixed up in a Fijian feast. And above all he knew that Sir Charles Jacquemart's daughter was almost criminally irresponsible if she meddled in Fijian-Indian affairs. And yet he was in love. If Toni engaged in folly, it was his job to protect her from the consequences. "I'll go along," he said quietly.

Twice during the day he regretted his assent and thought of telling Sir Charles about his daughter's impending indiscretion; but he knew that if he did, he would surrender any chance he might have of marrying this delectable and headstrong girl. Yet his sense of propriety was so ingrained that he had to warn somebody, so he slipped into Lady Jacquemart's room shortly after lunch and blurted out the evening schedule.

For once Lady Maud did not joke. "Will Toni be safe?" she asked soberly.

"Normally I'd say so. But Harvey has been threatened by fanatical Indians."

"So there's a spice of danger?"

"Yes."

"Then," Lady Maud announced firmly, "go ahead. This may convince Toni you're a man and not a mouse." And she slapped him on the seat of his pants.

At dusk, this odd quartet drove fifteen miles into the hills of Fiji. The rain fell mournfully about them and the car lights shone upon great jungle streamers that encroached upon the road. The night was so dark and the feel of the jungle so close upon them that each of the girls huddled against her escort.

And then, suddenly, the car turned into a village square, a horn blew, and giant Fijians tumbled out into murky light. A strong voice shouted, "Joe Harvey come!"

Men of the village who had worked for Joe appeared and carried the girls into a huge native house where many people were gathered. McGurn tried to walk under his own command, but found the footing impossible. "It's soapstone," Joe

164

laughed, as he slipped and sloshed along the village tracks. He had been there before.

Inside the jungle house, three pressure lamps, hung from the roof, made the place bright. Strands of sennit, miles long, had been woven into the roof, and now this roof danced with golden patterns that enchanted the eye. Toni Jacquemart looked about her as the men put her down. The great feel of the tropical night was upon her. "It's glorious," she said. Then, with a sense of what was right, she went to the chief and said, "We are pleased to be your guests."

The natives cheered this felicity and cheered again when Joe Harvey produced four bottles of gin, strictly forbidden to the Fijis. The chief placed the four bottles in a line before him and cried many words in Fijian. Then another old man spoke and dedicated the gin to the guests, and to the night's festivities.

It was apparent that Joe was a great favorite with these men, for they joked at his expense and when he could catch the meaning of their Fiji words, he cussed them soundly, and they drank gin together.

Pata and Toni formed a fast friendship and sat together at the long and beautifully woven frond mat that served as table. Soon, the chief yelled at his women, and they yelled back. Toni said afterwards that there had never been a meal served like that before. One woman ambled in with a pot full of dalo which she slammed on the table. Then for ten minutes nothing happened. The chief yelled some more, and another villager shuffled in with some boiled fish. It took an hour to serve the meal and another hour to eat it. The *pièce de résistance* was a dalo pudding with coconut and brown rice. It was chewy and delicious.

"I've been a pig!" Toni cried, and impulsively she leaned over and embraced Pata's shoulders. The chief applauded and embraced Joe. Then there was much shouting and an old woman brought in a large bowl. She sat cross-legged before it and began to knead a whitish powder into a cloth sack. This she plunged into the water and swished it back and forth many times. Finally, a dirty, pale-white fluid resulted.

"Yaqona!" Joe cried, and the chief ordered him to be served.

A young girl kneeled in stately manner before the ceremonial bowl and was handed a dipperful of the whitish liquid. Solemnly, she bore it to Harvey, who solemnly took it. The girl kneeled on the ground and clapped her hands twice.

Gravely, Joe lifted the dipper to his lips and in a mighty effort put the contents down in one draught.

"Mala!" shouted the Fijians in applause.

The serving maid next attended Pata and then Toni, who also handled hers in one gulp. The chief was impressed. Now it was McGurn's turn. He took the dipper and gingerly tasted the unpleasant-looking liquid. It was slimy to the tongue, earthy-tasting and mildly tingling at the gums. It took him three tries to drain the bowl. He did not like yaqona.

Now the evening was started, and slowly the natives began to hum songs or even to break into words. Harvey, with a gin bottle in one hand and his other upon the chief's arm, reverently began to sing the haunting phrases of *Isa Lei*. "Ahhhhhh!" cried the natives in approval. Toni caught up the immortal phrases of this best of all island songs and for a moment the two alien voices sang the great lament of Fiji. Then, as if the song had been intended for finer powers, the natives began to join in.

When the antiphonal chorus was reached, the hut seemed to explode with grandeur. The mighty, deep-probing voices of the basses carried the aching song far back in time, when suddenly the high, wailing voices of the women would throw it against the present night. When the long chord of conclusion was reached, Joe cried, "Again," and this time one woman sang the melody and all the others in the hut harmonized upon her refrain until the chorus was reached, when the full power of the basses was let loose. Even Louis McGurn was deeply moved, and Toni, seeing this, reached down and kissed his hand.

She became the heroine of the evening a few minutes later when the next round of yaqona was started, this time with a chief as server. Joe whispered to her, "When you finish the drink sing out *Dairo*."

"What's it mean?" Toni asked.

"You'll see!" So when she had gurgled down the last drop of yaqona, she cried loudly, "Dairo!"

McGurn thought a riot had started. The amazed chief dropped the bowl while six or seven native men leaped to their feet and started to shout violently. Soon, the entire Fijian population of the hut had centered on Toni, screaming imprecations at her.

"What have I done?" she pleaded.

Joe was laughing hilariously. "It's their totem," he said. "When you use it that way, it means, 'The yaqona was pretty good, what there was of it.'"

166

While Joe explained, the senior chief ordered the whole bowl of liquor brought to Toni's feet. Then, with a large ladle, he filled a large bowl and personally thrust it at the white girl.

"You've got to drink it!" Joe assured her.

With misgivings, she put it to her lips and took one long swig after another. Finally, somewhat dizzy, she handed back the empty bowl. The chiefs cheered and the women squealed their delight.

"Is good?" the senior chief demanded.

"Very good!" Toni said.

Then, as Louis was served his portion, she jabbed him and cried, "I dare you to yell *Dairo*." He looked at her as if to say, "Don't be foolish," so she nudged him again.

He had a very clear understanding that unless he cried *Dairo*, he would never marry Toni Jacquemart. He also knew that if he passed this test, she would apply no others, for she was in no way vicious, so in a half voice, not intending to offend, he whispered *Dairo*.

This time, it was no mere woman who had offended the tribe. In an instant, McGurn's coat and shirt had been pulled off, and all the women of the hut were lashing at him with small switches. Then he was handed a huge bowl of the dirty water. He drank until his ears popped, but he did hand back an empty vessel.

The cheers for his performance were loud. The chief himself shook his hand, and the great beauty of that last night started from that moment. The singing became like the sounding of organ music in a strange jungle, and the rain on the roof—incessant rain that seemed to accompany the revelry rather than to depress it—was a lullaby to the senses.

Toward morning, the entire village gathered in a long farewell to their good friend, Joe Harvey. The men were drunk with little gin and much singing. They would sleep all day. And the Indians in the valley would work.

In the car, as they drove to the airport from which Joe would leave this land forever, Toni finally made up her mind. She allowed McGurn to pull her toward him and after a moment of decent hesitation kissed him. Proudly she whispered, "You were quite a man tonight." Then she laughed and confided, "Up to now I've been afraid of you."

"Afraid?" he echoed.

"Yes. Afraid you were a stuffy, dull person."

"I am," he confessed.

"But I thought you were hopelessly dull. You aren't."

Then, as the day broke and the airport loomed ahead, they forgot their own love, for they saw Pata Cadi crying. This was her last hour, as it was their first. Impulsively, Toni broke into tears and clasped the little Indian girl to her while Joe went in to weigh his gear. When he came out, he kissed Toni on the cheek, and said, "You made the night a real festival." He grasped McGurn's hand and said, "You were a real sport, fellow. I'm glad for both of us that nothing happened."

Then his bravado left him, for he was standing face to face with Pata Cadi. He could remember her as she had lain beside him on his pillow. "May you have all happiness," he began, but his voice broke, and he clutched her tiny body to his.

"And may all that you do prosper," she whispered. The roaring engines warming up drowned out her other words.

Tears in his eyes, blond-headed Joe Harvey climbed aboard the plane that would take him away from Fiji. Rain swept down upon the field and through his shimmering window, he waved good-bye to his friends. He watched Pata as long as he could, but by the goodness of God, he had lost sight of her when Ramcheck Devidas Billimoria broke madly from behind a shed and plunged a writhing stiletto deep into her throat.

But Louis McGurn, horrified, was there to see the fanatical knife swirl in the air again. Then, as if driven by a force outside himself, he forgot his stiff white shirt and his diplomat's mission. He lunged furiously at Billimoria, knocking him to the ground. He was pounding his fists at the horrible face when the airport police intervened.

During the useless dash in the ambulance McGurn kept thinking, "I saw it all coming, and I could do nothing." Bitterly he recalled his warning to Harvey and the young man's insolent prophecy, "I'm the kind that doesn't get hurt."

McGurn was sick with fear of what might happen in Fiji because of this morning. Then Pata Cadi coughed. A foam of blood rose to her thin lips and for the second time that day McGurn acted instinctively. He fell on his knees beside her, clutched her frail hands and begged her, in an agonized voice, not to die. She looked at him but could not speak.

When death came, horrible and gurgling, he felt the terror of a strange land closing in upon him. Always before he had considered problems—the Israeli problem, the Indian problem—as subjects for neat intellectual reports to Washington. But now he saw Pata Cadi as a human being, a rare and

168

true person. In a naked humility such as he had never known before, he looked up at Toni Jacquemart with beseeching eyes. "What shall I do?" he mumbled.

It was not until they reached Lady Maud at the G.P.H. that they began to get the murder into perspective. She was firm. She said to Toni, "You've had a dreadful shock, girl. Go to bed and drink several cups of hot Bovril."

With McGurn she was more direct. "You predicted this. You did what you could to prevent it. Now you must dismiss it as an incident. Tragic but inevitable."

"An incident?" McGurn cried.

"As predictable as the tides. I've lived through six of 'em."

"But I might have done something more!" he accused himself.

"More! Don't be an ass!" She poured him a cup of tea and prepared to leave the hotel.

"Where are you going?" he asked pleadingly.

"I'm going to the Governor," she said firmly. "S'Chalz will rant about honor and propriety. He'll surely volunteer to disqualify himself in the Patel case. I've got to get there first and stop such folly. Time comes when a man can be too demmed honorable."

Majestically she swept out of the hotel, and McGurn felt as if the source of his strength had disappeared. He did not even recover his spirits when a messenger appeared with his long-delayed cable from Boston. He sat fingering it and wondered how Joe Harvey would hear of Pata Cadi's death. In a bar some day. A stranger would shout, "Boy, do I know Fiji? Say I heard the damnedest story down there. Seems there was this American . . ." Well, it would serve him right.

He wondered if Americans would ever learn to behave in alien lands. He recalled an arrogant colonel he had known in France. "Hell!" the colonel had boasted, "six energetic Americans could run this place like it ought to be run." Well, he mused grimly, they'll have their chance.

He was interrupted by Lady Maud's return. "The Governor was a dear," she reported. "Very sensible man." Then she asked abruptly, "Have you proposed to Toni?"

"At this time?" McGurn asked.

"Certainly! This is the right time. Marriage is always the child of crisis. When the world is shaking, people marry for security." She collapsed into a chair and shouted for some tea. As she poured it she whispered, "For example, S'Chalz had no intention in the world of marrying me. Had his eye

169

on a French widow. I've never admitted to anyone what I had to do to trap him, but he's been quite happy with me."

At this point the mynah birds discovered a swarm of insects in the weeping figs and there was a furious clatter. "Those wretched birds!" Lady Maud cried. "Everyone of 'em's a murderer." Then she clutched McGurn's arm. "Go in and see Toni. Now."

He walked to the door but found that Toni was sleeping. He started to leave but Lady Maud gave him a firm shove. So he wakened the girl and said, "Will you marry me?"

She blinked several times and then blushed deeply. "I was going to ask you—at lunch." She drew his hand to her lips and kissed it, whispering, "At the airport ... you were very brave."

Overcome with his love for the girl, he fumbled in his pocket. This was the appropriate moment! Proudly he produced the cable and announced, "Wonderful news! You won't have to be Mrs. McGurn!"

"But I want to be!" she protested.

"Read this!" he cried triumphantly. "The court has changed my name. I'm Louis Richardson now."

Lady Maud, in the doorway, saw her daughter's face grow pale. She knew that Toni was on the point of breaking off the whole engagement with this terribly stuffy man. But with an imperious eye Lady Maud stopped her daughter as if to say, "Marry him. All men are fools, but he's the best we've been able to find."

So Toni Jacquemart reached up and kissed Louis on the ear. "Toni Richardson," she mused. "Well, not exciting, but not bad."

"It's an English name," he explained. "You see, I'm really of English stock. From Surrey."

Guadalcanal

In the South Pacific there is an island, dark and brooding. It is not large as islands go, nor yet so small as to be forgotten when one has seen it.

It is inhospitable. Around its entire shore there is no harbor, no welcoming anchorage. Disease abounds in many forms, and often the climate is oppressive.

This curious and brutal island is not even known by its right name. Old planters call it Solomon Island. It is really Guadalcanal (Wady-al-Canar), but in its corruption it has become one of the blood-honored names in American history: Guadalcanal.

Here the great Pacific enemy was met. In small numbers at first, like the early whispering of an orchestra, and then in terrible crescendo, Japan and the United States hurled men and resources into the battle. At night single soldiers slugged it out hand to hand. In daylight hundreds of the world's finest planes clashed in mortal combat, while always the battleships and cruisers were aprowl, springing sometimes into tremendous conflict.

The battle for Guadalcanal should never lightly be termed a victory. Here our Navy took its worst defeat in history, absorbed its most humiliating shame. At Savo we had our cruisers, on whom the operation depended, poised ready for action. We knew a Jap assault force was forming to the north. We had its speed, its direction, its intention. Yet we let it slip into the very shadow of our guns and destroy the backbone of our sea force.

Our Marines tasted bitter medicine, too. At Henderson Field, on Bloody Ridge and at the Matanikau River they learned what it was to waver under fire. Aloft our Air Forces absorbed a daily punishment from the superior Zeros. The time came when two Americans had to go aloft to meet forty Japs. At Guadalcanal great men lost their lives, Admirals Scott and Callaghan among them.

Then, in the full bitterness of battle, we rallied. At first the Navy had to rely upon trickery and courage. Admiral Halsey radioed his tactician Fletcher: "Our educated guess is that the Tokyo Express will attempt reinforcements from Rabaul. They must be stopped at any cost. Repeat. Any cost." Finally

171

our sea strength accumulated and we smashed the express forever.

In the air Joe Foss and his men held off superior Zeros— "If you're alone and meet a Zero, run like hell, because you're outnumbered"—until the P-38's arrived and crushed the meatballs. In one day Army pilots shot down 110 Jap planes.

On the ground the Marines and the Army finally pushed the Japs right into the sea. The enemy commander reported: "I had 30,000 of the finest men. 10,000 were killed. 10,000 starved to death. 10,000 were evacuated, too sick to fight." Guadalcanal was a momentous victory, but it was purchased at great price.

To me—and to many like me—Guadalcanal has a significance that is hard to explain. For years we had been told, "America is soft. W.P.A. and C.C.C. have ruined the young men. This generation has no vital spark." We believed these rumors, in part, and what was more important, our enemies believed them. Across the world critics looked at us and reported: "Sports loving, luxury minded, whimpering in depression, unregimented." The fatal word was passed: "America is through. She's a pushover."

At Guadalcanal my generation threw back the answer. I was stationed there during the war, and I have walked the trails Americans crawled along, flown in their fiery skies and followed the furrows of the sea where their small boats went out to fight battleships. I am proud—vengefully proud, if you will—of what my generation accomplished at Guadalcanal.

Now when I hear Europeans condemn happy-go-lucky young Americans as soft, purposeless, or without courage, I smile. I learned different in the Solomons.

Guadalcanal lies at the foot of The Slot, that strange body of water set off on each side by long islands. Planes still fly The Slot. Each fortnight a lonely C-47 with bucket seats flies down from Rabaul to Guadal. At Torokina, on Bougainville, the plane dips low across the Laruma, still in flood, and lands at the fighter strip on the shores of Empress Augusta Bay. A few Australians rush out for letters. They're probing the jungle for stray materials and often turn up equipment worth thousands. Our fantastic fragment of Bougainville—we held 6% with 5,000 troops; the Japs held 94% with 40,000—shows few scars of our occupation. Some roads have washed away. Two rivulets cut right across the bomber strips at Piva, where we suffered our only full-fledged retreat in the Pacific war. High on a precipitous cliff—"How could any human beings drag cannon up there?"—the Japs unlimbered a daily barrage that made the fields untenable. And Mount Bagana has become a major volcano, with important eruptions of ash and lava.

From Torokina the C-47 flies south directly over once deadly Buin and Kahili, where Jap anti-aircraft specialists knocked down many of our planes. Now we can see the Treasuries, which had a special significance for me. I was stationed on nearby Stirling, a dot in the ocean surrounded by Japs impotent to attack, because we had the planes and they hadn't.

One day word reached us that the enemy had infiltrated Mono Island next door. An Australian patrol set out to investigate, and I went along. We found no Japs, but on the topmost point of Mono we stumbled into a filthy, unpleasant village bearing one of the loveliest names I'd ever heard: Bali-ha'i. From my pocket I drew a scrap of paper, soggy with sweat, and thought: "I'll take a note of that name. It has a musical quality." Years later, Rodgers and Hammerstein were to think the same.

Now we are over The Slot. I cannot describe this home of great battles except to say that for me it is the most beautiful I know in the world. This may offend those who struggled in its skies. It may cause a shudder to those who fell into its waters and paddled their way on rafts to dismal islands. But during the war I flew The Slot, and so help me it was beautiful, passionately wonderful with craggy islands, spangled lagoons and towering clouds. Now that war has gone, it is even more so.

To the left lies shadowy Choiseul, where silent patrols passed in the dark and did no fighting. The Japs held their end of the island; the Allies held theirs. It was from here that a much-relieved pilot who had come through two dog fights radioed his course in plain language:

Hey diddle diddle
Right down the middle!

Then suddenly the New Georgia group appears on the right. There is circular Kolombangara of the stately curves. Fleecy clouds hang over it, blue coral surrounds it, and at its feet, in fathoms of water, lie many Japs and their arrogant ships.

Now below us is one of the wonders of the Pacific, Marovo Lagoon. It runs along the north side of New Georgia, an arm of the sea cut off by an arresting and varied coral reef. Some of the fringing islands are long and narrow, like water snakes. Others are jewels. Still others are stars or coronets. Sometimes the water barely covers great patches of silvery coral. At other points the growing reef breaks the waves and a few coconut palms cling to the new-made sand. At Marovo the sea is endlessly varied, angry blue where the waves break, placid yellow above the coral, and dazzling white at the sand's edge. The lagoon is hemmed in by trees of all descriptions and visited by birds from across the Pacific. Once seen, with pillars of cloud reflected in its quiet waters, it can never be forgotten.

The Russells are still cut into a dozen vivid patterns by sea channels. Here are the largest coconut groves in the Pacific, occupying entire islands. From aloft the palms are like green stars on a purple sea.

Then to the left lies Tulagi, where P.T. boats hid during the day to sally forth with deadly accuracy at night. Here on a dominating hill was Halsey's deeply disturbing sign:

Admiral Halsey says:

> "Kill Japs. Kill Japs.
> Kill More Japs."

YOU WILL HELP TO KILL THE YELLOW BASTARDS IF YOU DO YOUR JOB WELL.

It was erected by men whose comrades had been tortured, beheaded and sometimes eaten. War in The Slot was brutal.

Beyond lies Purvis Bay, empty and silent in the hot sunlight. No more do the great ships of the fleet huddle here. No more do roistering commanders, home from raids against the Jap, roar down the steps from the Iron Bottom Bay Club. No more aloft the Jap planes, their crimson meatball flashing in the sun. No more the screaming Grumman plunging into the sea.

And at quiet Halavo, where the Black Cats went out to save more than 800 pilots adrift in the ocean, vines creep over the huts where brave men lived.

Below us now is the grave of ships, Iron Bottom Bay. More than a hundred major warships lie rusting in the deep waters of this undefined portion of the sea. Off Savo, still sleeping like a tired woman, off Esperance, the cape of no hope for the Japanese, and at Tassafaronga, where the fleets engaged in fury, the sea is placid, satiated with great ships.

174

Then the heart constricts! At least the American heart must always hesitate, for ahead lies Guadalcanal!

It is strange that so famous an island should be so often misrepresented. Most misconceptions arose during the war when frenzied correspondents sought easy copy and coined such inappropriate phrases as: impenetrable jungle, steaming tropical nights, uninhabitable, rain-soaked morass and lurking dangers.

Actually, Guadalcanal is divided into three parts, and the colorful adjectives apply only to the first two, where no Americans served. First there is a southern coastal belt which is hot and which contains most of the 12,000 natives; next a central mountainous strip with forbidding peaks rising to more than 8,000 feet; and finally a hospitable northern plain, ten to fifteen miles deep. Experts believe that this broad, flat land where the Americans were could support a European or Asiatic population of more than 50,000.

It is astonishing to discover that agriculturally the only limiting factor is lack of rain! At Kukum the rainfall is only 62 inches a year (same as Mobile, Alabama), and during July and August falls to less than 3 inches a month. The heaviest rainfall at any point occupied by Americans was 80 inches at the Tenaru (like Juneau, Alaska).

The temperatures can be brutally hot, but not at night. Actually, the temperature almost never goes above 95. The record is 102. But the sun is directly overhead, and 95 feels like 105! The humidity is high, usually over 80. But nights are cool—cold over 100 feet high—and a blanket is often appreciated, even at the beach. Guadalcanal at night is never so swelteringly hot as either New York or Washington after a real scorcher.

When seen aloft, the island is spectacularly beautiful. The mountains are arresting with their varied cliffs. River valleys are dramatic as they plunge toward the plains. But one feature is both unique and startling. At spasmodic intervals across the island the soil is such that trees will not grow. Therefore great kunai plains develop, and even at the tops of mountains there are breathtaking sweeps of superb grassy fields, rolling delicately like expensive golf links.

Full-grown jungle crowds down upon the open fields, but at the critical line of inhospitable soil the trees stop like a battalion commanded to halt. These vacant areas exist on the northern plain in considerable number. One mile east of where Americans landed there is a huge pasture reaching miles inland with rarely a tree. Our agricultural experts bull-

175

dozed away the kunai and built a farm that became rather spectacular. Black soil like the chernozem of Russia went at least sixteen feet deep and yielded three or four crops a year, enough to provide fresh vegetables to many troops. If overfarmed, the soil quickly lost fertility. But it recovered equally quickly, if planted with nitrogenous crops that were allowed to rot. The only drawback: not enough rain.

A trusted observer of exactly what Guadalcanal is like, is rangy, good-looking, talkative A. D. Bugbee from Honolulu. A thirty-eight-year-old Army civilian expert, he has served on the island for the last three years and says, "I like it here. Asked to be reassigned after my first tour. Good water, good fishing, cool nights, regular mail, and a first-class English doctor." He also has a skiff with a murderous airplane propellor that pushes it up the Lunga River at twenty-six miles an hour. He adds, "I've walked through almost every part of the island. Sometimes it's tough going, but usually enjoyable. That's why I do it." He shoots crocodiles for sport, wild pigs for food, and keeps plenty of soft drinks on ice. "My friends in the States write and say, 'Three years on Guadalcanal? You must be a hero!' Don't you dare tell 'em I ain't. But why should I worry? They wouldn't believe you." Of course, Bugbee is not pursued by Jap snipers.

But I wanted to recall exactly how Guadalcanal seemed in the old days when you crept through the bush with C-Rations. I went out one brutally hot day and walked some six miles up and around the Matanikau River. This was where the Marines were knocked back at one time, where the Army did much heavy fighting.

The trees and vines were not bad, for there had been no rain for many days. One could easily walk if he took his time, and the bugs—for this was daytime—were not unbearable.

The heat was. Within ten steps I started to perspire and in fifteen minutes I was a soggy mass. At the end of three miles not a stitch was dry. Even the insides of my shoes were wet. It's hard to describe the last three miles. I thought my stomach would collapse from lack of water. Never have I been so maddeningly thirsty.

Where the last hour's worth of perspiration came from I shall never know. The heat was so intense that even under a toque I was beginning to feel faint, and at last I had to scoop a drink from the Matanikau. It was as good as icewater and announced itself to my muscles each inch of the way down my gullet.

176

Now Guadalcanal was oppressive. I tried to imagine what it must have been like to the men who hated it, and I was sorry that anyone, American or Jap, had ever been forced to live under such conditions. I understood why even rugged Japanese troops had collapsed and died in that stifling mid-day heat, how they starved in this impersonal sea of greenness. Add constant malaria for quaking fevers, and this was forbidding terrain. Twigs crackled, and I needed no flight of fancy to know how increased the terror would have been with Jap snipers lashed in the crotches of the silent trees.

It took me three hours to walk six miles. When I was finished I had the jock itch, the beginnings of prickly heat, and near sun stroke. I was limp from excessive perspiration and my arm tasted acid, not salty. Had I stayed there beside the Matanikau until dark—as our men did—the mosquitoes would have been at me and the stinging bugs. And two weeks later I was to learn how really tough the Matanikau had been.

When I reached the road I looked back at the peaceful river. I should not want to fight there alone, with no medicine and no food, no tent, no communication with my friends. I acknowledged once more what a rotten, sweaty, frightening battlefield Guadalcanal had been. There was unending honor to the men who conquered it.

The worst of my Matanikau venture was the virulent attack of Spring Fever that followed. This tropical disease ran rampant among American officers during the war, and, when mixed with alcoholism, was irremediable. The patient gets up bright and chipper at seven, but at ten he feels drowsy and lies down for a nap. He wakes at twelve in time for lunch, following which everyone in his right senses takes a siesta. The officer passes out cold, like a dead mackerel, and wakens at four. After a swim and a good dinner he is wide awake and a brilliant conversationalist, but about nine he hits the hay. It's called Spring Fever when you pound your mattress more than twelve hours a day. I was never a champion sack hound because I found that if I slept more than sixteen hours a day, I had a little trouble dropping off at night.

The sharpest comment ever made about Guadalcanal was that of the sergeant who hated the place. On V-J day he rushed in and cried, "Nnnyahhh! Everybody sayin' how smart the English are in foreign affairs. We just offered to give them back this hole. And they took it!"

Why they took it in the first place is a mystery, for it has been a deficit protectorate ever since. They do not own the

177

islands and must one day turn them over to the natives for self-government. This might take place within a hundred years.

When they resumed control, the British were faced with a dilemma: "Where shall the capital be?" They had to choose between the destroyed capital at Tulagi (good harbor, rotten climate) and some new location on Guadalcanal (no harbor, superior climate). After inflamed debate they chose the latter and drew up plans for an ideal tropical town at Honiara. Americans familiar with Guadalcanal will insist, "There's no such place." Up to 1945 there wasn't, but there is now.

Leave Henderson Field and go west along Highway 50 past Fighter One, past Kukum Docks, across the Matanikau, and on to Point Cruz, where the ammunition dump was. At the base of Point Cruz, which forms the meager semblance of a harbor, Honiara has been built. The word means "where the wind blows," which, as the planter observed "is so perfect a name for a capital that any comment from me would be superfluous."

Honiara will be a better town than Tulagi ever was. King-size quonsets have been moved in for barracks, and grass shacks have been tucked away under broad trees to serve temporarily as government offices. Behind the town is a high ridge where lovely homes are being built in breezes that keep them permanently cool and mosquito-proof.

At Honiara there are no signs of war. A good saloon is operated by one of Guadal's old identities, Kenneth Houston Dalrymple Hay. An hilarious Chinaman, Ho Man, keeps the restaurant, which almost folded because "more than seven hundred dollars' worth of china and silverware was stolen the first ten months." Ho Man's menu is gruesome. He is reputed to be an excellent cook, but Guadalcanal has a most precarious food supply—ships don't call any more—and when I was his guest Ho Man hadn't seen meat, potatoes, fresh vegetables or onions for three months. As each hopeless day passed he became more despondent and instead of exercising his skill on what was at hand, raged at fate and banged whatever he could find into a skillet of hot lard. It seems theatrical, but when I got back to Guadal my first dinner with Ho Man consisted of Spam! Also my second through tenth.

There were other more notable dinners in the fine homes on the ridge. Captain Frank Moore, of Australia, is Inspector of Police. He's about forty, wears a close-clipped moustache, and has a beautiful wife. His house at the top of a cliff commands a startling view of The Slot, and in the large circular living room life can be very pleasant.

Drinks are at six, anything you can name. Formal dress is required: handsome gowns for women, whites with black silk cummerbunds for men. The Peter Hindles are there. He's from South Africa and is in charge of lands and mines, some of which are suspected of hiding pretty good gold. The guest of honor is Edward John Hugo Colchester-Wemyss (rhymes with seems), the new Chief of Police lately arrived from service in Jamaica. He's the imposing-colonel type who has known the Empire in its days of glory. "History repeats!" he cries. "England was at her greatest in the reign of Queen Elizabeth. I make bold to predict that she will be even greater in the reign of the new Elizabeth!"

Handsome young MacKenzie-Pollock, glittering in kilts and sporran, is the newer type of colonial servant. His wife is also a doctor and assists at the hospital. Talk turns to life in the tropics and MacKenzie-Pollock says in terrific brogue: "Mind you! White men are not intended to live within ten degrees of the equator." His energetic wife agrees. "I'm ashamed of myself," she admits. "I used to bounce out of bed at dawn after six hours' sleep. Now I rise at seven and take an afternoon nap."

The meal is impeccably served by a wide-eyed nine-year-old native boy. Four courses, wine, good bread, and liqueurs. Not until later do you remember that Guadalcanal has been without food for three months. Everything you've eaten has been improvised. The British would rather eat bully beef than lose dignity in native eyes by going out to hunt wild pigs!

Captain Moore and his colleagues are having a tough time living down certain bad breaks they suffered during the war. Natives watched them flee before the Japs. They saw them desert the Chinese at Tulagi—"No Oriental women or children to board evacuation boats"—and by the fortunes of war it was the Americans who came with fabulous equipment to recapture the islands. More important, they saw that our Negro troops lived the same as white men. It has been aptly said: "For forty years the English used social aloofness to impress the native. In one afternoon the Americans did a better job with a Texas Negro driving a bulldozer." The impact of Americans was profound, affecting even the story of the Crucifixion as narrated by a native pastor: "Master he look down he see Picaninny belong Him in pain too much. He sign out, 'Son, how's things?' Picaninny belong Him sing out, 'O.K., Boss!' "

On the island of Malaita, one of the untamed centers of the Pacific, a new problem has arisen. During the war certain Americans informed the Malaita savages that when peace came there would be a new order in which black men would govern and every native would receive the better part of a shipload of things like trucks and refrigerators. Upon these promises was formed the Marching Rule (Marxian Rule). Adherents refuse to be numbered in the census, to work, to pay taxes or to listen to the British, whom they threaten to club in the head if they came to Malaita.

The Marching Rule men are confused on one point. They think it's America that's leading the Communists. Accordingly, they've approached American soldiers with sums up to $4,000 if they will become field generals in the war against the British!

Actually, there are few islands in the Pacific better governed than the Solomons. True, there is much stuffiness about English on any island, including their own. They derive so much pleasure from doing things the hard, time-honored way that they often overlook essentials. For example, in Honiara's main street a very large Jap shell is periodically uncovered by the road grader, whereupon a big sign is erected: UNEXPLOSIVE BOMB. TAKE CARE, which is one of the best signs in the Pacific. The next trip of the grader covers the bomb again, and the sign is packed away. When I asked what would happen if the grader detonated the bomb, an official thought for a moment and replied, "There'd be a tremendous bang, I should think."

But Americans who scoff at the British system have one stubborn fact to explain. Bougainville, New Britain, New Ireland and New Guinea are better islands in every respect than the Solomons. Their natives are more susceptible to development. But those islands have been governed first by the brutal Germans and next by the confused Australians. When war broke, these German-Australian-trained natives killed missionaries, betrayed coastwatchers and sold American pilots to Jap soldiers who beheaded them.

On British islands not one white man was betrayed. Not one. The fidelity of the Solomon Islanders was unbelievable. Hundreds of Americans live today because these brave savages fished them from the sea, led them through Jap lines and carried them in their canoes to safety. Sergeant Vouza was the type. The Japs tortured him for hours to make him betray white positions. He refused. They lashed him to a tree and used him for bayonet practice. He received some twenty stabs and fainted. By a miracle he lived and was cut down by friends. "What did you think?" they asked. "I thought it was my duty," he said.

I knew many fine men in the Solomons. Dr. Fox was a 98-pound missionary who served at a remote spot. A brilliant linguist, he wished to write the definitive treatise on native grammar. To do so, he tried to project himself into the native mind, hiring himself out as a plantation house boy and living with the other servants. He didn't get the feeling of being a native. Finally he said to his master, "Will you please call me a bloody fool and kick me in the pants?" The white man was astounded, so the fragile little missionary explained, "I want to know exactly how the native feels." This planter had long hated missionaries, so with relish he backed off and let fire. Dr. Fox rubbed his bottom, thought for a moment, and said sorrowfully, "Too bad. I still don't get the feeling."

The American who left the greatest imprint on Guadalcanal was John Burke, of New York. He was six-feet two, weighed about 260, and told a leading naval captain in my presence, "You get in my way, Captain, and I'll break you!" At five o'clock each afternoon he used to consume three huge malted milks, six candy bars and four steins of beer. Then he would have a gargantuan meal. He was crazy about the jungle and on one trip with me took along only a toothbrush and a copy of the New York *Social Register*. He sat for hours inside his mosquito net unraveling the intertwinings of leading families. He dreamed of leading an insurrection of the Malaita men, who idolized him. But three weeks after I left, he and my staff flew our old C-47 into the side of a mountain. They were all killed.

The story of Paul Mason seems unbelievable, but only a tithe of it has been told. Says a friend, "Paul was so little and insignificant no one would give him a job in peacetime. We thought he wasn't quite bright, a five-foot runt of a man with a squint." He became a coastwatcher behind Jap lines on Bougainville. His exploits were heroic. He swam two and a half miles through sharks' waters to warn a submarine. He organized a native army which killed hundreds of Japs. At one time General Kanda reported to Tokyo: "Mason is our greatest enemy in this area." A crate of bloodhounds was shipped in to get him, but he radioed for American planes to bomb them on the pier. The planes came and Mason reported: "Dogs destroyed. Proceeding." When Admiral Halsey met him for the first time, Halsey said, "You stay seated. In your presence I'll stand." He was decorated by three governments, was perhaps the bravest man in the Pacific. It was partially through his efforts that Admiral Yamamoto was shot down at Kieta. The Yanks had broken the Jap code and knew he was landing for an inspection, but not when. Mason sent his cook into Kieta to work for the Japs. Soon the cook returned with electrifying news: "Numbawan Japoni bilong soda water (sea), he come!" And as Yamamoto left, our P-38's nailed him. Now Mason is running a small plantation on Bougainville. Reports his friend: "They figured that if he could do all that, he could be trusted to cut copra, even if he is a little squirt."

The American who completely captured Guadalcanal was Carole Landis! She arrived one blistering day with Jack Benny, and when she appeared in a glorious form-fitting gown, there was a breathless hush and then a cacophony of whistles. In her acts she kissed a sergeant, who fainted. My chief whispered, "I'd enlist all over again for one chance like that." She was a tonic, a bright, bubbling girl whose very appearance made you feel good. After the show she disappeared with a Navy ensign she had known in the States, and the Army went crazy. When the culprits were finally found Army brass thundered that the ensign must be court-martialed, but the Navy commander said, "You're excused, son. You've gone through enough already."

Today the island contains many surprises. The used portion of Highway 50 is better now than it was in 1945. Many of the bridges have collapsed. Quonset huts left in the bush have sometimes been completely covered with vines. Those that have been painted look better than they did originally.

The chapel has fallen in, the cemetery is gone, only the white steeple remains. The docks at Kukum are crumbling, and the infamous Hotel De Gink, after five years of complete abandonment, looks about as clean as it did in its heyday, which isn't saying much.

Wild life has come back to its former haunts. Magnificent birds—parakeets, hawks, heron, quail, frigate birds—are abundant. Wild pigs invade the airfields. Crocodiles infest the rivers. And the flying foxes, with no one to shoot them, have grown bold and plump. But there is one tragedy. Each island unit used to have a couple of bouncing little puppies. They are dogs, now, and have gone wild. They have crossbred into repugnant creatures and have become a major pest. They will all be shot.

Henderson Field is a continuing miracle. In recent years it has received little attention, yet it remains an almost perfect coral strip. I traveled the length of it—6200 unequaled feet of coral—in a battered jeep at 55 miles an hour. It was like a table top. Even the original Jap strip is serviceable. Explains Captain Martin, commanding the closing-down unit of seventeen men, "The Japs probably selected the very best site in the entire Solomons. The drainage is remarkable."

The only military installation still occupied is ComAir-SoPac on the hill above Henderson Field. Here Captain Martin occupies Admiral Fitch's old quarters and eats off Navy dishes with four impressive stars. "You'll observe," he says with Army satisfaction, "that they're all chipped."

Visiting Guadalcanal is like standing on the shores of Spain and looking toward Trafalgar, like walking the fields of Gettysburg. The entire island is a monument to the courage of free men who threw back the rampaging enemy. Although I knew it well during the war, I was moved to deep spiritual excitement when I saw it again, and I feel certain that any American visitor will have the same reaction. For beyond its people, beyond its governmental problems—even beyond the battle records—Guadalcanal must always have a unique place in American history.

Today Guadalcanal is a quiet, sleeping place of great beauty. It was not always so.

The Story

To me—and to many like me—Guadalcanal has a significance that is hard to explain.

Everyone who writes is besieged by people who report breathlessly, "I know the most wonderful story! But unfortunately I can't write. So I'll tell you the plot. Then you can dress it up and we'll both become rich!"

Writers learn to avoid such enthusiasts. The amateur's ready-made plot is invariably a pathetic chaos. To infuse meaning into its jumbled accidents would require not a writer but a magician.

One hot, sticky evening on Guadalcanal a stranger sidled up to me and said, "I been lookin' for you. Got a wonderful story to tell you. Write it down proper and we'll both be famous." And he revealed such a story as haunts me still.

At first I was disposed to flee this man. He was tall, cadaverous, completely bald and possessed of deep-set eyes. He was, I judged, about sixty and he bore the marks of having lived in the tropics for many years. His toque sat on the back of his head. He wore no socks, and his pants were soiled where he had wiped much sweat from his palms.

As I started to leave he grabbed my arm and said, "Wait! You haven't heard the story."

He led me, protesting, to the island bar, from whose verandah I could see The Slot and distant Savo and the dusty huts of Honiara. My guide leaned forward until his face was close to mine and said, "M'name's Larcom. Been in these islands forty years. And, Mister, I have a story to tell you . . ."

"Drink?" I asked.

"Say! I'd like that!" But he frowned and leaned closer, confiding, "The Governor put me on rations. I can't have any more today. But if you . . ."

"I'll have a whiskey," I called to the Malaita boy behind the bar. He brought it and set it down impartially between Larcom and me. Then he smiled, showing his immense white teeth.

Larcom tossed the whiskey down, shivered, and looked about him surreptitiously. Then he whispered, "There's a valley on this island. Haunted." He paused dramatically to study the effect of this cataclysmic news. I stared at him as if waiting for him to continue.

This unnerved him. He had expected a more violent reaction, so he began again: "There's a valley on Guadalcanal and during the war there were some queer stories told about it. But, Mister, nobody ever told the real story." Again he paused theatrically, watching me carefully. This time I had to show some reaction.

"What's it about?"

"Gold."

"I've heard a dozen stories about lost gold mines."

Larcom grabbed my arm again and cried, "Yes! But this one isn't lost!"

"You know where it is?" I asked.

"No," he said triumphantly, leaning back to enjoy my confusion. After a moment he pushed his lean face into mine and said, "It's not lost and I don't know where it is because, like I said, this is a made-up story."

I had to admit that Larcom had produced at least a striking approach and I ordered him another whiskey. Knowing that he had me on the hook, he sipped his drink slowly and leered at me. Then he leaned back expansively and stared out across the purple sea lanes that led to Tulagi. I was prepared for some astonishing yarn, but what Larcom told me was merely another of the dreadful romances cooked up by people who never read much when they were young. It was a complete waste of time.

It seems an American Marine was shot down in 1942 and after wandering through the Guadalcanal jungle stumbled upon a haunted valley whose mountains gleamed with gold. Back at his base he organized a searching party, but he was never again able to find that golden valley.

There was a lot more to the yarn, but it got worse. Finally Larcom reached the part where the frenzied Marine flew his plane into a mountainside, and as he burned to death the valley shone like gold. Larcom's face glowed in ecstasy and his whole body was in a palpitation of excitement as he waited my verdict.

"That's quite a story," I said, and he leaned far forward, gripping my arm again.

"You'll write it all down?" he asked eagerly.

"I'm afraid not." The electric tension in the old planter vanished, and I was both sorry and ashamed. "It's not in my line," I explained.

185

"What do you mean?" he cried. "You're an American. That flier was one, too."

"But that doesn't mean I could write the story."

"Look, Mister!" he whispered in bitter forcefulness. "This is the greatest story ever happened on Guadalcanal. And you're goin' to write it."

"You don't understand," I laughed. "To write a book a man has got to feel the story himself."

Larcom leaned back astonished. "You mean you don't feel this story? I must of left part of it out!" And he leaned forward breathlessly to repeat the whole painful yarn.

Much as I hated to, I interrupted him and rose to leave the bar. This so startled him that he moved with me, as if he were a mechanical doll attached to my shoulders. "Mister!" he pleaded. "You don't understand. I'm givin' you the entire plot. Complete. All you have to do," he said deprecatingly, "is write it down."

I now realized that I had to get rid of this monomaniac and actually left the pleasant bar. He paddled along behind me and said hurriedly, "I understand. I know you artist blokes. You're not in the mood yet. So I'm goin' to help you."

"Mr. Larcom," I protested.

He shook his long hand in my nose. "No mister with me! Plain Larcom, because we're goin' to see a great deal of each other. While I'm helpin' you with the book, that is."

Firmly I said, "I'm not going to write it."

With equal firmness Larcom insisted, "But you are! Tomorrow morning I'll call for you and I'll take you in to that valley. And when you see how mysterious . . ."

Again I protested, but he would not listen. He said I was to look for him next morning at the Chinese restaurant. As he left me in the roadway he looked deeply confident. "When you see this valley," he called back, "the story will come to you in a flash."

I returned to the bar, pondering the common belief that stories are born "in a flash." A good story is the result of painstaking artistry, as Rachel Field knew when she said that a writer is precisely like a master cook. He has many kettles simmering at the back of the stove, when for some unaccountable reason one of them begins to boil. That's the kettle he works on. But the others are still back there simmering with their precious complement of herbs and vegetables and sturdy meat. For no cook should ever rush into a kitchen and expect, unprepared, to make a tasty dish.

186

But as I sat there thinking of the many pots simmering on the back of my stove—and never one near to a decent boil—an elderly man in a black alpaca coat came and sat with me. He was a government man, long in service, and he had the warm face of a person who has never had enough power to hurt others.

"My apologies," he said. "Dennison. I'm the Colony's financial agent." He started to buy drinks, but I replied that since I was the intruder here he must let me catch this round, to which he readily assented, for salaries on Guadalcanal are dismally low and the cost of beer is high.

"I wouldn't intrude, you know," he said, licking the beer off his moustache, one of those shaggy English affairs that make one think irresistibly of scissors, "but I must explain that frightful bore Larcom."

"He's rather insistent," I agreed.

"Jolly good! Insistent! Yes, that's the word for Larcom."

"What's wrong with him?"

"Everything. A recluse. Lives inland on some godforsaken stretch of copra land. Eternally feuding with the government. Hates the government."

"Why?"

"Always something. Right now he's feuding about his native boy Vata. We know damned well Vata killed two men on Florida, but Larcom substantiates a ridiculous alibi. So what can we do?"

"Is he harmful?" I asked.

"Not exactly. Just a bloody nuisance. Was he pestering you with his novel? I thought so!"

"He wants to show me the valley. Tomorrow."

Dennison laughed and I felt a real sense of brotherhood with this elderly servant of the Empire. "If you want to win our gratitude," he began.

"Who's ours?"

"The government's. I think the Governor would give you a rather handsome reward if you'd take Larcom into his haunted valley and jolly well lose him."

"I've no intention of going anywhere with that Ancient Mariner."

"Ancient Mariner! That's very good. The Governor will enjoy that," and Dennison insisted upon ordering another round. "I know you'll pardon the intrusion," he said gently, "but Americans often have such strange ideas of we Britons. I didn't want you to think that Larcom ..." He started to chuckle and sipped the beer off his moustache. "Ancient Mariner!"

I had forgotten Larcom by next morning and was well into an essay I was writing on island governments when there was a sharp knock at my door. It was the planter, his toque leaning back on his head, his dirty white pants insolently drooping and his shirt barely buttoned.

"Where were you?" he demanded.

"When?"

"At breakfast. We made a deal."

"What do you mean?" I asked.

"The valley. Look."

He pointed down a dusty road that led from my shack to the waterfront, and there, some forty yards offshore, rode a small schooner. "We're waiting for you," he said.

I was about to protest that I could not disappear on a silly business about a haunted island when he pointed again, and for the first time I saw, in a single gaze, as it were, gaunt Larcom, his schooner riding in The Slot, and the dark jungle. In that moment I had a flash of premonition that here was a story, some immense yarn of tropical life that would illuminate Guadalcanal for all the thousands of Americans who had served on that bitter island; for I knew that although stories are never born in a flash, the cord of meaning which ties a story together may be so discovered.

"I'll be right with you," I said.

The fiery planter—you could sense that he would have to be at war with any government—led me down to Honiara's wharf and into a filthy dinghy manned by a huge native in khaki shorts.

"This is Vata," Larcom said. "Good man."

All that day we sailed eastward, keeping in sight the brooding mountains where so many battles had been fought. Dark, ominous Vata conned the boat and at dusk we hove to at the edge of a jungle that crept down to the sea. As night fell we could hear forest noises and the distant splash of flying fish as they dipped back into the sea.

Then it came. Larcom pulled a chair close to mine and said, "I've been thinkin' about our story all day. I see why it didn't command your interest. No sex."

I must have groaned aloud, for he snapped his fingers and cried, "There's a way we can handle that! Because in the jungle this Marine meets a white princess."

"How did she get there?" I asked.

"That's what you've got to figure out," he said.

188

I changed the subject. "How did you start your feud with the government?" I asked.

"All governments are composed of idiots," he snapped impatiently, eager to be back on the trail of his jungle princess, white.

"Then why do you stay here?" I pressed.

"It's my home," he said with some dignity. "I've been away from here only three times since I arrived. Once to Noumea; that's French, you know. Once to Sydney. Once to Bougainville, for you Johnnies. Why should I leave my home because the Colonial Office sends out one broken-down hack after another to torment me?"

He started to disclose further elaborations of his plot but I begged weariness and said, "I want to be fresh in the morning. To see your haunted valley."

He failed to catch the irony of my comment and cried, "And when you see it, Mister, our story will write itself!"

In the morning Larcom, giant Vata and I plunged into the jungle and pushed our sticky way inland for several miles. Larcom was much older than I, but he had twice the energy. Sometimes he would run back to keep me posted as to our progress, and finally we reached a most ordinary jungle clearing lined by tall trees, framed to the south by hills which might conceivably be termed mountains, and noticeable for a complete lack of moving air. Could this be the breathless valley that had so captivated Larcom?

I looked at him and it was apparent that he was as inspired as Byron had been by the valleys of Greece. In real agitation he called, "The big scene comes when your American stumbles into this mysterious valley!"

He continued to babble instructions as to how I must write the book and I concluded reluctantly that I had wasted two days on a complete bore. The flash I had experienced the morning before had been misleading. There was no story in Larcom.

Then I saw Vata at some distance preparing lunch and I said, "You stay here, Larcom. I'll study the valley from over there."

"I'll come along and show you where he meets the princess!"

"No!" I shouted. Then I added, "I want to see if I could spot you at this distance."

Like an obedient bird dog he froze, the gaunt figure of a tropical planter, and I sat down near Vata wondering how I could speed my return to Honiara when the black murderer said something calculated to send me, like a bloodhound, back to the trail of Larcom's story.

The huge native was trying to knock the top off a can of bully beef and I handed him my knife. As he gave it back we both happened to look at an odd clearing where the valley seemed to penetrate into the jungle. It looked like the nave of an immense cathedral and I was about to remark on this when Vata said, "That where Master Larcom he meet the Jew."

Now this last word was so unusual for a savage like Vata to use that I dropped the knife. "What did you say?" I asked.

"The Jew," he explained, recovering the knife.

"What Jew?"

"The American Jew," Vata said.

Then try as I might, I could get no more from the sullen man. I looked across the valley and there stood Larcom, erect and motionless as I had left him. I started back to question him about this astonishing news of Vata's, but the native leaped in front of me and whispered, "Please, Master. You not tell Master Larcom I say anything."

"But . . ."

"Please!" Vata repeated, and he stood above me like a dark giant, my knife in his hands. I agreed and he summoned Larcom.

"Could you see me?" he asked.

"Yes," I said.

"It's important, because the Marine has got to see the Princess."

Back on the schooner I had to use all my ingenuity to parry Larcom's demand that I make a decision about his novel. It was obvious that I could do nothing with the trash he offered, yet it was equally obvious that in his ascetic frame he carried a story of immense proportions.

So I said, "What's this about a trip to Bougainville?"

"Most of us old hands served up there during the war."

"What did you do?"

"Only what dozens of others did."

"What?"

He became acutely embarrassed and bit by bit I developed the truth. He had been a coastwatcher. "Were you ever in tight spots?" I asked.

"Me? It was my job to avoid tight spots."

At this point I was startled by the sudden appearance of Vata, who thrust his hand into my face. I saw a small blue box, its edges frayed, but as I reached for it Larcom leaped up and knocked it onto the deck.

A medal rolled out. An American medal awarded for great bravery. It lay there in the dying sunlight, its bright ribbons shimmering like the sound of trumpets. When I picked it up I saw that the box contained a letter, signed by Admiral Chester Nimitz.

"Bougainville?" I asked.

"About fifteen of us got them, I guess," Larcom said diffidently. He started to stuff the medal back into the box when he suddenly caught his breath and cried, "Hell!" He reached out and poked black Vata a tremendous blow in the ribs, then slapped him on the shoulder. "This medal is his!" he explained, kicking it along the deck toward the native. "The Americans handed medals out like cigarettes."

He made me move far forward, away from Vata, and elaborated his plot. "The Marine will be from Brooklyn," he said.

"Why Brooklyn?" I asked.

"I saw lots of movies durin' the war. Your men enjoyed it when the actors were from Brooklyn. But you'll have to help me with the dialogue. I've never been to Brooklyn."

"Neither have I."

In the growing dusk I could see Larcom's jaw drop. "You haven't been to Brooklyn?" he asked in a whisper.

"No."

There was a long silence, but the man's ingenuity could not be dampened. "Tell you what! We'll make him from Chicago. Son of an important gangster."

"I've never been to Chicago, either."

This stopped him for a moment, after which he rasped, "You ever been to Texas?"

"Yes."

"Good," he snorted. "I noticed they always laughed at Texas, too."

Abruptly I asked, "What were you doing in Noumea?"

The answer was spontaneous, "Business."

I told him that I had to have some time to think about this story, and he understood that, leaving me completely alone the rest of the night; but when I wakened on deck next morning before sunrise, there was Larcom, staring down at me, his face angular and contorted in the weird light.

"What do you think?" he inquired.

I had to tell him the truth. "I don't think I can do it," I said.

191

"You think some more," he said soothingly. "I'll see you at the bar tonight."

When I reached the Honiara pub that evening Larcom had not yet arrived, and Dennison greeted me with a warm cheerio. "Heard you went jungle probing!" he cried, joining me.

"Yes," I said. "And what's this about an American Jew?"

The question was explosive. Dennison surprised me by putting down his beer and shouting, "Men! He's heard about Fietelbaum!"

Immediately half a dozen men clustered about my table and began asking questions: Did I know Fietelbaum in the States? Did Fietelbaum ever actually tell President Truman to go to hell?

"What's this all about?" I asked.

So Dennison leaned on the arm of a chair and in an Oxford accent told me of a strange man who had come to Guadalcanal, and as he spoke I gained the very clear impression that everyone in the bar had acquired an unprecedented respect for the millionaire suit maker, Mannie Fietelbaum.

Said Dennison, "He appeared one day on a plane from Kwajalein. His first remark was, 'Money is no objection.' He had an ugly head of red hair which he kept combing with his fingers. He was very fat and he sweated incessantly. He had come to us on a terrible mission, for he was convinced that where the American Government had failed, where we here on Guadalcanal had failed, he could succeed. Somewhere in the jungle he could find the body of his son."

"In the war?"

"A pilot. It fell to me to tell him that the British Government had searched the valleys in vain, but Fietelbaum said, 'Money is no objection' and organized a safari. It was pathetic."

Now night had fallen over the island and there was a tinkle of glass as the Malaita boy tended bar. Dennison said, "What made the story doubly grotesque was that the boy had been killed in 1942. One of the first. In a jungle like ours there would be no possible remains."

There was an uneasy pause, then a new voice, an Australian's, said, "Maybe you know about Fietelbaum's boy. We understand he was famous in your football."

"Fietelbaum? Never heard of him."

"That wasn't the boy's name. He changed his to Foot."

"You mean Lew Foot? Of Columbia?"

"Yes. Lew Foot."

"One of the best. Great passer. What we call a triple-threat man."

"I know," Dennison said. "The best of our lads went first, too."

"What happened?" I asked. "About the old man?"

"It was heartbreaking," Dennison said. "He had a scrawled map sent him by some young blighter from the squadron. Searches had been made, of course."

The Australian added, "So in 1950—that's eight years later—Fietelbaum arrives. I told him how the jungle devours all things and asked him what he hoped to recover. He snapped, 'My son.' "

"Did he find the boy?" I asked.

"No. He probed every part of the island. We would not see him for many days. Then he would mysteriously appear in this bar and would drink immense quantities of beer. It would stream out of his pores and he would wipe his hair with his hand and say, 'What a man needs with good beer is some pastrami.' "

"What was that about President Truman?"

"Oh, yes!" Dennison explained. "Blighter pestered the American Government something frightful, I hear. Mind you, he had a right to. But when they finally had to terminate the correspondence he announced to all his friends, 'I'm going out there and find my boy. When I do I'll march in and tell President Truman to go to hell!' "

"But he never found the kid?" I asked.

The crowd about my table grew quiet and I sensed that someone was standing behind me. I looked up and it was Larcom. Unobtrusively the government clerks withdrew and the gaunt man sat down with me.

"What have they been tellin' you?" he asked. And the way in which he spoke, the scorn—and envious fear—he poured into the word *they* disclosed an entire island tragedy: the irreconcilable planter versus encroaching government.

"They were telling me about Fietelbaum," I said.

"He has nothing to do with the book."

"How did you happen to meet him in the jungle?"

The sweat of anger began to break out on Larcom's thin face, and you felt it didn't belong there. "God damn it!" he cried. Immediately he lowered his voice and said impatiently, "I was walking through the jungle."

"Why?" I pressed.

Larcom squirmed. "Because I wanted to meet him."

"Why?"

Nervously Larcom reached for his day's ration of whiskey and tossed it down. "Is this questioning necessary?" he asked.

"Absolutely," I said.

"Why? It has nothing to do with the story."

I thought if I were perfectly honest with Larcom I might find out what this was all about. "Mr. Larcom," I said, "people who don't write always think it's easy if you have some magic touch. Well, have you ever seen a great painting?"

I expected this to stump him but he promptly said, "Yes. When I was in Sydney."

"The artist never puts on his canvas just one pure color. He underpaints."

"What's that?" Larcom asked, much interested.

"Suppose you want blue. First you put on maybe some brown. Then some green. Some red. Perhaps a touch of white. On top of it all goes the blue. So that when you look at it, the blue sparkles. Like real nature. But all the time you were meddling around with brown and red, that's what you were after. That blue."

Larcom considered this for a moment and said, "So you writer blokes collect a bunch of ideas. And all the time it's something else you're after."

"Yes."

"What're you after now?"

"A story."

"The one I told you?"

"Perhaps."

"But why are you interested in the Jew?"

"I'm not. I'm interested in you."

"And you think the Jew has something to do with me?"

"I'm sure of it."

"What do you want to know?"

"Why did you go into the jungle to track down a man you'd never seen?"

Larcom leaned back in his chair and studied the Guadalcanal night. He thought a long time, wondering which of the many veils that covered him he might with impunity remove. Then, with a gesture of supreme disgust, he waved his hands toward the government men assembled in the bar and said, "Who could talk here? Among these spies?"

He led me along a silent road and onto the planks of the Honiara wharf, where we sat with our feet dangling over. He said, "I mind when there were a hundred ships in those waters. They're still there, on the bottom now."

194

"I served here," I said. "The Lunga region was like a city."

"We must have been here at the same time."

"But what about Fietelbaum?"

"I can't explain it. One night I came into this pier with some copra. I took my money and went into the bar. All I heard was the government officials laughing about this rich American. Right then I began to like him. Because when the government boys laugh at a man . . . he's apt to be all right."

"That's why you wanted to meet Fietelbaum."

"No. That came later."

"When?"

"Toward the end of the evening one of the government men said Fietelbaum must be crazy. Trying to find the body of his son after these years. That was when I knew I must help him."

"Why?"

The thin planter spoke very slowly, selecting his words with care. "If I had a son . . . dead for a country I did not love . . . I should not want him to lie . . . nameless . . . alone . . . forgotten . . ."

"What do you mean? A country Fietelbaum did not love?"

Now Larcom spoke with a flood of words. "How could he say he loved your country? Sometimes Americans aren't very kind to little round men with thick hair who have to elbow their way to the top. Fietelbaum's own son had to change his name. When other rich boys escaped the draft, his boy had to go. When he went to Washington and pounded on Army desks, they laughed because he was a funny-looking figure. He had no reason to love America."

"So you went out to help him."

"Yes!" Larcom cried belligerently. "You happy men who've known all the good things, you won't understand this. But a man can grow to hate the world he must live in."

"What happened when you found Fietelbaum?"

"Simply that from then on the men in the bar"—and he made a jabbing stab in the darkness as if all his enemies were that night clustered in the Honiara bar—"they had two of us to laugh at. Fietelbaum and the outcast planter. But I was absolutely determined to find that wrecked plane."

"Why did you feel that doing so would somehow . . . vindicate you?"

Larcom stopped abruptly and sucked in his breath. "Never thought of it that way. Now you mention it, I guess it did play a part. Revenge on all the stupid men who came out here to torment me."

"Torment you?" I repeated.

He ignored the question. "Fietelbaum had a scrawled map sent him by another pilot in the boy's squadron. It showed a river and a mountain with an X where the plane went down. There was also an arrow pointing to the mountain: 'Late sun looks like gold.' "

Now I gasped. For that was where he had found the germ of his ridiculous yarn. Here he had been, involved in some story of massive grandeur—the outcast fighting in his heart against the smaller men who belonged—but he could not see that. No he had to make up some gilt-and-spit fable. But I was to discover that I would never know Larcom, for he immediately proved my speculation false. He said, "When I saw the mention of gold I knew where the boy's body must be. You see, I've been planning this story of mine for years. Thirty years ago I came back to Guadalcanal in total despair. I would have destroyed myself, but one afternoon I too saw the golden mountain."

"Did you find the wrecked plane there?"

"Yes."

I waited for him to add something, but his report of the Fietelbaum case was ended. "Now that's out of the way," he said briskly, "we can get on with the book."

"I've got to think it over," I parried.

To my surprise this satisfied him and he rowed off to his schooner, where Vata reached down with immense hands to pull him aboard.

The bar was now closed, so I could not return there, but I was so involved in this complex of events that I had to talk with someone. So I made my way through the silent tropical darkness and up the steep hill to the plateau where the government officials live. There the cool breeze refreshed me and I saw that a light still burned on Dennison's porch.

"You must forgive me," I apologized.

"Only too glad!" Dennison cried, combing out his moustache and puttering about to find London magazines and a bottle of gin. We sat facing the glorious sweep of stars and dark ocean and distant shadowy islands.

"All they actually found, those two," he said with an involuntary shiver, "were some buttons and a cap brim. Still, that satisfied Fietelbaum."

Casually, as if to imply that I had no real interest in Larcom, I observed, "This Larcom. A queer duck."

"Very. Always fighting with the government. I must say I

bear him no grudge. You see, I happened to be the only one who did not scorn him when he returned from Noumea."

"Noumea?"

"Ah, yes! A most dismal affair. One of those things that can sour a man for life."

"Such as?"

"When Larcom first arrived on Guadalcanal ... about 1913 I'd say ... pitched right in, you know. Very fine worker. But four years later he faced the inevitable island problem. He needed a woman."

"He take a native wife?"

"No fear! Not he! A vessel put into Tulagi en route to Sydney, and since Larcom knew some young ladies there of good breeding, he went back to test his luck."

"Did one of the Sydney girls agree to marry him?"

"Never got to Sydney. Boat put into Noumea. It was the hell hole of the Pacific. Convicts, prostitutes, murderers. It was a vile place, Noumea."

"Larcom lose his money?"

"Much worse. He lost his heart. A convict's woman. Married her and brought her back to Guadalcanal."

Then Larcom's agony became clear. The stiff British families had refused him admittance to their homes. There had undoubtedly been scenes whose scars became evident whenever he spoke with contempt of "the government men."

"You guessed it," Dennison said, bustling about for some ice. He interrupted his account by showing me a newly bound volume of the *Oxford Book of English Verse*. "Quite a decent job, what?" he asked.

"How did Mrs. Larcom react?"

"We were quite convinced that she was a French prostitute, which of course she was, and no one would speak to her. When she entered the stores—there was silence. We British can be very cruel, you know."

"How long did that last?"

"Not long. This girl Renée had known a much different life. The beer halls, the wild excitement of Noumea. One day a ship put into Tulagi. An American freighter picking up copra. She ran off with one of the sailors. A foul-mouthed, swarthy man from Brooklyn."

"So that was the end of Mrs. Larcom!"

"Indeed it was not! If it had been as simple as that Larcom might have recovered. After all, many men lose their wives. No, as the ship was leaving, Renée appeared on deck stark naked. She screamed horrible insults at everyone. She

197

had dug up all the island scandals and aired them in frightful words. The sailors cheered her on, and in that way she left Guadalcanal."

As Dennison related this his hands began to twist and after a moment he said quietly, "She did not even spare me, although I alone had spoken to her. She knew that I was in love with the Governor's wife. Naked, she hurled this information at the waterfront. I have always suspected that was why I did not progress in the service, as I had planned."

Dennison shook his head gravely as he recalled the ancient debacle and I asked, "Why did Larcom stay here?"

"Habit. Why did I stay on? Habit."

"So he lives with his bitterness?"

"Men do the same in Liverpool." From the querulousness in Dennison's voice I knew it was time to leave. By some odd shift the conversation was no longer Dennison and I probing Larcom; it had become Larcom and Dennison protecting themselves from the stranger.

Yet when I stumped down the hill, when I saw below me the shadowy suggestion of Honiara mysteriously new, forever primitive, I felt a great twisting in my heart. Somewhere in the story of Larcom there was a core of meaning, that terribly precious jewel that all writers seek.

So I hurried down the dark road, past the barracks, past the new post office with the bright intertwined GR, and onto the frail wharf. Before me unfolded one of the imperative sights of the world: a jungle night with stars aloft, a tropical sea with shimmering iridescence, dim islands rising in the distance, a boat with lights. In that moment I understood all the men who ever come to the tropics. I could speak with Melville and Rupert Brooke and Louis Becke. How distant the schooner seemed, how remote from time.

"Haloo!" I cried. "Haloo there, Larcom."

There was no sound in reply, not even an echo. There was no motion, no new light.

"Haloo, Larcom!"

On shore, among the dark huts, a light showed. An immense black figure appeared beneath the bending palms.

"You? Master? You want get ship?"

"I'm seeking Mr. Larcom."

Breathtakingly, before me loomed Vata. "Master Larcom he no stop long ship. He stop long shore." He put his hands to his mouth and gave a long, mournful cry. We listened in the darkness and could hear only the lapping of water on the
198

sea-shelled coast of Guadalcanal. Mysteriously Vata announced, "Master he come."

I looked ashore and there appeared the angular form of Larcom. I was drawn to it mightily, and as I started to run along the wharf, the tall figure at the other end ran to meet me.

"Larcom!" I cried.

"By God, its you!"

As if we had needed each other we met midway along the wharf and shook hands eagerly, as if we had not been talking less than three hours ago.

"I wanted to see you," I blurted out.

"Everything's settled," he announced joyfully. "It was remarkable. When I got back to the ship it all came crystal clear."

"What did?" I asked eagerly.

"The plot for our story."

"Oh," I said.

He ignored the disappointment in my voice and babbled, "I never understood about writing books until you mentioned using many colors to get the right one. My story was too drab. Now it's fixed."

"How?" I asked, disgusted that I had been diverted back to the old channel.

"I have a wonderful idea to catch the reader's interest."

"What?"

"Just this. We go back to Brooklyn."

"What do you mean?"

"Like before. I said the young Marine was from Brooklyn. You said you couldn't talk Brooklyn. All right. When you get back, visit Brooklyn and listen how they talk. It's very distinctive."

Something warned me that I ought to stop Larcom right there, but he was quivering with volcanic emotion. "The boy's from Brooklyn. But that's not all. No, sir! Because you see . . . his mother used to live on Guadalcanal!"

He stepped back to invite my comment. What could I say? Tentatively I asked, "How does that help the story?"

He gripped my wrist with terrible strength. "Don't you understand?" he half screamed. "The lad's mother lived on this island! All the time he was growing up she used to tell him stories about it. Then he comes back and recognizes the places she had described. Look! We could even have him save his company because he knows where a certain river is. His mother told him all about it!"

He stopped and asked in a hoarse, hopeful whisper, "Wouldn't that make any book successful?"

"How did his mother get from Guadalcanal to Brooklyn?"

"I thought you'd ask that," he said gleefully. "You see, it's simple. She was the wife of an explorer. Like the Martin Johnsons. She was out here." He waited. "Well? What do you think?"

I had to be honest. "Your made-up story ... it's pretty bad. But your real story ..."

"What do you mean?" he asked sharply.

"The story about you," I said. "About your Noumea wife. How she ran off to Brooklyn. The lonely years that followed. And then your sense of identification with Fietelbaum. If you are willing, Larcom, we can make an immense story."

The cadaverous planter stepped away and said, with furious venom, "You idiot! You damned stinking fool! You've guessed none of it right. I'll write the book myself."

Quivering with fury he left me, but as he reached the launch he turned in anger and shouted, "So you think I felt a bond of affection for Fietelbaum! Ask your tattle-tales at the bar what I did to Fietelbaum when his plane left." Then he added derisively, "You bloody dreamer!"

I was furious with myself for having caused an open breach with this man who had wanted me as a friend. I returned to my shack and lay most of the night staring at the single light on his schooner, riding in the mists of Iron Bottom Bay.

In the morning I hurried to the Chinaman's for coffee, and since there were no white men abroad at that hour I tackled the Chinaman as he fried the morning ration of Spam.

"You know Larcom?"

"Sure, me know. He no good."

"You know Mr. Fietelbaum?"

The Oriental face burst into a sunny smile. "Sure, he good fella too much. Each day he rent my jeep. Twenty-five dollars! Whoopee!"

"Were you at the plane when Mr. Fietelbaum left?"

"Sure! He give me twenty-five more dollars drive him there."

"Was Larcom there, too?"

"Yes."

"What happened?"

The Chinaman looked back at his skillet and would say

nothing. I downed my battery acid, asked him about Hong Kong and then asked again, "What did Larcom do?"

"He bad fella too much! He come up with paper in hand. Check for thousand dollars."

"Where'd he get it?"

"Mr. Fietelbaum send it to him. For helping find son in jungle."

"Then what happened?"

"Larcom tear check in small pieces. Push them in Mr. Fietelbaum's face."

"Did Larcom say anything?"

"He swear. He say he bloody God Damn well not take bloody God damn money for work like that. Police drag him away."

"What did Mr. Fietelbaum do?"

"Tears come to his eyes. He run up to where police hold Larcom."

"Then what?"

"Mr. Fietelbaum—he good too much—he stoop and kiss Larcom on hand and say, 'Forgive me.' "

"Why did he say that?" I pressed.

"Maybe they know something together," the cook suggested. "They good friends, because when Mr. Fietelbaum grab his hand, Larcom cry, 'For God's sake, no!' Then he run away from police and we not see him many months."

I left the smelly restaurant and walked along the dusty roads of Honiara until the government offices opened. Then I burst in on Dennison and cried, "I'm sorry as hell I kept you up last night. But sometimes I get fixations. Terrible, gnawing ideas. Ninety-nine of them are a waste of time. But the hundredth! That's what keeps me going."

"Sure, old fellow!" the expansive clerk said, sucking his moustache. "Used to do a bit of watercolor myself. Many an essay before you strike the thing."

"I'm trying to piece together some things Larcom has told me. Under what circumstances did he go to Sydney?"

"The most astonishing, I sh'd say."

"Such as?"

"His son, Raoul."

"Son?" I echoed.

"Yes. The French whore left him a baby when she absconded. He was the pride of Larcom's life. Fine chappie. I taught him Latin. He won a bursary in Australia, and I must say I felt rather proud."

A native messenger appeared and said, in perfect English,

"Sir, the Governor has asked me to inform you that he is still waiting for those reports."

"Oh, dear!" Dennison cried. "Oh, dear me!" He grabbed up a sheaf of papers tied in red and blue ribbons and hurried off like a schoolboy. In a moment he returned and said apologetically, "Very methodical, the Governor." Quickly he added, "What we need in the tropics, of course. Very methodical."

"Why did Larcom go to Sydney?" I asked.

"Ah, yes! In 1939 the lad volunteered to join the British Army. Larcom used all his savings to go down to see the boy off. He was a grave sight when he left here. A Chinese tailor in Tulagi made him a proper suit. He looked abominable. But even those of us who despised the man had a moment of compassion when we saw him go grimly forth to say farewell to Raoul."

"Why do you say 'compassion'?"

"Because Larcom hated England. He hated what the English system had done to him. Yet he knew that Raoul had no such feelings. The boy loved distant England, and with a willing heart he went to fight for a land he had never seen."

"How did Larcom take that?"

"For once in his life he behaved like a decent man. He did not try to dissuade his son."

I left Dennison's neat office with a new knowledge of Larcom, the lonely man whose life had been tied up with his son, but I was not prepared for what happened as I stepped out into the road, for there was the tall planter, waiting for me with a greasy notebook under his arm.

"You must read this," he said. "I lied to you that first night. Because I have the novel all written. What I really wanted was for you to touch it up and find a publisher."

He insisted that I sit right down on a log—the bar was not yet open—and read his masterpiece. I opened the cover and read the title page: *The Mountain of Gold.* I turned the page and there, beautifully handlettered, was the inscription: To Raoul, With Love.

The first paragraph read as follows: "When Harry McGonnigle left Brooklyn little did he realize that ere long he would be plunged into the depth of one of the most big adventures ever recorded in the history of mankind. Harry McGonnigle was a fine, handsome, upstanding young Marine pilot who knew no fear. His country was at war and who was he to stay cowardly at home even though his father objected at the idea of his son fighting a war, especially airplanes?" Then came a freshly inked insert, added the night before: *"I forgot to say that Harry's mother once lived on Guadalcanal."*

Resolutely I handed the manuscript back to Mr. Larcom. I think he saw in my eyes the inescapable conclusion that it was hopeless.

"So it's no good?" he asked bluntly.

"That's right."

"What's the matter with it?"

"It's hard for me to say. Maybe an illustration will explain. You've heard of Alexander Dumas? *The Three Musketeers.* Well, one day a young man came to him and cried, 'I have the most superb idea for a novel!' Dumas asked, 'You have a good plot?' The young man kissed his fingers and exclaimed, 'A plot that is all excitement. Characters that breathe. Settings that bedazzle the eye. And the suspense is truly unbearable!' Dumas clapped him on the shoulder and cried, 'Good! Now all you need to make it a novel is 200,000 words.' "

For the first time in our acquaintance Mr. Larcom laughed. "You mean I don't have the words?"

"That's right."

Now he really guffawed. "You should get a job telling people bad news. You make it palatable."

"The bar's opening," I said, and we had a couple of whiskeys. We had a rare hour together, the tension of the book no longer coming between us, and I was inspired to say, "You must not regret the hours you spent writing your book. It has been like a medicine for you."

"How do you mean?" he asked.

"It prepared you for when Fietelbaum arrived, looking for his dead son. You could sympathize with him, having lost your own boy in the war."

With great control Larcom put down his glass. Coldly, in a colorless voice, he said, "You are still an idiot. Raoul was not killed in the war. He served throughout with great gallantry."

"Then what happened to him, Larcom? You must tell me, for Raoul is now eating away your heart as his mother did during those long years of bitterness."

"There is nothing to tell," he said austerely, preparing to go.

"Do you know where he is? Now?"

"Yes. In Jerusalem."

For a moment I was bewildered. I was so close to the

truth about this man that I could not bear to see him leave. "Larcom!" I called. "Wait a minute!"

"Good-bye," he said in his ashen voice. "It was good knowing you."

"Wait!" I cried, but he started off for the wharf. I ran along beside him saying, "Don't go like this, man. In these days you've come to know me as a friend. Don't pull the veils of bitterness and hate about yourself again."

"What is it you want?" he demanded, but in his voice I could hear that he wanted to talk further with me.

I said, "There's a powerful story. In you. Think of the Americans to whom Guadalcanal is a sacred name!"

"I offered you a story," he said, hammering his notebook with his fist. "You turned it down."

"But tell me just one thing."

"What?"

"Why did you track down Fietelbaum? What impelled you?"

Again there came the weighty pause. Could he trust me? Would I understand? Then the decision: "There is no explanation." With that he strode onto the wharf.

"No!" I shouted. "Damn it, Larcom, you mustn't run away like this. You're no outcast. You're a passionate human being. Don't let the clerks of this island . . ."

Contemptuously he said, "You're still guessing." And within ten minutes he had cast off the schooner and was coasting down the gloomy shores of Guadalcanal, seeking out the plantation to which he had brought his French whore, from which he had sent his English son. I never saw him again.

But on the last day, as I waited for my plane in the blinding heat of Henderson Field—that empty, sanctified strip of coral—the Governor of Guadalcanal came to bid me good-bye.

Apsley-Grieve was the perfect symbol of all that Larcom had hated: cold, aloof, opinionated, capable, relentless in enforcing English moral and social systems. He bowed stiffly, said he hoped my stay had been profitable. Then he surprised me by adding apologetically, "You know, sometimes we feel we hold Guadalcanal in trust for you Yanks. It's your national shrine, not ours."

I tried to counter with some felicity, but he interrupted. "Damned sorry if that bounder Larcom annoyed you. But please discount any unfavorable reports you heard about his treatment of your countryman Fietelbaum . . . I mean, the scene here at the Field ... Most distressing, you know. What I mean to say is, he cursed Fietelbaum and tried to strike him in the face. Well, point I'm making, poor devil's to be excused. What you must bear in mind is something that's not generally known. While Fietelbaum was in the jungle searching for his son, Larcom got news that his son ... Raoul, you know ... Splendid chap ... Apple of the old man's eye and properly so. Raoul was murdered while on duty in Jerusalem. The Stern Gang, you know."

Apsley-Grieve's cold voice was like the gray report of history.

"What happened then?" I asked.

"We were most apprehensive. Larcom rushed into the jungle with that murderous Vata. Swore he'd assassinate Fietelbaum. But when they finally met, some kind of miracle took place. Queer fish, Larcom. Beat the bush for two months till he found all that was left of Fietelbaum's son. Some buttons and a cap brim. You see, the cable had reported that after the bomb explosion in Jerusalem there was no trace of his own son, Raoul. No trace at all."

Espiritu Santo

During the War men who served on the bad islands had two unquestioned beliefs. When the Americans left, the local people would revert to the old somnolence. And the jungle would quickly devour everything that we had accomplished. Espiritu Santo is a good place to test these two theories.

In the early stages of war, Santo was our biggest base. In 1942 we landed ships at the edge of a jungle so dense that it even invaded land which was uncovered at low tide. In two months we had a flourishing city that soon grew to a population of 100,000. I say "city" because Santo had more public services than many American cities. A telephone system with seven exchanges and 570 distinct distribution boards, a superb interlocking teletype network, a radio station, miles of fine roads, forty-three movies, a PX department store, industrial shops of all descriptions, an optical laboratory, four huge hospitals, a mammoth steam laundry, and on the edge of everything a full-fledged Masonic temple!

At one end of this vast installation there were a few homes occupied by Frenchmen, and a few grubby tropical stores. Farther out were the hovels in which indentured Tonkinese slept after working the plantations. And beyond them, in the bush, lived some of the world's most primitive savages. How did peace affect these people? A visit to postwar Santo is a revelation!

Along the foreshore stretches a newborn tropical town of about fifteen hundred. There's a hotel, a half dozen tailors, two barbers, a shoemaker, two movies and a dance hall. The town, called Luganville, probably sets a record in length per population. It runs for six miles, never more than one house deep. It is terribly inconvenient, since the postoffice is three miles from the business center. Automobiles are a necessity and gasoline is 80¢ a gallon. Says one resident, "In Luganville everywhere is on the outskirts of town."

A social and economic revolution has occurred in Santo. The Tonkinese have been set free and now have all civil privileges. They won't work for planters, whom they hate, and they won't patronize the established stores because they have opened shops of their own. They run the taxis and own the barbershops. They are ingrained in Santo life and the white men foresee another Pacific tragedy. Like the Chinese in Tahiti and the Indians in Fiji, the Tonks seem destined to oust the natives.

The black men have also changed considerably. Those about Luganville now wear tailor-made shorts ($2.25) and T-shirts (85¢). They work a few days and then knock off for a good time. Although the law forbids it, the Tonkinese sell bootleg whiskey to them, and pathetic figures lurching along the road are common. Some of the natives have bought trucks, which they run as taxis for their friends, filling the trucks to the last inch with singing, shouting, arm-waving blacks. Even in the deepest jungle the American invasion had an effect. Stone-age families now have gasoline drums for water, army blankets, and cartridge cases to be used as trunks.

The white man has profited from the material comforts which he has newly gained. He often has two cars, a refrigerator, two or three big quonsets and all sorts of Yankee odds and ends. In addition he usually has a couple of thousand American dollars stashed away, less than the avaricious Tonks, but still a good nest egg.

Life in Santo is delightful, free, riotous, happy. Take the Club Civile, for example. The officer's mess at the P. T. base has been completely refurnished and enlarged. The paneled walls have been waxed, expensive paint has been used to make the dining room a medley of bright color, and draperies of good quality set off the windows.

The food is terrific! At dinner you sit in an upholstered chair at a table with a bright red cloth. Before you, amid the sparkling glassware, is a nest of plates. Navy silver, brightly polished, is lined up. The soup is split pea with croutons baked in oil. The second course is a local fish, cooked in wine and served with a delicate French sauce. The next course is a brief one, asparagus in oil and vinegar. Now you are down to two plates and the main dish arrives: steak with golden French fries and a chicory salad. Red wine is served, and there are five cruets with different condiments.

For dessert you get a French cheese or a piece of pastry, following which, if you wish it, a liqueur. Probably no American town of 1,500 could provide such a meal.

The game room has a poker table with a green felt cover, darts, bridge tables and a bar. A lounge, which stops eight feet from the water's edge, is enclosed in glass and provides a magnificent view of the channel.

After a sojourn in British islands, one aspect of life at the

Club Civile is arresting. People of all colors belong. There are Melanesian half-castes, Martiniques of high color, and tomboy Tahitian girls. It is disturbing to remember that in a British colony these people would live beyond the pale, despised by whites, hated by natives. Although I have not settled in my mind what the relationship between Pacific races should be, I feel, when I see the uninhibited happiness of a French gathering, that brotherhood has been attained.

But to see Santo at its boisterous best you must go to the movies. In a huge quonset by the sea, a full-fledged cinema operates with an American projectionist, Metro-Goldwyn-Mayer films and individual wooden seats.

There is a show each Wednesday and Saturday, with some talk of a Sunday matinee. Europeans pay 40¢, Tonkinese 32¢, and natives—who would never be allowed near a British cinema—21¢. The house is packed. Four short items are shown, during which the whole place roars with laughter at comedy or shrieks with delight at scenes of really violent disasters.

The main feature starts and then, at some critical point, the lights come up and everybody scrambles outside to the refreshment bar. Here six waiters dish up beer, ice cream, cookies, soft drinks and candy. An old Tonk woman in a peach-basket hat tosses down a lemonade while across from her a native in blue-duck shorts gulps a beer which some white has bought for him. The intermission lasts about forty minutes and then the show continues. On Saturday nights, when the movie ends, the seats are pushed back, jazz records are played, and everybody has a whale of a dance till 3 or 4 in the morning.

The proprietor of this amusement palace is one of the great characters of the Pacific. On Guadalcanal I complained that I hadn't seen an alligator. My host consoled me. "Don't worry. At Santo you'll see Tom Harris."

Actually, he's a wonderful veteran of the rough old days. He's knocked about the island for thirty years, been thrown out of same, been a trader for Burns Philp—known as Bloody Pirates—and bought up plantations. He has a face like Punch, a belly laugh like Falstaff. He was a wonderful friend to the American forces who alternated between raiding him for selling grog to enlisted men and awarding him letters of commendation. He knew most of the important figures and has a treasured batch of war correspondence:

December 18, 1943

Dear Mr. Harris:

Admiral Sherman is playing golf this afternoon on the Santo links, and if it is not too much to ask could we have a couple of your boys as caddies? We will pick them up at 3:10.

A. F. HOWARD

Now launched in a new career as impresario, Harris has built up a solid aesthetic philosophy. "The best plot is a man, a horse, a villain and a lost mine. My people don't go for this talk-talk society stuff. One of the worst flops I ever had was Hedy Lamarr and June Allyson in *Her Highness and the Bellboy*. But give us a good Western! My word, they tear the place down. A good chase, with some revolver play, is about the best, although hanging from a cliff is good, too. I guess the finest picture I ever saw was *Winners of the West*, a thirteen-part serial. The Europeans ridiculed it at first, but by the fourth episode everybody on the island was trying to get in. They stood outside and looked through the doors. When a scene ended with the hero about to be killed, the noise was so great it deafened me. Europeans yelled louder than the natives!"

Harris says the only other really good picture is one with airplanes, although he will go for a gangster picture if it has enough gunplay and murder. "But," he insists, "what we need is Westerns!"

It is interesting to speculate that considering all the people in the world, perhaps the only universal dramatic form ever conceived is the formalized Western. In China, in Italy, in Fiji and in the States, the people who really love movies prefer two men on horseback, galloping over the desert, firing at each other.

Harris has also evolved a new theory on intermissions. "My plan is to have them as long as the customers will buy anything. This eight-minute stuff is ridiculous! I give my people twenty-five minutes, maybe thirty. If they seem to be spending well I allow them up to three-quarters of an hour. In this way they go back to the feature in a good frame of mind. They're not hungry."

The American projectionist came to Harris by chance. Ray Jenkins is a quiet, balding fellow from Hollywood. He's 30 years old and of all the troops who were stationed on Santo—perhaps half a million at one time or other—he's the only one who came back. "I like the climate and the people,"

209

he says. During the war he spent two years at Ship Repair, about a quarter of a mile from where he now works. He says, "Santo is like Southern California, except it's damper. If you take enough quinine you don't have any trouble." Since all newcomers neither French nor British must opt which of Santo's two legal systems he will live under, Ray has chosen to be a Britisher. "They're more like us," he says.

The business of having two governments—called the Condominium and universally burlesqued as the Pandemonium—is one of the most fantastic phenomena in the Pacific.

Imagine the New Hebrides with a population of less than 45,000 having two complete governments in which every office in the one is duplicated in the other! There are two systems of money, French and Australian, two types of postage stamps, a French system of law in favor of the planter, a British code which protects the native. The comic-opera confusions are so hilarious they practically justify the exorbitant expense.

Says a British planter, "Suppose the British try to make me do something. I run right away to the French with tears in my eyes like a martyr and ask, 'Have you surrendered the islands to the British? They're making a monkey out of you.' So the French get mad and protect me. French planters do the same thing with the British."

Another reports, "At a murder trial I was an assessor, a cross between a civilian judge and a juryman. There was a French judge who didn't speak English, and an English judge who didn't speak French. The interpreter would ask the native a pidgin question, then translate it into French for the French assessors and into English for the rest. The French judge wished to question the native's reply, so he asked a question, which was interpreted to the English judge and then put into pidgin for the accused. And the interpreter never really understood the native, who didn't know what all the fuss was about. We hung him anyway. He was undoubtedly guilty."

Yet ridiculous as this farce is, it was once justified. France and Britain faced each other on many moot points about the world. A disturbance might cause a complete rupture. Therefore a compromise was reached over the New Hebrides, and this may have saved the peace of Europe. Certainly it helped preserve the alliance of these two powers against Germany in 1914.

Today the Condominium is indefensible. "In fact," says Tom Harris, "there's only one good thing about the system. Neither government can ever levy an income tax!" Like most islanders, he thinks the New Hebrides should be turned over to the French.

Two problems may force booming Luganville back to the decay which Americans predicted. The first, strangely enough, concerns jeeps. The cliché symbol of the South Pacific used to be a palm tree by a lagoon. Now it's an over-age jeep bounding along bumpy roads. What will happen when they wear out? On every island Chinese make new cover tops, but no spare mechanized parts can be bought from the United States because of dollar trouble. Many predict that after a splurge of fun, the islanders will have to travel as they did before: by launch.

The second headache is money. Where is it going to come from? Copra plantations are rotting because there is no labor, and a substitute economy has not been discovered. For the present everyone is taking in his neighbor's wash, spending the American dollars scrounged during the War. When this ends, what? In the meantime the people of Santo are having a whale of a time.

It's good to see the New Hebrides happy, for in the past they were perhaps the most infamous blot on white civilization and certainly equal to the African slave coast, since the crimes of the Hebrides were committed after a public conscience had stopped the African trade.

Originally these islands contained a million natives, some say more. Each valley supported its villages where cannibals ate only grown men killed in battle. Now the population is about 40,000. One island dropped from 12,000 people to 256 in a few decades. By and large, the great numbers of dead were killed by white men.

Three brutally vicious practices caused the great decline. First and most horrible was the planned introduction into difficult islands of new diseases. A freebooter would catch a native, wait till he caught either measles or whooping cough, and then plop him on some island. Sometimes in less than a month 50% of the population would die, mainly because they lay in sea water to subdue their dreadful fevers, a practice which worked with malaria but not with the new plagues. And when the ships got back to Australia, the captains would narrate in public their cleverness in getting even with natives who were not willing to become slaves.

Second was the slave trade, called blackbirding. Ships prowled the islands kidnapping natives into virtual slavery on the sugar fields of Northern Australia, where the practice was protected and encouraged by colonial laws. A neat trick was to bolt a huge water tank to the bottom of the hold. Large bunches of natives were asked to shift it and were ridiculed when they couldn't do so. More boys were called to show the white man. Then the hatches were lowered and the ship would be off to sell the cargo in Australia. This happened as late as 1901.

On one such ship the shanghaied blacks created a disturbance, so the crew opened the hatches and spent the night firing rifles into the mass of slaves. One man held a light so the others could aim. They killed sixty and severely wounded sixteen, all of whom were tossed overboard on the grounds that "they would have died anyway." And a civilized court in 1872 dismissed charges because a black man could not testify against a white!

The third cause of depopulation was the sandalwood trade. Southern islands in the group had the great misfortune to contain this aromatic tree which commanded such a high price in China. A completely craven group of outlaws stormed ashore to get it. They murdered, burned and forced the natives into jungle slavery. The sandalwood islands never recovered.

Naturally the natives retaliated. Today there is an island known as Erromango of the Martyrs. Here six missionaries, one after the other, were clubbed to death, yet other missionaries ultimately stopped the terrible violence of these islands. In many parts of the Pacific missionaries have been a bane, but all their excesses are outweighed by the fact that in the New Hebrides they alone tried to redress the crimes sanctioned by the public.

Native memories are long, and there is still resentment against the white man. Today it is reflected in the Jon Frum movement. This remarkable society was founded as the result of religious confusion. A new religion entered the islands and made great promises in order to lure natives from the old. They went, but soon found that each church was defrauding them so they reasoned, "All the time we go to John the Baptist. Now we go from him." Hence the name. The movement is militant, obstructionist and confused, another of the native ferments that are spreading across the Pacific, some directed by Communism, others, like Jon Frum, not.

If Americans guessed wrong about the effect of war on the people of the New Hebrides, they were equally wrong about the jungle. It has not reabsorbed the island. Every road is still passable, even the narrow one that led to the remote swamp where men were trained in jungle fighting. Many quonsets are standing in their old positions and look pretty much as they did five years ago. The air fields, except Bomber 2 which has been torn up, are still used, and NAB (Naval Advanced Base) is a thriving Tonkinese village, incredibly dirty. Where buildings have been torn down the jungle has rushed in and covered the sites, but for the most part the tropical obliteration Americans predicted has not eventuated.

The word jungle, say the purists, should never be used. It has an emotional coloring and no precise meaning. The scientific term is "the tropical rain forest." This term accurately describes most of the so-called jungles of the South Pacific, for they are not the frightful places that many would have us believe. Most often the rain forests are composed of very tall trees which form canopies over land that is rather fun to travel. The rain forest is much more like a warm Canadian woods than it is like a jungle.

I know rain forests that are like beautiful parks with no undergrowth, others that seem to be cathedrals with sunlight slanting through the rose windows. Brilliant birds fly through the solemn spaces, and I am always struck by the silent majesty of such sanctuaries and agree that to call them jungle is misleading.

But there is another kind of rain forest that is neither inspiring nor majestic, and the vast forests of Espiritu Santo are in that category. Here each tree is burdened with parasites. The sky is never seen, the ground never free of crawling growth. Malignant vines clutch at the intruder. Extensive swamps suck down his feet, and the atmosphere is rank.

Let me explain just what the Santo forest is like. At the end of a road there is a cascade which was much enjoyed by American troops. From this road a trail leads to a spot some four hundred yards above the waterfall. Once I used that trail and came to where I could hear the cascade tumbling down. I was inclined to cut across the short intervening distance and come back by the road, but an Army officer with me felt we had not the time for such a trip, so we retraced our steps to the highway.

The next day three men followed that same trail, came to the same spot, heard the noisy waters. They took the short cut, and when they had gone fifty feet from the trail realized that the going would be tough. Great vines impeded their way; dense growth of all kinds hemmed them in; so they decided to return to the trail, but in that short distance they had become lost.

For two days they tried to gain the cascade. They could

hear it sometimes, but from which direction the sound came they could not tell. If they climbed a tree to survey the ground, they could never get above the tangled canopy.

The nights were fearful. Insects of all kind attacked them. Mosquitoes flocked about their faces. There was an armadillo-like millipede six inches long that exuded an alkali which ate away the skin wherever it touched. Thin feelers of the lawyer cane, sometimes forty feet long, tore at them with inverted fish hooks. There were prickly vines, itch plants, poisonous leaves. If they stepped upon a fallen log, it crumbled into dust. If in stumbling they scratched themselves on the rotten wood, the sore festered in six hours and might not heal for six months. They could not drink the water. They could not see the stars. And if they infected one of their thousand bites they ran the risk of blood poisoning.

At the end of the two days one of these boys was dead. Another was out of his mind, and the third had stumbled into a coastal village. Through all their experience they were within three miles of 100,000 men.

Perhaps the purists are right. Perhaps such malignant forests, so poisonous to men, are technically no different from the more clement forests where one may stroll with pleasure. But it seems to me there is a word in our language for the forests of Santo, and I shall use it: JUNGLE. Five times I helped organize searching parties for G.I.'s lost in the Santo jungles. Three times we found the men.

Toward the end of my second visit to Santo, I was beginning to think that I knew at least the outlines of tropical life. I had lived on dozens of rough islands, gone into the jungle as I wished, and shared many experiences with people who live in the hot lands. But I was about to encounter an aspect of equatorial life that taught me how little I really understood.

It started one evening at six. I was walking along the beach when a great pain shot through my eyeballs as if someone had beaten me on the head with a club. I staggered for a moment and the pain subsided.

For more than an hour nothing happened, and then at dinner I felt the connecting tissue in my joints collapse. My limbs seemed to be hung onto my body with flapping wire. I had never before experienced anything like this and sat very still, waiting until I could regain control of my muscles.

All that night I shivered in uncontrollable spasms and sweated furiously. My throat became raw and I heard ringing sounds in my head. In the morning I was taken to the

214

hospital, where I turned in a fancy temperature that pleased the nurse and scared me. I had malaria. On my mission up the Watavihan River I had acquired the often-fatal Guadalcanal fever.

The pretty white mission hospital in Santo is run on the principle that the human bottom is a pincushion. As one famous beachcomber said of it, "They shot me from every angle."

Still, it was interesting to be sick in pidgin. The shirt is to be taken off? "Lipt him up calico." The tongue looks better now? "Ah, he good fellow too much." I rediscovered the adage that the only perfect climate for a human being is bed, and I settled back to some of the most patient care I had ever known.

But as I lay in bed I thought: I shall get over this quickly with modern medicine, but not five miles from here are natives who have never been free of malaria. The Melanesian savage is inoculated at birth and never discovers what a malaria-free life might be.

The shaking comes, the pain behind the eyes, the great fever. The naked man huddles in his hut and does not complain, for all men have fever.

At forty the savage is an old, old man. At forty-five he is usually dead. His most prized possession was the tattered blanket he once found in a dump. It had been his only medicine.

There is a more dreadful aspect of malaria. If the dead corpuscles coagulate in the brain, death is instantaneous. But even then the worst has not been said. Usually the dead corpuscles do not attack the brain. They crowd into the kidneys. Then the patient, who thinks he has merely another case of fever, urinates and reels back in horror. The urine is smoky black! He has blackwater fever. In racking pain he dies, his kidneys dissolved, his head a receptacle of molten lead.

There are now medicines which cure more than fifty per cent of blackwater cases, but the disease, once described as "the only way the islands had of striking back at the white men who had debauched them," is still fatal if treatment is not prompt. And in the jungle, where there is no medicine, the native always dies.

Americans did much for Santo, and all the inhabitants admit it, but we left one harrowing scar that will never be forgotten: Million Dollar Point.

At the east end of the island there was a huge coral pit, later converted into a dump. When the war ended all new rolling stock was moved into this dump. There were tractors, uncrated new jeeps, earth-moving machinery, ambulances—anything you could think of on wheels. The Frenchmen eyed this collection enviously. Overtures were made to buy it, but always at the last minute the deal fell through. The French say the Americans were afraid to follow orders.

The Americans knew the French were stalling, sure they would get the lot for nothing. A deadline was set and the French allowed it to pass, even though the terms were about 8¢ on the dollar.

So a ramp was built into the sea and bewildered mechanics climbed aboard the great earth-moving monsters, the road graders, the heavy trucks. Ignitions went on. The engines coughed, and the giant procession crawled along the ramp. At the last moment the mechanics jumped free and the lumbering dinosaurs of modern industry plunged into the sea. There was a hiss as engine blocks cracked, and a rising column of water standing for a moment like a monument in a weird graveyard. The wealth was gone.

A British subject says, "It continued for days. Those warehouses of canned food, the cloth, the tools, and most of all the jeeps! There were men who watched with tears in their eyes. Million Dollar Point, we call it. Not even the Americans could explain what they were doing. One day they oiled the engines carefully. The next they threw them into the sea. How could governments permit such a thing to happen?"

Of all the islands in the Pacific, Santo has made the most profound impression on me. There are lovelier islands, true, but the main reason why I like Santo is its zany life. On the day I left I was entertained at lunch by the commissioner for native affairs, the resident liaison officer of the British Government, the collector of taxes, the chief of immigration, the administrator of housing, the commandant of the army garrison, the secretary of the council, and the protector of French interests. It was a small luncheon, because all of the above officials were one man, a delightful French philosopher I had once known in Tahiti. As the plane came he sighed mournfully and said, "You must be very sorry to leave so happy an island. Where everybody dances and gets drunk and the chief of police never makes a fuss." He was also the chief of police, and he was right. I was sorry to leave.

The Good Life

*A social and economic revolution has occurred in
Santo. The Tonkinese have been set free of their
indentures and now have all civil privileges.*

Not long ago I was sent from Efate to investigate a rather
astonishing report which had reached the British half of the
Condominium Government. I proceeded aboard a small
schooner which fortunately was putting in at the very plantation I intended visiting.

At dawn two mornings later I caught my first glimpse of
La Fécondité, the famous establishment of Jean Perouse,
who was the cause of my embarrassing inspection. La Fécondité was well named, for great copra plantings ran right to
the water's edge, except where a belvedere had been built
over the fringes of a placid bay. There a fine pavilion stood
with iron chairs and a long table, where diners could enjoy
their dinner in the evening while they watched the lights
along a superb reach of channel. Behind the belvedere stood
an imposing house, built in the colonial style with many
verandahs, and behind it clustered a half dozen small red-
and-white cook houses, card rooms, dining quarters and
American refrigerator units. Deeper in the jungle, beyond a
small stream, were ranged forty of the dismal huts inhabited
by the Tonkinese laborers, and beyond them were the famous
cacao groves that had made Jean Perouse a wealthy man.

He had given us trouble before. During the war, American
Military Police were constantly raiding La Fécondité, and
Perouse was charged with almost every kind of offense. We
discovered, however, that he maintained good relations with
American commanding officers, so that as fast as the M.P.'s
arrested him, the responsible officers set him free, and it was
in this way that he assembled the finest collection of
American heavy equipment in the Hebrides.

But it was not regarding material things that I was seeking
M. Perouse. I left the schooner, climbed the steps to the
belvedere and proceeded to the main house. There I was met
by a ruddy faced man of fifty-five, well preserved, handsome,
hearty in what one might call the British fashion. He spoke
to me first in French, but, since I am only adequate in that
language, promptly switched to English.

I was brief. "M. Perouse," I said. "It has been brought to

217

our attention that you are harboring on your plantation a young woman who is—shall we say?—wanted in Australia."

He appreciated my candor and greeted me with a disarming grin. "Come in, Mr. Crompton," he said. "Would you be averse to a whiskey so early in the morning?" He was most generous and led me to a large room exquisitely furnished in bamboo, where he placed a full bottle at my elbow. Then he apologized and asked me to excuse him for a moment, since, as he explained, he always tried to listen to the morning news from Los Angeles.

The radio was dull that day. You know, the usual dreadful stuff from America. Gangsters killing people and strikers rioting. When it was finished he said, "Rather boring, Crompton, but I did get to like the damned Americans when they were here. Now what can I do for you?"

"About the Australian girl," I reminded him. "I've got to lodge a formal protest and to ask that she be sent back to Australia."

M. Perouse laughed heartily and said, "Old man, you're too late. Your pretty has flown the coop! She returned two weeks ago."

This rather took me aback, but I said, "How in the world did she ever get up here in the first place?"

"Simple," he laughed contentedly as he recalled the incident. "I live here alone. That is not good. So I wrote to a trusted friend in Sydney and said, 'Surely there must be some pretty girl down there who would enjoy a long vacation on a real tropical island.' To my surprise, and I may add satisfaction, Phyllis arrived on the next plane."

I have to admit that I gulped and asked, "What?"

"Yes," he said frankly. "There are many lonely men in the world. Even more lonely women. I could afford to pay the plane fare, so what was more natural?"

"You mean an Australian girl. . . . She spoke English?"

"But naturally! Fine girl, too. Not well educated, perhaps, but a fine girl. Sang soprano."

I hardly knew what to say. I've lived in the New Hebrides long enough to realize that no Englishman will ever completely understand the French mind. Of course, that wretched affair at Oran when we had to sink the French fleet didn't help, either, but the more I study the French the more convinced I become that their way of life is certainly not appropriate for decent Englishmen.

I said, "So the girl Phyllis Crump has returned to Sydney?"

"Yes, Mr. Crompton, she has." I asked for a few additional particulars about this most irregular affair and then, since the schooner had not yet left the channel, I proposed to rejoin it and thus save several days of unpleasant travel. But as I was about to go there was a commotion outside the house and M. Perouse asked to be excused. He was gone but a moment. Then he returned with a scrawny Tonkinese foreman.

"This is Nguyen Bo," he said, introducing the Oriental to me as if he were a gentleman.

"I've heard of Nguyen," I said, for this was the Tonkinese who was causing the French Government so much trouble about the repatriation claims.

"Better stop with us," Perouse suggested. "You may be interested in this."

"If you'll excuse me," I said, not wishing to be involved in any way with the Tonkinese problem. The French had brought these Orientals into the New Hebrides years ago under an ironclad agreement to repatriate them to Tonkin when their indentures were discharged. Now, faced with postwar troubles in Tonkin and having no ships, the French were autocratically extending the contracts. It was a ugly situation in which I, as British civil servant, must express no opinion.

But M. Perouse insisted. "Forget the schooner. I'll drive you down to the wharf. Sit down, Nguyen."

I had to admit, as I listened to the Tonkinese, that he presented his case admirably. He said, as I recall, that his people were willing to go on working for the French under certain conditions. More rice, a pig a week for ten families, whitewash for the huts and pay in cash. The critical point, however, was their freedom to work for whom they wanted, even if it entailed travel from one island to another.

M. Perouse told Nguyen that he considered the terms reasonable, but that the French were inflexible on two of the points. No pay in French money. No freedom to leave present contracts. Nguyen said, "But you accept the terms, do you not?"

"Of course!" Perouse said. "Haven't we always got along together at La Fécondité?"

"With you, yes," the Tonkinese promptly replied. "But the Government?"

"The Government?" M. Perouse shrugged his shoulders. "The Government is always wrong." Then he added, much to my discomfort, "In times of change all governments are always wrong."

Nguyen then asked, "What are we going to do?"

Perouse replied, "Those that work for me have no complaint. The rest must be patient."

Nguyen said, "Not much longer. Soon there will be trouble."

"Nguyen!" Perouse shouted. "Don't be a fool. Because if trouble comes I shall side with the white men. Remember that."

"With you no trouble," the Tonkinese leader insisted. "With the Government, yes."

There was a moment of tension and then M. Perouse laughed. "Well, I warned you."

Nguyen laughed, too. "And I warned the French Government."

I report this conversation in detail so that you will more clearly understand what happened later. Specifically, however, on that day there was no ill will between the men, and in the presence of Nguyen Bo, M. Perouse said to me, "I hope you'll report honestly what the situation is." This was decidedly improper for him to have said and I told him so.

"M. Perouse," I protested. "And you, too, Nguyen. You must consider that I was not present at this discussion. Officially I know nothing about it."

This time I rose in earnest, but as Nguyen Bo left, a native rushed up in a jeep crying, "Mastuh! Plane he come!"

"I'll be damned!" the hearty Frenchman cried. "Come along, Crompton. Important business!"

He pushed the black driver out of the jeep and after I had managed to climb aboard—what a horrid vehicle!—he drove like mad along his coral road. I noticed, when the dust permitted me to look, that his establishment was the only one in these parts actually cleared and in full production. He had wire fence to keep his cattle in, several American army trucks, six quonsets and an ice plant. I asked him how it was that his lands looked so good, and he said, "I can always get coons or Tonks to work for me. I give them good pay and extra rice."

It seemed that we would miss the plane's arrival, for as we neared the edge of his plantation we were blocked by a road grader. "Where did you get that monstrous thing?" I asked.

"Handsome, isn't it?" he asked with much pride. "I got that for teaching a fat American colonel how to shoot flying fox." I affected not to have heard this, but M. Perouse slapped me on the shoulder. "Come, my friend," he said. "Your country and mine, they did great things together in the

220

old days. Now, for a while, we are finished. It is the time of the Yankees. Look! Anyone who can build a machine like that deserves to rule the world—for a few years."

I simply refused to acknowledge such blasphemy and by my manner I indicated as much. It may be true that Britain—I shall not speak for France—is undergoing present difficulties, occasioned I must say mostly by a Labor Government, but I should never wish it said of me that even in the darkest days did I for one moment believe or even fancy that what we have known as British leadership could decline one jot or tittle.

M. Perouse accepted my rebuke, not graciously, perhaps, for he stopped pointedly by the grader and patted it fondly, saying, in French, "My little sweetheart of the fat colonel!" Then he plunged his foot down on the accelerator and we fairly bounced along. "I mustn't be late," he chanted. "Not today of all days."

We arrived at the seaplane base just as the PBY came in for a very wet landing. When the tug went out to unload the passengers there was a moment of great commotion, following which a girl of about twenty stuck her head through the hatchway, screaming, "Hiya, Monsoor! We made it!" Beside her a redheaded girl, who looked as if she hadn't bathed in three days, peered at the dock and shouted, "Coo! That's him in the helmet! Yoo hoo, Monsoor Peroose!"

I am ashamed to add that the distasteful picture was completed by M. Perouse, who jumped up and down shouting, "Flora! Gracie! Over here!"

The next half hour was a nightmare. The two girls made a great noise as they came ashore, each with a cheap guitar. They were, I will concede, rather pretty in a vulgar sort of way. During the first five minutes they informed M. Perouse, whom they had never met before, that Phyllis Crump had skipped out on a Dutch steamer before the police could catch her. "Phyllis was a darling," the redheaded girl, Gracie Dalrymple, said. Then the other regrettable person, Flora Keats, laughed and said, "Phyllis thought this was the best island in the world, Monsoor."

"It is!" Perouse agreed, and that was where I left them. In all fairness I must explain that these girls were Australian and not English.

In the next four or five months we heard many reports about M. Perouse and his two visitors. Each week-end there was a gay party at La Fécondité. The girls became famous as guitar players and, I am ashamed to add, as consumers of practically all the alcohol the French could provide. Yet strange as it seems there were no reports of obnoxious drunkenness, but you must remember that French officials are notoriously lax in checking upon such details.

That was the way things continued for about half a year. In Efate we British took no official notice of the girls, because M. Perouse lived under French law, and it was no concern of ours what he did to wreck the morals of his community. Many persons have made fun at the expense of the Condominium Government, but I am proud to say that this spirit of laissez-faire of which I have been speaking has permitted two great nations to live side by side in peace for more than fifty years, and that I think is no small accomplishment, even though I do sometimes feel the amity has been preserved principally through the willingness of us British to overlook some fairly irritating behavior on the part of the French.

For example, about this time two Tonkinese workmen on an island near La Fécondité were murdered, and since only Frenchmen were involved, there was some dissatisfaction when I was dispatched from Efate to inquire into the particulars. It was not a pretty story; indeed it was not. A brutal French planter had decided that the Tonkinese were being pampered, so on his own recognizance he had cut the rice ration. The Tonks had protested and in the confusion of argument two men were killed. No one could say who had done the shooting, so no one was charged with the murders.

French gendarmes moved onto the small island and evacuated all Tonkinese to the mainland, where M. Perouse hired them at the wages they requested. He issued a double ration of rice and spent long hours with Nguyen Bo, explaining what rights the Tonkinese had so long as they behaved themselves.

This time I participated officially in all negotiations, and much as I had to deplore the way M. Perouse lived, I was nevertheless impressed by the scope of his thinking and by his fair play. At times he seemed more like an Englishman than a Frenchman.

While the negotiations were in progress he insisted that I stop with him and I am somewhat embarrassed to admit that never during my entire service in the New Hebrides did I enjoy myself so much. La Fécondité was a most charming place. It had curtains at the windows, polished floors and wonderful food. Normally I do not drink wine with my meals, but M. Perouse offered such excellent vintages that I could not refuse. At first I found it awkward to sit at the same table with Gracie and Flora, but under M. Perouse's kindly tutelage they had lost much of the garishness I noticed that first day at the plane.

I recall two aspects of my stay with special pleasure. The singing was magnificent. The two girls each played the guitar, a rather trifling instrument, but when it accompanied their hearty voices the result was rather pleasing. Planters came from many miles to attend the musical evenings, and I shall pass over without comment the fact that occasionally one of them spent the night, nor do I think it proper for me to discuss what seemed to be the arrangements between M. Perouse and his two guests.

The second reassuring aspect of my stay was the substantial work accomplished by my host in bringing to the attention of all French planters the critical nature of the Tonkinese problem. Once he had Nguyen Bo meet with four Frenchmen who up to that time had been adamant in their refusal to consider any contract revision. Occasionally, much against my will, I was brought into these meetings and I recall vividly a speech by M. Perouse, in the course of which he reasoned, "We are all seeking the good life. Each of us calls it by some different name. My father conceived it as *Liberté, Egalité, Fraternité*. Our English friend here calls it fair play. What the Tonkinese call it, I don't know. But we had better find out."

An official who had served in Indo-China said haughtily, "The only reasoning they understand is a rifle jammed down their throats." This infuriated M. Perouse, who called for Nguyen Bo, but the official said he would leave La Fécondité that night if he were forced to discuss anything with a damned Oriental bastard. M. Perouse looked at him sadly and said, "Our English cousins once said that about Indians. Now it's the Indians who won't talk with the British."

The French official jumped to his feet. "Am I to understand, M. Perouse, that you are willing to release the contracts?"

"No!" Perouse cried sharply. "By God, I'm not willing to release these men. I made a fortune out of the yellow devils and if they were stupid enough to honor the old contract I'd make another." Then he dropped his voice and said, "I am not willing to release them. But even less am I willing to murder them for a few francs."

There was a moment of silence and the *fonctionnaire* asked, "Who spoke of murder?"

"Anyone who thinks he can keep backward races backward much longer."

I could have cheered M. Perouse for that statement, but of course it would have been most improper for me to have done so. As a matter of fact, I would subsequently have been disgusted with myself had I publicly approved the man in view of what was to happen next day.

M. Perouse called for me right after breakfast and said, "Mr. Crompton, I have a most difficult problem and I must enlist your aid."

"Certainly," I said, for I was beginning to like the cut of this man's jib.

"It's about money," he said.

At this I gasped, for he was reputed to be wealthy, whereas I made only a few pounds ... Well, since it's a matter of public record I make four hundred eighty pounds a year plus living expenses, which with prices what they are is truly inadequate. "I'm sorry," I said with what I hope was honest frankness.

"I didn't mean a loan," he laughed. "I mean I want to buy some pounds to be delivered in Sydney."

"That's not difficult," I assured him. "How many?"

He replied, "I want each of the girls to have a thousand pounds, clear."

"The girls?" I gasped.

"Yes. They're going home. On today's plane." He became very melancholy and rang for the servant to bring the girls in. I immediately begged to be excused, but he wouldn't hear of it.

Gracie and Flora appeared in their best dresses, and M. Perouse said, "Girls, I've arranged with Mr. Crompton for each of you to get a thousand pounds when you land in Sydney."

Flora kissed M. Perouse and Gracie kissed me, adding, "That's mighty sweet of you, Herbert." Normally I dislike being called by my first name, but we had all enjoyed such a splendid time at La Fécondité that I did not protest. I was, however, totally disgusted and even outraged by what happened next.

M. Perouse made a little speech in which he said, "I am desolate about your departure, but as I explained I am at heart a Frenchman and much as I love the English language I am not at ease in it. As I grow older I want to have French things about me. French wines. French songs. The good French language of my youth." Then all three of them began

224

to weep, M. Perouse too. I was humiliated, but still I hadn't heard the worst, for he added tearfully, "I have a Marseillaise girl coming up on the next Trapas plane."

The girls cried some more and said they hoped he would be very happy. When they boarded the seaplane, the girls screamed back to the crowded deck, "Au revoir, Monsoor Jean!" and Gracie embarrassed me frightfully by shouting, "Thanks for the thousand quid, Herbert!" I considered trying to explain to those on the dock that I was not giving her the money, but everyone was weeping, so I said nothing.

At this point I was willing never to see M. Perouse again, for I could scarcely countenance the things he did, and this matter of throwing out the Australian girls to make way for a Marseillaise was so absurd as to be revolting, and not solely because the losers happened to be of British stock but rather because it seemed an offense against the decencies. In fact, my association with M. Perouse had corrupted me to the point where I was beginning to think that a man need merely wave his hand and beautiful girls would come running, but I reflected that my host's three million francs probably had a lot to do with it.

Much as I wished to leave La Fécondité, my Government directed me to report further on the likelihood of fresh labor troubles, and so reluctantly I returned to the plantation, where I interviewed this chap Nguyen Bo. Again I took pains to remind him that the British Government was not officially involved, in that the French were solely responsible for Oriental affairs, but I did let him know that I was interested in the problem so far as basic justice was concerned.

Nguyen Bo, when interviewed alone, was an astonishing person, astonishing. He weighed not over eight stone, had black teeth from betel juice, sharp little eyes and a nervousness one does not customarily associate with Orientals. It was his living quarters, however, which affected me most.

As you know, when the Tonkinese were first brought into our islands the planters devised a cheap, rapidly constructed type of housing for them. A lozenge-like foundation thirty feet long and eleven feet wide was built of coconut logs and coral. Across the middle a solid wall was erected, creating two living spaces fifteen feet by eleven, each with a curved lip. Into every one of these halves a complete Tonkinese family was moved, and since to build windows in the walls would have cost extra money, the hordes of yellow people lived in unventilated squalor. Although I am more aware than most of the many stupid mistakes we English have made

225

around the world—for example, many of my superiors have, I am ashamed to say, been very ordinary men—I do not honestly believe that in any colony of ours we would have permitted this particular offense against human beings.

Nguyen Bo's half-lozenge was a revelation. It was white-washed, very clean, most orderly and withal somewhat attractive. He said, "My wife, two daughters and three sons live here." I could say nothing.

He went on to tell me that his people were still pressing for the same points, which he did not bore me with by repeating. He said there was no disposition to cause trouble, but that some of his friends had spirited out a long report to the United Nations at Lake Success. I tried to hide my surprise and asked if the French knew of this and he said, "Not yet."

I then tried to ascertain how an unlettered Tonkinese, smothered in a jungle, could have heard of the United Nations, let alone submit a report. I questioned him directly on this and discovered that it had been smuggled out by Gracie Dalrymple. She was the redheaded girl from Sydney. "She couldn't have written it," I argued, for lovely as Gracie's singing voice was, I doubt if she could write her own name. Thereupon Nguyen assured me that it had been written in French, from which I deduced that Jean Perouse himself must have been the author. Nguyen Bo would not confirm my guess and begged me not to mention it to anyone else, lest it reflect discredit on the Frenchman as a kind of traitor to his class, and this is the first time I have divulged my belief, although subsequent events have more than substantiated my rather shrewd deduction.

As I was leaving the lozenge there was a great commotion about the big house of La Fécondité and I saw to my amazement that a piano was being moved in! It had come from Sydney on the last *Morinda* and must have cost a fortune. As I watched its progress through the door, M. Perouse rushed out with a cablegram and cried, "Danielle said there was only one thing needed for her complete happiness. A piano!"

"Who is Danielle?" I inquired.

"La Marseillaise!" he cried ecstatically. Then he showed me the cable. Danielle said that since she had never before been in the South Pacific, and since the trip out was a very long one—this was a most remarkable and expensive cable, sent collect—and since she feared loneliness she was bringing along another girl who sang with her in the café. But they had to have a piano!

On the next Trapas the two girls arrived. They were tall, sparkling-eyed and very French. Danielle was the prettier of the two, but Alceste had the finer sense of humor, a trait which I prize greatly. Even before they landed they completely captivated everyone on the dock, and for the next weeks La Fécondité was the gayest it had ever been.

Danielle played the piano competently and Alceste joined with her in delightful French songs, although I must in all fairness say that their voices were somewhat pinched in comparison with the fine, strong voices of the Australian girls. All the unattached young Frenchmen of the island, and some of the attached ones as well, made La Fécondité their headquarters, and even though the French girls did not accept me with quite the openhearted friendship the Australians had extended, I nevertheless grew to consider myself a member of the household. I may add that I now kept my luggage at La Fécondité, where M. Perouse had kindly allocated me a permanent room.

The big event naturally was Bastille Day, a typically French holiday, but one in which all men of good will can properly join, since a triumph of human freedom in one corner of the world is a triumph everywhere. I therefore decided to stay for the festivities and on July 12 guests began to assemble from many plantations, but I saw with alarm that many of the men were arriving with guns. One of the planters said, "Sooner or later there's going to be trouble," and he intimated that he and his friends would know what to do.

An entire room was set aside for alcohol, to which I am addicted in moderation, not to the point certainly of being an embarrassment either to myself or others. The day of the thirteenth was spent mostly in drinking, since it would have been ungracious to have launched formal festivities before all the guests had arrived.

That evening, at the close of a long and pleasant day in which I must say I upheld my half of the Condominium, I was recovering in the belvedere, where the cool breezes helped clear my head, but I looked up the channel and saw a most distressing sight. From a nearby island two large canoes had set out for the upper reaches of La Fécondité. At first I assumed they were filled with natives bringing in more fish or chicken for the feast next day, but as I studied the craft I realized with apprehension that each canoe was loaded brimful with Tonkinese! I watched for some moments and saw two rather clumsy barges, each jammed to the Plimsoll line with Orientals.

Seeking not to alarm anyone, I left the belvedere quietly and found M. Perouse, in a rather intoxicated condition, beating time while Danielle sang French cabaret songs. With some difficulty I got him to his feet and asked the girl to leave us alone for a moment.

"M. Perouse," I whispered. "If I can judge correctly, more than two hundred Tonkinese have converged on La Fécondité."

He looked at me, first with rather bleary eyes and then with increasingly steady ones. "Mr. Crompton," he said slowly. "Are you sober enough to drive me a few miles?"

"Certainly," I said, for although I may not have covered myself with distinction as a government official in the New Hebrides, I must honestly admit that I have yet to find the Frenchman who has ever, as the Americans say, "put me under the table."

It was a macabre drive. Around us the jungle seemed to resent our coming. Long runners of vine slipped across the road and our headlights cast weird reflections on huge leaves. As we drove, M. Perouse became quite sober and said, "Crompton, I hope I haven't let you in for something messy. Are you armed?"

"No," I said.

"Good," he replied. "I prefer them to see that I have no weapons."

We now started to overtake straggling Tonkinese workmen, each carrying some kind of implement, but none, as far as I could see, with guns. When they first saw the jeep they stared in open animosity, but when they discovered that it was M. Perouse they watched our progress with passive masks.

We came at last to a large coconut grove where several bonfires had been lit. The smoke, curling upward, was grotesque. M. Perouse left the jeep, a stocky, handsome figure of a man. He went right up to a group of Tonkinese and started to argue with them. In a few moments he called me over to verify some points.

I said that La Fécondité was filled with planters who had assembled to celebrate Bastille Day. I assured them that the French had not collected an arsenal for an attack upon the Tonkinese.

"We saw guns!" they replied.

"A few," I said. "Like you, the Frenchmen are frightened."

"Can we believe that?"

228

"Look for yourselves. We are not armed."

One of the Tonks cried, "But what about the jeep?"

A dozen men ran over and ransacked the car, finding only a bottle of vermouth which M. Perouse had forgotten. "You can have it," he said, and for a moment there was a bit of merriment to relieve the tension.

But as the Tonkinese passed the bottle, there was a sound of rifles in the distance and in a moment Nguyen Bo rushed up in a truck. "They are attacking our huts!" he shouted.

Immediately there was great confusion, during which the Tonkinese grabbed both M. Perouse and me. "Nguyen!" Perouse shouted, but the noise was so great that the Tonkinese leader did not hear. So each of us shouted and finally he came to where we were held prisoners.

"Nguyen," M. Perouse pleaded. "If trouble has started only you and I can stop it. Please work with me."

The little man reflected for a moment and said no. The French had begun this . . .

"How can you be so sure?"

"Only the French have rifles."

"But look over there, Nguyen. Four of your men have guns."

"M. Perouse!" the wiry man interrupted. "It is the Tonkinese who are dead. I know, because one of them was my wife."

There was a deathly silence as this news passed among the enraged workmen, but Perouse would not be deflected from his purpose. "All the more reason, my friend, why you and I should prevent more shooting." He shook himself loose and went to his wizened little foreman. "Nguyen," he said quietly, "we must go."

We climbed into the jeep while four Tonkinese with rifles hung onto the frame. Nguyen said they would kill us if there was any trickery. To this M. Perouse did not even reply.

We reached the northern end of the Tonkinese hovels to find the entire population in a state of hysteria. Some drunken planters had detected the passage of many workmen through the jungle. The Orientals were challenged and some fool discharged his rifle. A Tonkinese was killed, perhaps a planter, too. Then a group of planters had rushed out of the big house and had begun to shoot wildly. Two more Tonkinese were killed in the native huts, one of them Nguyen Bo's wife. Now there was desultory firing in the distance.

Nguyen and Perouse studied each other. Finally the

Frenchman said, "My friend, this had to happen. You and I know that. Now we must stop it."

He left me as hostage, a not unwilling one if my staying could help prevent bloodshed, while he and Nguyen, followed by the four riflemen, started down the trail on foot. At the top of his voice Perouse kept shouting, "My friends! Hold your fire!" I last saw him going forward, his hands in the air, pleading for a truce.

It was not until next day that I learned what happened. As the six men approached the plantation a Frenchman cried, "Perouse, you stinking traitor!" Some enraged fool shot into the crowd and killed Nguyen Bo, whereupon the Tonkinese riflemen aimed at Perouse, who fell into the dust of the very plantation he had spent years in perfecting.

I shall gloss over my own experiences. When news of the tragedy reached my guards I was beaten a bit but I suffered no real harm. After two days I was released, and when I staggered back to La Fécondité my heart stopped for a moment.

The Tonkinese had fired one corner of the big house. The Frenchmen had wrecked two of the small kiosks. There was no sign of life and the ambulance driver said, "It was a very bad night. All Tonkinese are under arrest. We have issued guns to the white men."

At the hospital, the doctor said there was nothing wrong with me except bruise and shock. He said he would, however, keep me with him for some days as a precaution. I was led to a small room, where to my amazed delight I found Jean Perouse propped up in bed.

He was badly wounded, a portion of his face having been blown away. But with one unbandaged eye and one corner of his mouth he grinned. Through jaws wired together he said, "We accomplished little, old man."

We lay there for many days because it seemed that one of the kicks at my kidneys had caused a minor infection. M. Perouse said that he had never understood why people could not live together peacefully. He told me that only one good thing had come out of that terrible night. The laws binding Tonkinese to expired contracts had been rescinded. He explained that a report had reached the United Nations and in self-defense the French Government had revoked the law.

He added that the piano had been wrecked and that he was considered to be a traitor by his countrymen, none of whom came to see him. I said I could not understand such a judgment against a man who was obviously acting in the common good. He laughed and said, "Times change and opinions follow. In a year it'll be forgotten, because this time I was right."

Tears came to his cheek and I thought that his ostracism had cut deeper than he admitted, but he said, "The worst blow is that Danielle and Alceste have not even bothered to visit me. Who can blame them? They must believe what their friends say. Danielle is marrying a planter in Efate. Alceste is singing in Noumea." He folded his hands and seemed so dispirited that I forebore reminding him that the Australian girls Flora and Gracie would never have deserted him that way in a time of danger because it is not the British custom to do so.

I did not see M. Perouse again for nearly a year. Then it became my duty to deliver some papers to him regarding the arrest of Phyllis Crump in Singapore. It seems she had with her four French railway bonds which had been traced to La Fécondité, from where she must have stolen them.

I had been instructed to deliver the documents in person, since the complaint had to be signed before a witness, and as soon as I entered the gates to La Fécondité I felt my spirits rise. There was the same clean wire, the scraped roads, the well-tended cacao with its leaves glistening in the sunlight. At the Tonkinese quarters new whitewash had been applied and all the middle walls had been knocked out so that each family could have double space.

I must admit that I found petty pleasure in the fact that whereas all other plantations seemed to lack labor, my friend—for I have grown proud to call M. Perouse my friend even though his inherited patterns of behavior are often offensive to British sensibilities—had all he needed.

La Fécondité flourished. Damage had been repaired and the very sight of this productive land made my spirits soar, but as I stood there surveying the scenes I had grown to love, I heard a strange sound from within the house, as if a once-fine piano were being played out of tune. I listened for some moments but could not discern what it was that I was hearing. Finally I knocked on the door, and the haunting sounds stopped.

M. Perouse appeared, and for a moment I suffered an involuntary shock, for the left side of his face was a nasty scar. He sensed my discomfort and ran his hand across the scar, saying, "It doesn't hurt, Crompton. I was fortunate."

He took me into his spacious living room, which was more polished and attractive than ever. I came immediately to the point, as is my custom on official visits, and showed him the reports from the Singapore police. He studied them casually and then broke into a wide grin which pulled up the scarred lips.

"Four railway bonds," he laughed. "All these many papers about four railway bonds! Which I gave to the young lady."

I was unable to dissuade him from this story and said that I would have to have a sworn deposition from him to that effect. "But naturally!" he said with great affability. "Write what is necessary and I'll swear to it."

I could not myself take such a light view of legal procedures which in their day have saved many innocent lives and helped preserve the civilized decencies, but I composed some lies which sounded plausible and he signed them. Then we needed a witness to attest the signature and he said, "Some of the French planters will be coming out tonight, but let's get the business finished now." He rang a bell and a native girl appeared. "You run catchim Quoyn," he said.

I was dreadfully embarrassed when the Tonkinese arrived, an intelligent-looking young man who was introduced as the new forman of La Fécondité. In a whispered consultation I had to inform M. Perouse that in a Singapore court the signature of some unknown Oriental named Quoyn would be worse than useless. It would prejudice the deposition.

I never saw M. Perouse so infuriated. He jumped up and stormed at me, "Do we never learn? Why do we die? Why do we bother to try to make the world a better place? So that some judge in Singapore can say Mr. John Doe is an honorable name because it is common in Liverpool, but Quoyn is not, because the damned stupid judge can't pronounce it?"

I have not repeated his exact phrasing, which was shocking even to me. The upshot was that he grabbed the depositions and would have destroyed them had I not said, "M. Perouse! If you do not send the clearance, Miss Crump may get a long jail sentence."

I can see him yet. He stood there, a man terribly disfigured, his entire body trembling with rage. Slowly he dropped the papers and fell back into his chair. He said a few words in Tonkinese to Quoyn, who smiled and left. He was silent for a long time and said, "Thank you, my friend. The very least I can do for Phyllis is to get a decent French signature. She was a very good girl, Phyllis. She sang like a thrush."

Night came on and we sat there. In the dusk he said, "I think we shall never learn, Crompton. We have a new *fonc-*

tionnaire now, straight from Paris, a man with an unbelievable record for courage against the Nazis. Yet he says unofficially that what we should have done was shoot our yellow bastards right and left when we had the chance." He poured a stiff brandy, which I must say I appreciated. Then he became more relaxed and said, "Yet look at us a year after the big affair! A few have lost money. None of us can order the Tonks about as we used to. But by God everyone has a better life."

He became actually expansive and said, "Crompton, you never liked music much, but are you up to some now?"

I protested that on the contrary I enjoyed music very much, providing it wasn't that blatant American jazz, and that I would relish some right then. I rose to tune the radio but he said, "No! Never use that if the real thing is at hand."

He called for the servant and said, "You can tell the girls to come in now," and from the interior of the house appeared two beautiful little Tonkinese girls whom I judged to be about twenty and eighteen. They were dressed in European style, but with Tonkinese hairdo. He introduced them and said we were ready for some music.

In a manner which betrayed their familiarity with the house, for in fact they lived there, the girls went to a cupboard and produced two odd instruments that I had never seen before. With tiny hammers they began to play the strange, elfin music I had heard earlier that afternoon.

M. Perouse leaned back and smiled at the girls, whose beautifully placid faces did not change expression as they tinkled forth a new tune. "You've got to acquire a liking for it," my host said.

"The girls?" I whispered. "Who are they?"

"The daughters of Nguyen Bo," he replied. "They were orphans, you see. It was the least I could do for an old friend." He listened to more of the music and then said he would like them to sing. They laughed nervously and said they did not like to perform before strangers.

"Crompton's no stranger!" he cried emphatically, slapping the younger girl on the bottom. As their thin reedy voices blended in an old French song he sighed and whispered, "If you seek the good life, Crompton, you must be prepared to accept many new things."

New Zealand

New Zealand is probably the most beautiful country on earth. The official school history says that when Richard John Seddon, the great Prime Minister, died, "he passed on to a better place even than God's own Country."

The New Zealander finds it difficult to believe that there could be a better land than his, either on earth or in heaven. He is always ready to boast of four national distinctions. "We have a land of unmatched beauty. (True) We have demonstrated that two races of different color can inhabit one land in peace and honor. (True) We showed the world how to pass social legislation for the good of all. (True) And today we enjoy the highest standard of living known by any nation. (False)"

As regards the first claim, the natural beauty of New Zealand is difficult to believe. Its two islands, no larger than Colorado, combine all types of alluring scenery, all kinds of climates. Consider what you could see in one day's travel.

At the northern tip of North Island you find a dazzling tropical beach sixty miles long. (New Zealanders call it Ninety Mile Beach.) It ends in a cluster of handsome islands around which sport immense marlin and swordfish. Farther south are prehistoric sub-tropical forests with towering kauri pines that took 1500 years to mature. In the center of North Island is a brooding desert surmounted by three majestic volcanoes, one or the other of which seems always to be active, spouting lava ash by day and beacon fires at night. At Rotorua the wonders of Yellowstone Park are challenged, for here geysers play, mud pools bubble and hot waters tumble down over colored terraces.

On the west coast you will see Mount Egmont, rising in beauty, the perfect snow-capped cone of a dead volcano, cloud wreathed and pointed like Fujiyama. But in New Zealand you always say, "Fujiyama looks a lot like Mount Egmont."

Now you leave the North Island and fly south across Cook Strait, where vast mountains sank into the sea until only their tips remained aloft. Here earth and ocean mingle in astonishing beauty, varied, twisted, glowing in the sunlight.

Ahead lies South Island, where the real beauty of New

Zealand is found. Here Mount Cook rises more than 12,000 feet, perpetually glaciated, with huge fingers of ice reaching almost into the sea. Nearby are the Southern Alps, immense rows of jagged peaks beneath which nestle dozens of wonderful lakes, each serving as a mirror for some great range of mountains.

On the coast, near the glaciers, you find dramatic evidence of New Zealand's turbulent geological history. During millions of years this land rose and fell repeatedly. When it lay under the sea, sand covered it. When it was thrust upward, limestone deposits collected. Finally the resulting rocks were forced high into the air, where howling winds eroded the sandstone layers and left tall rounded pillars of limestone wafers piled one upon the other, appropriately called The Pancakes. And then, since New Zealand scenery is completely prodigal in its wonders, the hungry Tasman Sea ate huge caverns beneath The Pancakes into which tides roar, bursting upward through crevices and shooting thin strands of spray high into the air.

Farther south lies Milford Sound, first and finest of the fjords. Cutting deep inland, it is enclosed by brooding and majestic peaks. High waterfalls plunge from mountain plateaus directly into its waters, and jagged bays probe into dark forests. At the head of one such indentation Sutherland Falls leaps nearly 2,000 feet down into a solemn glen, one of the superb waterfalls of the world. Almost inaccessible, it is reached by means of a difficult trail labeled on maps "The World's Finest Walk." Along ten casual miles I counted forty sheer granite cliffs, each at least 800 feet high, three of them dropping precipitously for more than a thousand feet. I also saw at least 200 waterfalls, some of them hundreds of feet high. One unnamed one—there are so many wonders in this part of New Zealand that they are not even recorded—fell 300 feet and then leaped backward, borne aloft on surging currents of air. Another zigzagged eight times to get down a cliff face. A third fell some hundred feet, then dashed upon a huge projecting boulder which split the fall and threw each half high into the air, so that the falling plumes looked like two Grecians horses plunging into battle. At no point in the ten miles did I fail to see at least three waterfalls. Frequently more than ten were visible. And this was in the dry season!

In the same ten miles there were other spectacular phenomena so far unnamed: a cataract that had gnawed its way sixty feet through solid rock, leaving at the land's surface a gorge only 36 inches across; a tiny lake of perfect ultramarine; a balanced boulder bigger than a cathedral; a walled valley hidden in circles of granite cliff. And often above me flamed that most brilliant tree, the pohutukawa, at the end of whose branches grow massive clusters of scarlet flowers, so that sometimes the forest seemed to be on fire.

On even the best maps the land south of Milford Sound is marked UNEXPLORED. New Zealand has dozens of fjords still to be opened to travel. It has hundreds of natural wonders still to be discovered. One who knows the region said, "For the rest of this century my country could open up each year some new spectacle that would astonish the eye."

Proof of this came dramatically in 1949. New Zealand is geologically a recent land and has few animals that resemble those found elsewhere. It does, however, have some that are unique. Among those still living is the kiwi, a long-billed, flightless bird that has become the national symbol. (New Zealand fighting men are Kiwis.) Now almost extinct, the kiwi is famous for two qualities: it feeds by stomping its feet over worm holes to imitate rain, thus luring the hors d'oeurve into position; and it lays an egg of ridiculous size. If a hen were to do comparatively as well, chicken eggs would be 14 inches long and would weigh three pounds each!

The most famous of New Zealand's extinct creatures was the moa, a gigantic bird that towered above the heads of men who liked its rich meat so much they exterminated it about 150 years ago. (There's a great fight on about this, some scholars maintaining that moas were never seen after 1350.) Another of the extinct birds was the notornis, a beautiful turkey-like creature with blue-green feathers and a brilliant red toucan-like bill. The last one was seen in 1898, a previous specimen having been eaten by shipwrecked sailors some years before.

Then in 1949 some explorers in the wild southern valleys came upon a family of notornis that had miraculously survived. Cautious investigators probed the area and discovered perhaps fifty of the handsome fowl. A surge of excitement swept across the scientific world and other expeditions were hastily outfitted. Warned the Government: "It is ridiculous to call these excursions moa hunts. No moa could possibly be alive in New Zealand." But the scientists point out that there used to be a dwarf moa and in most bars you can get even money that sooner or later a moa is going to turn up in those southern valleys marked UNEXPLORED.

The first human beings to see this compact wonderland of New Zealand were a mysterious unidentified people who left

236

carvings on the walls of caves. Scientists are divided as to whether these rude artists were ancestors of the famous Moriois who were found here later and whose history is terrible to contemplate. Profoundly peaceful, they outlawed war and settled arguments by play-duels, the mock battle ending whenever a contestant cried, "Behold! I bleed!" For centuries they lived in quiet peace. Then the warlike Maoris fell upon them, killed the men, carried off the women. In 1930 there was only one Moriori left alive. He was a grotesque fellow, Tommy Solomon, weighing 588 pounds. He liked to ride horses and always carried with him a small ladder by which to mount. In 1933 Tommy Solomon died, completely wiping out a distinct human race of which it was said, "They were gentle, therefore they perished."

The Maoris, who took their place, were certainly not gentle and they are not even close to perishing. They won New Zealand by some of the bravest exploits in maritime history. About the year 900 an intrepid Polynesian named Kupe drifted down to New Zealand from Tahiti and on his return established in Polynesian memory a description of a favored land called The Long White Cloud. In 1350 a great fleet of canoes migrated from Polynesia and brought permanent settlers to New Zealand.

Regarding this hegira more specific information is recorded than is known about Columbus' voyage some 150 years later. Today each Maori tribe traces its ancestry back to one of the original canoes and takes its name therefrom. For example, the Tainui tribe can relate proudly that the canoe Tainui was 70 feet long, captained by Hoturoa, that it sailed on the fourth night of December in 1350, and that "Taikehu was in charge of the great paddle Huahuaterangi." The name of each paddler is remembered, plus the fact that the canoe's priest turned out to be a thieving rascal who ran off with Hoturoa's daughter. Even the chant that kept hope alive is recited: "Seek ye the way! Though the distance be great, though the way be long, keep thy course, O son! Across the waters is thy path."

The Maoris were wonderfully capable settlers, and are today the best off of all Polynesian peoples. They are darker, perhaps because of intermarriage with native tribes. They are more healthy, for their climate is better. And they are more gifted in self-government, because they stood boldly toe-to-toe with English invaders and slugged it out to a standstill. The Maoris were never totally defeated, so a sagacious treaty was devised whereby two vastly different civilizations could live together in mutual respect. The spirit of this Treaty of Waitongi still animates relations between Maori and Pakeha, as the white man is known. At the time of signing a native chief exclaimed, "The shadow of our land goes to Queen Victoria, but the substance remains with us." Surely one day the Maoris will merge into the white stream that engulfs them, but for the present they cling boldly to their Maorihood, slowly acquiring the skills and tricks necessary for survival in a white man's world.

In the meantime they have a good life. They elect their own members of Parliament, who vote the straight Labor line because it was Labor that passed the law which gives parents $1.50 a week for each child. (Maoris call this the Stallion Fee.) Maoris can marry whites, live where they wish, enter whatever professions they prefer. As proof of their citizenship they fought with renowned bravery in both world wars, marching to battle singing their "Maori Battalion Song."

But you don't live long in New Zealand without discovering that the Maori-Pakeha relationship is not all pleasant. A good deal of hypocrisy obscures realities. Many Maori villages are in fact slums. Sensitive Maoris confide that they never really feel at ease among whites, who shout public acceptance but practice private ostracism. As one complete realist said, "White men don't marry our girls much any more, because Maori brides no longer inherit huge landed estates." Even so, the relationship between brown and white in New Zealand is far superior to that between black and white in America.

And the Maoris have a good time! At elections they often vote six or seven times if they particularly favor a candidate. They are great practical jokers, a favorite jest being to pick one's teeth in the face of an enemy, thus signifying, "The flesh of your ancestors is caught in my teeth." As a learned judge of Maori land disputes reported, "If Maori A claims land that once belonged to B's family, there is one bit of evidence that supersedes all others. Can A prove that some ancestor of his killed and ate B's ancestor? If so, the land clearly belongs to A."

Maoris have only vague concepts of private property. "The first Maori up in the morning is the best dressed." It is not uncommon for a man who has bought a fine hat to give it ungrudgingly to the first friend who admires it. Says the white man: "The New Zealand Maori is the finest man on earth. But don't lend him anything!"

There is one aspect of Maori culture that is a sheer delight, one of those perfect art forms that haunts the memory with true loveliness. Young Maori girls, dressed in knotted cord blouses and skirts made of flax stems, become adept in swinging poi balls, made of compressed rushes tied to strings. (Short poi, six-inch strings; long poi, eighteen inches.) In delicate rhythms, sometimes brushing their skirts so as to yield an extra beat, teams of girls execute prolonged and intricate drills.

On festive days they do the canoe poi. Then, with each girl whirling two short poi, they seat themselves upon the ground so as to represent their tribal canoe. In back of them a chief rushes up and down flourishing a greenstone club and urging them on. Somewhere in the shadows an old woman stands, chanting through blue-tattooed lips some wild Polynesian account of the great migration.

Now, in their canoe, the girls make the poi balls fly. At first it seems nothing, merely another dance. Then slowly the poi take on the rhythms of the sea. Shoulders begin to weave as if hands carried great paddles. The chief rants and cries. Always the mournful woman chants in her husky voice.

Now the poi balls whirr in the air, striking beaded skirts, tapping against the body. The entire audience is sailing in that ancestral canoe and the night is tense with the sound of the poi balls. Suddenly the woman moans. In silence the girls fall backwards, as their ancestors had once collapsed from near starvation. There is now no sound but that of the mysterious poi balls, echoing the tiny slap of waves against the historic canoe. Then the chief shouts. The old woman screams the last measure of the chant. The girls revive, and the trembling poi balls leap to a beat of joy. And there is no one in the room who cannot see that early vision of the Long White Cloud!

The white men who share New Zealand with the Maoris are all of British stock—English as far south as Christchurch, Scots the rest of the way—and no matter for how many generations a family has lived in New Zealand, everyone still speaks of going Home, and they proudly insist, "We are more English than the English." Perhaps New Zealand's position at the very antipodes from England has led them to cling tenaciously to every fragment of their English ancestry. This has both good and bad results. New Zealand has a more homogeneous population than any other major country, and in the last war the only four illiterate New Zealanders were found. On the other hand, gifted young people tend to run away from their own land, back to the security of England. Katherine Mansfield, the gifted storyteller, David Low, the cartoonist, and Lord Rutherford, the atomic trail blazer, are only three of thousands who fled their homeland.

Every outstanding prime minister has been born outside New Zealand, and it is interesting to read the boast carved into the beautiful memorial church at Cave: "1928. It is noteworthy that all the men engaged in the building of this Church were British-born." This yearning for the womb of England combined with life in a vivid new land has resulted in a nation which is most conservative in social life yet completely radical in social legislation.

This discrepancy can be explained historically. The first serious settlers arrived in 1840, so that New Zealand is the youngest of nations. These settlers came from conservative, Victorian England and they tolerated no nonsense about "brave new worlds." It was their proudly expressed determination to transfer "old societies to new places," and a conscious plan was devised whereby settlers could be kept within sacrosanct social levels, ranging downward from "wealthy gentry of good family" to the laboring lower classes. As late as 1857 one of the gentry begged New Zealand to avoid the errors of the United States democracy and to follow instead a system whereby men of property and intelligence ruled as they deemed wise. To this end the price of land was rigged abnormally high so as to prevent laborers from catching a foothold on the social ladder. During one depression an arch-conservative government saw nothing lamentable in the flight of more than 100,000 New Zealanders to Australia, where they could find land and food!

Reaction was inevitable, and under Richard John Seddon, a forceful immigrant workingman who rose to be Prime Minister, New Zealand passed the great liberal laws that laid its reputation for being in the forefront of social legislation. Federal votes for women, universal suffrage, forced arbitration of labor disputes, old-age pensions and a nationwide system of child care were all first provided in New Zealand. From a nation established for the benefit of wealthy men, the country expanded into what it still is: a workingman's paradise. There were, however, temporary retreats from Seddon's program, and in the early 1930's a bewildered and incompetent conservative government could think up no way to fight the depression.

Listen to what a workingman has to say about that period. Tom Neill is now over 60 and has retired to a small farm in

240

the South Island. He is a tall fellow, handsome and mystically convinced about the rights of labor. In his small cottage, immaculately clean, he lives on a government pension and helps his vigorous wife take care of his chickens. His home contains a kind of altar: the glowing fireplace above which hangs the portrait of an unpretentious man in a black suit.

Neill says, "I started work when I was 12. In a cheese factory. Five in the morning till six at night. Seven days a week. Often we had to work till ten or eleven at night, but our wages were the same. Three dollars a week and no overtime. Later on I became manager. Then I worked daily from six till nine at night. I had an accident and lay in hospital a long time. I lost every cent I owned and could never get started again."

Mrs. Neill serves a tea of hot scones, six kinds of cake, and thick cream. She says, "I worked at home till I was 31. Then, thank God, Tom found me and took me away. My parents couldn't give me any pay because they earned none. I was never away from the farm till I was 18. The only entertainment I can even remember was church lantern slides, mostly upside down. I went to town once a year, but until I was past 25 I never had more than three dollars a year to spend on myself."

Tom continues. "When the depression came I got a job shoveling a ditch. There were two men working in our gang, strapping blokes they were. I noticed they always ate their lunch to one side. I, being older, said, 'Look here! Eat with us!' And they were ashamed to come over, for all they had was boiled potato skins. The meat of the potato they left at home for the kiddies." Tom unclenches his hands and says, "I tell you, the rich man's government had only one thought. Get us unemployed out of the cities so we wouldn't create riots. The prime minister said, 'Labor has taken the cuts without protest. Give them another.'"

Tom has cruel memories of the depression but soon the anger leaves him. He looks up at the portrait over the fireplace and says, "That simple workingman up there threw the government out and set up a Labor cabinet that saved this nation. I don't care what anyone says about Michael Joseph Savage. I was near defeated when he came to power. I can still hear what he said in those first days: 'The Government will pay Christmas benefits to all needy families.'"

The social services provided by Savage's determined ministry are remarkable. There is an old-age benefit with liberal allowances plus a superannuation income for anyone who cannot otherwise qualify. There is a widow's benefit, an orphan's benefit and a family allowance of $1.50 a week for each child up to 16 years of age, extendable if needed. There are benefits for coal miners and for chronic invalids. There is unemployment insurance and a hilarious Emergency Benefit which was explained in this way: "Suppose your wife is in love with another man. You won't agree to a divorce, so they burn down your store. Obviously you've suffered a catastrophe. The store I mean. But you're not covered by any of the preceeding benefits. That's where the Emergency Fund comes in."

Recent governments have added war pensions and a special fund for ex-soldiers "who, even though never wounded, are aging prematurely." Every New Zealander receives free a complete medical service, including doctors, surgeons, drugs, certain patent medicines, hospitalization, maternity care, X-rays, massage, nursing—and artificial eyes and limbs at one-fifth cost. But to understand the spirit of social legislation in New Zealand you must read the directions regarding soldiers' pensions: "Boards are instructed that when contradictions appear in records, the claimant shall receive benefit of any doubt."

The cost of this security is very high, not in money, for the deductions are modest. A man with a wife and one child pays on a $3000 salary $275 social security and $360 income tax. (In the United States he would pay $45 for social security and $185 in income tax.) It is rather the cost in restrictive legislation that seems paralyzing. Consider the case of Mr. C. G. Moore, a happy and popular haberdasher in Greymouth.

Mr. Moore must have his shop open at 9:00 A.M. and closed at 5:30. He may neither open at 8 nor stay open till 6. Hours are set by the Government. The wages he can pay his help are stated in law and he must not deviate from them. Recently he got into trouble because the Government found he was paying a foreman less than prescribed. He pointed out that he allowed the foreman a commission on volume. Then he really was in trouble, for that put the wage above the legal limit!

Mr. Moore's son works for him and must by law belong to a union; he may not work voluntarily at night. Hours for tea and lunch are legal matters, as are vacations. A government inspector may visit the shop at any time and call for more heat, less heat, more clean towels, more space for drinking tea. And a rigid forty hour week is mandatory.

The prices Mr. Moore may charge are set by the Government, which also insists that the books be kept according to their system (double entry) and be available for inspection at any moment. To buy stock Mr. Moore does not simply import it from England. He must apply for an import license, and the Government lists what may be bought and where. A woman in Greymouth recently read about a hayfever remedy made of rose petals. Unthinkingly she sent a letter to Australia, ordering some. When the medicine arrived the Government impounded it and raised the merry devil about sending money out of New Zealand without permission.

If Mr. Moore had some money in London he would have to leave it there, since the Government must maintain a favorable balance in Britain. Same applies to any money he might have in Australia. Several young girls in Greymouth married Americans during the war. Their mothers may not visit them unless "the New Zealand girl has a child and the grandmother is over 65," when the Government may permit foreign travel.

If the Moores want to build a home, the Government will issue a permit if the home does not exceed 1300 square feet of floor space. If they wanted to sell the house they have, the Labor Government would say what the price would be. And if Mrs. Moore keeps more than twenty-four chickens, she must register them with the Government, which will buy the eggs at its price. It is little wonder that New Zealand voters finally tossed Labor out by a resounding majority.

Yet it would be a grave mistake to interpret this as a retreat from liberalism. Before the election the new prime minister pledged that he would alter none of the basic laws. If he were to do so, it is probable that his party would be thrown out of office within a month. New Zealand is still a liberal country. What the new party did was to lift some of the onerous restrictions. Like Michael Joseph Savage before them they gave the people a Christmas present: unlimited whipping cream for private use. Mrs. Moore promptly mixed up some Pavlova pies, which she hadn't been able to make for years under the Labor Government. Into a sugared shell she poured thick cream, covering it with a double meringue, maraschino cherries and brandied peaches. I am happy to say that I ate four-fifths of the first one. With its wonderful taste in my mouth I said, "C. G., you've made a lot of money. You have a son to watch the store. Why don't you travel?"

He thought a moment and considered the good, easygoing life he had. "Where would a man want to go?" he asked.

The typical New Zealander is rather shorter than the

243

average American, and slimmer, too. He wears gray flannel trousers, an expensive sleeveless sweater, and a trim sports coat. When he dresses up it's in a stiff, high-breasted dark suit with vest, which he never discards, even on sweltering days. He is quiet, modest, eager to defend his honor and addicted to dreadful jokes: "*Q.* What jumps from branch to branch and wears a bowler hat? *A.* The manager of ten chain stores."

Along with the Spaniard, he is probably the most conservative white man still living. He is rarely at ease in public with his wife, whose new-found freedoms have not yet been clearly defined. In print he invariably refers to girls by initials, leading to the impassioned message I saw scrawled in schoolboy writing within a carved heart: "T. Davies is nice." He abhors American boasting but indulges in what might be called reverse-braggadocio: "Although the author would not dare to presume even the scantiest knowledge of the subject, yet he must confess to a not altogether inconsiderable experience in the field." He badly overuses such words as frightful, beastly, wretched, horrid, miserable and awful. If he has a trivial headache he will say proudly, "Really, I've got the most frightful head," whereas if he actually has a splitter he'll say, "Rather a nasty twitch." But don't fool yourself. When he says that, he wants sympathy!

He is most unsentimental, which probably explains why there has been no first-rate art of any kind produced in New Zealand to date. Yet he can become maudlin if you mention the gallant All Blacks, two famous Rugby teams (all-black jerseys with silver badges) who went to Europe and massacred the opposition.

He speaks softly, using precise English even on road signs: TWO DECEPTIVE BENDS. He is troubled by the intrusion of Australian and American speech forms, yet he himself has many odd expressions and would be astonished to learn that anyone else thought them amusing. Food is never delicious; it's beautiful. A good fried fish with lemon butter is apt to be especially beautiful. Assume is often pronounced with an h; controversy is accented on the *tro*, capitalism on the *pit;* food is tucker; a man's wage is his screw. Thirteen, fourteen, etc., are pronounced with d's, as thurdeen. Uncertainty is expressed by a drawled "Ah dunno," and you never speak with a man; you have a yarn to him. Anything good is wizard; you don't make sandwiches, you cut them; you never go to the hospital, you go to hospital; and the refrigerator is invariably the frij. Nor does the New Zealander often say yes or no. It's usually "Ah no," and "Ah yes," the latter sometimes being pronounced yay-yissss.

There are four sure ways to infuriate a New Zealander. The first is to call his land New Zillan. The second is to confuse the islands. If he's from North Island you must say, "Those South Island blokes are pretty stuffy." If he's from the South you say, "Auckland men are all right, but they seem a bit unsound. Too American." The North Island is progressive, Labor, industrial and butter. South Island is Conservative National, agricultural and sheep. North Island is the smaller, the less beautiful, the more developed and the more heavily populated, with two-thirds of the 1,700,000 total population. (Detroit's population is 1,838,000.) South Islanders pride themselves on being better educated, more loyal to England and more substantial in all ways. For many years South Island's conservative substantiality was recognized by giving it a bonus of several seats in Parliament beyond those its population warranted, but Labor governments changed this, and now the Auckland area alone has as many seats as all South Island.

The third way in which to invite trouble is to confuse New Zealand with Australia. They lie 1400 miles apart and it takes three days by ship to get from one to the other. They have no political connections except loyalty to a common king and membership in the Commonwealth. Actually, New Zealand is much more like Canada than like Australia, whose goods may not enter without permission. Each country uses pounds-shilling-pence, but the New Zealand coinage is worth 25% more than the Australian. New Zealand has no separate state governments; Australia has a federation of six states plus an immense federal territory, plus an over-all national parliament. Furthermore, Australia has thirty times as much territory as New Zealand and five times as many people. But New Zealanders claim that they are better educated, read more books and have a greater per capita wealth. Australia has much the better radio stations; New Zealand much the better newspapers. New Zealanders call Australians Aussies and are in turn called Pig Islanders, from the porkers landed by Captain Cook, "thus forming," says the Australian, "the parent stock from which the present inhabitants have sprung." The two nations have a common defense policy and an agreement, The Anzac Pact, defining their common policies in the Pacific; but even so relations became badly strained when England and America hailed the popular song "Now Is the

245

Hour" as Australian. It's a Maori folk song, and any New Zealander will put up his dukes if you claim otherwise!

But the one unforgivable offense to a New Zealander is to speak disparagingly of the Crown or of the tie to England. King George VI is the personal King of New Zealand. (He also happens to be King of England.) The devotion of New Zealanders to the Royal Family is unique. Country newspapers carry in their society columns casual items like this: "Today Queen Elizabeth poured out the tea for a bricklayer's wife, a stoker's wife and a dairy worker at a gathering at Sandringham Women's Institute, of which she is President. Princess Margaret served the wives of a verger, a motor mechanic and a farm worker."

Yet New Zealand has suffered two inconsolable tragedies regarding the Royal Family. Edward, Prince of Wales, loved the land and was the most popular visitor ever to tour the islands. His betrayal of the Crown has left a lasting hurt, and although people rarely speak of him, it is obvious that he has wrenched their loyalties. In 1942 the clerk of a crowded hotel could call querulously to the manager, "Would it be proper, do you think, to let American soldiers occupy Prince Edward's suite?" He had stopped there one night two decades ago.

No king of New Zealand has ever visited his Dominion while ruling, although several have while still serving as Prince of Wales. In 1949 King George planned to do so, but illness prevented the tour. It is difficult to comprehend what this postponement meant. In Christchurch all buildings on the Square were to have been cleaned. With the King not coming there was no reason to proceed. In tiny Timaru the main street was to have been repaved for the Royal limousine. Now it is still bumpy. Plumbing was to have gone into hotels that had none, carpets into bare hallways, and paint onto racetrack stands. All New Zealand was going to get a face lifting, but none of it was completed, for the King was not coming to see. In early 1950 plans were announced for a substitute tour in '52. New Zealand went wild with joy, and the old plumbing diagrams were dusted off.

New Zealand pays no taxes to England, is completely free of laws passed by the British Parliament, has its own coinage and is free to exclude British goods if it sees fit. New Zealand enjoys a national existence completely free of English domination, except that curiously she prefers to use the Privy Council in London as the supreme court of appeal.

Yet the love that binds New Zealand to England is immeasurable. When Britain went to war in 1914, a Conservative New Zealand prime minister declared war a few minutes later. In 1939 a Labor prime minister did the same. To have acted otherwise would have been unthinkable. When peace came, New Zealand gave hungry Britain an outright gift of $28,000,000, then allocated almost all butter, the best beef and the finest mutton to the motherland. The number of food parcels still mailed each week is enormous. I met an old woman who takes a tin can, packs the bottom with lard, fills it half full of fresh eggs, pours in more lard, tops it off with a slab of bacon and sews it into a stocking for posting to London. Then she herself eats oatmeal.

Few Americans appreciate the tremendous sacrifices made by New Zealand in the last two wars. Among the Allies she had the highest percentage of men in arms—much higher than the United States—the greatest percentage overseas, and the largest percentage killed. She rushed the cream of her manhood into Africa and Crete and Narvik and Singapore. Then she watched helplessly as the Japs crept down the islands until only the miracle of Coral Sea prevented actual invasion. So many New Zealanders were overseas that even women were conscripted into labor corps and told where they must work. Many American families learned how terrible it was to have men overseas for three years. New Zealand men were gone five years, or more.

Bernard Freyberg was born in England of undistinguished parents and soon emigrated to New Zealand, where he became a dentist. He was not too successful and quit to serve as a mercenary soldier under Pancho Villa. While in the Mexican desert he heard that England had gone to war. Rushing across the Atlantic he joined the New Zealand forces in London in time to serve at Gallipoli, where under intense Turkish fire he swam the Hellespont towing a barge full of flares which lighted the way for invasion. Later, in France, while suffering from four bullet wounds, he led three forlorn charges and in a fourth took a fortified village. Later he performed other wild feats and won all the medals a soldier could win. He was hailed by Sir James Barrie, a specialist in these matters, as "the bravest soldier in the war." Now he has returned to New Zealand as the personal representative of the King, a post previously held by titled nobodies. Even the conservative press applauded the appointment, observing, "Sir Bernard is a happy choice, even if somewhat revolutionary."

Today when Freyberg stands stiffly at attention during

247

public functions he is often attended by a stumpy, square-jawed chap who is generally conceded to have been the bravest soldier in World War II. Charles Upham was a schoolteacher, but his behavior under fire seems incredible. Once he rose from a raging attack of dysentery to lead his men against insuperable odds, "thus becoming the first skeleton ever to win the Victoria Cross." In fact, he is the only fighting man ever to win two Victoria Crosses in a row, and he was even recommended for a third! But the generals said halt: "Three would be too many, even for a New Zealander." When he returned home his nation offered him a gift of $30,000, but he refused saying, "Set up a scholarship for the children of the blokes who didn't get back." Now he tends cows on his small farm, a quiet, sawed-off chap who might serve as the model for the typical New Zealander we've been talking about.

The nation lives by trading agricultural products to Great Britain. The first Merino sheep were landed by Captain Cook in 1773, and within a hundred years the wool industry supported the country. Smart scientists discovered that New Zealand's grass could be the world's best except for a lack of cobalt in the soil. Now the blue mineral is added each year, sometimes by airplane, and the pasturage is spectacularly rich.

Great sheep ranches, called stations, run Merinos on the sides of mountain ranges. Lilybank is typical, a station of 70,-000 acres and 6,000 sheep nestled between 10,000-foot peaks at the head of a superb lake. In the fall (April–June) the Merinos are mustered out of the mountains for eye clipping—so they can see—and belly stripping—so their shaggy wool won't freeze into the snow. To do the rounding up teams of three comb the mountains. Top man walks along the slopes at the 7,000-foot line, tossing stones at the sheep to keep them moving downhill. He signals his two companions by setting fires on mountain peaks, and upon him depends the thoroughness of the muster.

During winter (July–September) the men of Lilybank do the hard work of a sheep station. Sometimes on foot, often on snowshoes, they snow-rake or scuff tracks through blizzards so that sheep can follow them to caches of feed. Fortunately, the Merino has learned to live through snow that would kill other sheep and has the good habit, if totally stranded, of eating wool off the backs of other sheep to stay alive. Even so, during a winter of bad snow Lilybank may lose up to 25 per cent of its flock and in 1895 lost every one.

In spring (October–December) Lilybank becomes a flowering wonderland, and since Merinos lamb best when left alone, the men rebuild fences, cull out bad stock and clean up the station.

In Summer (January–March) the shearing takes place. Since the climate is rugged, all shearing is done by hand so as to leave about an inch of wool to warm the sheep. This is slow work, for a stripping machine could handle 160 sheep while hand clippers take care of 100. But since few Merinos are ever sold for meat, careful clipping is the most important part of the year's work.

The profit would be greater if it were not for the kea, a magnificent native parrot with a two-inch scimitar beak and a passion for sheep fat. In teams the keas hunt down ewes. A big bird will dart down, fix his talons in the wool and then slash his beak deep into the ewe's back muscles. The terrified animal starts to dash about, whereupon the rest of the team screams with infuriating joy. Again and again the cruel rider shifts position and slashes at the back until the agonized sheep falls prostrate, when the keas strip off the kidney fat and leave the animal to die. It is understandable why station hands will track a kea crew for days.

Today the dairy industry of North Island has passed wool in national importance, and many New Zealanders predict that soon huge refrigerator ships will run between Auckland and San Francisco carrying "our beautiful butter north."

But no matter how important dairying becomes, the sheep industry will always be remembered as the one which gave New Zealand its character. The lore of the top man, tramping the lonely peaks, is strong in New Zealand blood. For example, touching Lilybank on the east, high among mountain passes, is the most famous of stations, Mesopotamia. Here in 1860 appeared a scrawny Englishman with $12,000 of his father's money. He had many wild and moving experiences, including a hundred-mile dash through a snowstorm to the land office where he defended his station against a fraudulent claim, after which "he astonished everyone by working off his excitement playing Bach's Fugues for two hours." He was obsessed by the mountains that fringed Mesopotamia, and from his speculations concerning what might lie beyond them grew *Erewhon*, by Samuel Butler. The young social dreamer was successful as a station owner and in three years doubled his investment, yet locally he is remembered for the fact that when he built his thatched hut he stupidly placed the thatches upside down so that all the rain ran inside, "an extraordinary thing for so clever a man to do."

New Zealand's legendary hero also came from the sheep country and gave his name to vast reaches of magnificent upland moors. In 1845 Queen Victoria visited Aberdeen in Scotland, and the city fathers, wishing to provide an unforgettable feast, advertised for some prime cattle, whereupon an enterprising young Scot named John Mackenzie went from one farm to another and stole the prize steers, delivering them boldly for the Queen's table. Then he hopped the next boat for Australia.

He wound up in New Zealand and disappeared into the unexplored wastelands where sheep were beginning to graze. He became a poetic figure, moving among the great mountains with a mournful bullock and a mute dog. At rivers he would hold fast to the bullock's tail and ferry across. At night he pitched his camp where no men had been before.

Soon rich station owners began to miss their sheep, and it was deduced that John Mackenzie was driving them off in thousand-lot hauls. Rewards were offered, but sly John and his dog were too cautious. Then they were caught with more than a thousand marked sheep. The crafty Scot escaped but was captured at the coast as he tried to board a ship. He knocked his jailer out with a length of leg chain and was recaptured only after having a bullet pumped through him. Twice thereafter he broke loose and once he was dragged back to prison trussed up like a pig. Finally the Government decided it would be cheaper to pardon him than to have him wrecking the jail each month, so John Mackenzie was banished from New Zealand, but it is rumored that he sneaked back to his wild upland moors where his ghost may still be seen at times, tramping the barren Mackenzie Country with his silent dog and mournful bullock.

The modern New Zealander is apt to be impatient with the sheep men. Now the emphasis is all upon manufacturing, with the nation trying vainly to make all sorts of items which common sense would tell her to import from either England or Australia. (Any importation from America is inconceivable at present.) The result is close to economic stagnation and has resulted in a marked decline from what was once "the highest standard of living yet attained by all the people of any nation."

The competition for labor is ridiculous. Employers must bribe help to work and are lucky if beginners stay long enough to learn a trade. Consider one advertisement of thirty-nine lines, begging girls to come to work. Twenty-five relate to the bonus system, the newly decorated tea room, provisions for time off, assurance of constant radio music during working hours plus the plea, "Bring your parents with you if you would like their opinion of the working conditions." The ad ends: "What Girl Could Ask For More?"

Apparently many do, because another shop offers, in addition to the above: free permanent waves, daily carfare, taxis home on late nights, tickets to the movies twice a week, and—illegally—an extra two weeks' pay above vacation pay if the girls will consent to report to work on Monday after the annual holiday!

A totally inadequate labor force plus a rigid 40-hour week means that New Zealand is underproduced in everything except mutton, butter and wool. For example, the country has immense deposits of coal, yet coal is often imported from Australia or even the United States. There is abundance of wool, but carpeting is simply not available. There are fine forests, but no lumber; great wealth, but not enough homes.

At Foxdown Farm near Timaru I watched Bob Ford work 1200 acres, run 3200 Romney sheep for mutton and 100 Aberdeen-Angus cattle for beef. He had no hired help. Could get none. Bob and his wife worked fourteen hours a day, seven days a week. They made a pile of money, but they were burning themselves out.

The result is that New Zealand's once-high standard of living has drooped pitifully. In ten homes where husbands earned what would be $8,000 a year in America, only one wife had both a refrigerator and a washing machine. In three homes there was neither, yet both husband and wife desperately wanted both. None available.

Until recently New Zealanders refused to believe that their living standards had slipped. Then, in 1950, they played host to the Empire Games, which brought newsmen from all parts of the Commonwealth. The result was some of the most shocking criticism a country has ever had to absorb, and all of it delivered by members of the family. An Australian: "I get an over-all impression of gloom and depression. All public services are shockingly out of date." A Londoner: "Even our English cities, with austerity and restrictions, are immeasurably more cheerful, better equipped and better serviced for out-of-town visitors." Another Australian: "The transport system is painfully obsolete." A Canadian: "New Zealand does not have a single public restaurant that would be classed as anything better than third-rate in Vancouver." Another Canadian: "Service in stores and shops is poor. Goods are shoddy ... If this is a vicious indictment of Auckland as a tourist town, it is vicious only because it is the only honest impression one can take away." An American: "In five days I visited five cities and could not find a single hotel room. I slept in dingy rooms or in none at all. What was disturbing was that hotel clerks were outraged that any sensible human being should simply step up to a hotel desk and expect a room!"

New Zealand was shocked by the reports of its friends. In the discussions that followed this seemed to be the common explanation: "Everyone's got it too easy. We've all got minimum wages, social security. Nobody gives a hang."

Actually, many thoughtful New Zealanders have known for a long time that their socialistic paradise wouldn't stand up under careful scrutiny. There is much that is truly wonderful in New Zealand, much that is third class. Only very had work will eliminate the latter.

The question then arises: "Who will do the work?" New Zealand is dangerously underpopulated. (World average 41 per square mile. United States 48. Japan 532. New Zealand 16.) Steps are being taken to increase immigration, but the fact that New Zealand is exclusively British means that only British immigrants are welcome. In Dunedin a committee facing this problem seriously passed the three following resolutions: (1) Our population lack is critical. Something must be done. (2) But since we are of British stock, only British immigrants should be sought. (3) And since Australia is so much worse off than we (less than three to the square mile) let's wait until they get all they need!

Tragically, of every hundred Englishmen who do arrive as immigrants, as many as forty go right back home. Their reasons: no houses to live in; the beer is too weak; we can't stand those dreadful New Zealand week-ends.

These latter are an astonishing phenomenon. Because of the forty-hour week, no stores of any kind—except fruit, candy, hot food—may open on Saturday. You cannot buy groceries, meat, milk, or bread. No haircuts, no doctor visits, no dentist, no shoes repaired. You can buy gasoline only in proved emergencies and then from only one station in each city. You also need an emergency to warrant sending a telegram after 12 noon. Telephone and train services are curtailed. Few restaurants are open. Life comes to a deathly standstill. The best description came from a workingman:

"We have two Sundays a week, except that on Saturday we have horse racing." The result of knocking two full days out of every week, plus working only about thirty-three hours out of the forty-hour week, is that economic production has inevitably deteriorated. It is quite possible that the social legislation of Seddon and Savage has reached the point of diminishing returns.

Yet I myself cannot wholly subscribe to the harsh criticisms of the British visitors. Life in New Zealand is wonderfully pleasant. Each home has a garden of glorious flowers. Evergreen trees abound and make the landscape lovely. The sea is always available and no home can be far from mountains and clear lakes. New Zealand food is superb, even if the cooking is apt to be pretty dreadful. There are, however, five unique delicacies: soup made from sautéed toheroa clams, pronounced by the Prince of Wales to be "the finest soup ever made," an understatement; grilled mutton bird, a baby sea fowl whose parents cram its rubber belly with so many fresh fish that it cannot move, so that when it is cooked it taste like chicken with a streak of trout; Colonial Goose, which is strong mutton sliced wafer thin and served with onion stuffing and an almost black gravy; the best little teacakes in the world; and whitebait. Gourmets can go into trances over a mess of fresh whitebait, pitched into a batter of whipped eggs with a touch of onion and fried into a thick, brown fritter.

The relaxation of life in New Zealand is appealing. In addition to the two Sundays there are frequent stops for tea, a willingness to yarn at any time, plus an unbounded hospitality. New Zealand children are kept in school uniforms till they are seventeen or eighteen on the theory that if a boy is in knee pants till that age he won't be in a hurry to mature into a criminal. The plan works, for the crime rate is low.

The care of children has always been a special New Zealand concern. In the late nineteenth century, Truby King, a childless doctor at a mental institution, became fascinated by his hobby of feeding pigs, on whom he developed scientific nutrition tables. After adopting a waif he found that his pig principles worked equally well on humans, and within a few years he had pioneered child-care centers under the direction of the Plunket Society, so named after the wife of a Governor-General. Later, young girls were encouraged to study child care and today Karitanes—named after the hill where Truby King worked—study for sixteen months the problem of "Helping the mother and saving the child." When a Karitane reports, and they are in great demand, she assumes sole charge of the child and soon she has it gurgling and fat. Karitanes are neither nurses nor servants. They usually marry young and make wonderful mothers. To them is given much credit for the fact that New Zealand babies are unusually healthy.

Actually, all young things seem to grow fabulously in this country. Animals have been brought here from all over the world, and because New Zealand had no natural predatory creatures, introduced animals have multiplied enormously. American deer increased so freely that now the Government must hire cullers who roam the valleys shooting does, whose carcasses are not even gathered. The rabbit is a national pest, having made deserts out of much of the South Island. Goats, pigs, opossums, sparrows, hawks and even wallabies (midget kangaroos) have all found New Zealand a bonanza and are now pests. Even plants run wild in this fertile land. Gorse was brought in to decorate gardens, and in a few years the magnificent yellow shrub was a national menace, engulfing whole fields like a sweeping golden flame.

But there was one introduction which has made New Zealand famous wherever sportsmen gather. The rainbow trout was brought down from Canada and the United States. Instantly it took to the cold, dashing rivers where no predators fed upon its young. Soon the famous game fish grew to gigantic size and New Zealand became known, quite properly, as the Sportsman's Paradise. To see this wonderland at its best you must stop a while at Alan Pye's Huka Lodge, at the northern end of Lake Taupo.

Here, beside the swift-flowing Waikato River near a gorge where waters roar between rocks, Pye has built a fisherman's retreat that can have few equals anywhere. In a homey lodge he serves remarkable meals: fresh chicken, trout for breakfast, all the eggs you can eat, steak, always two immense desserts with four pitchers of cream that has to be ladled out. Nearby a thermal spring pumps mildly sulphurous hot water into a deep pool walled off by evergreens so that fishermen and their wives can go bathing nude.

But the food and hot baths are not the attraction at Huka Lodge, for in the river and in Lake Taupo abound monstrous rainbows. The average fish caught at Pye's weighs about seven pounds, and each will feed four people. Above the fire are two mounted beauties that tipped the scales at more than 12, but Pye himself, a red-faced weather-bitten Irishman—all famous New Zealanders were born somewhere else—says,

"Those fish are not to be regarded. The champion picked out of this river was 26 pounds. And mark you, the flesh was firm. They aren't lazy, the New Zealand trout."

For years Pye has conducted a running feud with the Tongariro crowd upstream. They fish the legendary Tongariro River, termed "the most perfect reach of trout water ever known," where each pool bears a famous name: Vera's, Swirl, Nursing, Stump, Log and Mud. Pye used to insist that Tongariro trout were overrated, but in recent years he has said little, for evil luck has fallen upon the Tongariro pools.

To the west three great volcanoes have been throwing torrents of volcanic ash into the air, and prevailing winds have carried it across the river. Its effect upon the superlative Tongariro trout is unpredictable; for the present the fish have grown sluggish. The water near Pye's lodge is so far unaffected, but he does not gloat. For if the volcanoes continue to erupt, the ash could well destroy all the trout.

In the meantime, Pye provides near perfect fishing for $5 a day, all expenses covered. He also has a remarkable cottage which costs more and which provides the finest accommodation in New Zealand. He will not tell you how he happens to have such quarters, for he has not yet got over the shock of acquiring them.

It happened this way. About fifteen years ago a handsome United States naval officer became fascinated by the fishing at Pye's and prevailed upon Alan to lease a corner of land by the river. Here a super fishing lodge was built and decorated at princely expense. Year after year the young officer, now a full commander, came vacationing to try the trout. When war broke out he served with distinction as liaison with New Zealand forces.

Then peace came and with it the shocking news from New York! The handsome naval officer, this favored man, had been proved beyond doubt to be involved in a worldwide narcotics ring, to which he was himself a slave. By God's grace he died shortly after the story broke, and now his fishing lodge, more beautiful than ever, stands by the trout-filled Waikato, waiting for other fishermen.

I have known New Zealand in many weathers and I have served with its quiet men in most corners of the Pacific. I have never met people more deeply convinced than theirs in the one good land. But whenever I think I understand even slightly what makes this radical-conservative country tick, I am brought up sharp by some new experience. When I started to write this essay I went for one last look at a city I have grown to love: placid Christchurch with its English cathedral and terribly stuffy manner. Here on the broad plains of Canterbury I felt that I had come at last to the true meaning of New Zealand: English forever, reluctant to move ahead, confirmed in the defense of human dignity. Then I turned one more corner and stumbled upon the fastest-growing religion in conservative Christchurch. There it was! A store-front chapel with the pastor's Model T Ford parked outside and on the walls the mystical words: PEACE! PEACE! PEACE! FATHER DIVINE!

Until They Sail

> *New Zealand rushed the cream of her manhood into Africa and Crete; then watched helplessly as Japan crept down the islands.*

The last time the family ever met together was in August of 1939, when father returned to New Zealand for Barbara's wedding. He brought the *Nestor* into Wellington Harbor, where a great fuss was made over the British warship, for a spirit of great excitement then pervaded the country.

That very night he boarded the South Island ferry and experienced that vague and ancient delight of feeling the old boat pitch and toss upon the first waters he had ever sailed. A stranger approached him as he stood by the rail and said, "My apologies, sir. But aren't you Captain Harry Neville of Christchurch?"

Neville immediately stiffened to discourage familiarity and grunted that he was. The stranger slapped his arms together in the cold wintry breeze and asked, "Shall we be giving Jerry hell again?"

Captain Neville was not a tall man, but when he drew back his head in British Navy style and stared down his nose at the intruder, the latter could do nothing but apologize for his inquisitiveness and go below. His place, however, was taken almost immediately by a very thin woman who cried, "It's Captain Harry Neville! You home for Barbara's wedding?"

He ticked his braided visor and indicated that her guess was correct. The woman laughed and said, "I'll wager you've never met the young man. Let me assure you, Captain, he's a splendid type. Splendid."

She beamed at Neville, who against his will, relaxed and asked, "You know the boy?"

"Know him?" she echoed. "He's my nephew!"

With due modesty she assured the captain that Barbara's intended husband came from one of Christchurch's finest families. She said, "Mark's handsome, like his father. You wouldn't know his father, but he was my brother. Mark attended a very fine school." She dropped her voice modestly and added, "In England, you know." Then she asked apprehensively, "Surely, there won't be another war, will there?"

Captain Neville stared at her precisely as before and in

some confusion she left. For more than an hour he peered into the darkness of Cook Strait. He loved this turbulent water. Even its name was clean and simple. Had a good English ring. As a boy, upon this ferry, he had decided to strike for a commission in the Royal Navy. It would be difficult, he knew then, but he also knew that the best New Zealand men had always struck for the Navy, the real Navy that is, the Royal Navy out of London and Plymouth.

He had made it, an awkward little tow-headed youth from New Zealand competing with the best young men of England. Then, in the succeeding years, he had often returned to New Zealand, always to sail across Cook Strait to his home in Christchurch. It was on this ferry that he had heard of Anne's birth during First World War. Later, he had been chasing Count Luckner through the South Pacific when he got the leave during which his second child, Barbara, had been conceived. In years of peace he had often left his various commands to spend some time with his family at Christchurch, so that his wife teased him with a quiet joke. "Nine months after Harry's leave there's bound to be a new child."

"Navy tradition," he had growled. "Dammit, Sara, Englishmen have been serving at sea for centuries." They had named their first daughter Anne, after Harry's mother. The second child was Barbara after Sara's sister. Having started with the alphabet, Sara, who believed in omens, insisted that the third child be Christopher, the next Delia, and the baby Evelyn. At first this nonsense had offended Harry Neville, but on distant stations it helped him to keep the children straight, and during the night watch he could run down the family in order. Anne was his favorite, tall, serious, reserved. Barbara was the energetic one and it was appropriate that she should be the first to marry. Christopher was a good lad, but Harry never mentioned to his family the secret disappointment he felt in Kit. He had hoped the boy might follow him in the British Fleet, but Kit hadn't the ability. He wasn't stupid. Harry was first to insist that Kit wasn't stupid, but he wasn't top-flight either, and the home fleet could accept only the cream; so Christopher was now in the New Zealand Army, a ragtag and bobtail in Captain Harry's judgment. Next there was Delia . . . He always stopped at her name. She was the glorious beauty, but no one could ever be certain of Delia. She would be eighteen now, he figured, and vaguely he wished that it were Delia rather than Barbara who was being married, because everyone knew that Barbara could take care of herself. Then he broke into a quiet chuckle. Evelyn! Bright, happy, outspoken, born long after the others. Any father would be proud of such a child. He had last seen her as a pig-tailed girl of eight gravely telling him that Edward was now king and that every good Englishman owed strict allegiance to their new King Edward.

A seaman presented himself, saluted, and said that the ferry captain, hearing that Captain Harry Neville, R.N., was aboard, wished to extend the hospitality of the bridge. At first Neville was disposed to send his regrets, but he felt that as an officer of the Fleet he had certain obligations, so he drew his greatcoat about his shoulders and stamped up the ladder.

"Cap'n Neville," he mumbled, saluting.

The ferry captin was in no way obsequious. "Shall we be having trouble with the Boche?" he asked directly.

Now Neville felt himself to be talking with an equal. "Jerry's acting a bit stiff," he said cautiously. "Knows he can't whip us, but his aircraft might knock us about a bit."

"Very determined adversary, the Boche."

The two sea captains nodded sagely and then Neville excused himself and turned in. The morning was clean and fair. He hurried on deck to greet Littleton Harbor, a deep, winding volcanic cut in the side of a massive hill. It was, he thought, the best harbor he knew. The harbor of Christchurch.

In great excitement he piled his gear aboard a creaking train that tunneled through the hill to deliver the ferry passengers to Christchurch proper. When the whistle blew and the train actually started to move, Neville's excitement increased, for getting home in troubled times was very good, but when he finally stood before his family—all five children and sniffling Sara—he was as coldly erect as they had always remembered him.

Sedately he shook hands with his wife and then planted a kiss on the forehead of each of his four daughters. With a brisk snap he shook Christopher's hand and said, "I see you're in the Army."

His son laughed. "Hadn't brains enough to get into the so-called senior service."

Captain Neville froze to attention. He had always been repelled and offended by Army jokes against the Royal Navy. "I would be pleased," he said, "if you would not use that ridiculous phrase."

"Oh father!" Barbara protested. "Sometimes the Navy is a pain in the neck."

Captain Neville stared at his daughter. Less than a year later Barbara recalled this look when word reached Christchurch that Harry Neville's light cruiser *Nestor* had faced up to the *Graf Spee* and had driven the heavier German from the convoy routes. True, both the *Nestor* and its captain had been lost, but many navy letters reached Neville's family, and each said the same thing: "We who knew Harry never anticipated that he would do other than preserve the best traditions of his service."

His death was a terrible blow to his wife. Sara Neville had never been a strong woman, but she had been so dedicated to her husband that she had always conserved her energy for his infrequent visits. Then she blossomed into a gay sprite, chaffing him, idolizing him, drawing him out about his various exploits. But when he left she relapsed into pregnancy and invalidism.

It now became apparent to the family that she would never recover from her husband's death. The Nevilles lived in a modest cottage in Ferrymead, a suburb chosen because it overlooked a broad and salty estuary. When they were young, the children had gazed upon this arm of the sea, imagining that they were in contact with their father's ship. Now their mother sat day after day, staring vacantly at the ocean which had played so powerful a part in her life.

There was an extended family discussion as to whether Anne or Barbara should assume responsibility for the home at Ferrymead, but since Anne had a good job in a Christchurch store, it was decided that Barbara should become the mother, for although she was married she had no home of her own. Her husband had behaved as New Zealand men will. Shy, brave, morbidly attached to England where he had been educated, Mark Forbes had volunteered for duty on the day Germany marched into Poland, and now he served in Africa.

So his wife Barbara took over the cottage at Ferrymead and purchased a large map of Europe—plus the north coast of Africa—and on it she followed the fortunes of war, guessing at where Mark might be. They had known each other briefly, had lived together less than a month, and Barbara sometimes had a feeling of unreality as she placed a slender pin to represent a slender man she scarcely knew.

She had been housemother only a few months when Christopher, too, left New Zealand. At twenty he was a cocky, witty lad quite unlike his father. He astounded his sisters on his last night at home by leaning back with his feet on the ottoman and announcing, "Anne, when you quit work tomorrow I want you to walk along Colombo Street and assure all the sheilas that Kit'll be home before long."

Anne frowned and said, "That's a most beastly word, Kit."

"I agree," he laughed. "But all the same, you give the sheilas my message."

At the station when Christopher left, Anne said, "Now behave yourself, Kit. Remember that people will know you're Father's son."

"You remember to tell the sheilas!" Kit teased, and Anne sniffed in her handkerchief, whispering to Barbara that she was worried about Kit, he was so irreverent.

Barbara didn't worry about Kit. She worried about her older sister. Anne was twenty-six and knew no young men, preferred knowing none. That night Barbara wrote to Mark in Africa: "I'm sure no man can even understand how a girl feels when her older sister is determined to stay an old maid. Anne is one of the finest girls I've known. She was the one who saved me. As you pointed out, I have a beastly temper at times, but it would have been unbearable except for Anne's patient instruction. If I'm even fifty percent civilized it's because of her. That's why it hurts me terribly when I see her shutting up her life like a old house by the sea, closing it against a winter that might never end. Then I think of you, Mark, and of how you saved me from becoming such a person, and I am forever indebted. When I move your straight and very erect pin about at night, guessing where you are, I love you very, very much."

In the morning after this letter Barbara tried to discuss with Anne this problem of getting married, but Anne blushed deeply and said she would have thought that Barbara would have had other things to worry about. This rebuff, and others, made Barbara wonder if Anne were deficient in emotion, but this likelihood was dispelled when news arrived of Christopher's death at Narvik, in Norway. Barbara was not at home when the telegram arrived, and the full brunt of it fell upon Anne.

She guessed at once that either Kit or Mark had been killed and for a moment she held the message in her hand. Then, with a deep breath, she ripped it open and devoured the contents in a glance. Quickly, as if caught spying on death, she refolded the telegram and pressed it back into shape. Young Kit was dead. The sheilas on Colombo Street should know of this. Everyone in Ferrymead should know that happy young Kit was dead.

Carefully she stuffed the telegram into her pocket and then dressed for the street. Barbara met her at the door and said brightly, "Where you off to, darling? Before you go, help me with these packages." Then, seeing the dull look in her sister's eyes she asked, "Anne! What's the matter? Is it Mother?"

She dropped her packages and dashed into the front room where she saw with relief that her mother was still staring at the estuary. "Afternoon, my darling!" Barbara whispered, patting her mother's white hands.

"Hello Anne," the wandering woman said in a very tired voice. She could no longer differentiate among her children.

"I was afraid you were ill," Barbara said.

"I'm all right."

Relieved, Barbara returned to the kitchen, but there she saw Anne staring at her from the doorway, the scattered packages still on the floor. "What is it, Anne?" she cried.

Anne took the telegram from her pocket and carried it, like a ghost, to the kitchen table. She let it fall and then sank into a chair. "It's Kit," she mumbled. "He's dead."

Barbara unfolded the message with shaking hands and read it twice. She put her hand to her forehead and muttered, "Narvik? Narvik? We hadn't even a pin at Narvik." She went to her map and searched vainly for the unknown name. "It's not on the map," she said.

At this time Anne began to cry, asking, "What does it matter where they die? They'll all die in some horrible lost village."

"Oh Anne! Please!"

"It's all right with you, Barbara. You don't seem to have any feelings."

"Darling!" Barbara cried, falling to her knees beside her striken sister. "I lie awake at night and pray. I know what terror is. I've prayed for Father and Kit."

"And one by one," Anne sobbed. "One by one they'll be lost. What is this meaningless business about?"

"You've got to have faith that there is meaning to it," Barbara whispered.

"Why? How? Our men running off to die in Norway and Africa ..." She stopped and looked up in horror. "Oh, Barbara! Forgive me. I'm sick with fear."

"We have a right to go on hoping that there is meaning to it," Barbara said, hiding even in her own mind the word Africa. "Have you told Mother?"

"No," Anne said. "Will you tell the others?"

Barbara said that she would, and forthwith started to get supper. She found this kitchen, with its warm and cheery fire, its table soiled with much use, a comforting place to be in time of death. There had been much life and goodness in this kitchen, and she had grown to understand why women came to look upon the least attractive room in their home as home itself. "Please God," she whispered to herself as she worked, "let me have a kitchen like this some day with Mark." Immediately she shivered as she thought of telling Delia and Evelyn about Kit's death.

But when Delia burst into the kitchen, with a fine happy grin there was no thought of death. "It's happened!" she cried.

"What has?" Barbara asked, lighting a burner for tea.

"I'm engaged!" Delia shouted, twirling about the room. She stopped suddenly and asked, "Isn't anyone pleased? What's the matter with you two?"

Quickly Barbara caught up the telegram and said, "We're delighted, Deel. Aren't we, Anne? But who's the ..." She stopped, embarrassed that she should have to ask the name of the man to whom her own sister had become engaged. "Who's the lucky man?" she asked weakly.

Delia sensed the impropriety of her announcement and stuck out her thin, firm chin. Raising her blonde head defiantly she said, "Cobber Phil, who else?"

Anne gasped, but Barbara promptly covered the insult by crying, "Cobber Phil! He'll be a jolly sort to have about the house."

But not even Barbara could force any real enthusiasm into her congratulations. She knew Cobber Phil, an uncouth, unwashed, very un-English young man who had knocked about Australia a bit—whence his name—picking up the worst color of that strange land but none of its character. No one liked Cobber Phil, except possibly Delia, and if Captain Harry had lived or if Sara Neville were in possession of her mind, a man like the Cobber would never have been permitted to enter the house. But war had denuded New Zealand of decent men, and Barbara said, "Cobber's a jolly sort."

Then followed a cruel, silent moment during which each sister in the kitchen understood exactly what the other felt. Barbara, sensing this to be a critical moment in Delia's life within the family, laughed and said, "We're happy for you, Deel. When will you be married?"

It seemed, for a moment, as if this easy question would permit Delia to swing back into normal small talk about the wedding, but Anne broke the spell by asking acidly, "Yes, when will the marriage be?"

Delia flushed and snapped at her critical sister, "What's bothering you, Anne? You parading the fact you hate men? I don't."

"I know you don't," Anne said, adding unfairly, "and the only thing wrong with me is that Kit's dead."

Delia stared at Anne for a shocked second and then held out her hands to Barbara. "I've been so afraid about Kit. Ever since Father . . ."

She sat down dazedly and brushed her hair back from her forehead. "What shall we do about Evelyn?" she asked.

On the spur of the moment Barbara said, "You'd better tell her, Deel. You're closer to her than we are."

So when Evelyn, then twelve, came up the steps, Barbara led Anne from the kitchen. They could hear the little girl crying and Anne said, "I don't like leaving Evelyn with Delia."

"Why not?"

"The less Deel has to do with the child the better."

"I agree," Barbara said. "But Delia needs us very much right now."

"There's no good worrying about Delia," Anne said. "She's lost."

"Oh, Anne! How rotten! Even to think that."

"Wait," Anne said. "You'll see."

To her surprise Barbara caught Anne by the shoulders and whispered harshly, "Look here! Delia is going to be married in this house. You and I are going to be nice to Cobber Phil and make him think he's one of us. It's our only chance to save Delia . . . from . . . well, from becoming a very unpleasant person."

It was hard for the Nevilles to stomach Cobber Phil. He sucked his teeth, laughed at his own stories and called Anne "old girl." He was the kind of New Zealander who made the girls regret their ancestors had left England. With no knowledge of English ways and no command of the English tongue, he leaned back in Captain Neville's old chair, plopped his feet on the ottoman and offered free advice to Lord Wavell as to the conduct of desert warfare.

Now even euphemisms were surrendered. Anne stormed one night after Cobber Phil had advised her how to knit socks, "The only reason I tolerate that boor, Barbara, is to keep my sister off the streets." This time Barbara did not argue back.

There was considerable relief, therefore, when Cobber Phil was drafted and sent to garrison duty in Singapore. "A fine spot for him," Anne said when the ferry had left. "He's so far from the fighting he can't do anybody any harm." She did, however, comment on a fact that she was sure Barbara, too, had noticed. Delia seemed to be as pleased as the rest that her husband was finally off to war.

As a gesture Anne brought home a cheap little map of the Pacific and a very bright red pin which indicated the Cobber in Singapore. He sent illiterate letters reporting that "the Chinese girls who came down from Shanghai are very immortal." Delia laughed and said, "That Cobber!" She said she was happy he'd drawn Singapore instead of Africa.

For it was now that the New Zealand armies started the great oscillating battle across the desert. The pins in Barbara's map moved with sickening speed toward Alexandria, then with bounding fervor back toward Tobruk, and in one such surging battle Mark Forbes was killed.

When the news reached Ferrymead, Barbara was half-alerted for it, but she found that no one could be totally brave when such information was afoot. It was, actually, more than she could bear. At first she tried behaving normally with her sisters, but it was no use. She threw her hands over her eyes and cried, "I hardly knew him." Her grief embarrassed Anne, who excused herself and went back to the store. It was Delia who took over. She led Barbara to a sofa and covered her with an afghan. Then she sent Evelyn to school and returned to kneel by her sister.

"You'd better get to your job," Barbara warned.

"I'm chucking the job," Delia said, straightening the afghan.

"You're what?"

"Don't get excited, Babs. It's just that Christchurch ... It seems so awful."

"I know."

"The men all away. Dying in places you've never heard of."

"It's all for a purpose," Barbara insisted. "Daddy was no fool." She paused and added, "Neither was Kit ... nor Mark."

"Did you lie awake at night ... wondering?"

"Of course I did, Deel!"

"You never liked Cobber Phil much, did you? I mean you and Anne?"

"We didn't know him well," Barbara evaded.

"I didn't know him, either. Lately I've discovered that I hardly feel married at all."

Barbara was frightened. Quickly she said, "When Cobber comes home all that will change. He'll live here with us . . ."

"He'll have to," Delia confessed. "He'll never keep a job very long."

"That's all right!" Barbara insisted. "He's a lot of fun. And the family's got to stick together." She held Delia's delicately beautiful head in her arms, and for a moment the two girls recaptured the old fellowship they had known as youngsters, when they sailed small boats on the estuary while Anne stood on shore nervously predicting catastrophe.

Delia said, "You were right. I see it now. Cobber Phil's a ridiculous man. How could I ever have married him?"

Barbara asked, "Are you taking a new job?"

"Yes."

"Doing what?"

"I'm going to Wellington. The Navy Office."

"But Deel! Wellington! Why?"

"Because I can't bear Christchurch another day."

"Darling, listen carefully. It's when times are bad that we must stick with our friends. It's not a good idea . . . you in Wellington . . . alone."

"Pretty soon the Manpower Commission is going to freeze us in our jobs. I won't be frozen in Christchurch. I won't!"

Barbara rose on one elbow and placed her arm about Deel. "What has happened?" she asked soberly.

Delia started to cry into the crook of her sister's arm. "You wouldn't understand. It's the terrible loneliness of Christchurch. Of all New Zealand. A country without men. You walk down Colombo Street after tea. All women. Nothing but Kit's sheilas. It's like suspending life for two years. And it'll go on and on."

Barbara relaxed her hold and sank back upon the sofa. What Deel had said was true. A nation without men. They had slipped away quietly at first, the professionals like her father, then the willing young heroes like her brother, next the gallant ones like Mark, and finally even the ne'er-do wells like Cobber Phil. They had been sucked out of the valleys and the seaports, leaving behind a civilization that was ugly and barren. It was a brave civilization—chin up, old girl— but it was barren.

266

Barbara contemplated her next remark for a long time. It might sever Delia from the family permanently. On the other hand, it might be just the word of caution that would save the girl. "Deel," she said cautiously, "I think you're going to Wellington because there'll be men there. Deel, you're terribly attractive. Do be careful, darling."

Delia rose from the floor, brushed off her dress and said nothing. She was twenty, not so tall as Anne, nor so rounded as Barbara. She had naturally blonde hair which she wore short about her exquisitely molded head. Her very thin lips were parted in a hesitant smile which showed her very white teeth. But Barbara noticed only how translucent Delia's skin was, how perilously near the surface her blood vessels were. Impulsively Barbara rose from the sofa and embraced her sister. "Deel," she whispered, "do be careful. With so many of us dead, you are the one person left . . ."

But before Delia could escape Christchurch the entire Pacific exploded with the terrifying abruptness of Pearl Harbor. At first there was a flush of joy when it was realized that at last America had to join the battle, assuring ultimate victory. But this elation changed to a cold and creeping fear when it became apparent that Japan was going to conquer, almost unopposed, the islands north of New Zealand. Day by day, with horrible speed, like a spider dashing down upon its prey, the Japanese swept south, almost to the gates of New Zealand.

Singapore fell, and word crept home that thousands of men had been slaughtered or forced into jungle labor gangs where they died without medicine. The Government officially informed Delia that Cobber Phil was missing.

Anne said, "Most missing men . . . that is, if they aren't at sea . . . Well, anyway, most missing men turn up safe, Deel."

Barbara, who knew that Cobber's disappearance might be a boon to her sister, elected to say nothing, but then was astonished at her callousness and said, "I think Cobber will be all right. I think he'll be back here with us some day."

There now seemed to be always that aching pain in the kitchen at Ferrymead as the Japs came closer and closer. There was a special agony in New Zealand at this time because of the fact that her defenselessness had been caused by her own gallantry. Captain Harry Neville's *Nestor* might have helped oppose the Jap fleet, but it had sunk in the South Atlantic, protecting England. Mark Forbes might have helped defend Auckland, but he had died in the desert defending Alexandria. Kit was dead in Norway and even the Cobber

267

was lost in Singapore, defending God knows what. At home there was nothing. Nothing.

The days of that dreadful autumn were rainy, cold and dismal. Barbara tried her best—in the house of five women and no men—to keep spirits alive. She baked special goodies for their teas, instituted a program of reading each night at least four poems from *The Oxford Book of English Verse,* but the love lyrics were so lacerating to the heart that by common consent this was stopped. And week by week the Japs came closer.

The great tenseness of the time was broken by Delia's abrupt departure for Wellington. She did not even bid her sisters good-bye, but fled the lonely cottage by the estuary.

And then titanic hope burst like a mighty spring flower all across New Zealand. The first Marine Division landed from America, and with it came astonishing stores of equipment, superb young men, and hope.

There had been in the entire history of the world nothing quite like this. To be sure, supporting armies had often landed on allied lands to help local forces, but never before had a strange army come to take the place of every available man. Never before had all the military population of a nation gone off to blazing foreign fields in support of a friend, only to have the enemy sneak down upon the undefended homeland.

An impassioned sigh of deliverance went up from New Zealand. They saw in the powerful and handsome First-MarDiv the flower of American strength, comparable to the acme of New Zealand strength that had been the first to leave for Africa. It was always the finest men who left home in time of war, and New Zealand recognized this fact.

The Neville girls would never forget their first sight of the Americans. Evelyn, then fourteen and an increasingly lovely child, came bursting into the kitchen screaming, "You should see them!"

"Who?" Barbara asked quietly.

"The Yanks!"

Instinctively there was a catch in Barbara's throat. Then, prosaically, she said, "Well it's about time. They've been about it long enough."

The two girls bundled their mother up so her feet would not freeze and then they slipped off to the city, where they found a convoy of military trucks in the central square. Lounging upon them were the tallest, cleanest-teethed, smilingest men Barbara had ever seen. Against her will tears came into her eyes and Evelyn teased, "You silly! What are you crying for? I think they're cute!"

This chance remark was Barbara's first warning. And when she looked up from drying her eyes to find that one of the Americans was making signs to Evelyn, she whisked her sister home and said, "Look here, young lady. There'll be no making signs at soldiers." Evelyn laughed at the warning but nevertheless appeared in the kitchen some time later with the startling news: "Four girls in Ferrymead are pregnant."

"Evelyn! Where'd you pick up such language?"

"They're pregnant," Evelyn replied. "Do you suppose they'll marry the Yanks?"

"No," Barbara said simply. "That's what so terrible about war, Evelyn. They don't usually marry."

Articles of complaint began to appear in the newspapers concerning the conduct of the American troops and one night Anne came home flushed and trembling. "A great oaf! Couldn't even speak the language. Pestered me in the store and then grabbed me as I was leaving. Leered at me and said, 'You and me would be terrific in the hay, baby.' I'm going to call the police!"

"Please, Anne. This is war."

"That's no excuse."

"No, it isn't an excuse. But it is an explanation."

"Barbara! Are you condoning these barbarians? Do you think New Zealand men are behaving like that in London?"

"Yes," Barbara said firmly. "In a different way, perhaps, but yes."

Anne's disgust with the Americans became complete when word trickled back to Ferrymead that Delia was living with a Marine in Wellington, and soon Barbara became aware that a shocking change had taken place in New Zealand life. Daughters of impeccable families began to contract strange alliances with American soldiers. For more than thirty months there had been no men in the land, and here were dashing young fellows with free and easy ways and plenty of money. It was indeed more than average human beings could tolerate. Anne heard from a friend in Auckland that the New Zealand Government had made an arrangement with the American generals whereby mothers of illegitimate children would be paid allowances deducted officially from the father's military pay. This callous decision shocked the nation and some older men even banded together and administered thrashings to individual Americans.

One night Anne said, "That delightful Kennery girl is going

269

to have a baby. The world I know seems to be vanishing. Just a little while ago Daddy and Mums and all of us were a unit. Now the whole fiber of the nation is disintegrating. I wish the Americans would leave and never return."

And then, just as Anne's antagonism threatened to become general, the Americans did leave. They headed north to a jungled island that would soon acquire an immortal connotation both in America and New Zealand: Guadalcanal.

There were few households in either the North or the South Island that did not know some American boy who now fought on that desolate island. When the casualties were posted they were read, sometimes, more eagerly in Auckland and Wellington than they were in New York or Dallas. Then, as the Yanks secured their foothold on Guadalcanal, the second American invasion of New Zealand began. In many ways it was worse than the first, for it was deeply emotional, more hopelessly confused.

From the feverish jungles of Guadalcanal, where there were no remedies for malaria, the sick and wounded were evacuated to New Zealand. Flyers who had been boldly aloft for five times the prescribed numbers of hours limped down to Wellington for rest and recuperation. To Christchurch and the cold valleys of the south came Americans who were simply worn out.

They bought with them an intolerable arrogance. Having fought a very dangerous war, they were sure no other soldiers from countries like New Zealand had ever done so. In bars they shouted, "You ought to be goddamned thankful we saved this godforsaken wreck of a country. Where were your men?" And from the jungles came Americans who had seen no woman for three months. They met New Zealand girls who had seen no men for three years, and if the girls were happy to see strangers who had saved the country from Japan, they were known as pigs. Bright, confused and hungry girls like Delia were pigs.

The burden of these insults fell very heavily on Anne. Americans would come in to buy underwear at one of her counters and they would say, "I want something frilly for my pig about this broad." Then they would poke their fingers through the imitation silk and complain, "Why in the States you'd pay maybe twenty cents for junk like this." At first Anne tried to explain that for nearly four years her country had been at war, that everything had been sent to England; but she stopped when the Americans asked, "Why should you send stuff to England? Why should you knuckle down to their king? Don't you New Zealanders have any guts?"

Anne therefore felt a surge of patriotic joy when news reached Ferrymead that Cobber Phil was living. A prisoner in Malaya, he scrawled a naïve letter which he had smuggled through the lines: "Im all right. Left leg gone. No pain. Beat the yella bastids. Youre Cobber."

She said, "I'm going to take this to Delia. I'm fed up with Christchurch right now. Too many Yankee heroes."

She left on the ferry one stormy night and was feeling battered about when she checked in at Delia's hotel. She found the Prince George crowded with important-looking Americans and considered, for a moment, leaving, but instead she went up to Delia's room.

It was quite unlike any Anne had seen in the stuffy Christchurch hotels. It was big and clean and modern, decorated in light colors. Delia was dressed in excellent new clothes and wore her hair long, with a ribbon in back.

The girls embraced with nervous uncertainty and Delia started to comb her hair. "Are you visiting in Wellington?" she asked casually, sitting on a big double bed which dominated the room.

"No. I brought some news."

"For me?" Delia asked suspiciously.

"Yes."

"From Singapore?"

"Yes."

"Cobber! He's alive!"

"Yes. Lost his left leg, but he's alive."

"Thank God!" the younger girl cried. "He's a strange little guy, Anne, and you never liked him . . ."

"I'm growing to understand him," Anne said quickly.

"I've prayed for that crazy little man every night," Delia said.

"Cobber's not so little," Anne protested.

"Compared to the Yanks, he is."

Anne sucked in her breath and went to the window. "We were thinking . . . Barbara and I, that is . . . We were thinking that now you might want to come home."

"I can't," Delia said.

"But what about Cobber?"

"I think Cobber'd understand," Delia said nervously.

"God, Deel! What's happened to you?"

"I don't think you would understand, Anne."

The older girl felt dizzy and sat in an expensive armchair.

She pressed her forehead to control herself and then said slowly, "You don't seem like the same girl, Deel. I've never told Barbara, but word's come to Christchurch that you've been living with Americans. Not just one. Different ones . . ."

Delia rose from the bed and paced the room, clutching at her own shoulders. "It's impossible to understand—for you, that is. But please try, because I love you and Barbara very much. I'm only twenty-two. Cobber's been away—how long? He'll stay away God only knows how much longer. I know you don't like Americans. They're not English and all that. But I would crawl on my knees to get to America—with almost any one of them."

"Delia! You mustn't . . ."

"But I'm married and they're going off to the islands. We see one another until they sail."

Anne was shaken by Delia's hopeless confession. "You must be careful, Deel. Won't you please come home with me?"

"No."

Anne was about to deliver some kind of ultimatum when the door banged open and a tall, broad-shouldered man burst into the room shouting, "Hiya, Baby! Poppa's back!"

Delia, forgetting Anne, dashed across the room and leaped into his arms. "Andy! You made it!" And she kissed him on the eyes and lips.

"Made it?" the stranger shouted. "I told the commandant he could damned well . . ." He saw Anne and stopped. "Who's the queen?"

"Oh, this is my sister. Anne, this is Andy."

The American dropped Delia on the bed as if she were a toy doll. He cocked his hands on his hips and studied Anne. "Deel said she had a sister, but she didn't say the sister was a goddess. Divinely tall et cetera."

Delia laughed and said, "Don't believe anything this galoot says."

"Galoot?" Anne asked.

"That's Yank for cobber."

The American grabbed Anne by the arm and said, "This cobber insists you have lunch with us." Then he stopped and studied a moment. "Whaddaya think, Deel? Safe to take a Queen like this down among them wolves?"

"I think," said Deel, "it's the only way we'll get to that J.P.B. officers' club."

"What do you mean?" Anne asked.

"The J.P.B. has everything sewed up in Wellington," Deel

explained. "Maybe one of the chairborne heroes will ask you to visit their club."

"What's the J.P.B ?" Anne asked.

As they picked their way through the crowded dining room Andy looked sourly at the array of handsome, polished, important-looking American officers who filled the tables and whispered, "That's the J.P.B. Joint Purchasing Board. They buy everything that's edible for the troops up north. They are Mister God."

When they were seated Delia said, "They're the desk soldiers. Andy's a fighting man, so they don't like him much."

But this time Andy seemed quite attractive to the J.P.B. men. One after another spoke overeffusively to him and finally, as he had anticipated, a particularly suave and well-fed J.P.B. man sat casually at the table and said, "Good old Andy! When are you chaps pushing out? I don't believe I've met this young lady before."

Andy said, "This is Miss Anne Neville, of Christchurch."

"Lovely city, Christchurch!" the J.P.B. man said. "Most attractive in New Zealand, I think. I stayed there when I was buying potatoes at Timaru. I especially liked the square. Say! Why don't you three have lunch with me?"

He led them to a special J.P.B. section, where the food was better and where ration books were not needed. "Call me Bill," he said.

Delia came directly to the point. "I was hoping to show my sister the officers' club."

"Why not?" the J.P.B. man assured them. "In fact, I've been working too hard lately and I was planning to take the afternoon off. How'd you like to tour the city with me?"

Out on the street the J.P.B. man whistled and an enlisted Marine drove up with a polished Buick. Bill said the man could have the day off, he'd drive. Then, to Anne's surprise, he held the car door open until she got in. This had never happened to her before. Ill at ease in a car with left-hand drive, she started on her tour of the city. Once she looked into the mirror and saw Delia, with tears in her eyes, staring at the American who rode beside her. They were pathetically in love and she looked straight ahead.

"Our work is pretty grueling," the J.P.B. man said. "Contact with the public all day long. True, we get three pounds a day to live on . . ."

"You mean one man gets three pounds a day?" Anne gasped.

"Yes. But we have to buy many more things out of that.

And then the gooks try to ..." He stopped abruptly. "I'm sorry, Miss Neville. I apologize for using that word. You see, I work with the dockhands sometimes ..."

At tea time he pulled the Buick up at the slick club, where it became apparent why the J.P.B. men needed so much money. There were slot machines, all kinds of drinks and expensive gifts for girls. "This is for you!" Bill said, giving Anne a carton of American cigarettes. When she refused them he said, "We get them for practically nothing. A deal we have on."

After tea he turned on the juke box and carefully held her chair while she rose. She could never remember having seen a New Zealander do that for a girl, and when they got back to the Prince George a bellboy arrived with a bouquet of roses, the first flowers she had ever received. The card read, "Roses for a lady who doesn't need them. Bill."

At dinner, Anne, somewhat breathless, noticed the J.P.B. men carefully. They were polished men, not like the boors she had met in the store at Christchurch. They wore spotless uniforms, highly polished shoes and clean smiles. She particularly noticed that they didn't speak in loud voices. But as Bill returned to the street to signal for the Buick, two Maoris became confused. One stopped to let Bill pass, but the other kept moving and had no choice but to bump ever so slightly into Delia.

Instinctively, like an infuriated animal, Bill shot out his right fist and knocked the offending Maori down. "Don't knock into white girls, you damned nigger!" he cried.

When she got back to Christchurch Anne could not explain exactly what had happened next. "All I recall is that suddenly thirty or forty New Zealanders . . . Barbara, I was never so proud of New Zealanders in my life. One of them shouted, 'You'll not call our Maoris niggers!' There was a terrible fight."

"What happened?"

"I think my J.P.B. man would have got away. But I tripped him!"

"Cheers! Then what?"

"Then you'd have been surprised. Oh, Barbara." She bit her lip and started twice to explain. Finally she sat down and said, "Suddenly I was sorry. I was so terribly, horribly sorry for Deel."

"For Delia?"

"Yes. Poor little Deel. Because in the morning her Marine sailed. They had known he was going but they didn't tell me.

He had taken a big risk to get away from camp. It was to have been a perfect dance, one last night."

"What did he do?"

"What could he do? He jumped into the fight and helped the other American."

"What happened?"

"The military police arrested him. He was taken back to camp for discipline. Deel never saw him again."

Barbara sighed and poured her sister a fresh cup of tea. "I thought you were going up to Wellington to give little Deel the devil."

"I don't know what's happening any more, Barbara. Deel and her American were pathetically happy together. And I wrecked their last night. That's all I know."

She also knew that she was scathingly angry about how the J.P.B. man had treated the two Maoris, and when she finished reporting to Barbara she sat down and wrote a bitter letter denouncing such behavior and sent it to the Christchurch paper. She said she hoped that for the good name of her country, every New Zealander would publicly rebuff any Americans who tried to introduce race discrimination. Her letter had a surprising result.

Early next morning an olive-drab staff car stopped before the cottage and a young Marine lieutenant inquired for Miss Anne Neville. He doffed his cap, bowed and said, "I've come from Headquarters . . . to apologize on behalf of the Marine Corps."

"What for?" Anne asked. "Come in."

"Your letter. In the paper. The General was outraged. See." He handed Anne a mimeographed notice which began, *"Yesterday a New Zealand citizen complained with reason, of American behavior on a delicate and important subject."*

The young man said, "It's been distributed to all units, Miss Neville. It's an order."

"What is?"

He showed her: *"If any further instances occur of disrespect to Maoris, severe disciplinary action will follow."*

He coughed nervously and said, "Actually, America appreciates deeply the courtesies your country has extended us. We know our intrusion is bound to cause minor frictions. We regret that, indeed we do."

"Thank you," Anne said. "Thank you very much."

"The General wanted to know if you wished to make a specific complaint."

"No. I've forgotten it."

"I'm glad, because if you named names the General would just about massacre them."

"I don't want that. I wrote in anger, but it's all over now."

"I'm really glad, because I can appreciate your resentment better than some. I was educated in England. New Zealand is very much like England."

"You were?" Anne cried. "Oh Barbara! The lieutenant says he was educated in England!"

Barbara stopped her work with the dishes and sat with her sister. "Anne and I were educated there too," she said. "Father always said a naval officer didn't make enough to live on, but he'd see we went Home for schooling."

"I knew some splendid New Zealanders at Oxford," the American said.

"Were you a Rhodes Scholar?" Anne asked.

"Yes. I live in Oklahoma and the competition wasn't too keen there."

"You went to Oxford!" Anne repeated. "Barbara, let's have some tea!"

"Oh!" Barbara cried. "Look at the clock!"

"Have I been keeping you?" the lieutenant asked.

"Gracious! I'm late!"

"Could I drive you . . ."

The next two months were like an aching, lovely dream. During every free hour Anne Neville and Richard Bates were together. He spoke endlessly of his days at Oxford and she queried him about out-of-the way towns she had visited on her lengthy visit Home. Once she said, "My memories of Home are very persistent, but I have never felt that my life would be as meaningful in England as it is here." He laughed and said, "It's the same with me. I prized Oxford but it was Oklahoma I really loved."

His effect on the cottage at Ferrymead was electric. He took most of his meals there, and the three girls were delighted to have a man to care for, and a very decent man at that. Evelyn brought him the paper. Barbara fed him too much food, and Anne ransacked the cellar for odd books he might like to see. In the evenings they often sat together, the four of them, with Mrs. Neville in her own mysterious corner, talking and having a rare time. Frequently he took Anne to some military dance or other and late one night Evelyn jumped into bed with Barbara and poked her in the ribs.

"Babs!" the youngster cried. "You'd never believe it!"

"Believe what?" Barbara asked sleepily.

"Iceberg Annie! She's out front necking her head off."

276

"Of course I believe it!" Barbara said sharply. "Now get to bed."

"I think it's wonderful!" Evelyn said. "Our Annie and an American!"

"Get out of here!" But when the child left, Barbara crept to the window. Below, in the staff car, she could see Anne in an evening dress, kissing and talking and talking and kissing. Barbara thought it was very appropriate, very warm and appropriate.

During the next few days Evelyn turned the conversation constantly to love. What did Lieutenant Bates think of all the marriages that were taking place in New Zealand? Did Lieutenant Bates see the story about the Wellington girl who had taken one look at her husband's home in California and hurried right back to New Zealand? Finally the American pushed his chair back from the tea table and said, "I was going to ask Barbara if it would be all right for me to marry Anne. But you seem to be the most concerned. Have I your permission?"

"You bet!" Evelyn cried.

Barbara, acting as mother, asked when Richard thought the marriage should take place. He said he'd have to get special permission from Admiral Halsey, but that such permission was being granted to Marines who might be sailing north.

The next days had an autumnal beauty about them. Bates spent most of his time at the cottage, and the three sisters accepted him as a member of the family, as if he were already married. Once he asked Barbara if she would like him to bring along a Marine who might like to meet her. She said no, explaining that she did not yet feel like a woman again. "I'm sort of an ageless mother. Or a new bride. I keep thinking that my husband is going to return at any moment." She added, "It's very curious what war does."

"I know," Bates said. "Before I met you and Anne I had fallen into the habit of calling everyone here a gook. I could never have done that in peace time."

"When are you going to marry the gook?" Evelyn asked.

"Halsey hasn't acted upon my request," the Marine replied, "but it ought to be soon."

But before the wedding could take place the FirstMarDiv shipped out. They left, Anne thought, willingly and yet with a premonition of catastrophe. They were in the bars and movies on Wednesday. But by Thursday morning the ships had quietly sailed.

Then followed days of silent waiting, breathless expectation before the radio, during which Anne was several times inspired to talk frankly with Barbara, telling her of scorching fears; but there had always been something about the Neville family that forbade the sharing of secrets, and now Anne wondered if that was not the reason for her mother's sitting dumbly in the rocking chair. Once she came perilously close to honest talk when she said to Barbara, "There's a lot wrong with our stiff British conventions. I'm rather glad I'm going to marry an easygoing American."

But when the name of the island to which Bates had gone was announced, Tarawa, she had an instant intuition that she would never marry him. When the first enormous casualties were announced—totals only, not names—a ghastly pall settled over many New Zealand families and more than a hundred excellent young women like Anne Neville, whose marriages had been delayed by the red tape of war, broke down wherever they were and went sobbing to their sisters or fathers or mothers.

Anne said dully, "I'm going to have a baby."

Barbara continued washing dishes and said, "I think Dick'll come through all right."

Anne said, "We both knew the ships were sailing soon. Some other island."

Barbara stopped her work and said, "Darling! You don't have to justify yourself to me."

Anne said, "I had a strange thought. I was glad that Mother wouldn't be able to know. Everything has changed so much."

Barbara laughed. "You underestimate Mother. She knew what war was. One after another."

Anne said, "What should we do if Dick doesn't get back?"

Barbara said, "He will. It would be unfair if this family lost anyone else."

As in a hundred similar homes, Anne said, "I'll have the baby. Right here if you'll let me."

Barbara laughed again. "Let you! Whose home do you think it is?"

Anne laughed and said, "You do all the dishes."

Then followed a curious barbarism of war. In anxious America the names of the dead Marines on Tarawa were rushed onto the front pages of village newspapers. There the pictures of dead heroes were displayed in a kind of public agony; and many small towns that had predicted nothing but disaster for some young no-good now proudly published his picture and nobody in the entire town gave a damn, except that it made their village important for a day.

But in New Zealand, where the Marines were intimately a part of the population, the notice of death did not arrive, for it was unprecedented to hold that any soldier could have owed allegiance to two different nations. So Anne Neville lived a desperate fear, afraid to call the American headquarters, for she was not married to her Marine.

She received an ugly fright one morning when an American staff car pulled up at the cottage. A major in his middle thirties, pompous and plump, knocked at the door and announced himself as Major Harding. "Is Miss Anne Neville at home?"

Anne, in whom pregnancy had started in earnest, felt faint and was unable to speak, but Barbara, standing beside her, said, "This is my sister. She's Anne Neville."

With extraordinary politeness the major found two chairs. Then, sitting very straight on a third, he said, "You must take this interview very seriously. A great deal depends upon this interview."

"Please!" Barbara said. "What is this all about?"

Ignoring Barbara the major stared at Anne and asked, "Your age?"

"She's thirty," Barbara said.

"Please!" the major said stiffly. "Would Miss Anne Neville please reply? Born?"

"Ferrymead," Barbara responded.

The major carefully placed his pen in his notebook and said, "The record must be precise. And in your sister's own words. Otherwise we shall be able to do nothing for her. Your father living?"

"No," Anne said cautiously.

"His occupation when living?"

"A captain!" Barbara exploded. "A captain in the Royal Navy!"

The major wrote rapidly. "That is important! That's going to help a great deal. Your religion?"

"Church of England," Anne said.

"I guess that's what we call Episcopalian," the major said. "I'm Baptist, myself. You girls lived here for some time?"

"Thirty years," Barbara snapped.

"Ever been in jail?"

"No!"

"Look, Miss Neville. I don't like this any more than you

do. Besides, I'm asking your sister. Would your minister be willing to swear that you were of good Christian reputation?"

"Yes," Anne said quietly.

The major sighed and smiled at the sisters. "That's that. Dreadful questions, but I'm going to break a confidence and say right out that you're as good as married."

"What do you mean?" Anne asked.

"Miss Neville!" the major said, rising and extending his hand, "in ten minutes I'm going to cable Noumea and recommend, without qualification, your marriage to Lieutenant Bates. And in the meantime the American Government wants to give you this present."

Anne unfolded the parcel and read the book's title: *W.P.A. Guide to Oklahoma.* "What's this?" she asked.

"If you're going to live in Oklahoma, we want you to learn about it first. So you'll be prepared when you get there. And tomorrow night you're invited to the Young Eagles Club."

"The what?" Barbara asked.

But the major was already in his good-bye spiel. "I think America is very lucky, getting a fine good-looking girl like you. Yes, sir, rules or no rules, I'm telling you now, you're practically an American, Miss Neville!"

"Then maybe you could help us?" Barbara asked hesitatingly.

"At your service! Once you pass the investigation we'll do anything within reason. We want you to like America."

"Anne's future husband . . . Lieutenant Bates . . . he's on Tarawa."

The pompousness and the major-ness evaporated and Harding banged his leg. "Oh, damn it!" he groaned. "Why won't they let us have those lists?"

"Is there any way you could find out?"

"No!" he snapped. "You'd think we had no rights here in New Zealand. They won't let us have the lists."

"Is there anything we might do?" Barbara asked.

"Not a damn thing," the major sighed. Then suddenly he jammed his hat on his head and asked, "Is that the phone, there on the corner?"

"Yes," Barbara said, leading him to the bright-red kiosk.

Major Harding pushed his way in, jangled the hook and stuck his head out the door. "How do you work these damned gook phones?" he asked.

Barbara laughed and said, "They're difficult." Then she showed him how to deposit the pennies, and listened as he stormed at headquarters about the casualty lists from
280

Tarawa. "Damn it!" she heard him shout, "these are fine girls. The one I interviewed this morning is as fine as any American girl you'd ever meet. She's got a right to know." He slammed the receiver and said, "I'm disgusted. I was a lawyer in Chicago, and I thought I knew what red tape was."

"If you hear, please let us know."

"Let you know! Sister, I'm going to cable Halsey direct!" Before he said good-bye to Anne he whispered to Barbara, "This damned routine is getting me down. Checking on marriages when you aren't sure there's ever going to be one."

"Have you met this situation before?" Barbara asked.

He looked down at her with the worn-out patience of a businessman trying to explain to his wife what had happened at the office. "Have I met it? Lady, the last four marriages I've investigated, we don't know whether the husband got through Tarawa or not." He shook Anne's hand and then Barbara's. "You girls were swell. This is a hell of a job they gave me, isn't it?"

He climbed back into the staff car and started forth to interview another Christchurch girl who wanted to marry an American who might or might not still be living. When he waved from the rear door Anne said, "Life with people like that might be fun."

Barbara laughed and said, "I thought I'd scream if he called me Lady one more time. Say!" she said, leafing through the book on Oklahoma. "I thought where you're going was a city. Look at all this land!"

The next evening Major Harding appeared after tea and said, "The Young Eagles Club is meeting in Christchurch tonight, and with your permission I'd like to take you in."

"There's no news about Dick?"

"None. This Young Eagles Club sounds funny, but it's a good idea. Wish you'd come along."

"What is it?" Anne asked.

"American Government is very eager that you girls marrying Americans understand your new country. The consul is going to speak tonight about conditions in the western part of the country."

"I'd rather not, Major."

"I wish you would," he said quietly. "You see, there's a lot of fables abroad about our country. We like to keep the record clear."

"Your men brag enough about it," Barbara interjected.

The major turned and spoke directly to her. "You misunderstand! The Eagles Club—there's one in every city—try

281

to correct misinformation. After all," he laughed, "America isn't like you see in the movies. At the Eagles Club we try to tell the truth."

"I'd like to hear such a meeting!" Barbara said.

Stuffily the major explained, "But you're not eligible. It's only for girls who are going to marry Americans."

He led Anne to the staff car and carefully held the door for her. Evelyn said, "If all Americans do that for girls, no wonder they're such dynamite!"

Barbara asked her sister to sit down. "You've got to watch your language, Evelyn."

"I didn't swear!" the vivacious youngster replied.

"I don't mean swearing so much as your slovenly way of speaking. Your use of so many American words."

"I sort of go for it!" Evelyn replied.

"But where do you learn such words?"

"I hear the Americans talking. Stores. Places."

"Evelyn! Have you been meeting . . . soldiers, I mean?"

The younger girl thought for a moment and said, "Well, not meeting, exactly. But I see a certain Yank after school."

"Oh, darling! You're only fifteen!"

"Lots of girls walk with American soldiers. They're very nice."

"Look, darling! You've been awfully sweet with me, being patient when I acted like a mother. For two more years, Evelyn, believe in what I tell you. Don't go with soldiers."

"But Iceberg Annie went with one and everything turned out swell."

"Not so swell, maybe," Barbara replied, grimacing at the ugly word. "Because Anne is going to have a baby."

Evelyn drew back and stared across the table. She started to speak and then rose slowly and started to help with the dishes. "I'll do what you say, Mums!" she laughed nervously. Then she asked, "Will Anne have the baby?"

"Of course!"

"Because I think Dick Bates is alive."

"Of course he is!"

When Anne returned, Evelyn fetched her a chair and the three girls sat about the kitchen table discussing the Young Eagles Club. "It was really amazing!" Anne said. "There must have been two hundred of us, all planning to go to America. The consul explained how much different America was from the movies. Then the head chaplain from Wellington assured us that America wasn't like the movies. And finally the colonel said Americans didn't all have the luxuries you see in the movies."

"Sounds like they only had one record," Evelyn said.

"Wasn't it boring?" Barbara asked.

"Strangely, no. Because each man so obviously wanted us to like his country. And there was one exciting bit when a big map of the States was brought in. The two Callendar girls are marrying Yanks, you know. The consul asked them to stand up. The older girl—she's the one with buck teeth—is going to live in California. The one who's marrying a Catholic boy will live in Boston. The consul asked each girl to stand up front with her finger in her city. Then he said the average American family would be able to visit back and forth between two cities that far apart perhaps once in four years. He said it would cost—oh, something like three hundred pounds. Then he laughed and said, 'So you sisters better give up any idea of nagging your husbands for a visit every summer. Unless your husbands are rich, like in the movies.' "

"Then he laughed, ha ha?" Evelyn asked.

"Yes, but you gained the impression everyone was trying to tell the truth."

"That's easy!" Evelyn explained. "They know the G.I.'s have lied to lots of our girls and they're afraid the New Zealanders will tell the truth first."

For the first time in several days Anne laughed. "I think you're right! Because one of the girls asked a special question. She said she was marrying a Negro from Georgia and what would it be like in America? Like marrying a Maori?"

"How did they answer that one?" Evelyn asked.

"The consul coughed, but the head chaplain spoke right up. 'If I were you, my dear, I wouldn't go through with such a marriage.'

" 'Why not?' the girl asked.

" 'Because your life will be an intolerable misery,' the chaplain said."

"It must have been exciting," Barbara said.

"It was, in special ways. I sat beside two girls whose men were on Tarawa. We could almost hear one another praying."

Early next morning the staff car stopped at Ferrymead. The major seemed afraid to get out and Evelyn, watching at the window, whispered to Barbara, "Oh, my God!"

There was a knock at the door and Major Harding said

bluntly, "We got the list. Lieutenant Bates was killed. At Tarawa."

It was Barbara who started to cry. Anne simply sat down and stared at the major, who said, "We demanded the lists and we got them. A great many men were killed."

"Thank you, Major," Barbara sniffed. She indicated that he was to leave.

"No," he said stubbornly. "I can't leave like this. People should not be alone at a time like this."

"Please," Barbara begged.

"No, Mrs. Forbes, there's a great deal I can do for you. After all, your sister is practically an American now." He started to open a briefcase.

"You bring your papers back this afternoon," Barbara said.

When he had left, the three girls—almost as if by signal—started to care for their mother. With unusual attention they bathed and fed her, talked with her about the weather, and placed her chair so she could study the estuary. At the end Anne said, "I'm going to lie down."

Evelyn said, "I'll be off to school, and, Babs, I won't walk with the Americans."

Anne stopped. "What's this about Americans?"

"Oh, I just met a nice Yank at the store. We've been walking together."

"You seem very young," Anne said in a whisper.

"Barbara thought so, too," Evelyn laughed.

"Let's agree on one thing," Anne said, taking Evelyn's two hands. "Let agree that if later on you do want to talk with a soldier, you'll bring him right out here."

"That's fair enough!" Evelyn agreed.

But when she was gone Barbara said, "Anne! You've ruined it! She agreed not to see any Americans till she was seventeen."

"How silly!" Anne laughed with nervous uncertainty. "Evelyn's almost a grown girl. Sooner or later, if the occupation keeps up . . ."

"I'll call the store and tell them you'll not be in. That you won't be in any more," Barbara said, escaping from a thought which had begun to agitate her mind.

"Nonsense, Barbara! I'll work like anyone else."

"No. You'll stay here and watch Evelyn and Mother. I'll take your job. Now lie down."

As Anne did so she looked up and said, "I do wish that Delia were here. I never understood Delia." Then she hugged the pillow to her face and made believe she had fallen asleep.

Barbara tiptoed out of the cottage and went to the telephone kiosk, where she talked with Anne's employer. The man growled, "She can't just quit. She's got to clear it with Manpower."

"I'm taking her place," Barbara explained.

"You'll have to clear it with Manpower," the voice warned.

When Evelyn reached home that night she said, "See! I came straight home." There was a touch of bitterness in her make-believe childishness and Barbara said quickly, "It's exactly as Anne proposed, dear. If you want to talk with an American soldier, you bring him here. In your own home."

"I thought you said two years?"

"Anne's proposal was wiser. You see, darling, you're not grown up yet and you're not a child."

"It's just that there aren't any boys I know . . . They've all gone to war."

Barbara was shocked. She had thought of Evelyn always as a child, and she had ignored the fact that war was as cruel to children growing into adulthood as to anyone else. Then suddenly little Evelyn threw her arms across the table and began to sob violently. "What's happened?" Barbara cried.

"Nothing. Just that Daddy's gone and Kit and your Mark and now Dick. Everyone I've loved has been killed." She kept her face against the table, but her shoulders twisted in a manner that tore at Barbara's heart.

"You've got to believe that it all adds to some purpose," the older girl said.

"Don't be so goddamned brave!" Evelyn sniffed. "Even Deel's gone! And I feel like the devil, Babs."

"I know," her sister argued. "I've been so concerned about myself I've forgotten you were growing . . ."

Evelyn wiped her eyes and asked, "Where's Anne?"

"The major and a chaplain came to take her to another meeting of the Young Eagles. They said she was an American now, more than ever."

"Pretty soon she'll be packing a gat," Evelyn said. The two sisters thought this very funny but Evelyn stopped laughing abruptly and asked, "Babs! Could I bring Max home? You wouldn't be . . . ashamed of me?"

"No, darling! Of course not!"

Quickly the younger girl ran to the kitchen door and cried, "Yooo, Max! It's all right!"

From the darkness appeared a small wiry G.I. with a uniform that didn't fit too well and sharp, penetrating eyes. "This is Max Murphy!" Evelyn said proudly.

Max said he was from New York City, "Biggest burg in the world." He fell comfortably into Captain Neville's old chair and propped his feet on the ottoman.

"Would you care for some tea, Max?" Barbara asked.

"Boy!" he said, picking his teeth. "This is some country. Nothin' but tea."

"Don't you like tea?" Barbara asked solicitously, acting the mother who desperately wants to like her only daughter's first beau.

"Me? I despise tea. If you ask me too much tea is why the teeth of New Zealand is so rotten."

Barbara gulped. This was a very touchy subject. She herself had excellent teeth, but she had to acknowledge that her countrymen did not. In fact the dental health of New Zealand was shocking, but she thought it ungenerous of Max Murphy to say so.

"Tell me, what do you New Zealanders think?" Max asked.

"About what?" Barbara inquired.

"About us Americans coming in and saving your country? Where was your men?"

Barbara was about to explain, bitterly, where her men were, but she happened to look at Evelyn and the girl was so delighted to have Max there in the comfortable chair, handing out his opinions, that Barbara could say nothing. There was not time enough in the world, she realized, to explain to such Americans where the men of New Zealand were. The only thing to do was to be patient and hope that they would learn.

"It's a tough war!" Max continued, wolfing the sugar cookies—there was so little sugar in New Zealand that it was always kept for American G.I.'s—and trying to blow smoke rings. "You probably wouldn't believe it, but I been away from home for more than a year!"

When Max left, Barbara asked Evelyn, "Which battles was he in?"

"Oh, he's never been in any. He's been stationed in Hawaii. Don't you think he's cute?"

"Yes," Barbara said. That night she prayed that the Americans would invade some new island—in a hurry.

Reluctantly, however, she had to turn over to Anne the supervision of Evelyn's dates with Max, for when she reported to Manpower she was told bluntly and irrevocably

286

that she could not work at Anne's old job. She must serve as nurse in the hospital for the criminal insane.

"Neither have the others," the commissioners said.

"I'll appeal."

"The appeal is not granted."

"You handle the appeals, too?"

"We must. This is a total emergency."

"But I've never been a nurse!" Barbara protested.

"I know," Barbara said.

The manpower shortage was so acute that she had to start work the next morning. Her work was so horrifying that she preferred never to speak of it. The hospital matron said, "It's our only choice, Mrs. Forbes. You've been married. We can't give such work to naïve girls."

The bed pans did not bother Barbara, not even when the idiot inmates spilled them along the corridors, but the old men who had lost their minds completely were such cruel relics of the handsome New Zealand men she had known that sometimes she felt as if she could not work another day. And at night when she got home, there would be Max Murphy, lolling in the comfortable chair, eating up all the sugar.

When Anne's baby was born, Max went into the bedroom to see the ugly little girl and returned to his chair soberly shaking his head. In a whispered voice he pointed out that in America nice girls didn't have babies without being married. He said his mother would break his sister's back if she went around having babies. And furthermore his older brother would crucify the man responsible; that is, after his brother got out of reform school he would crucify the guy.

Max also reported that he had seen the last brides' ship leave for the States, and in his opinion most of the girls on board were pigs. Barbara blushed at this, but Max quickly added, "There were also some nice girls like you and Evelyn, but not many. Most of them was pigs."

Barbara would have been unable to stand both Max and the hospital, had not Major Harding begun stopping at the cottage. He came at first to report that Lieutenant Richard Bates had left no insurance for Anne, but that if she wanted to apply to the committee on illegitimate children she could get a government allowance.

"We don't need that," Barbara said.

The major stayed that night and talked with the girls for a long time. Later, his presence slowed Max down a bit and Barbara once went so far as to inquire if there was any way that Max could be eased out of Christchurch.

"I'll look into it," the major said.

But pleasant as it was to have the stiff and somewhat unsure American officer there—he brought immense stores of presents from the PX—it was also trying at times. He often spoke of his Chicago experiences but inevitably wound up with his impressions of New Zealand. "At first I couldn't see this country. 'What in hell,' I asked myself, 'are these people doing in Europe when they can't even protect their own country from the Japs?'"

"How did you answer yourself?" Barbara asked, leaning wearily on her elbows.

"Well, Anne explained about how you feel toward the British Empire, and although it seems pretty stupid, I have to respect you. This country has guts."

At other times the major would dandle the baby on his knee and coo, "You're an American kid, you are. You're as good as any American baby born this year."

Anne laughed at this when the major was gone and said she was sure he thought exactly like a Nazi: "This Polish baby had a German father, so it's sacred to the Fuehrer!"

"I'm too tired to be amused by the supermen," Barbara replied, but she was pleased when Major Harding insisted that she go to the movies with him. At the door, as Anne and Evelyn were admiring her before she left to join the major in the staff car, she suddenly held out her ugly red hands. The nails were broken from scrubbing floors, the cuticle had disappeared in lye and harsh soaps. "I'd almost forgotten I was a woman," she said.

Evelyn cried, "Wait a minute!" and brought her a pair of gloves, but in the cinema Major Harding slowly pulled the gloves off and took her hands. His fingers felt the roughness and there was a moment of agonizing suspense, after which he drew the hand to his lips in the darkness and whispered, "You New Zealand girls fight right with your men."

But the cinema was a dreadful bust, because it showed Errol Flynn winning the war in Burma and murmurs of protest rose to sharp cries of derision. Many New Zealanders walked out, and next evening Major Harding waited on the doorstep, poking his head around the corner of the door, asking, "Can an American come in?" He had the papers, which were filled with angry complaint against the stupidity of the American film.

"So help me," he said. "I never knew there were any British troops in Burma."

"We don't want praise," Barbara explained wearily.

288

"Really we don't. But we've fought on all the fronts in the world. It's humiliating to see Errol Flynn . . ."

"Thank heavens he wasn't an American born!" Major Harding said. Then, awkwardly, he took a parcel from his pocket and handed it to Barbara. Eagerly she opened it and took out two bottles of an American hand lotion. At first she was outraged, and then her curiosity triumphed and she poured a little on her palm.

"I was outside the door last night when you were showing your hands," he said. "It's very hard for a stranger to understand a new country."

Barbara laughed and said she hated girls who accepted presents from the American PX but there just wasn't . . . She would have cried, but instead she ran into the bedroom and placed the bottles on her dresser. Then she said to the major that she forgave the Americans their PX's and even their films.

There was one American, however, whom she could never forgive. Night after night brash young Max Murphy came to Ferrymead and sat with his feet on the ottoman, delivering his opinions of New Zealand. "Until I rode on a New Zealand train I didn't know what murder was. When the train stops everybody piles out for tea and sandwiches"—he pronounced it *sangriches*—"and if you get caught in the middle you're a dead duck."

"We happen to like tea," Barbara explained wearily.

"But why don't you have diners on your trains? In America we do."

"Custom, Max. You have diners. We don't."

"But it's not diners I'm worried about," he said sagaciously, gormandizing the sugar cookies that Evelyn dutifully brought him. "It's the disrespect New Zealand men show their women."

"Oh, dear!" Barbara sighed inwardly. "Here we go again! The puritanical American!"

"What I mean is," Max explained, "like when the train stops. Men knock women over to get their tea first. Now in America . . ."

Barbara fled the kitchen and went in to attend her mother, but even in the darkened room she could hear Max belaboring the point that in America men respected women. Barbara had noticed this strange obsession before, the frontier-like worship of women coupled with totally confused attitudes toward sex: women were to be idolized, but they must jump into bed if a man whistled, and if they did they were pigs.

289

Barbara tucked in her mother's blankets and laughed nervously. "I'm glad I'm not an American girl. Imagine trying to please Max Murphy."

When she entered the kitchen, Max was saying, "Thing that gets me is the immorality of New Zealand women. They have babies . . . "

He looked up and saw Barbara's unmasked glare. Quickly he changed the subject and said, "You hear the story about the New Zealand waitress who was bragging about her new boy friend? 'He comes to me table and orders tea, which I serves very hot. Do you think he pours it in his saucer to blow on it like an uneducated lout? No bloody fear! Not him! He leaves it in the cup and fans it real polite, wiv' his hat.' " Max doubled up with laughter and Evelyn, delighted to have him with her in the kitchen, cried, "Max! Where do you get all your stories?"

That was enough for Barbara. "You shouldn't use that word, Max."

"What word? Bloody?" He roared with laughter and said, "In America there's nothing wrong with bloody."

"In New Zealand there is."

"That's what's wrong with New Zealand . . ."

"I think it would be better if you didn't come here any more, Max."

Evelyn jumped up and cried, "Oh Barbara!"

"No need to get sore," Max said pettishly. "Just because I said bloody."

"It's not that," Barbara explained patiently. "It's just that . . . Well, Evelyn has to study harder."

"I don't need to be hit by a ton of bricks," Max said in bravado. "I get a hint. I know when I'm not wanted."

"That's right," Barbara said firmly. She scooped up the rest of the cookies and stuffed them in a bag. "You take these, Max. You've been very sweet to Evelyn. Let us know . . ." She stopped short. She had been about to say, "Let us know if you ever get into any real fighting," but she knew that in wartime one never goads that wound, not even in fun. "Let us know when you get safely home."

"Can't be soon enough for me," Max said sheepishly. Then he shook Evelyn's hand and said, "You're a very good kid. For a New Zealander."

When he was gone Evelyn burst into tears and cried, "That was dirty rotten! I'm going to see him whenever I want to."

"Of course you will, darling!" Barbara assured her.

"Then why did you send him away?"

290

Barbara finished washing up the tea things and then sat with her sister. "Surely you and I know that Max was a dreadful person. You know he's dull. Foolish. A braggart."

Evelyn looked down at the floor for a moment and then admitted softly, "I know all that, Babs. But he's the only boy I've ever met. They're all away."

Nothing Evelyn might have said could have moved Barbara so deeply. She wanted to console her sister, for Evelyn had spoken this day's truth. Max Murphy was the best boy available. In the happy years when a girl should be knocking about with boys, listening to their boasts, surveying their natures, there had been none in the land; and now though she was old enough to fall in love, even the first-rate Americans had moved north to the terrible islands. Barbara said quietly, "The war's got to end soon. Didn't I used to see you walking with a very nice boy? Tommy somebody?"

Evelyn looked up quickly. "Did you think Tommy was nice?"

"Yes, I did rather."

"Oh, I did, too!"

"Where is Tommy?"

"He's in Italy."

There was an awkward pause and Evelyn started to cry. "Tell you what!" Barbara said. "The minute Tommy gets home we'll have him over here. Imagine! He'll be able to tell us all about Africa and Italy."

Evelyn wiped her eyes and confessed, "I kissed Max. Several times."

"Was it fun?"

"Yes . . . But I have to admit, he was a terrible drip."

"I thought so."

"He used to tell me every day, 'If we hadn'ta moved in, this country woulda been sitting ducks for the Japs. Where were your men?' Where in hell did he think they were?"

"Take it easy!" Barbara laughed.

"Oh ho!" Evelyn chuckled. "Look who's telling me about Americans! Look who was kissing one half to death last night!"

Barbara blushed and said, "Major Harding is different."

"I'll say he is. Tell me the truth! Are you going to marry him?"

"We've not discussed it. Probably not."

"Why?"

"I shouldn't like to live in America."

Evelyn changed the subject. "If you knew all along that Max was a drip, why didn't you say so?"

"Because girls have got to discover some things for themselves."

And next morning the Neville sisters discovered how long their emotions had been imprisoned. For Major Holland appeared at Ferrymead with the news that Max Murphy had insisted upon transfer north. "I guess he had a fight with Evelyn because he told me confidentially that all New Zealand girls were pigs."

"We appreciate your telling us," Anne said.

"But that isn't what I came out for! Listen!"

They stood quietly in the kitchen and caught the sound of whistles blowing in the distance. Then car horns began to whine and Barbara saw women dashing out into the street.

"It's over!" Major Harding said.

"What?" Anne asked desperately, afraid to form the words.

"The war! The war in Europe!"

Barbara sat down and put her hands over her face. England, their Home, had been saved. The crusade that had seemed so quixotic had ended as her father and husband had said it must end. This was radiant news, and in a moment she joined her sisters in their hectic celebration.

Twice Major Harding tried to remind the girls that the war in the Pacific was still critical, but Barbara and Anne would not consider this. That was America's affair. Their war—the real war, as New Zealanders called it—was over! A great national sigh accompanied by prayers, riots, broken heads and raided saloons went up. The war was over!

Major Harding drove the girls down into the square, where a frenzy developed. After watching what seemed to him an irrational and premature celebration he excused himself. "I feel as out of place as an Englishman at a Fourth-of-July picnic." Late that night the Neville girls went home, tired and hoarse. Their war was over.

Then the first contingent of soldiers arrived from the Italian front. Their transport docked at Wellington and there was some talk of flying the South Island troops down to Christchurch, but there was national protest, for it was recognized that a plane disaster, after five years absence overseas, would be intolerable. So the ferry was crammed with Enzedders, and in the morning it arrived at Littleton. The heroes of South Island marched onto a special train that hauled under the mountain and into Christchurch, where in

292

the distance they heard a fine skirling sound: the bagpipes of home.

Slowly the train chugged to a halt, and the pipes played a lament for the missing dead, then a piercing march, and the men of Tobruk, Benghazi, Crete, Cassino swung into the square. They were neither cocky nor victorious nor afraid nor tearful. They were just men who had been away at their jobs for five years. There were not even any cheers, only the click of metaled heels upon the stones and the whispers of women. The Lord Mayor looked straight ahead, and Major Harding, the American representative, saluted stiffly. Then Barbara became aware that Evelyn was crying. The younger girl whispered, "Look, Babs. That's Tommy. How tall he's grown."

The next days were like the radiant sun of autumn, when the harvest is in. Tommy appeared at the cottage and sat with his feet on the ottoman, eating all the sugar cookies the girls could bake. Major Harding was wonderful, drawing Tommy out about the war and admitting candidly, "You could never call me a hero, Tom. I sat right here in New Zealand, better fed than I'd have been at home."

"I could of done with some of that food!" Tommy said.

"What was it like in Italy?" Evelyn asked.

"Ah, that was a tough one! Even the Yanks were stopped, and they had all the equipment."

"Did you like Italy?" Barbara asked.

Tommy stuffed the last cookie into his mouth and said seriously, "I tell you, Mrs. Forbes, those Italian sheilas were disgraceful. They were so immoral you wouldn't believe it."

"I can believe it," Barbara said, pouring some more tea.

Evelyn proudly produced a pair of socks she had knitted, but Tommy raised his hand imperiously and announced, "I'll never wear another knitted thing in me life!"

"I'd like them," Major Harding said, so Evelyn gave them to Barbara who gave them to the major.

Then Tommy made a startling proposal. "The Enzed Government is offering all returned men month passes on trains and planes. They want us to see the land we were fighting for. Wives can go along. So I saw the bloke and he said it would be all right if Evelyn went up to Auckland with me, and we'd be married at my uncle's."

"Of course she can go," Barbara said promptly.

Anne asked, "Do you think it would be . . ."

"When did you plan to leave?" Barbara asked.

She and Anne took what money they had and bought

293

Evelyn all the things contained in a proper trousseau. They dressed her in a neat tweed traveling suit and had her stand in the kitchen while they admired her.

"She's exquisite," Anne said proudly.

Then Major Harding drove them to the airport, where the young couple climbed aboard the plane. As it rose into the air, Barbara felt as if part of her were flying off, and she thought how apoplectic her father would have been, in his Navy blues, if his baby Evelyn had proposed leaving on a honeymoon, the last day of which would see the wedding; but a curious event distracted her from further contemplation of changing times, for at the airport she had picked up a Wellington paper.

For some months past it had been her habit to read the tragic advertisements that were beginning to appear in New Zealand papers: "Hennessy, Harold. First Marine Division. Does any New Zealand girl living near Paekakariki have a portrait of my son killed on Guadalcanal? Family has none. Mrs. K. L. Hennessy, Trafalgar Road, Shaker Heights, Ohio."

Barbara read these strange and shadowy messages with macabre fascination, as if she had written them: "Forbes, Mark. Third New Zealand Force. Does any wine seller in Cairo remember Mark Forbes? If so communicate his wife. Please, please communicate, for she has forgotten how he smiled."

But on this day she read: "Bates, Richard Gaines. First Marine Division. Did any New Zealand family know my son killed at Tarawa? If so please communicate with his mother, Mrs. R. D. Bates, Clifton Terrace, Oklahoma City, Oklahoma."

Quickly she crumpled the newspaper so that Anne would not see the message and upon arriving home she hurried to her room and locked the door. Then she wrote a long airmail letter: "My sister would never have told you this, Mrs. Bates, but she has a baby girl. I can't describe how lovely this child is, nor how elfin-like she resembles your son. Lest you surmise this is a trick, let me assure you that Anne's father was a distinguished captain in the Royal Navy. If you find back copies of newspapers you can read about him and the *Nestor* in their fight with the *Graf Spee*. I wish I could send a photograph of your son, but we have none. His memory was so alive with us that we had no need of pictures."

She tried to guess what Mrs. Bates in Oklahoma City would want to know, and the letter ran to three careful pages, ending, "Normally I would not tell you these things in a first letter, but I too lost my husband and my father in the war, and I think you will want to know the truth without preliminary courtesies."

She posted the letter and then reported to the Manpower Commission. She said that with the pressures relieved she hoped she might be excused from further work at the insane hospital. The secretary stared at her icily and asked why she sought this favor.

"Because I'm very tired, and I must stay at home for a while."

To her surprise the secretary stopped scowling and said, "And you're right! You girls have done yeoman service. Time you let up." He whipped out a thermometer and jammed it under her tongue. "You look sick," he said.

But her temperature was normal and he growled, "Nothing but exhaustion. Go home and sleep." Then he scowled at her again.

She stayed about the cottage, hoping to intercept any letters that might come from Oklahoma City, but she was outsmarted, for one morning a dignified gentleman in a black suit arrived and asked for Miss Anne Neville. When she appeared he handed her six hundred pounds. "It's from the bank," he said solemnly. "We received this cable." He bowed and Anne read aloud: BELOVED DAUGHTER. COME HOME AT ONCE. BRING CHILD. FUNDS WITH THIS CABLE. MOTHER.

When the frocked messenger had gone, Anne broke into tears and cried, "Forgive me, Babs, for not telling you."

"Not telling me what?"

"About my letter to Mrs. Bates."

"What letter?"

"I hate secrets, but shortly after Evelyn left a girl at the store brought me an advertisement in the Wellington papers . . . I've saved it." She produced a worn clipping: *Bates, Richard Gaines.* Quietly she confessed, "I was afraid Mrs. Bates might be some horrible . . ." Suddenly she pressed her hand to her face and cried, "The baby! How did she know I had a baby!" She grabbed the cable and read again BRING CHILD. "Oh! She's had the American consul snooping . . ."

While Barbara explained, Major Harding appeared. He was in high spirits and had a big basket of food. "A celebration!"

"Whatever for?" Barbara asked.

"Our new American daughter!" he shouted, bowing low to Anne. "Oklahoma's own!"

"How did you find out?" Anne asked suspiciously.

"Everybody in New Zealand knows! Boy, you got pull!" He showed her a telegram he'd received from the ambassador, REPRESENTATIVE HALLORAN OKLAHOMA DEMANDS IMMEDIATE PASSAGE STATES ANNE NEVILLE CHRISTCHURCH AND DAUGHTER. EXPEDITE.

Barbara took the telegram and studied it. It was so American. Somebody had known somebody and somebody had damned well better expedite. She liked the telegram. Sometimes things should be done that way. Expedite.

Major Harding was saying, "Now Anne, there's going to be a lot about America you won't like. We don't treat our Negroes the way you do your Maoris. What I mean is . . ."

The girls interrupted, crying in unison, "America isn't like the movies!"

"This isn't a meeting of the Young Eagles Club," Barbara teased.

"And even if your country is horrid, I'm going," Anne announced firmly.

But a letter from Mrs. Bates indicated that Oklahoma, at least, would not be horrid. She wrote: "If you two had connived to win my heart completely nothing could have succeeded better than your two letters, Anne's so afraid, Barbara's so confident. When I finished them I felt I knew you both. I'm enclosing a picture of our house, because I've heard that many New Zealand girls have been deceived by Americans. I must warn you that we are not wealthy, but you and the baby need never want. Further, if this won't make you ashamed of me, I think it would be best if we made believe that you and Dick were married. I don't care a hang, but in some ways Oklahoma City is still a small town." On the photograph was the added warning, "The porch has been torn down and the place doesn't look quite so nice. No help."

When Anne's departure was imminent Major Harding presented her with a toy pistol. "You pack it this way, Babe," he explained. He also taught her to snarl out of the corner of her mouth and said that when she met Mrs. Bates she was to drop her bags, extend her arms and shout in a clear voice, "Hiya, Toots!" But later that night Barbara heard Anne explaining to the major that "Oklahoma City is the petroleum center of the world. All the major companies have offices there, Texaco, Standard Oil, Shell."

When Anne finally took the baby and left for America, Barbara experienced a dull heaviness of spirit. It was cruel, she thought, what had happened to her country. First the finest men had left for five years and now the finest girls were departing forever. There could be no healing the wounds New Zealand had suffered. The scars would grow shut. They might even grow smooth to the exploring finger, but the under-structure had been damaged. There could be no healing that.

It was while in the grip of such melancholy reflection that Barbara called Delia in Wellington, but a man answered the phone and reported that he had the room for the week-end, because Deel was up in Auckland seeing a troop ship off. Okinawa or some place like that, he guessed. Well, wherever the Yanks were going to hit next.

So Barbara composed a long letter, filled with information about Evelyn's marriage and Anne's departure for America. She concluded, "Now that war seems to be nearing the end they'll surely find Cobber in one of the prison camps, and I want to tell you again, Deel, that you and Cobber are to live with us." She added, "That will give Cobber time to find a job," but the sentence seemed to harass old wounds, so she wrote the last page over again, omitting the gratuitous insult to Cobber.

To her surprise, Deel answered the letter in person. She appeared much thinner and yet more beautiful than ever. "I'm so glad you invited me down, Babs. It's hell up there, waiting for news of your man."

"I think Cobber's all right," Barbara assured her.

"I didn't mean him. Joe's at Okinawa."

"You must forget these Americans, Deel."

"How can I? I've never lived before."

"Cobber's going to be home soon."

Delia brushed the hair back from her forehead and confessed, "How could I ever live with Cobber again? I can't even remember him!"

Barbara sat with her sister and said, "That's normal, in war, Deel. You know how much I loved Mark? I cannot even remember how he looked."

For more than a week the two girls worked happily about the cottage, not thinking, not worrying. They simply did the chores of a house and gossiped. It was Delia's opinion that Anne was the best off of the lot. "A home in America, a baby. And I'll bet she'll marry some Yank, too."

"Do you think so?" Barbara asked.

"Sure. Those Americans are hungry to marry girls like Anne. Four of them have proposed to me."

Then the rugged news from Okinawa began to appear in the papers, and the happy interlude at Ferrymead was ended. Deel wept and said, "If Joe's killed I think I'll die." But he got through and on his battle leave finagled a ride all the way to Wellington, where Delia was waiting. When she left Christchurch she said, "I don't know how this is going to end, but if Joe wants me to come to California as char lady in his restaurant, I'll go."

The cottage at Ferrymead seemed desolate now, with only Barbara and her infantile mother. The solitude was broken in the evenings by Major Harding, who brought food and cigarettes and a shawl for Mrs. Neville. Now Barbara started to study him with special care, for it was apparent to each of them that when his duty in New Zealand ended, he would ask her to go with him to America. It was not that they were in love, she reasoned. He had found comfort in the cottage, and when people were over thirty such comfort was almost more important than love.

She found John Harding to be a strange assembly of contradictions. He was less winning than Anne's Dick Bates and much less revolting than Evelyn's Max Murphy. He was an average American man, unsure of himself emotionally, afraid of women, yet completely enslaved by them. Sometimes the puzzled look on his face indicated that he knew she was making fun of him, and yet she liked him immensely, for he was also an average American in that he was both generous and kind. In fact they had a fight about presents from the PX. On one memorable evening she had come close to crying. It was over the nylons.

He had big-dealed six pairs and delivered them in a gift box. Barbara opened the package and studied the sheer beauty of stockings—like all New Zealand girls she had worn none for five years, despising the black cotton ones released by the Government—so she was keenly eager to accept them. But a galling phrase of Max Murphy's haunted her and she said, "Sorry, John, but I've decided not to be a chocolate-bar beauty."

Major Harding dropped the package and said, "That's a hell of a thing to say!"

"I mean just that! You Yanks have been parading your PX stuff too long. Now you take these stockings . . ."

He grabbed her and pulled some papers from his pockets. "PX stuff, eh? Why, damn it, I spent six months getting these flown out here. And you're going to take them!" He picked up the stockings and shouted, "I got them for you because I happen to love you."

She kissed him and pushed the stockings away. "And I can't accept because . . . well, I'm beginning to love you."

He laughed and said he guessed he understood. He'd seen a hundred men fall in love with New Zealand girls, but he never thought it would happen to him. "The fools come down here on leave, and they're big heroes. Everything is gook this and gook that. Then what happens?"

The major was very fond of hearing himself talk, especially when he could act out several parts, so Barbara asked, "What happens?"

"On the last week they come running to me and cry, 'Major, can you wire the admiral for special permission for me to get married?' "

"And what do you say?" Barbara asked.

"I always pour it on. I ask, 'You? Married to a gook?' "

"And they say?"

"They break down and say, 'Major! I never knew what love was till I came down here.' " There was an embarrassed pause. Then he added with a rush, "I guess they're getting even with me. Because I never knew what love was till I watched you and your sisters."

"What do you mean?" Barbara asked, no longer teasing.

"I guess it's what men think about when they think of marriage. People living together and not spending too much money and having a good, quiet time. You don't see much of that in America, any more."

Their courtship was interrupted by a cyclonic event which showed Barbara a new aspect of her major. The Japs surrendered, and although New Zealanders took the event rather casually, the Americans in the country—wherever more than two were gathered—touched off an epic celebration. Major Harding appeared with a nurse at Ferrymead and told Barbara that the nurse would take care of Mrs. Neville while they painted the town. They wound up at a café where three other Yanks were drinking bootleg whiskey, and the drunker the men got the more they insisted upon making heroic speeches. Major Harding's was the best.

He addressed the crowd in the café and said, "You won your war in Europe. Very gallant. We won ours in the Pacific. Now I want every calendar maker here and abroad to print this day in red henceforth. Why? Not to please us. Oh, no! America don't need to be soft soaped, but to remind all the bastards in the world that they can push New Zealand

and America just so far." He glared menacingly about the room for a challenger, but none appeared and he ended feebly, "Print the date in red, that's all."

"A lovely speech," Barbara assured him.

But the Major felt that somehow his effort had fallen flat and he rose with a shout and cried, "I feel constrained to throw a bottle through the window," and before anyone could stop him he had done just that. The police were called, but some New Zealand soldiers in the crowd said the major was all right, he'd pay.

Next day he appeared red-eyed at the cottage and asked, "Did I make a fool of myself last night?"

"No! I like you best when you're all Yank."

"In New York, too, they take a very dim view of bottles through windows."

"Everyone forgave you."

"I'm glad. Because the news has come, and I wouldn't like to leave with people ashamed of me."

"Are you leaving?" Barbara asked carefully.

"I'm sailing home next month."

"You must be very happy."

"I am. The admiral's given me some leave. I'm going down to Queenstown to see the lake." He blushed and added, "I was hoping you'd come along."

Barbara evaded the fundamental question by pointing out that she could not leave her mother. "I've thought of that," he said. "I've arranged for the nurse we had last night."

Now there was no evading. "The real reason I said I wouldn't go is that I'm the New Zealand girl who isn't falling all over herself to run off with a Yank."

The major blushed and said, "I'm sorry." He was about to leave when an unfortunate break trapped Barbara and forced her to reconsider the whole question; for Delia arrived from Wellington with the news that Cobber Phil was being flown home from the Japanese prison in Malaya. The official list reported him as blind in one eye from beatings about the face and missing his left leg from gangrene. Delia was pale and immediately asked if Barbara would leave the cottage for a while until she'd had a chance to talk with Cobber. "Leave us alone for a couple of days."

"What I was suggesting," the major said. "I've asked her to come on down to Queenstown."

In spite of her anxiety Delia could not forbear studying the American and she beamed her approval. "A fine idea, I think!" she said.

"And I've just said that I think Americans in uniform are disgraceful. They think any girl is dying to play around with them."

"I'm sorry," the major said. "As you know, that wasn't my intention."

He left at once and Delia said reproachfully, "You sure washed that up fine."

"I meant to."

"Well, I meant it when I said I wanted to be alone with Cobber."

"What are you going to tell him?"

"Tell him? Nothing! I don't owe Cobber anything."

"But you do! He's your husband."

"Don't be silly. He's no more my husband than some boy I met five years ago."

"The fact remains he's married to you."

"That doesn't erase what's happened, Babs. You may as well know it. I'm asking Cobber for a divorce."

"You can't!"

"Yes I can. Because I've found the Yanks are my kind of people."

"But Cobber's a sick man."

"He'll understand."

"Deel, you can't wash away responsibilities like that."

"My responsibilities are with Joe. I'm going to California."

"Deel, why do you suppose I've stayed here in the cottage year after year? Because this was my responsibility. You'd better find out what yours is."

"And you'd better figure out what's best for you, too. This major is crazy about you, Babs. You'd better go with him now, or it'll be too late. I've seen girls in Wellington break their hearts. Too late."

"I don't run off with Yanks," Barbara protested furiously.

"Well, ten thousand did, and they all have electric washers now."

"That's horrid!"

"And true. Why mutilate yourself, Babs? You love the guy . . ."

"Your American language sounds frightful, Deel."

"It's a language I like. I'm going to speak it the rest of my life."

"By God! You must not do such a thing!"

The sisters argued for two days, and Delia convinced Barbara that she had no desire to be hard or to hurt Cobber or to behave immorally. She said simply, "It's just that I've met the kind of man I can respect. The kind I want to live with."

"But you must consider Cobber," Barbara protested.

"I've thought it all out," Delia assured her. "And I do wish you'd leave the cottage, because this is going to be difficult enough, without you here siding with him."

And so, repelled by Delia's actions, Barbara was driven to reconsider the invitation to Queenstown. She was not prepared to say that she wanted to marry the American, and yet she was eager to admit that knowing him had been most pleasant. His unfeelingness in bluntly proposing a nuptial flight was merely part of the superman attitude inculcated in all Americans by their prolonged stay among women who had been without men for years. She used one of Delia's words: "He's a dope, but he's a kind and gentle dope."

To her surprise she said to Delia, "But even if I did want to go down there and tell him I'll marry him, how would I find him!"

"At the Kentish Arms," Delia said.

"How do you know?"

"He told me."

"Why?"

"Because I told him you'd change your mind."

Delia bustled her sister onto the train, and as it pulled southward Barbara became aware of how exhausted the years had made her. Too, she had forgotten the great beauty of her land, and now she lay back and feasted on the swirling valleys, the wild ocean hammering at the coast, the towering glaciers reaching down from the sky. She felt, at times, as if all the agony of the preceeding years had been meaningful if such a land had been preserved. From time to time she would catch the eye of some New Zealand soldier who had fought long years across the desert and in the fjords, and she would know that he was thinking the same thoughts: here was the great land, here was the realm of beauty.

Then she would be jolted from her reverie by a tea stop, when a thousand berserk passengers would catapult from the train to grab massive cups of steaming tea accompanied by soggy biscuits. It was worth a woman's life to be caught in that hungry eruption, and once as Barbara was smashed back against the wall by a huge farmer coming home from market, she recalled wryly Max Murphy's insolent description of a New Zealand tea stop: "Murder, with cream and sugar." She laughed and admitted that even Max was right sometimes . . . "The drip."

302

At Invercargill, cold and barren land's end, she caught a bus which would take her to the magnificent uplands. Now she relaxed and fought against the thoughts that assailed her mind, "I am like a woman who has lost all shame and is chasing . . ." She halted that. She was not a woman without shame. She was a woman slowly falling in love with a strange man from an even stranger country. She was going to Queenstown to tell him so. That was all. "If Father could read the history of his daughters . . ." She halted that, too. Captain Neville knew war. He knew war at sea, where the greater agony comes before the ship sails. She thought, "I guess Pops would understand." Then she sank back and watched the brooding valleys creep high toward the Alps. She would think no more. She was emotionally exhausted.

She was therefore unprepared for what she encountered at the Kentish Arms, for when she found Major Harding he was accompanied by a red-headed girl who had obviously come along for his last leave. And the girl was wearing nylon stockings.

There was a moment of shocked silence as Barbara and the major stood face to face. The red-head understood at once and asked apologetically, "Is this the lady you were telling me about?"

"Wait! Barbara!" the major cried.

He overtook her at the bridge where the tame trout come to feed, but she turned on him sharply and said, "Go away. I'll leave on the morning bus."

"She's just a girl who's worked at our office. She means nothing."

"Just a pal!" Barbara cried.

"She's not even sharing the same room with me."

"But she's wearing nylon stockings."

"You wouldn't take them."

The scene was revolting to Barbara, but she was caught in its rising tempo, and to her own surprise she shouted, "You brassy conquerors! You conceited men who think every girl . . ."

"At least listen to what I have to say!"

"You stupid supermen!" she cried. Then she sensed how ridiculous it was for her to say this when she had followed for hundreds of miles one of the men she was reviling. "Oh, go away!" she sniffed, seeking for her handkerchief.

She turned and fled up the street, finding an unheated hotel with a vacant and musty room. She crawled between the shivering sheets and reflected. "Well, anyway, I'd have made

a rotten American. I have too much sense of humor."
Amused at her own behavior, and congratulating herself on
her providential escape, she went to sleep.

In the morning she was awakened by sharp hammering at
her door and shortly became aware that she was in
Queenstown and that Major Harding was outside. She commanded him to go away, but he burst into the room and announced in a frightened voice, "It's Delia."

She drew a robe about her throat and asked from behind
it, "What about her?"

"American Headquarters tracked me down. The police
wanted me."

"Oh, God! What's happened to Deel?"

"Her husband came home. From Singapore. And three
hours later he killed her."

Barbara sank her face into the robe and tried to stop her
ears to the next ghastly sentences: "The police want you to
hurry back. He cut off her head with a saber."

Major Harding waited in the hallway until she was dressed.
He kept talking to her through the opened door, assuring her
that she would have been helpless to prevent the tragedy.
That was precisely the wrong thing to say, for when she
joined him she was reminded of the fact that if it had not
been for him, she would not have come to Queenstown, and
if it had not been for other Americans, Deel would not now
be dead.

"Get away from me!" she muttered with unconcealed
loathing, and she did not see him again until they met in
court, she sitting with the Crown's witnesses, he with the
defense.

The trial of Cobber Phil Friskett was the first of several in
which New Zealand soldiers were charged with the murder of
wives who had consorted with Americans during the occupation, and as such it aroused a bitter and pervading interest.
The judge, to whom war had been a chess game played on
some distant board, seemed sternly determined to hang Cobber as a warning to other returning husbands; but the clamor
of the population was all for an acquittal.

Barbara, inwardly thanking God that her parents were past
knowing what was happening, was one of the first witnesses.
She delivered platitudes defending her sister as a fine girl and
perjuries defending her as a respectable wife. Other witnesses
volunteered the information that Cobber Phil was a man of
vile temper who had threatened, in prison camp, to "stab his

wife a thousand times if she had played around with them Yanks."

A damning case was built up against the crippled soldier, who glowered hatefully at the jury, and it seemed the man must die when the American officer, Major John Harding, took the stand. Keeping his eyes averted from Barbara, he testified that he had known the dead girl. But not personally.

"It was the other Americans who knew her—personally?" Cobber's lawyer asked.

"Yes."

"How did you become acquainted with her?"

"I was sent to investigate."

"Investigate?"

"Yes. That was my job."

"But investigate what?"

"Her marriage."

"Her marriage to Friskett? What interest of yours was that?"

"Not her marriage to Friskett. To a Marine."

"An American Marine?"

"Yes. An American Marine wanted to marry her."

"But she was already married."

"Yes, but she didn't tell the Marine. He applied for permission to marry."

"And you were sent to investigate?"

"Yes."

"Was that customary?"

"Always."

The defense lawyer concluded that this was the spot to make his first point, so he asked, "You investigated all New Zealand girls who wanted to marry Americans?"

"That's right."

"Why?"

"Well . . ."

"Speak up. Tell us why."

"Because we didn't . . . That is, the State Department didn't want . . . well, riff-raff. They didn't want riff-raff coming into the country."

"Riff-raff? I don't believe I know that word."

"It means, well—undesirables."

"Oh! Undesirables! The State Department didn't want undesirables . . . like . . . say . . . gangsters, or racketeers, or hold-up men, or counterfeiters. Of course you wouldn't want people like that in America."

There was immediate objection, but the counsel had made

305

his point. Cobber Phil was no longer on trial. It was the Americans who had invaded his home.

"Now, Major Harding, what kind of woman did you find Delia Friskett to be?"

"Attractive . . . Intelligent."

"I mean morally."

"Well, not knowing she was married I judged her to be . . . well . . . satisfactory."

"What did you think later?"

"I didn't think anything, sir."

"Quite correct. It wasn't your job to think. But what did you report?"

"That she had been living with a lieutenant before she met the Marine who wanted to marry her."

"An American lieutenant?"

"Yes."

"And before that it was some other American?"

"Yes."

"And another, and another, and another?"

"Yes."

"Speak up, Major. I said three anothers."

"Yes."

"Now I am going to ask you, Major, how many Americans in all did you report Delia Friskett as having been intimate with?"

Major Harding looked beseechingly at Barbara and said in a low voice, "Seven."

"I do apologize, Major, but you must speak up."

"Seven."

There was no sound in the courtroom as the spectators stared at the American offering testimony that would save the New Zealander. But the Crown had its suspicions and asked, "Later on you made acquaintance of other members of the deceased's family. Is that correct?"

"Yes."

"Where?"

"Here in Christchurch."

"Did you ever tell them of their sister's behavior in Wellington?"

"No."

"Is it true at one time you even contemplated marrying one of the deceased's sisters?"

"Yes."

"Yet you never told her of your investigation of her sister."

306

"No."

"I suggest that you didn't because there was no such evidence. I suggest that you, a military man, are lying to protect the defendant, also a military man."

Immediately the defense asked, "Major why did you not tell the other members of the family what you have told us today in court?"

"Because the other members of the family were not like their sister."

The statement had a terrible finality, and after it was spoken no one could doubt that Cobber Phil, the first of the soldier murderers, would go free.

As Barbara left the courtroom she instinctively avoided the bench where Major Harding would be, and she walked along the cool and reassuring streets of Christchurch. She was content, now, that John Harding's testimony had proved her to be a liar. There had been too much killing, and she was glad that Cobber Phil would go free. For more than six years her life had been a hopeless turmoil of death and occupation and victory. Now the good, clean air of peace was blowing down from the mountains, and for a moment she felt young again, as if she were a schoolgirl bright with promise, walking with pigtails and black stockings to her school. She thought, "I must have been a stupid girl. I certainly didn't learn much." Then she had a thought that some day the people of Christchurch would understand exactly what this war was about. Someone would write a great novel, perhaps, and it would all be clear. She hoped that on that day she would comprehend, too, but for the present she was tired and would not try.

She went into a milkbar, one of those curious innovations made popular during the American occupation, and as she ordered a lemon she mused on how strange it was that the one lasting memento of those violent men were the milkbars where you could buy sweet ice creams.

She smiled at the conceit and took from her coat a letter she had skimmed once that day, but only hurriedly. It was from Oklahoma City and it ended, "The strangeness has begun to wear off. Veronica is in pre-kindergarten, would you believe it? Mrs. Bates and I are sure that some of the women in town have begun to guess that I was never actually married, and you'd be amused at the clever questions they ask trying to trap me. But once they're satisfied that I've been a bad girl they're perfectly lovely to me. I'm surprised to report that I'm having a splendid time, and Mrs. Bates astonishes me, really she does. A friend of hers has a son, he's about forty and served with the Air Force at some English base. As soon as he heard my English accent he invited me to the country club, and three weeks now I've said no, but last night Mrs. Bates said, and I'm using her exact words, 'You ought to think about forming some lasting friendships. I won't live forever and I'd feel more easy if Veronica had a solid home to grow up in.' Then I think she called her friend, because a little while later I was invited to the country club again. And this time I said yes."

Barbara folded the letter carefully and thought, "I'll read it again when I get home." She was tenderly amused at how American Anne was becoming, Anne, the most English of them all.

And then as she stepped back onto the sidewalk and started with crushing weariness to walk out to the lonely cottage, she stopped suddenly in the midst of all the people and whispered, "Oh, God! Don't let him sneak away to Chicago without seeing me. Don't let him, God!"

Australia

Australia is the only nation that absorbs an entire continent. It is a vast country, about the size of the United States. It is also a violent land, often alluring, often forbidding. And it is empty, with no more inhabitants than the city of New York.

At dusk, your plane rushes toward Australia, and the heavens come alive with color. The dying sun inflames the clouds. Then, in the darkness, the great empty continent looms up. In the distance, a lighthouse flashes. You can feel the loneliness that engulfs this mighty land.

Then suddenly below you explode the million lights of Sydney. On half a hundred hillsides, down many bays, you see the brilliance of metropolitan Sydney, with a population of almost two million. Few approaches to the nations of the world can be so spectacular, so portentous of what is to come.

Here is a land of untold capacities! Its deserts are more cruel than the Sahara, yet they abound in mineral wealth. Its people are courageous, yet more than two-thirds of them huddle within twenty miles of the sea, while the dead heart of their continent lies barren.

Australia is a wonderful land, challenging and empty. Its unknown future inspires the imagination of all who see the lovely cities and the majestic plains.

Australia's future is uncertain because she stands, like a bewildered woman, at the schizophrenic moment. She is bedazzled by flattering choices, frightened by oppressive dilemmas. She has no clear idea of what she wants to become.

Formerly an agricultural nation, Australia is now dabbling in manufactures in the dubious hope of becoming self-sufficient. There is an Australian airplane whose pilots, when they went against the Japs, wirelessed Melbourne, "We who are about to die, salute you." There is a fine Australian car, some talk of a television set. Prices reflect the older economy. The best filet mignon you ever tasted is 29 cents a pound. On the other hand, a good suit of clothes, made of Australian wool which has been made into cloth in England costs $85. An electric mixer for the kitchen is $70, and a very average refrigerator is $475. But a haircut is 18¢.

Always intensely loyal to England, Australia now acknowledges that for defense she must rely upon America. This creates a psychic wrench, which is compensated by extra attention to odd little English customs. Tropic hotels announce:

IN ORDER TO MAINTAIN
THE DECENCIES
GENTLEMEN WILL APPEAR AT ALL MEALS
ATTIRED
IN TIE AND COAT

In sweltering Cairns, only 17 degrees off the Equator, conservative men dress as they would in London. And Sunday is like a Philadelphia Sunday—cubed.

Nor can Australia decide what part of the world she belongs to. Up to 1919, she imagined herself a part of Europe, an English shire once removed. Then came the "Australasian period," when it was believed that white Australians were destined to guide their teeming brown and yellow brothers to a civilized society. Now Australasia, as an idea is passé—even though a major bank is stuck with it—because Australians realize that if any guiding is done, it'll be the brown boys guiding the white. In the bitter days of 1942, when Japan was bombing Darwin at will, there was a brief period when Australians thought their destiny lay with Canada and the United States. Now, they're not sure where they belong.

Most important of all, Australia can't decide what her system of life should be. People shout for more production, but work about 35 hours a week. They insist that things be modern, but prefer the good old ways of doing things. They are intensely individualistic (the "Australian boxing glove" is the business end of a broken bottle), yet they surrender many enterprises to state socialism, which runs most of them at a loss. And although they must "populate or perish," they don't like foreign immigrants!

But they are the most hospitable English-speaking people on earth.

To get on in Australia, you must make two observations. Say, "You have the most beautiful bridge in the world" and "They tell me you trounced England again in cricket." The first statement will be a lie.

Sydney Bridge is big, utilitarian and the symbol of Australia, like the Statue of Liberty or the Eiffel Tower. But it is very ugly. No Australian will admit this. The war bride entering San Francisco was typical. The captain of the *Lurline* said, "Well, girls, here's your new home." The brides stared in silence and finally a lass from Adelaide spoke for all of them: "Sydney Bridge is better."

But Sydney Harbor is the finest I have ever seen, and that includes Acapulco. It is a thing of beauty, a fairytale body of water surrounded by little houses with red roofs. It is a superb lake set amid a nest of friendly hills.

Long promontories stretch out into the bay and form anchorages which no storm can molest. Three of the land fingers are public parts, so that no matter where you are in the busy harbor, you feel close to country parks.

Sydney itself is like London, but prettier. It consists of many small towns banded together in their common dependence upon the bridge. As you walk through Sydney, you feel that around the next corner you must come upon open countryside. But the city stretches for miles. Traffic is the city's curse, because there are no adequate streets. In the shopping district, even the sidewalks are lined with yellow to keep pedestrians from crushing one another. It has been suggested that shoppers walk north on one side of the street and south on the other. As one comedian says, "Apart from the traffic, there's only one thing wrong with Sydney—Melbourne!"

Where Sydney streets are treacherous, Melbourne's are almost unbelievably handsome. Three chains wide—that's 198 feet, three times the width of an average street—they are flowering wonderlands, with exotic trees down the middle. The blocks in this beautiful city of a million and a quarter people are very long, so following Bourke Street you get an alley, Little Bourke. Some years ago, one of these alleys, Little Lon, had a string of the best patronized candy shops in the world. Remarkably pretty girls tended them, with about sixpence-worth of stale goods for sale. The customers were always men, and as soon as one arrived, the candy store was closed. Now Little Lon has shops with more substantial, but not more appreciated, supplies.

Melbourne claims superiority over Sydney in four respects: its football is rougher, its girls are prettier, its loyalty to England is more constant and its beer is much better.

Australians must consume ten times as much beer as they do milk. Saloons, called hotels—with a crust of bread for a meal and a snarl if you ask for a room—are open only from ten in the morning to six. And from five o'clock on, an Australian hotel is like something out of Dante.

You've finished a day's work and drop into your favorite pub for a couple of quick ones. At the door a blast of foul air, smoke and shattering noise greets you. Around the bar—an oval perhaps 50 feet in length—is jammed a struggling mass of humanity. The barmaids are slinging schooners as fast as their hands will work. They work in a kind of mechanical daze and speak to no one.

You stand at the edge of the crowd and start to shout for your pint. No one notices you, so you start slowly to elbow your way up to the bar. Stale beer slops over you. You see a friend and shout at him. He bangs on the bar with his glass and finally gets hold of a pint for you. As he passes it back over the heads of others, some of it spills.

At quarter to six, a bouncer begins to bellow in a mournful chant, "Come on boys! Drink up! Drink up!" At five to six, he cries pleadingly, "Closing, boys, closing!" Men order frantically and those at the bar line up three or four. The bedlam increases. At six, the doors are slammed shut and a frightful gong begins to ring. Now the bouncer cries, "Please, drink up!" The lucky ones at the bar toss off one pint after another. In a corner, Tim O'Farrell carefully pours his beer into a growler. In a nation where there isn't enough of anything (except food), beer is the greatest shortage of all. Saloons save their bottled stuff for old friends, so when Tim has a mate in at night, he has to serve whatever stale booze he's been able to sneak out of the bar.

No Australian likes such a system. It is a dreadful travesty on the good fellowship of an English pub. Workingmen guzzle like animals and reel home drunk. Yet whenever late closing is put to a vote, it's defeated—by the women. They say, "Sure my husband comes home drunk. But he does come home."

The other thing Australians love is sport. In number of participants, tennis is the prime game, and the Aussies are convinced they'll retain the Davis Cup. The most colorful sport is surfing. On perfect beaches, where combers from the Pacific thunder in, the Australian family collects a fine coat of tan. "We're a nation of pagan sun-worshippers," complain ministers during the summer months.

Every beach is protected by Life Saving Clubs, and to see the handsomely outfitted young men parading like wooden soldiers as they go to drill is an exciting experience. R & R competitions—rescue and resuscitation—are held throughout the season. "Patients" swim madly to distant buoys, where they "drown." On the beach a team of five goes through motions as stylized as a ballet. The beltman—rescuer—swims like crazy out to the buoy, while the shore crew play out a long silken rope. Now they drag back the two swimmers and resuscitate the drowned man. On show days, it's a game. On other days, it saves thousands of lives.

Australian beaches have a special problem. The surf is so rough that many dentures are knocked loose. At low tides, the guards collect them and place them in rows, from which distraught owners can claim their own. But in recent years, bums have been slipping in, trying the chompers for size, and walking off with a set that fits.

Australia has a strong baseball league, with junior teams who wear uniforms donated by Bing Crosby. It's amusing to read that "two sides have a fixture as finalists for the major premiership." Girls play softball. Lacrosse and basketball are popular. Older men play bowls, "but your knee has to crick before you're old enough to make the team." On country stations, farmhands use a pitchfork to toss a ten-pound bag representing a sheaf of wheat over a bar. Champions toss it higher than fifty feet. Billiards is a mania with many, and Walter Lindrum was a greater champion in his game—pot the ball, scratch off it or carom—than Willie Hoppe was in his.

The great games are football and cricket. Australians play four kinds of football, each rougher than the other: soccer (11 men, kick the ball); rugby union (15 men, handle or kick); rugby league (13 men, rougher rules); and Australian rules (18 men, kick, run, dribble).

This last is a cross between throwing slaves into the Coliseum and a riot in an Irish pub. Body contact is violent, hospitalization frequent.

In fact, Australian sport is a man's occupation. Papers on Monday are a report of lacerations, who kicked whom, referees' explanations as to why the riot developed and formal protests. One Rules game in Sydney—it's really a Melbourne game—resulted in four fractures, a riot and the public censure of two officials.

Even cricket—that dullest of games—becomes murder when Australians are involved. For several years England had dominated play for the Ashes, cricket's mythical Davis Cup, but in the 1920's one of the world's most remarkable sportsman appeared in a small Australian town. He was Don Bradman, cricket's Babe Ruth, Ty Cobb and Joe DiMaggio rolled into one. He mesmerized the opposition. Sometimes he batted for days, scoring doubles and triple centuries.

He was knighted by the King for having practically murdered English bowlers. But they got even. In the 1930's they developed two bowlers of super speed who heaved the ball right at Bradman's head. When he tried to defend himself with his bat, the English captain posted half his team in the infield. And Bradman popped up.

This outrageous sportsmanship was indefensible—wasn't cricket, you know—but there was no rule against it. The Ashes deteriorated into a public brawl. At Adelaide, the English were razzed worse than the Giants are booed in Brooklyn. Books were written and there was some talk of dissolving the Empire.

Finally, the rules were changed. You could no longer pack the infield, but by this time Australia had two very fast bowlers and England none. So, in the 1948 tests, Australian bowlers banged murderous shots right at English heads, and more books were written. New rules were proposed, but the Aussies say, "No matter the rules! We'll still win!" Say the English, "Goodness! They play as if all they wanted was to win!" Reply the Aussies, "We do."

But to see the nation go mad, you must attend the Melbourne Cup, run at beautiful Flemington Race Track in early November. During the war an Australian stationed in New Guinea found himself in a jungle outpost when the Cup rolled around. There was no one to bet with, so he finally talked a naked savage into backing the favorite for a couple of bob. No self-respecting Australian is ever caught without "something going in the Cup." The betting mania on this race is unbelievable, for horse racing is the national sport, betting the national vice.

Lotteries are popular. State governments use them to support hospitals, and famous ones like The Golden Casket have been running for years. First prize in a big one might consist of two furnished homes, a $3000 sport car, and an income for life. Horse punters—as serious bettors are called—like doubles and all ups (parlays). A Melbourne clerk recently picked eight certain winners in a row and bet $6 all up. He won $65,000 for one afternoon's work!

But to see the national spirit at its best, one must visit Oak Park for the August meeting. Oak Park is a cattle station on the vast plains of the north. There is no town, no railway, nothing but a big open space where the maximum amount of fun can be had.

People begin to arrive six days before the races. They tent on station land. There's a dance every night in the wool shed. Women wear their best. Right promptly the men—some of them near millionaires—start "to lay the dust." They keep this up for six days, and then the serious drinking begins.

From places as far as 400 miles away, people charter planes to see this fabulous meeting. By race time, Oak Park looks like a gold-rush town. Sixteen important bookmakers arrive to place odds on anything. Only amateur jockeys and inexperienced horses are run, but the betting is astronomical. A caterer sets up a shack where he feeds two hundred a day. Fellows and girls dance all night and raise hell all day. It's Australia at the country races! Reported a friend with a faraway look, "Oak Park! Never in me life did I see such beautiful fist fights!"

But Australians can also achieve great things in harnessing their mighty land. In the Murray River Valley, they have discovered a dozen ways to use every drop of water they get. Great hydro-electric projects use the streams as they form. Irrigation is practiced to make utter desert lands flourish with fruits and cereals. Then dams store what's left for fields lower down.

In the Latrobe Valley, east of Melbourne, great deposits of brown coal have been uncovered and the wet, not-yet formed coal is burned in special furnaces that use the steam for power and the dried-out coal for briquettes. The entire valley has become an Australian T.V.A., a brilliant project with created villages, new industries and great promise.

The harnessing scheme I liked best was one some four hundred miles east of Oak Park. There, on a jungled table-land, I was led to the edge of a precipice and loaded into a swinging birdcage—called "The Flying Fox"—which swung out over a tremendous waterfall that roared some six hundred feet below me. Wind made the Fox sway sickeningly as spray leaped up from the black rocks below.

When I reached the other side, I was taken to a cable car—an old coal truck dangling from a single strand of wire—and dropped seven hundred feet straight down the cliff to the foot of the falls. It was a superb trip, if one looked up at the water.

There was nothing when I stopped but the rock floor of the huge canyon, but I was led behind some rocks and into a deep cave. There, completely protected from any kind of assault, was hidden a complete hydroelectric plant capable of generating 110,000 volts. It served an area of 400,000 square miles, yet even the penstocks delivering the head of water were buried deep in rock, up gloomy tunnels that sweated as I climbed them.

The Australian, like his newer projects, is a powerful man, primarily Irish and English. His ancestors were petty convicts—"Selected by some of the smartest judges in England"—who had to be sent to Australia after the American Revolution had ended the traffic to Pennsylvania and Georgia. The Australian's *Mayflower* is the famous *First Fleet* of eleven ships which landed in 1788.

The Australian loves freedom. He has fought for it and established his nation in the face of great obstacles. When Captain Bligh of the *Bounty* was sent out to knock some discipline into the local lads, they proved too tough for him. They told him to go on back home, and he did so.

An Australian journalist, long accustomed to the courtesies of American shops, returned to Melbourne and sought to buy his wife some chocolates. "Don't have any," the clerk snapped. "But there's a box in the window!" the journalist protested. The clerk stopped dead, cupped his hands and yelled, "Hi, Mabel! Come 'ere! It's the bloody Duke of Gloucester!"

A railroad crew in Queensland had a boss described as "the finest man who ever drew breath." But one utterly cantankerous workman set out to lay him low and one day did so. Said the others, "Jake was right. We was gettin' to like the boss too much."

When the famous actor, Robert Morley, gave Sydney stagehands the same aloof treatment he had dished out in London and New York, they said nothing. But opening night of *Edward, My Son* was a riot. Curtains didn't work, the phone behaved disgracefully, and when Morley switched a light, nothing happened. Said one, "We gave him the old Australian handshake."

You've never been insulted until you offend an Australian. Their scorn is vitriolic. They say proudly, "No bloody barstud can tell me how to do anything. But if you're man enough to do it yourself, well . . . I like a bloke who knows the tricks."

Australians prize this arrogance, even when directed against themselves. The journalist who was accused of mistaking himself for the Duke says, "I like it that way. When I was a lad, sheep shearers got three dollars for shearing a penful. And if the owner didn't like the results, he might not pay. You touched your cap, when you spoke to a man with money. Me? I touch my cap to nobody."

In order to understand Australian labor, it is necessary to visit Broken Hill. You leave Sydney and travel west by fast train. You cross the Blue Mountains and then penetrate desert waste for hundreds of miles. Names on your map refer only to stops where sheep may be loaded. You are in the Outback—the Never-Never—where wind rips across empty land. Monotony increases and you seem headed for nowhere.

Then suddenly, you see a gaunt mine shaft, and as you approach you find not desert but a green and tree-protected city of 27,000. Many visitors call Broken Hill a miracle. It is.

From its jagged crest have been taken multimillions in almost pure silver and lead. It was probably the richest single deposit of wealth ever discovered, and when tailings from silver mining were examined, they were found to contain new fortunes in zinc.

In 1905, a brilliant young engineer from London, described in the official history as "Mr. H. C. Hoover, who subsequently rose to the eminent position of the President of the United States," established processes by which the zinc could be won.

A closely held company controlled this fantastic wealth. It was named Broken Hill Proprietary—world famed as B.H.P.—and yearly dividends of more than 100% were common. Now B.H.P. has turned its attention to making steel and is the biggest producer south of the Equator, the most powerful corporation in Australia, comparable only to DuPont or Armstrong Vickers.

B.H.P. developed when most men thought that riches existed only to make rich men richer. Australian workmen were not of that opinion. In a series of protracted and brutal strikes, they established the principle that they were entitled to a substantial share of all profits.

Today, Broken Hill is one of the most completely unionized cities on earth. And the unions are considered ideal patterns for others to follow. There is little labor strife, no wildcatting, no irresponsible outside leaders to wreck production.

Credit for this goes to the Barrier Industrial Council, an advisory board to which all unions must belong. It is the sole bargaining authority. It conducts Union Badge Shows, when practically every workman in Broken Hill—hairdressers, blacksmiths, bakers, municipal employees, bartenders, reporters—displays his union badge.

To join one of the good unions in this ideal city, you must (1) have been born in Broken Hill; or (2) been educated there since the first grade; or (3) lived there for eight years. Thus there is no chance for radical outsiders to take over. Says management: "Those we have are radical enough!"

The city is a law to itself. It has thirty-nine bars which rarely close. "There's legal closing, of course, but it's open to a fluid interpretation." The Barrier Council assisted by the companies, have provided good doctors, a fine hospital, excellent education, race tracks, swimming pools, picnic grounds, honest gambling and public housing.

For example, Mrs. Velda Watters, aged 31, is married to a miner who works underground. She and Cyril were born in Broken Hill, but as a young man he did not fancy mining. He ran away with a circus, but he was gypped out of his pay so many times that Broken Hill stability began to look pretty good. He took a job with Zinc Corporation.

The Watters live in a small concrete-block house with a corrugated roof, which they bought for $11 a month. They are considering a newer house, which Zinc will finance. They have recently bought a Kelvinator through Zinc at a discount of $32.

They enjoy many industrial benefits resulting from the great strikes. For 36 cents a month, the family gets medical insurance including hospitalization, medicine and surgery. For another 14 cents, they get free dental care, but they must pay for any false teeth.

At Christmas, they get three-weeks' vacation with pay and a cheap ride on a Zinc train to Adelaide, where they can rent a seashore tent for 80 cents a week.

Cyril Watters makes about $65 a week plus all kinds of recreational facilities, a lending library, a pre-school kindergarten for his daughter, plus all the social services which labor has forced the state to provide: health insurance, charity hospitalization, free drugs, widow's pension of $5.26 a week plus $1.60 for each child. He has unemployment insurance, financial aid when his wife is pregnant, a child endowment of $1.60 a week for each child after the first. When he grows too old to work, he and his wife may, if they need help, move into an old folks' home where each married couple has a private flat, medical service, and $6.84 a week per person. At death, the state will provide Cyril Watters with a free grave and a Christian burial, if his family cannot do so.

In addition to such services, every man or woman connected in any way with mining at Broken Hill receives a lead bonus—about $27 a week, depending on the world price—irrespective of his other wages. This was won as a result of a strike and accounts for the restrictions on union membership.

Then, to complete the miracle of Broken Hill, the companies decided that some steps must be taken to halt the erosion that is crippling much of Australia. (Coastal towns are sometimes swept away by torrents of water that used to be held on the land by trees and roots.) At Broken Hill huge strips of trees have been planted, ground cover restored, and a magnificent flowering oasis created in the middle of desert land. This has been done by hauling water as far as 72 miles. It is no wonder that two local words dominate Broken Hill conversation: "It's a beaut day. It's a bonza town."

Cyril Watters has been worried recently with a touch of pleurisy, and his wife has wondered whether or not he should quit underground work. He also has an odd habit of riding home at night in the ambulance. This worries his wife, who knows that no matter what benefits the Barrier Council has won, mining is still a dangerous job. "If he gets good pay, he earns it."

Of course, even if Cyril did quit Zinc he wouldn't leave Broken Hill. A man would be crazy to leave that rollicking, impudent, wonderful place.

Australia is a worker's paradise. An employer with religious scruples wouldn't permit factory broadcasts of horse races. His girls quit. There are at least half a million unfilled jobs. Even the casual listener hears of many industries that would be launched "if I could get the help." An employer must actually beg people to work for him. One false step, and his whole force may walk out!

A glaring result of labor's domination is a critical underproduction of everything. Practically all items that go into building a house are unobtainable through normal channels. Bathtubs, toilets, tiles, telephones, cement and steel cannot be bought. As a result, the housing shortage is much worse than in America, for even the smallest town is brutally overcrowded.

I sat in the upper chamber of Victoria State Parliament when the Minister for Works was being questioned. "Why do we have insufficient schools?" Money has been budgeted for 250. "Why don't you build them?" No cement. No workmen if there were cement. "Why isn't the park roadway mended?" We have the funds but no workmen. "Why don't you build a breakwater to protect the shore?" We have the money but we can't get men to work so far from home.

319

One odd aspect of the forty-hour week is that many families find it almost impossible to shop. Stores close Saturdays and clerks won't work late one night a week. Housewives with jobs do all their marketing during lunch hour. When I asked a woman what she'd do if she wanted to buy a dress, she said, "I'd skip out during work." And if the boss caught you? "If he opened his mouth, I'd jolly well quit." The post office, where an immense amount of business is conducted—telegrams, telephones, social security, old-age pension—is open from 9 to 5, so that queues at lunch hour are staggering.

Actually, it's a thirty-five hour week. Employees are entitled to ten minutes smoko—Cigarette and tea—morning and afternoon. It usually runs to twenty minutes each time, and on Fridays clerks start to wind up the week's work shortly after lunch. In an expanding land that needs everything, Australia produces little.

Yet the resulting pattern of life is wonderfully pleasing. (Says one Australian critic: "All my people want is freedom, no work, a lottery ticket and a pint of beer.") I myself have been happier in Australia than in any other major nation except my own. Life is easy. The climate is superb. Nobody gets ulcers. And anyway, most people work too much.

Australian labor is militant on the point. They say, "We don't want an American speed-up system here. We don't want millionaires. We don't want chrome and we can do without night clubs. What if it did mean an extra three quid a week? We like Australia just as it is." And questions have already been asked in Parliament about baby-sitters. "Is this a device to exploit the worker?" There is a strong movement on to unionize baby sitters!

The under-utilization of Australia's industrial capacity would be all right if it concerned only Australians. But directly north and east of the great continent lie many islands and the mainland of Asia, all crowded with millions upon millions of brown people who can scarcely scrape together enough to eat.

In 1942, Japan could easily have invaded Australia. No one in the crowded islands will forget that. Since population often determines history, it is certain that the brown races will sooner or later challenge Australia again. The hot breath of Asia is upon Australia's neck, and only good fortune will keep her free.

One answer to the menace has been the White Australia policy, which almost every Australian, regardless of other commitments, defends with fanaticism. This policy demands that no one with colored blood be allowed citizenship. It is enforced with brutal consistency. On passport applications, white travelers are warned that any colored servants brought into the country must possess a return ticket. Chinese men who married Australian girls and who reared large families were thrown out of the country. An Englishman who had married a Tongan girl of royal blood was told he'd have to send her back. A priest came to the moment of marrying a couple when he discovered that the girl had Martinique blood. He could not proceed with the ceremony. Not even Maoris were permitted to take residence until New Zealand officially protested at such an insult to her citizens.

The white Australia policy started as an answer to the Chinese influx into gold fields and to the Solomon Island slaves in the sugar fields. The former were repatriated in shipload lots. The Islanders were crammed into schooners and evacuated. Says a white captain, "We put them ashore at any convenient island. They landed in strange places, wearing strange clothes, and with gold. For many it was instant death."

Along with the White Australia policy goes the acknowledgment that unless white people fill up the empty spaces, brown ones must. Therefore the Commonwealth maintains offices in Europe which beg settlers to emigrate. Considerable inducements are offered, but the number of takers is disappointing.

The quality is even more so. What Australia seeks is five or six million Englishmen with college educations, money in the bank and impeccable appearance to join them. Failing that, they'll accept Scots, Irish or Americans, in that order. If pressed, they'll accept settlers like the German Templars, a religious group who emigrated to Palestine in 1860, from where 540 moved recently to Australia, bringing with them $11,200,000. Obviously, there aren't many such emigrants.

The ones they do get come mostly from the Baltic States or from Central Europe. And they aren't much liked. Australians are not anti-Jewish. Their first native-born governor-general—the direct representative of the King—was a Jew. But they are anti-foreigner. They do not comprehend that America grew strong from a mixture of many nationalities. They insist Americans are English. A popular joke concerns the ranting American who cried, "You're on the wrong track, wanting only English settlers! Why, in my veins there runs the blood of Armenians, Russians, Turks,

Irish, Germans and Czechoslovakians." From the rear of the audience came a whisper of admiration: "By Jove! His mother was a sporting sort, what?"

One of the amusing aspects of the Australian attitude is the fact that the kind of Englishman they want would probably never consider emigrating to Australia. For years, the British stage has had a stock character: the Australian sheep millionaire, uncouth and barbarous of speech.

This question of speech is a great misfortune, for Australian pronunciation is hilarious. A train that is late again today is reported as "Lyte agyne todye." It is so repugnant to some ears that in New Zealand books have been written calling for a national commission to keep Australian pronunciation out of that Commonwealth. Educated Australians, of course, speak a most pleasing language, far removed either from the massacred A or the amusing affectation of their radio announcers. It is quite a relief, after a daytime of bastard Oxford, to hear a politician cry in the Parliamentary broadcasts, "It's a disgryce for Astrylia to tyke such a stand on immigrytion."

The whole problem of occupying the vast emptiness is highlighted in the case of Frank Jang. In 1930 he arrived from China and later on took up a farm that no white man had been able to make pay. In a few years, he had it out of the red. Then the Dominion Government ordered him deported. By this time, he had a wife and five children, the oldest nine years old.

Although Australians approve the White Australia policy, many of them condemn its heartless operation. The neighbors of Jang refused to let him be deported. Said they: "We need men desperately here in the empty North. Here's one who has proved he can farm." School teachers reported that no Jang child ever failed a subject. Businessmen informed the Government that when Jang's deportation order came through, the Chinese took all his money out of the bank and went personally to each of his creditors, paying all bills in cash. Conservative farmers circulated petitions begging the Government to make an exception in Jang's case. Reluctantly, the Government agreed to a six month's stay, providing Jang would leave the land and work in town.

This provoked a greater storm. Much of Australia that now lies idle could support human beings; and if the population increases, Australia might have a chance to withstand Asiatic aggressors. The men of Jang's district wanted him kept on the land. The Government said it would restudy the case.

Frank Jang illustrates all aspects of the struggle for population and the fight against Asia. Farmers see in him a man who can bring land into profitable cultivation. Neighbors see him as a fine citizen. But others see those five children, those ten yellow people under one roof—Jang also supports his younger brother, his step-mother and an old Chinese friend—and they recall how Asiatics have absorbed one island after another. Jang or no Jang, Australia shall not make that mistake. Out they must go! All of them!

The Australian is adamant only on labor freedom and the White Australia policy. In other respects, he is a generous, kind, reliable friend. Until you have stopped at some Outside station, you have not known hospitality. Australian friendliness—"Put on some tea! Open the beer!"—is the frontier type that once made the American South famous.

And the Australian is surely one of the best-fed human beings on earth. Everything is abundant. Steaks so thick, so rich that they seem unreal. Lemons as big as grapefruit, oranges as big as cantaloupes, paw paws that look like watermelons! Fruit of all kinds, cereals—pronounced sireals—lamb chops, fowl and wonderful fish. Australian oysters are good all year round and in the North have to be cut into four pieces, they are so monstrous. Lobster tails are common food, and roast beef is so ordinary that guests at hotels say, "What! Again?"

Only tea is a problem. Australia has no national anthem. If one is ever written, it should feature the tinkle of a tea cup. One gets tea seven times a day; in bed at 7; breakfast at 8; morning at 10; lunch at 1; afternoon at 4; dinner at 7; night cap at 10. I have been in amazing parts of Australia, including the front lines at Bougainville during the war, and I have never seen an Aussie miss his tea. Picnic grounds, zoo, race meetings and all outdoor events maintain a stand with the sign: "Hot Water. Fill Your Billy."

The Government pays a subsidy of 40 cents a pound for tea which sells for 46 cents a pound. Australians care very little for politics—you are fined if you don't vote—but it has been said that a government which dared to revoke the tea subsidy would be tossed out overnight.

The indifference to politics is hard to understand. Of seventeen married women from all levels of society, fifteen said, "I don't bother about elections. Except on late closing of saloons, I vote with my husband."

It is believed by many Australians that compulsory voting is a mistake. But others point out that Australia has many powerful Communists, and the compulsory vote at least ensures large democratic majorities. Critics remember the last national election. It had the bad luck to come during the big spring horse races. You hardly knew there was an election on!

Food is plentiful because of men like R. J. Doolin in Myall Downs. He has a small station of some 44,000 acres. (A big one would contain that many square miles. The biggest are as large as Colorado.) He runs 15,000 Merino sheep, two acres to the sheep, and feeds 800 short horns, seven acres to the steer. He grows 3,000 acres of Gabo wheat, a hard miller rich in gluten, 1,000 acres of sorghum, and another 1,000 of lucerne (alfalfa).

Mr. Doolin is known as a squatter, the proudest title in Australia. Squatocracy is made up of those families that went beyond the hills and settled vast farms. His station is one of the richest, and although he would pass for a small Indiana farmer, he is a wealthy man.

Myall Downs lies in flat to low-rolling land. Fields are immense, broken at intervals with broad bands of trees to halt erosion. They get 26 inches of rain a year and experience temperatures from 20 to 110 degrees. Doolin uses eight tractors, six reapers (called headers), four trucks and a jeep. The latter is used to reach the railhead fourteen miles away, for there are few roads here, only tracks across the bush.

Doolin runs this station with the help of four big, tough sons. Two of them were commissioned in the field during the last war and a fifth was killed in New Guinea. As his sons marry, Mr. Doolin builds each one a handsome, low, rambling home, complete with kerosene refrigeration, 32-volt electricity and all conveniences.

Myall is a busy station. Lambs begin to drop in September. Winter wheat is planted in May and June, harvested in the late spring (November, December). In August, eight skilled shearers are brought in with their helpers. And there is always the job of tending cattle, cutting sorghum, and keeping the place tidied up.

At night, the Doolin boys like to get out the jeep and hunt wild pigs that root through the wheat. With a powerful light, they spot the animal and crack at it with their rifles.

Mr. Doolin, who is technically a pastoralist—if he had a small holding, he would be a cow cocky; if he grew sugar cane, an agriculturalist; never a farmer—has not worked at

Myall much in recent years. He serves on the Federal Wheat Board, an authority which buys local crops and sells them abroad. Through his efforts a fair price is maintained ($1.04 a bushel) and foreign markets are sought.

Easter is the time at Myall Downs. Then the squatters move their entire families into Sydney for the autumn show of the Royal Agricultural Society. The Doolins stay at the Metropole, known as the Bushman's Pub. Here, in bleak splendor, a trio of elderly women plays classical music, while the squatters discuss the Show, which is a cross between a rowdy state fair and a sedate carnival. "But," says Doolin, "I'm always happy to get back home. It's the best land in the world."

He is right. The land of Australia is magnificent. It is grand in the manner that excites the imagination. At dawn the sun breaks out of the Pacific and speeds across the coastal plains. To the north fires are still burning in the vast sugar fields. To the south apples are ripening in Tasmania. Sydney and Melbourne are beginning to stir. A flood is roaring down to wreck the edges of a city. A continent is beginning to waken.

Soon the sun is upon the Dividing Range, where snow accumulates in winter. Then it dips into the country of a million sheep and flashes on to the scrub lands where gold was found, where silver and lead stood free in broken hills.

Now it races into the central deserts, vast empty spaces where lakes and rivers show on maps, but where there may be no water for years at a time. Children born here may reach seven before they see rain; their homes are washed away in mighty floods. A jackrabbit springs from his nest and leaps across the barren wastes. Soon another follows. They are Australia's scourge. In three years, a litter of six can increase to 9,600,000. Now a train of camels moves slowly with a store of goods for an Outback station. A lonely train puffs its way north to the middle of the continent, where even it surrenders.

The sunlight flashes on the poles of the Overland Telegraph Line. It was built against superhuman obstacles in the 1870's. By the time a section was completed, termites had eaten down the poles of the previous stretch. It was the lifeline of Australia, crossing from south to north, Adelaide to Darwin, for the code of the Outback permitted lost or exhausted wanderers to cut the telegraph wires. That meant the repair crews would reach them within a day!

Now the light strikes the great road, the Bitumen (called

325

bitch-a-mun). It was built during the war and connects Alice Springs with Darwin. Before it was surfaced, clouds of dust could be seen for twenty miles. It was no use speeding to get out of the dust. It wasn't made by the car ahead of you, but by the cars that went by last week.

Beyond the Bitumen, there is nothing—nothing but sand and lonely desert. Yet as the sun rides west, it picks out, even here, a station or two where some mad soul is trying to run a few cattle. With him are the aborigines, the half-castes. These are the people who were described by the first white man who studied them as "the miserablest on earth," an opinion that has never been challenged. They were so primitive that they did not even associate pregnancy with intercourse. They blamed night spirits!

Then the racing sun strikes the ultimate dead heart of the continent. From the Nullarbor Plains, in the south, through the Victoria Desert and the Gibson Desert, in the center and on northward, to the useless tropical wastes of the Leopold Ranges the light reveals—nothing. Heat is intense. There is no water. (At Kalgoorlie, they pipe it 360 miles to the mines.) To the south the lone railroad track runs for 800 miles with rarely a bend. You must remember this part of Australia when you hear, "It's as big as America! It could support a hundred million people." Men died on these plains when they tried to penetrate the limitless deserts. Looking at them, a wise Australian said, "There is only one difference between Australia and America: the Mississippi." Yes, if you could rip out that magnificent system—Missouri, Platte, Ohio, Tennessee, Arkansas, Red—and throw it into the heart of Australia you would have a wonderland, rich beyond compare. But there is no Mississippi. There is no river that always carries water. This is the heartbreak land.

With a rush of relief, the morning sun bursts upon the beauty of the western rim where Perth rests near the ocean. A bright poster announces: "Tonight. The Lovely Musical. Oklahoma. New York Cast."

In this mighty land strange animals live. For eons, Australia lay cut off from all other lands, so that its animals did not develop along customary patterns. They are all marsupials, who carry their young in pouches. The kangaroo, and its smaller cousin the wallaby, are pests, yet the kangaroo appears on the national seal. They are delightful creatures with faces much like rabbits. They hop about on huge hind legs, beg for peanuts, spar with their attenuated front feet and have a roistering good time. A mother, if chased when she has a joey in her pouch, will toss him in the bush and try to lead her pursuers away from the baby. But for all their attractiveness, the kangaroos eat too much grass and they are shot by professional hunters who sell the skins. Say the sheepmen, "When my beasts are starving, the 'roos are fat. They grub the grass out with their under teeth. I pay 70 cents a head, the same as I do for eagles."

"The platypus," says one naturalist, "must be seen to be believed, and when you see it, you believe it even less." It lives in eastern rivers, digging tunnels from below the waterline up into caves along the bank. It's a mammal, lays eggs, suckles its young although it has no teats—milk oozes out from the pores through the skin—has a bill like a duck, webbed feet, a beaver's tail. It carries poisonous spurs on its back feet, eats a pound of worms a day and produces a fur that is supposed to be the equal of sable.

The koala bear is, of course, not a bear at all. It's a crazy and wonderful comedian, perhaps the most completely winning of all animals. It has a flat, rubbery nose, pin-point eyes that seem perpetually startled, and hairy ears that stand at attention. It was the pattern for the teddy bear, and no more proper model for a child's toy could have been devised.

At birth, the koala climbs into a pouch and occasionally thereafter thrusts out an unconcerned head that nibbles at eucalyptus leaves. As he grows older, he climbs onto his mother's back to survey the world. It is difficult not to laugh when a group of koalas climb aimlessly from branch to branch, stopping now and then to nudge one another, while they stare at people with innocent wonder.

They live only upon eucalyptus, eating the tips of leaves and thus acquiring an unpleasant odor which protects them from predators. They are joyous creatures, protected by the state. And they are no longer threatened with extinction.

Less fortunate are two rare animals living in Tasmania, the island state. The Tasmanian devil is a small scavenger, about the size of a badger. The Tasmanian tiger is more formidable, a carnivorous marsupial that looks like a jackal. He has a long rat's tail, a zebra-striped rump and a face like a wolf. Each of these creatures may soon become extinct.

If they do so, they will follow a tragic pattern, for the original wild men of Tasmania also found it difficult to get along with white civilization. They were fierce, relentless enemies. They perpetrated retaliatory murders until white settlers had to root them out. Bands were organized to hunt them, and they were rounded up into compounds, where they refused to have children. In the early years of this century, the last Tasmanian native died. A unique race of human beings had become extinct.

A happier fellow is the kookaburra, a fat, gross brown and white bird that perches upright on rails or telephone wires. Occasionally, he throws back his head, opens his oversized bill, and emits an outrageous burst of raucous laughter. He is a rough and clumsy clown.

The continent is filled with other strange creatures: the beautiful lyre bird, whose feathered dance is magnificent; the wombat, whose pouch is set backwards so that dirt won't get into it when he digs tunnels; the stately black swan of Western Australia; the brumbies (wild horses); the dingoes (wild dogs of handsome mien who howl but do not bark); crocodiles whose skins are valuable; and the great wild Cape buffalo whose ancestors were brought in as beasts of burden. They are fantastic creatures well suited to a violent land.

Although the Outback is cruel, many rugged Australians have challenged it. In this, they have been helped by two remarkable agencies. The Bush Brothers are missionaries who wander back and forth across the waste lands. One had a parish of 300,000 square miles. Sometimes they hit a community where they baptize adults, marry them and then baptize their children, all in one afternoon. "They're great Christians, but they're not stuffy."

More spectacular are the Flying Doctors, also an outgrowth of missionary effort. Peter Stevenson, the manager of Durham Downs station, runs 15,000 cattle on his 3,600 square miles. His wife Lillian writes away each week for correspondence courses which she teaches her three children. On Sunday, there is a radio Sunday school.

Stevenson is helped by fourteen men, one of whom suffers serious injuries when a horse falls on him. The nearest doctor is 450 miles away at Broken Hill.

Stevenson goes into his living room where the pedal wireless stands. He pumps the pedals and finally gets short-wave contact with Broken Hill. The voice comes through faintly. "This is Frank Basden. The doctor is on a trip to Innamincka. I'll tell him."

From Broken Hill, the message is relayed north to fifty different pedal wireless sets established on remote stations. The doctor has left Innamincka and is heading for Tibooburra, where he visits the hospital at intervals. Finally, word reaches him, and the two-engine De Haviland turns north to Durham Downs, hundreds of miles distant.

Meanwhile, at the station, trucks have been lined about the field with their headlights ready. Mrs. Stevenson is tending the injured man, while a woman, two hundred miles away, says over the pedal, "Try putting on hot presses."

Shortly before dusk, the De Haviland appears from the south. All hands run out to the landing field and greet the young doctor as he climbs out. "Come in for some tea," they say, and he agrees. "Now the patient." They lead him to a half-caste—they are the best stock riders—who lies on a cot in a screened verandah. The doctor studies his injuries, and asks him to remove the clean white pajamas provided by Mrs. Stevenson.

There has been no fracture, no rupture. Everyone is relieved. The half-caste gets a sedative, because the sprain is painful. Then the doctor has a big station feed. Mrs. Stevenson gets on the pedal and informs Broken Hill that the doctor will stay with them for the night. She also exchanges local gossip—her neighbors are 25, 60, 80 and 105 miles away—over the pedal circuits, and everyone settles down for a long chat.

The doctor has brought six books from the lending library, a spool of blue silk, and other items ordered by the Stevensons on his last visit. He promises to bring glucose and a ham on his next.

In the morning, he leaves promptly. Mr. Stevenson winks at his wife. It's odd how the Flying Doctors always visit the Tibooburra hospital on race day. "It's a beaut morning!" they cry as he takes off. They may not see him again for months. But he is ready, 450 miles away.

The Outback colors all Australian life. Most of the best literature deals with settling the bush. Most of the paintings deal with it in one way or another. "In back of Bourke" refers to the great Never-Never. The constituency of Woop Woop is an imaginary place "where a cyclone could erase all human life and it wouldn't be discovered until the next election." But it is the fabled town of Snake Gully about which center the hilarious Outback yarns.

Here live Dad and Dave, two characters who originally appeared in a book called *On Our Selection* (Homestead). Dad is the Australian countryman, hard-pressed, hoping for rain, ragging the Government. He speaks in a drawl that yields about five words to the minute. Dave is the universal yokel whose courtship of Mabel is the basis for most Australian dirty stories.

Dave's great delight is to attend a Two Up school. Sneak-

329

ing far out behind a sand dune—for Two Up is a crime—Dave and his friends form a circle. Watchmen, called cockatoos, are posted on hilltops to warn against police. In the center of the ring, a man holds a small paddle called the kip. On it, he places two pennies. Breathless with excitement Dave says to the man next to him, "Two bob it comes heads." The kip is adroitly twisted upward. The pennies flash in the air and then fall onto the sand. A head and a tail. They are tossed again. This time, they're both heads, and Dave wins. Across the circle two other men exchange fifty pounds. The cockatoos sing out that all's well. Australia's greatest gambling game continues.

Said a Frenchman, "Australia is most religious. Everyone stands about a circle. A man in the middle throws up his hand and falls upon his knees. Then everybody bows and half the crowd cries out, 'Oh, Christ.' "

But Mum, Dave's mother, is not a humorous character. No Australian woman of the Outback is. She lives in a corrugated iron shack that has never seen paint. Although Dad and Dave buy tractors and headers, she often has no running water, no coal, no electricity, often no refrigeration, no indoor toilet, no new sink. In summer, she cooks over a wood stove when temperatures reach 120 degrees.

She is the heroine of Australia, and before the pedal wireless, she lived a life of loneliness and peril. No Australian writer has begun to capture her saga. But Mabel has no such aspirations. As fast as possible, she hightails it into Sydney. It has been truly said of Australia, "It's a heaven for men and dogs, hell for women and horses."

Women have an odd status in Australia. The great feminine reform that has swept Russia and the United States and which is now startling the British has not even started in Australia. Women are excluded from much of a man's life. They may not drink beer with him, except in extra-charge lounges that make any woman look immoral. They are not welcome in his clubs. They have the vote, but they don't really exercise it. They dress exceptionally well—David Jones' in Sydney is one of the largest buyers in the world of French fashions—but they are essentially of the nineteenth century.

Perhaps that is why so many American young men married them during the war. They were fresh, pretty, athletic, intelligent and above all, willing for the man of the family to be the man. Australian men don't want their women to change. Specifically, they don't want them to become too much like American women. "Beautiful, lovely, smart, but too bossy."

Australia is a man's country. It is not surprising, therefore, that art has had a bad time. Says a leading architect, "Up to 1935, a full-grown man who was interested in painting or music was obviously pathetic and to be spoken of in whispers." On the pediment of the national shrine in Melbourne, men are shown tending sheep. In an off corner, a woman is tending the arts. Until recently, art has played almost no part in the over-all national life. (Some minor artists have made a fair living and done passable work.) As a result, domestic architecture is atrocious. "We never have a straight line if we can tack on some gingerbread." In Queensland, because early settlers built their homes on stilts to protect against termites, people have done so ever since, when there were dozens of better ways to combat white ants. It has been said that one good architect in 1850 would have been more valuable to Australia than Broken Hill.

But this has changed radically in recent years. In the painters Dobell and Drysdale, Australia has artists of absolutely top magnitude. Tabloid newspapers run competitions in which young people sing Italian operatic arias for a chance to win scholarships in music. In Henry Handel Richardson, Eleanor Dark and Xavier Herbert, the nation has fine novelists; and the architects are working day and night to make the nation more attractive. Clean, straight homes are replacing the rococo. People who buy land are being begged not to chop down the trees. (In colonial times, the first thing a man did to start a home was to ringbark the trees. Today trees that would be worth $200 in any other country are ripped out before building starts.) In every form of art, there is awkward interest plus a knowledge of what is going on throughout the world.

In poetry, the Jindyworobaks—it means roughly *a campfire meeting place*—feel that Australian poetry can have meaning only if it returns to aboriginal patterns, as in the following lovely passage using the native word for dove:

> I would be unseen as Gul-ar-dark-ark calling
> out of the sky and tresses of the leaves,
> now that the fig lets fall her single flowers
> like stars to pass beyond my trailing hand.

Aboriginal words are also used effectively in naming sleeping cars: Allambi (quiet place), Tantini (sleeping), Weroni (quiet), and Dorai (to sleep).

Australian belles lettres have recently taken a terrific shellacking. There suddenly appeared a fiery natural poet, Ern Malley, who became a pet of the intellectuals. Nobody understood his work, but journals carried extravagant praise of his tortured rhythms. Then tragically he died and newspapers lamented the loss of "this authentic Australian voice." Then came the tempest, for Ern Malley had never lived at all, was a gigantic hoax. Two bored soldiers in New Guinea had made him up. His immortal verse? Clippings from the most horrible examples of tortured prose in army field manuals printed in short lines so as to resemble modern poetry.

Artists have a hard time making a living in Australia. What the nation needs is things: houses, trains, telephones, roads. Hugh Ramsay, in the 1890's, was the typical artist. Showing great promise as a painter, he scraped together a few pounds and studied in Paris. When he returned to Australia, he starved, and like bankrupt Rembrandt before him, painted his own portrait many times. Now they are tragic memorials, because you can trace in their gaunt lines sure proof that Ramsay was dying of tuberculosis. At 29, this immense talent was buried.

Ironically, shortly after his death, his brother discovered and sold Kiwi shoe polish, so that the family became very rich. They gave Hugh's pictures to various museums. But the artist was dead.

When I remarked that the Sydney museum—crammed with chauvinistic stuff—must be one of the most gloomy public buildings extant, a Melbourne friend exploded. "Don't say that. Australians love art. Come with me!" He took me to his own excellent museum, where a steady stream of visitors climbed the steps to the second floor. They went to the precious Van Eyck, one of the loveliest, and whispered to the guard. "Turn right," he whispered back. They went in silence to stand reverently before the stuffed skin of Phar Lap, "the greatest horse that ever lived." One man sniffed back his tears and said, "I still think American gamblers poisoned him in Kentucky." He blew his nose and went back past the Van Eyck to the street.

Australians are extremely world-minded. The average business leader has been to London, Paris, Rome, New York, San Francisco and Capetown plus other cities relating to his special interests. He makes the American businessman seem provincial.

One of the most frequent questions asked any visitor is:

"Are our accomplishments of world class?" Hotels are far below. Air service far above. Magazines way below in appearance, about equal in content. Newspapers about equal, except that there is no *Manchester Guardian* or *St. Louis Post-Dispatch*. Radio equals the standard with a fine national system plus commercial networks. Women's styles equal the standard. Restaurants, with some exceptions, do not. Government is above the standard. Roads are way below. Health services above. Swimming beaches far above, except for intruding sharks. Labor unions also above, except for those admittedly controlled by Communists. Hospitality far, far above.

Trains present a special problem. In colonial days, each governing unit thought it smart to have its own special gauge, so that today only rarely can a train from one state pass onto the tracks of another! Four different gauges are used from 2' 8½ " in the north to 5' 3" in the south.

A businessman who travels from Melbourne to Sydney leaves on the evening train at 6:30. But he can't turn in early, for there are no sleepers on the 5' 3" part of the trip. At 10:30, he reaches the 4' 8½ " section, and his sleeper is waiting. He grabs his bags—no porters—walks some two and a half blocks along a gusty platform, and climbs aboard. But even then he can't get to bed, because everyone wants to use the washroom at the same time. The Australian dismisses this with a shrug. "Night air," he grunts. "Very bracing!"

A royal commission has estimated that to unify gauges would take eleven years, 850,000 tons of unavailable steel, 12,000,000 new ties, and adjustments to 38,000 pieces of stock. Although some rationalization is taking place, the Australian is prepared to keep his trains as they are. "After all," he points out, "if you want speed, fly. Our planes are the best in the world."

If you sought two words to sum up Australia, they would be average and British. Australians love the average—not the mediocre—but the average wage, the average good bloke, the average happiness. There are few millionaires, almost no poverty. The cow cocky with a dozen head will argue with the squatter.

You can understand this best at the great memorial shrine in Melbourne. It is an impressive Assyrian mound to the dead of World War I. In Australia, it looks self-conscious. But in the shadows, on a vacant lot near the shrine, stands a small statue which no Australian can view without deep emotion. It's the "Man with the Donkey," and as statues go, it isn't much.

But it symbolizes a nation. At Gallipoli, a sour-faced Aussie called Simpson—it later turned out that wasn't even his name—was a bad case. Took orders from no one. When his mates were driven from the hills, he found himself an old donkey. He made more than a hundred trips right across No Man's Land, dragging in the wounded who would otherwise have died. His superiors warned him that if he persisted, he would be killed. On the twenty-fourth day, he was.

On Bougainville, I knew a murderous Aussie who took offense when some G.I.'s claimed that MacArthur was a better general than Blamey. This cobber offered to take on the crowd, one by one or Rafferty's Rules. Four days later, I learned that General Blamey was coming to inspect the troops. I told my friend the good news. He looked at me and spat. "Bugger the old barstud," he snarled. "Wattinell's he doin' up 'ere? Why don't he stop in bed and swill his booze?" That cut the general back to size.

There is one Australian, however, who is never content with the average: R. M. Ansett, whose story is hard to believe. He quit school after the eighth grade and finally wound up with a broken-down passenger car which operated as a bus between two country towns. At 26, he had so large a fleet that competitors sought government protection to keep him out of their areas.

He turned to aviation and in a few years had a training school, an airline and a reputation as a very hot pilot. He almost went broke and hadn't the money to pick up three much-needed Lockheeds when they reached the dock. Bankers wouldn't help. "Young fellow's overextended," they said.

He swung the deal himself and became one of Australia's big air companies. But war knocked this in the head and he devoted his planes to evacuation and training work. One of his pilots flew 23 hours a day moving people from Darwin when the Japs threatened.

In the meantime, he became fascinated by large, de-luxe motor buses, operated on a tour basis. He bought out an established company and immediately revolutionized a profitable business.

Australians love to travel. Ansett takes them anywhere, from Melbourne streets right to the dead heart of the continent. When he couldn't find decent hotels, he bought decrepit ones and made them over. When he couldn't buy, he built new ones, beautiful jobs definitely of world class. He became one of the most influential hotel men in the nation and spurred others to meet his standards.

Next he found that he was having trouble getting buses, so he decided to build his own. On chassis made in England, he attaches luxurious bodies with a hundred gadgets. They are so good that he even sells them to his competitors.

Then he re-established his air lines, so that today he runs many trips—say thirty luxurious days for $260, 5,000 miles—by a combination of private car, bus, airplane and cruising boat, with all stops at Ansett hotels.

His most startling venture, however, has been the purchase of several tropical islands near the Barrier Reef. On one of them, he has erected a hotel that will compare with any in the world. Modern, set beside a coral reef, facing a prospect of unmatched beauty, it provides each guest with a private cabana done in the flossiest style. "At present exchange," he said, "I can give American tourists a perfect tropical holiday with hot and cold bath, gourmet's meals, and perfect service for $33 a week."

His companies now control millions of dollars, thousands of people. And the remarkable thing is that he did it all before he was 40! Bankers still predict that he's got to go bust: "We've never operated like that before in Australia. Isn't sound." Ansett laughs.

"Maybe you've never heard of Sam Insull," I goaded.

"Sure I've heard of Insull," the thin, alert young man laughed. "I'm not making his mistakes. But assume that I did. Well, I can still drive a bus."

As for the fact that Australia is British, few Americans can understand this. Yet the same conditions and principles operate here as in New Zealand. Australia is economically, emotionally, spirtually and historically British.

An Australian will apologize for driving a Ford. It's unpatriotic to do so. "I've got to have one," he mumbles. "Damned English cars don't stand up on our roads. But even so, I prefer 'em."

In his will, a rich businessman says, "Any nurses, maids, or attendants coming into contact with my children shall be British or Australian born. My reason is that I am of Australian birth ... and wish that my children shall never become imbued with foreign ideas."

Australians who serve you a gargantuan meal often stop to apologize: "If we had the ships, we'd be sending this to England. They earned it, not we." An Australian who attended the cricket matches in England in 1948 says, "We prayed, with tears in our eyes, for an English victory against our own lads. It was no use. For eight years, the English blokes hadn't had enough to eat."

Each Australian state has a personal emissary of the King, in whose name the government is conducted. The Commonwealth also has a governor-general, and not even Labor's appointment of a party hack to that exalted post—formerly held by dukes of royal blood—made the institution cheap. Explained a tough old banker, "I swallowed me gorge and thought, 'Not even the person of a labor flunky can dim the King's prestige. He's here with us.' But in what a vessel!"

On the Melbourne shrine, the word AUSTRALIA never appears. The dedication is to "the honoured memory of the men and women who served the Empire." In the most revered chamber, the flag of honor is the Union Jack. The Australian flag stands to the left.

Economically, Australia's tie with England—they don't use the word Britain much—makes a lot of sense. Australian wool, meat, butter, wood and sugar are natural British imports. And British products like good cloth, crockery, heavy machinery, ships, and all the odds and ends of a commercial nation are needed in Australia. With no other country could the great continent carry on so purposeful an exchange of goods.

The devotion to things British can best be seen in Melbourne, where the Lord Mayor in his regal trappings has said, "As long as I'm in office, councillors shall appear at state functions in knee breeches, cocked hats and lace waistcoats." He is an excellent administrator and implies that when he's gone the Labor crowd—only ten out of thirty-three but growing—can wear overalls if they like.

In Melbourne, too, one can see the stately British procedure in Parliament. In the Legislative Council Chamber—an upper house elected by people who pay a certain amount of taxes—the party leader in wig, white stock and black robe sits at a desk containing an ornate hourglass. About him, on benches of brilliant red plush, sit the members. Above is suspended a canopy embellished with shells and a lion and unicorn. Behind is the throne chair with regal carvings kept empty in case the governor might wish to attend. Stately arches support a blue and gold ceiling.

Sessions start at 4:45, but are not broadcast as are the proceedings of the lower house—"It would be so frightfully dull"—but the Council does debate the rash laws of the lower house. They turn back legislation that is too liberal, and then the lower house passes it anyway.

Members receive about $2,200 a year and are elected for long terms. They get free railway passes and a vacation pass for their wives. They address one another in the archaic terms of parliamentary procedure, whereby one's mortal enemy becomes "My dear, dear friend, the honourable and gallant member for Woop Woop." Courtesies out of the way, the slaughter proceeds.

Nowhere can the British spirit be more finely studied than at the West Brighton Club in an unpretentious suburb of Melbourne. Here the leaders of the South, men of good fellowship whatever their calling, gather each Saturday night in hallowed ritual.

The bowling green is unsurpassed. The tennis courts are tended daily. The clubhouse was built eighty years ago and may never be changed. It is a low, rambling building with billiard rooms, a large bar, card nooks and a pot of cheese.

Members gather at six to discuss the day's doings. At seven, the elderly clerk—he's had the job for generations— becomes excited about the seating and checks it carefully with the president, who runs the largest internal airline in the world. Now members move into the dining hall, which is hung with mementoes of many wars. German propellers, giant brass shells, spears from New Guinea, helmets from France, and toques from the desert remind the members of how precariously the life of Empire has hung at times.

The food is incomparable. A ruddy-cheeked surgeon as wide as he is tall, well known in America, carves the roast. A leading architect serves the chicken. Grilled fish, five vegetables, four cheeses, a quart of beer per member, and oddments comprise the meal.

The talk is good. The waiting list for members is endless, for members never retire. A good dozen are over eighty, lusty, bright old men. A rejection from the club is binding for life. The last three who were blackballed were for typical reasons: one told smutty stories when a guest; one had welched on gambling debts; one lit his cigar before the toast to the King.

Finally, as the salad is being served—for thirty years, the same man has made the salad—the president rises and in a voice fraught with emotion cries, "Gentlemen, the King!" A shuffling of chairs, old faces looking up, and each member salutes the embowered corner where the three great portraits stand. In the middle, the King. To his right, Churchill. To his left—F.D.R.

A member starts the club song:

> One hundred years from now
> It'll all be the same.
> One hundred years from now . . .
> Somebody else will be in the soup,
> And the world will still go on.

Like the West Brighton club, Australia remembers America's part in the war. A fruit seller says, "It was glorious! I had five prices for a melon. Australian civilian, one bob. Australian army, two bob. American, three bob. American soldier with a girl, four bob. Marine with a very pretty girl. Sky's the limit!"

In a land bound with government red tape, citizens still laugh about the American colonel and the postmaster. Said the colonel, "The Japs may land at any time. We've got to have 16 phones." Replied the postmaster, "Ah, yes. Fill out these forms. In triplicate. And have them notorized." Patiently, the colonel did so. "It won't take long, will it?" he asked. The postmaster gleamed: "Perhaps two weeks. One mustn't rush Canberra, must one?" As the colonel left, the postmaster tucked the applications into a pouch which would go south, some days later. He had no sooner done so than his phone rang. It was the American colonel. "Thought I'd better tell you. The following sixteen call boxes have no telephones." And he rattled off the addresses of sixteen booths from which he ripped the necessary phones.

Americans astounded the Australians. The hard work, the good spirit, the efficiency and, above all, the tractors were marveled at. Many Australians dislike Americans, but you never find an engineer or contractor who doesn't say, "You chaps know how to do things." And anywhere in the North, people say frankly, "The Japs could have walked ashore. Our own government announced that it would sacrifice everything north of Brisbane. America saved us."

Today in Parliament it is admitted that Britain can no longer defend Australia, and it is obvious that Australia cannot do so alone. It is therefore openly acknowledged that future defense must rely upon American power.

At the same time, Australians don't trust America. Diehards cry, "The Yanks'll take over!" Cultural leaders say we are intellectual barbarians. Bright young things, many of them confessed Communists, stigmatize us "the champions of reaction." And people attached to England contend that any step toward America is treason, since it must be a step away from Britain.

Little points exacerbate. For example, there is no copyright agreement between Australia and America—because an Australian law left out a few simple words—and some American publishers pirate material. Therefore, all Americans are crooks.

In Labor's Federation House, Sydney, an artist-and-writer's union is holding a protest meeting. Carl Lyon, a handsome man of fifty, is speaking. "Three years ago, I had two comic strips running in several newspapers. Now I have only *Black McDermitt*. In one. Why? Because American strips are dumped on our market."

A short-story writer reports, "In Perth, I tried two weeks to sell a story. Finally, the editor showed me a 3,000-word American story complete with art work which he could buy for $1.02!"

A committee reports. "In the forty American comic books we studied, there was nothing but murder, rape, sexy drawings, sadism and gangsterism."

"How do they get in?" the chairman cries. "I thought there was a law."

Carl Lyon speaks. "Sure there's a law. But this trash is sold to New Zealand and London and then comes in as British."

The committee chairman continues: "And newspapers won't protest because if they don't run *Dick Tracy* and *Superman*, they lose sales." So American novels, technical books, and critical magazines reach Australia in limited quotas or not at all. We are represented by comic books.

Even so, Australians know a great deal about America. A favorite joke is, "You have the Democratic Party and Bob Hope. We have Labor and no hope." Newspapers often carry page-one headlines in this proportion: from Sydney, Melbourne, Canberra, 30%; from Europe, 30%; from New York (all U.S. stories are so dated) 40%.

American movies are almost as popular as English ones. An average program might be: 7:20 American newsreel; 7:30 another American newsreel; 7:40 English newsreel; 7:50 Mickey Mouse (cheers); 8:00 cowboy picture; 9:20 intermission with advertising slides; 9:30 intermission continues, but with advertising movies; 9:40 Australian newsreel; 9:50 color comedy (cheers); 10:00 Humphrey Bogart feature; 11:25 handsome color film of *God Save the King*. A program like that, if the patient lives, is bound to make Australians aware of what's going on in America.

But smart economists point out that if their country should ever move into the American orbit, it would be economic suicide. America would never absorb the raw materials that England now does. Our wool men, meat growers and timber producers would wreck Congress if we ever imported enough to keep Australia's economy alive. At present, we take some wool, lobster tails, tennis racquets, orchids, lead, zinc and gold. But not enough really to matter.

If international trade were arranged on ideal lines, a ship would leave Australia with raw materials for England; then carry to America manufactured items valuable because of British styling and polish; then pick up automobiles and heavy machinery for Australia. There appears no hope for such an arrangement. So Australia and America drift apart.

Wise Australians deplore this. They think it a tragedy that Japan is regarded as America's natural Pacific ally. "You can't trust them!" they warn. "They'll betray you again!" Responsible newspapers have proposed that American forces use the Outback deserts for atomic research. "Fifty thousand Americans would then visit us every year. They'd see that we are their natural allies."

There are other Australians—many, I fear—who are determined that Australia shall ally herself neither to England nor to the United States—but to Russia. I can foresee the day when Australia, faced by a resurgent Asia, will have to choose between Russia and America. It is apparent that this great continent-country is even now in grave danger of a permanent occupation by Asia. It could well be that under duress, Australia would prefer domination by Russia to annihilation by Indonesia, India or China. For the present, our fleet postpones the fatal decision.

I wish I could write these last words in red: Forget that Australia needs us. We need her. She is our forward friend. She is now what Hawaii was a generation ago: our first line of defense against trouble in Asia. We must cement our friendship with her. For in her, we have an ally that can be trusted, a splendid people who can be relied upon.

The Jungle

Australian women are essentially of the nineteenth century. Perhaps that is why so many American soldiers married them.

From the moment she stepped onto the wharf at Sydney, John Millstor looked at her with longing eyes. She was slim, very well groomed and provocatively pretty. She was nearly thirty-five, yet her manner was that of a much younger girl half shy, half sure of her beauty. "Any man would look twice at her," Millstor thought. He leaned against the bridge of the *Roviana* and hummed a satisfied little tune which kept time with the woman's confident steps. "And she's my wife!" he chuckled.

Now the wharfies noticed her approaching the ship. At first they said nothing, but as her long legs flashed past they began to whistle softly. Finally, when she took her first step onto the gangway a bold dock hand cried, "Ah, those Yankee women!"

In embarrassment she reached for the second step, but her fashionable skirt made this difficult and one of the wharfies bleated, "Oh you babe!" She blushed and started to run up the gangway, but again her skirt hampered her, and the rough Australian stevedores cheered.

When she reached the top step her husband, pipe in hand, came forward to greet her. The wharfies watched him kiss her and one shouted mockingly, "Oh, you lucky cobber!"

"Enthusiastic audience," Millstor laughed, taking his wife by the arm and leading her back along the deck to a cabin aft of the bridge.

"This is a trim little cruiser," she said approvingly.

"Cruiser!" he echoed. "A real Lloyds A-I bucket." He edged her past a bulkhead and up four steps. "Before you, the bridal suite!"

Liz Millstor studied the tiny cabin with the dirty floors. For a moment her heart failed. To have come all the way from Boston for a vacation on such a bucket! Then she controlled herself and said cheerfully, "Oh, John! It's a darling little boat." Impulsively she kissed him on the ear and cried, "A wonderful tramp steamer for a honeymoon!" She kissed him again. "Even if it is a second honeymoon, twelve years delayed."

"It's not really much of a cabin," her husband apologized. "But it does have running water. And that's something."

"It's everything!" she exulted, flicking the faucet with her graceful fingers. Then, as the water protestingly trickled out, she began to pirouette about the dismal cabin as if she were a *danseuse* jammed into some corner before the ballet started. "It's a darling room for lovers," she cried joyfully. And then abruptly she did the one thing best calculated to frighten her husband and kill his enthusiasm. She caught his two hands, kissed him on the lips and whispered, "Oh, we shall have a wonderful trip, shan't we?"

An involuntary shiver crossed Millstor's shoulders and for a moment he could not reply. Then in a much subdued voice, from which the gaiety had been dispelled, he said, "It'll be magnificent, darling." Then, as if not even his wife's words could completely subdue his anticipations, he said quietly, "I'll be standing by this post and I'll cry, 'Darling, here it is!' And you'll come protesting to the door. . . ."

His wife peeked around the edge of the door and raised her arm dramatically toward the horizon. "Guadalcanal!" she gasped in a mock-tragic voice.

John Millstor laughed. When he first proposed this trip Liz had scowled. "Oh, John! You're like a worn-out football hero creeping back to Notre Dame to drain another sip of glory from the dregs. You've got to stop reliving the war." She had gone to her cabinet of prized possessions and rummaged for the President's citation. "See," she teased. "Even Roosevelt, curse the name, says you're a hero. Isn't that good enough?"

He had tried to explain that he wanted to revisit Guadalcanal not because he had been a minor hero there but because it was a vital part of his personal history. "Don't you want to see it?" he had asked.

"Of course I want to, John dear," she had replied, adding sulkily, "but it does seem a little ostentatious to be the very first old grads arriving for reunion."

Even now, here in Sydney on the eve of departure, it still surprised John that he had stood firm. Usually, in recent years, he proposed many courses of action which his wife had studied with the impartiality of a judge. He noticed, however, that the decisions always went against him. This time he had been adamant. "I'm going to Guadalcanal this winter. Please come along."

"Why, of course, darling!" she had graciously surrendered. "We'll leave the noisy little brats with Mother and we'll have a South Seas holiday. Delicious!" He had not bothered to explore her usage of that inappropriate word, for he sensed that it implied ridicule of his nonsensical idea. But here she was in Australia. Even more astonishing, here she was on board Alec McNair's dirty old *Roviana*. John Millstor was content that things had worked out so well.

"Guadalcanal!" Liz repeated mockingly. "You must call me early that morning."

"What do you mean, 'morning'?" he asked blankly.

Kissing him on the ear to kill the insult, she whispered, "I'm sure you'll be up most of the night, looking for the island. Won't you?"

He thought for a moment and agreed somewhat stuffily. "Why, yes, I suppose I shall." But in that moment of time, while the evening ferries scuttled back and forth across beautiful Sydney Harbor, he was deeply impelled to try once more to explain what Guadalcanal still meant to him, and the urgency of sharing was so burning within him that now he might have succeeded where always before he had failed. But a strong, rough voice interrupted.

" 'Lo, John. 'Lo, Mrs. Millstor."

The Americans turned to greet Captain McNair. He was a huge man, about forty. His shoulders were broad, his eyes deep set. He had a striking black beard that reached a good five inches below his chin. He obviously liked being a sea captain. He stood there with his hands jammed down into his coat pockets. "I never thought we'd lure you aboard this scow," he rumbled, shaking Liz by the hand.

Instinctively John placed his arm about his wife and said, "She's a wonderful sport. Said she'd travel by the *Roviana* or not at all."

McNair chuckled. "I should've thought our refighting the war the other night would have scared you away. Sort of a sample of what you might have to put up with on the trip."

"Nonsense!" she replied. "I know you two men were heroes up there. And I'm mighty proud of you." Impartially she grabbed the elbows of her P.T. boat daredevil and the Australian coastal pilot who had guided Halsey's cruisers up The Slot.

McNair was embarrassed by her hand and stepped back to survey his insignificant ship. "You can see why they call these tubs the Goal Posters." Fore and aft twin booms had been erected for the discharge of diesel drums and the loading of copra. Each pair of booms was braced by a lateral crossbar that gave the appearance of a football goal post. "As a class," McNair boasted, "the Goal Posters are the worst ships afloat. And the *Roviana* is the worst of her class."

Liz laughed and said, "Now you're bragging. It's a delicious ship."

Her assumed familiarity with sea matters irritated McNair and he turned away from her to observe, "But you're right, John. For returning to Guadalcanal a Goal Poster has a certain aptness. After all, when you Johnnies first went up there you hadn't much better."

Then the two men entered into one of those reflective communions which so infuriated Liz Millstor. Once at dinner in Sydney her husband had broken such a dedicated silence by blurting out, "By God, McNair, we did make do with damned little."

The big Australian had banged his leg and cried, "But we had Clarence Miller, and he was worth more than a battleship."

John knew that Liz detested such conversations. She had explained why once in Boston. "They're slightly obscene. Like a woman who's suffered an awkward childbirth. She insists upon flaunting her unusual pain between the meat course and the salad. All right! She had the baby and now she's out dancing. You men went off to war. Now you're back home. Let's let it go at that."

But John Millstor could not do so. For him war had been an awakening of the spirit. Through it he had discovered what always before had eluded him: meaning. In fact, although he would not openly admit it, war had touched his emotions more profoundly than Liz had ever been able to— except for the first febrile weeks of marriage.

He didn't blame Liz. He had married her in 1937 when he knew practically nothing about other people or himself, and up till 1941 he guessed that he was enjoying a standard American kind of happiness. Then, on December 8th near Boston Common, he had come upon a group of hell-raising young fellows enlisting in the Navy, and something about their tough indifference made him realize that they still possessed many things he had somehow lost.

Impetuously, in a manner quite unprecedented for the Millstors of Boston, he had enlisted, and now as he recalled that quixotic gesture he had to acknowledge that he had enlisted just as much against Liz as against Tojo. He had derived a childish pleasure from announcing it to her. She had reached for a handkerchief and sniffed. "You enlisted!"

she gasped. "Oh, John! Couldn't you have got a commission? Think of the children."

"We have enough money, Liz ..."

"But, John! It's not the money. It's that you're ... Well, you're a college graduate. You're a responsible man in Boston." Then she had broken down and kissed him heartily. "And you're a gallant fool," she had sobbed.

Later, of course, she learned that many Harvard men had chosen to enlist. "Fashionable nonsense," she explained to her friends. Her pain was further assuaged when John rapidly became an officer "in something terribly important, you know." She rather guessed, and intimated as much to her circle, that it involved counter-intelligence.

"But Benny told you!" John had protested. "I'm in small boats!"

"Benny never told me," Liz insisted, but even if Benny had she would have elected not to believe that her husband was piddling around in landing craft. "Still," she wept on his last leave, "I guess you Millstors have been going off to wars for five generations." She had smiled bravely but had finally clung to him crying, "Oh, John! Do you think little Derek will be chasing off some day?"

"More'n likely," he had replied.

"Oh, damn!" she had groaned. "Now look, John Millstor! Don't you go being a hero! I want you back!"

The silence at the rail of the *Roviana* was broken by a rough little voice calling, "Cap'm, Cap'm?"

"It's Nella," McNair grunted with no enthusiasm.

For some days the Millstors had tried to comprehend Mrs. McNair and had failed. They could not understand why Alec had married her nor what now held them together. When she appeared on deck they understood even less.

She was a dumpy, oddly complexioned woman whom Liz had characterized as "the American farm wife sixty years ago." Certainly her habit of jumping whenever her husband spoke, her invariable reference to him as Cap'm stamped her as one of those nineteenth-century slaveys Liz had always despised. "Can you imagine!" she had laughed one night after a dinner with the McNairs. "A subjugation like that? Premature aging? Standing still while your husband forges ahead? Tied down by men's silly rules? Oh, John! I'd never make a good Australian wife. Please promise to take me back home."

"Evening," Mrs. McNair said in what was for her a sprightly voice. "Thought I'd miss the ship."

345

"I thought so too," McNair said gruffly.

"I'm only going as far as Guadalcanal," Mrs. McNair explained. Her husband turned his back on her and went to the bridge, whereupon the *Roviana* began slowly to stand out into mid-channel. For a moment there was that glorious clanging of bells that presages the good voyage, the protesting groan of the propeller, and the lights on shore shifting their positions for a last look at the voyagers.

Caught up in the strange beauty of a tramp steamer's leaving port, Millstor slipped his arm about his beautiful wife and exclaimed like a schoolboy viewing his first sunset on Boston wharves, "There's something wonderful about a boat setting out for the South Seas."

Liz pulled his excited lips against her cheek. "I'm so glad we came, John," she whispered. "It's so very good to see you breathless and relaxed all at the same time. I'm sorry if I didn't understand—back there in Boston. I do now."

This unexpected depth of emotion quite upset Millstor and he was about to acknowledge his appreciation of her sportsmanship when the spell—brief though it had been—was completely smashed, for his wife held his face against hers and whispered, "We shall have a perfectly wonderful trip, shan't we? Even with that awful woman aboard?"

"I'll go in and shave," Millstor said.

"There's no hurry," Liz teased.

"McNair said they ate promptly."

"I'll be there," she laughed brightly. "You scrape the barbed wire off."

"What I meant was," John called back, "let's get off on the right foot. Long voyage and all that."

Liz poked her head into the cabin and chortled, "Don't worry, fuss budget. I shan't wreck your military love affair with Cap'm." She gouged him in the ribs with a long forefinger. "Because I love you very much."

But even so, trouble started that night. Mrs. McNair stopped by and called in a husky voice, "You two! Better get a shuffle on. Cap'm likes to eat prompt." There was a sound of awkward feet and then silence.

Liz winced. "Seems we'll have a pretty rigid regime. Everything according to a timetable."

"Darling," her husband laughed, "if the British like to be stuffy . . . After all, they were wonderful allies."

"Sweetheart!" she interrupted, kissing him so that he fell backwards against the bed. "You're so generous in your ex-

346

cuses for other people. You're a dear, wonderful man and I'm going to be late for dinner."

"You wouldn't be, if you'd hurry," he half announced, half asked.

"All right!" she agreed. "Watch me hurry." But he noticed that she dragged even more than usual. When they reached the wardroom the McNairs and Mr. Morrison, the engineer, were already eating.

"Dinner's at six," McNair said gruffly, not rising to greet his guests. "Food's apt to be pretty good, so we humor the cook." He added this with a disarming grin, as if to take away the sting of his first remark.

Liz smiled generously and helped herself to the soup. "John was angry with me for being so slow," she confessed. "Especially after your wife was good enough to remind us." She beamed at the Australian woman, who did not smile back.

When dinner was over Captain McNair combed out his beard, leaned way back in his chair, and indicated that the steward could pass the cigars. At this signal Mrs. McNair rose quietly and started for her quarters, "so that the men might be alone with their cigars and port." She held out a hand to Liz and said, "Come! We'll tend to our knitting."

She could have found no more insulting phrase. Liz looked up with a face all innocence and said, "Thanks, I'll stay. I rather like cigar smoke."

There was a moment of audible tension during which Mrs. McNair blushed and looked to her husband for instructions which were delivered by a disgusted shake of his head. The little Australian woman left and closed the door.

The talk which followed was most uneasy. Mr. Morrison, always a taciturn man who smoked a pipe and grunted answers, ignored the amusing questions Liz asked about the ship. There was some talk of Guadalcanal, during which it was painfully apparent that Captain McNair wished his cabin cleared of women. This irritated Liz, so by artful flattery she finally thawed the bearded man into explaining how watches were changed aboard the *Roviana*. There was, however, no easy flow of conversation such as one imagines aboard a small ship plowing northward to the tropics.

After twenty such awkward minutes Captain McNair dispatched the steward to inform his wife that "the gentlemen had finished their cigars and awaited the ladies," whereupon Mrs. McNair appeared with the improbable news of a whale to starboard. Now there was light-hearted discussion of whales in Southern waters and Captain McNair grew eloquent as he told of the barque *Essex* which was completely stove in and sunk by a whale in 1819. "The beast attacked twice, altering course so as to intercept the ship head on." Mr. Morrison said he had seen a whale leap into the air and fall upon another whale, but he narrated the incident with such pointless hesitancy that no one could find further observation on the phenomenon. This did not annoy the engineer, who rose and went to a cupboard. Mrs. McNair clapped her hands and cried, "Good-oh, the squeeze box!"

Mr. Morrison took down an octagonal accordion, which he pulled out to its entire length in one mournful wail. He tested it for tone and then put it aside while he relit his pipe. Leaning back in his chair, his eyes closed, his countenance most doleful, he started a series of rollicking tunes. During the strathspeys and reels of his native Scotland he kept his right foot pumping madly, never changing the droop of his mouth.

Captain McNair marked time with his cigar and said expansively, "It's rare music for a ship, that." And for a moment John Millstor sensed the true camaraderie of a small ship at night. The last brandy was served and in the distance the lights of Australia sank beneath the western waves.

As the party broke up McNair artfully detained Millstor and said, "Your wife doesn't understand, John. Aboard a British ship it's customary for the women to retire . . ."

"I know," Millstor blushed. "In my family we used to do the same . . . But in recent years . . . things have changed."

"It's still a good custom," the Australian said, leaving abruptly for the bridge.

John recognized this as a rebuke, one which he was obligated to pass on to his wife lest there be an unpleasant scene later on. He moved along the deck to their cabin but when he reached the door he heard Liz singing some of the sea chanteys Mr. Morrison had played, his resolution left him and he stood beside the rail. How could he lecture his wife about social customs? The thought repelled him. In fact, long ago he had surrendered his rights to lecture her about anything. He tried to recall how he had been tricked into giving up his prerogatives, those rights which big Alec McNair had so obviously kept.

It had begun, John thought, on their honeymoon. They arrived at the family island off the coast of Maine, where Millstors had been taking their brides for generations, and suddenly Liz had clutched his arm with overwhelming tenderness and cried, "We shall have a wonderful marriage, shan't we,

John?" That was her first use of the rhetorical question, and as its bittersweet memory returned, here at the fringe of the Coral Sea, John cringed.

They had spent their wedding night discussing the attributes of a perfect marriage, and as John thought back to the vital decisions of that first skirmish he realized that right there he had begun his long retreat. Liz had said, "The most important thing in marriage is to have a true understanding. Even on the most trivial points." John was to discover that this meant he must talk everything over with his wife, who would then determine what should be done. He had grown to depend upon her judgment above his own, for by and large the Millstor men had never been brilliant.

Even now he could remember how frightened he had been when Liz had said, during their first year, "John! I'm worried."

"What about, darling?" he had gulped, for she had been pregnant at the time. "Is anything . . ."

"I don't mean about Hector," she laughed, patting her stomach. "I mean about us."

"Us?" he had repeated incredulously.

"Yes, John," she said tragically. "I am a good wife, aren't I?"

That was how it started. That was the gambit which had proved most efficient in eroding the spirit of a man. He pondered the dark waters at the stern of the *Roviana* and mused, "How did that go? She was worried about whether or not she was a good wife. I told her she was, but she listed a dozen things about herself that she didn't like. But the upshot of it all was that I quit smoking cigars. Let's see, how did it work out that way?"

In time he had become alert to his wife's military tactics. When she said, "We shall have a wonderful trip, shan't we?" it signified that she had certain specific ideas of what should be done and that the least expected of her husband was blind obedience to her strategy. If she confessed, "John, I'm worried. About us!" it presaged a manly, heart-to-heart talk, the first half hour of which consisted of a recital of her defects followed by three cruelly efficient minutes during which he agreed to give up something which offended her. The poker games, the class reunions, the fishing trip to Androscoggin, the old felt hats, the dinners with Ponsonby . . . All the marks of John Millstor as a man had slowly been erased and in their place had been drawn, in fine woman's script, the clean, handsome outlines of the world's most pathetic modern miracle: the typical American husband.

Liz was not selfish. John had to admit that. Nor was she spendthrift. She paid far less for clothes than most women and appeared twice as attractive: "I think it's a wife's duty to see to it that her husband dresses better than she does." With this in mind she pleaded, "John, we're making fifteen thousand a year now. Isn't it about time for us to buy your suits from J. Press?" He had protested that J. Press was the tailor for Harvard men who weren't quite sure of themselves but who had to make a reputation on Wall Street. "I like the suits at Filene's," he had insisted. But in the end he had gone to be fitted at J. Press's and had come away looking very repectable in conservative high lapels and expensive English suitings. Liz was delighted when her Boston friends said, "Really, John is getting to look too distinguished."

Shortly after she had rebuilt his wardrobe, he had enlisted in the Navy, and there came the humiliating day when he appeared in gob's uniform with the schoolboy's challenge, "Now, let's see what J. Press can do to these!" Liz had cried and cried, "You look so damned ordinary. And so brave." But when he became an officer she ordered a complete outfit from J. Press and did not comment when he ripped out the labels and scuffed up the coat. "He's still a darned convincing-looking officer," she said approvingly.

Now he stood at the railing and reviewed these sorties. He had come out of them changed, no longer a callow youngster. He was a successful lawyer, the husband of a desirable wife, the head of a family and a pillar in Boston society. He was all these things, and he knew it. But he also knew what he was not. He was no longer a man.

He proved this anew by shrugging his shoulders and going to the cabin where Liz sat brushing her hair. "A hundred strokes each night, and you'll never lose your husband," she always said.

"Liz," he began hesitatingly.

"Yes, darling?" she said brightly.

"You agreed that we'd always discuss things? Everything?"

"Why, of course, darling! Here, sit down." She moved over, but he sat on his own bed. "Not way over there!" she begged. "Whenever there's something unpleasant, we should face it together." She had always made a great point of "talking things out," "sharing one another's troubles," and "making adversity bring us closer together."

"It's not unpleasant," he laughed. "It's only that Captain McNair says there's a custom aboard British ships . . ."

"Oh, John!" she laughed. "You mean about the wardroom and all that?"

"Please, Liz. He takes it seriously."

"And he asked you to give me a lecture!" She laughed delightedly and kicked her bare foot into the air.

"He simply asked me to explain," John insisted.

"Oh, now!" she teased, catching him by the arm and pulling his face closer to hers. "We aren't going to let an old-fashioned Australian tyrant ruin our vacation, are we?"

For a moment Millstor was disposed to fight this thing out, but he was completely thrown off guard by his wife's next question: "Surely we don't want a marriage like the McNairs', do we? A browbeaten woman, a relic of feudal times? Oh, no!"

She dismissed the protest and at dinner next night affected not to notice when Mrs. McNair left dutifully before the cigars. The captain said nothing, but Liz noticed that in his indignation he crumbled the end of his cigar and had to ask for another.

Late that night a knock came at the Millstor door and Mrs. McNair said, "Could I see you for a moment, please?" John rose and the little Australian woman said, "Oh, I'm sorry. I meant the Missus." He could hear Liz wince at such an appellation, but he also heard her say sweetly, "I'll be right there, Mrs. McNair."

The captain's wife was brief. "Cap'm told me to tell you that please after dinner leave the wardroom for a few minutes. It's the custom."

"I am so sorry," Liz said, patting the older woman's arm. "You see, in America we don't treat our women that way."

There was a startled silence while Mrs. McNair considered what to do next. She pushed Liz's hand away and said bluntly, "If you women don't show your husbands such respect, maybe it's time you learned."

Liz laughed. "Perhaps our men prefer twentieth-century wives. Maybe they like us the way we are." Then, ashamed of herself for having punctured so plain a woman, she added, "I'm sorry, Mrs. McNair, but the custom seems strange to John and me."

"Oh!" the little woman cried. "Then your husband did speak to you about it?"

"But of course! We had a jolly laugh."

"The Cap'm wondered, that's all."

"Wondered? About what?"

"The Cap'm said Mr. Millstor was afraid to reproach you."

"Afraid?" Liz chuckled. "Oh, my dear! American husbands and wives aren't *afraid* of each other. We discuss everything."

"You do?" the Australian woman asked.

"Certainly we do. And John thinks the custom just as silly as I do. But thank you all the same, Mrs. McNair. You can be sure we never intended to embarrass the Cap'm."

She returned to her cabin and in the darkness laughingly described bedraggled little Mrs. McNair. "She's half frightened out of her wits by that man of hers!" She went to John's bed and kissed him several times, whispering, "This trip will do me a world of good. It'll make me appreciate you, dearest John. Won't it?"

Millstor faced dinner the next night with some trepidation. He had not been able to make Liz promise to retire before the cigars. In fact, he half foresaw what actually took place. The pause came, the captain said, "Well, my dear . . ." and Mrs. McNair rose to go. She extended her hand to Liz, who smiled sweetly at the captain and asked, "Is it true that waterspouts can damage a ship?"

Patiently McNair showed his wife to the door. Then, carefully closing it, he stood at the head of the table and said in a towering voice, "Mrs. Millstor, I asked you to leave the wardroom. My wife asked you, and if your husband is not scared to death of you, he asked you too. Now as captain of this ship I'm ordering you to get out! Join the ladies and leave this room to your betters!" With violent gestures he slammed the door open and stood there majestically while Liz Millstor rose, smiled at Mr. Morrison and said, "Of course, Captain." Delicately, as she had been taught years ago, she left the room, her head straight and high.

When she had left, McNair said bluntly, "Dammit all, John. I'm sorry. I apologize. But a ship's a ship."

Millstor was too astounded to reply. He stumbled to his feet and muttered something about seeing Liz. A great paw reached out and forced him back into his seat. "Don't be a damned fool!" McNair roared. Then, cutting Millstor off from the door, he said slowly, "Mr. Morrison, I checked those figures about diesels. You were right."

"Aye," the Scotsman said. "I knew it at the time."

Twenty minutes later the two women returned. Mrs. Millstor was slightly flushed and very lovely. She smiled at Captain McNair and said, "The coffee was delicious. You should compliment the steward."

"I shall," McNair said, holding her chair.

When the last strains of the accordion died away—much to John Millstor's regret—he and Liz made their way to their cramped cabin. He anticipated a frightful scene but his wife merely laughed. "It was like something out of *East Lynne*," she said. "And oh, John! That poor whipped little woman. Do you know what she told me? Her name is Citronella! Her mother lived way out in the Australian Never-Never and saw the name in a book. Mrs. McNair actually laughed and said she guessed it was the only beautiful thing her mother had ever known." Liz pressed her ears close to her head and laughed nervously. "It's medieval!" she shuddered and kissed John thankfully. He drew back from what he feared was to be a heart-to-heart talk, the upshot of which would be instructions to punch Alex McNair in the nose. Instead, Liz surprised him by turning out the light and sighing, "Those poor Australian wives! Can you imagine people living like that? In the twentieth century?"

During the next days Liz changed completely. No more arguments in the wardroom, no more pressure on her husband. She became the happy, delectable woman John had always cherished. They stood in the prow for hours watching the flying fish whip the ocean with the iridescent, unbelievable tails. "It's very peaceful," Liz said approvingly.

In such relaxed contentment they neared the New Hebrides and McNair produced a nest of charts. "We've two days to spare," he said. "As I remember you in Guadalcanal, John, you loved to hike. How'd you like to see the Big Nambas country?"

"That would be something!" Millstor cried.

"We could get up there in a day, spend the night, and come back."

"What are the Big Nambas?" Liz interjected.

"The last real savages in the Pacific," McNair explained.

"I'd enjoy seeing them," Liz said promptly.

McNair laughed. "Too dangerous. No woman could climb . . ."

"Tell him, John," Liz interrupted. "Tell him I can outclimb you any day in the week."

"She can, too," John agreed.

"It's very rough terrain," McNair said. "Do you really think your wife ought to risk it?"

"She's game to go anywhere," Millstor said.

"If you approve, all right," McNair said reluctantly.

When the *Roviana* hove to off Malekula, Liz was aghast at the forbidding quality of the land. "Look at that jungle!" she whispered, afraid that McNair might hear her surprise. "John! It creeps right down into the water!" She shivered apprehensively as she saw the twisting parasites drooping from each tree. Then she pulled on her heavy socks, saddle shoes, old skirt and thick panties. "If I have to come down sliding," she joked, "I want it to be the panties and not me." She wore a man's shirt, John's, and a red bandanna, also his, twisted tightly about her ears.

"You look well prepared," Mrs. McNair said acidly.

"I do wish you were coming along," Liz lied.

"If you get back alive, maybe I'll go next time." She returned to her job of handing the food baskets down into the pinnace.

When they got ashore, the steward, who had made the trip before, led the way to the trail that immediately started upward. In a few moments everyone in the party was drenched in heavy perspiration which was not to stop flowing for two days.

They had gone only a short distance inland when they came upon one of those cruel jungle sights that give the islands their macabre quality. "Look at this!" Liz cried.

McNair flicked the moisture from his thick beard and said, "It's a strangler fig."

"How sickening!" Liz gulped, stepping back to stare at a massive tree. But her husband did not look upward at the revolting spectacle, for he saw something more arresting. When Liz moved backward she bumped against the huge rough hand of Alec McNair as it pointed toward the jungle tragedy. Neither she nor McNair pulled away, and for a long moment the Australian's hand pressed against her bosom.

"You've got to expect unpleasant sights in the jungle," McNair said.

Above them towered a giant kauri pine, one of the finest trees in the world, rich in sap and cabinet wood. Long ago it had been attacked by a single thin strand of parasitic fig. For a generation the kauri had been unaware of its doom, and then one day the fig was established, with a thousand aerial roots drifting down to the jungle floor. Slowly and with diabolical intention the once innocuous fig began to grow laterally, like molten lava spreading over a mountain. In ghastly sheets of bark it enclosed the kauri. Limb after limb of the giant tree was strangled off. Next the trunk itself was

354

attacked and with malignant power the parasite enclosed the huge tree in a garment of steel, an inescapable vise which methodically killed all life within its grasp.

Now the kauri was dead. It still stood, held up by the parasitic growth that had usurped its life. But the once-great monarch was rotting in the jungle heat, while the strangler fig, with no roots of its own attached to the soil, flourished.

"How awful!" Liz whispered, still standing close to McNair.

Her husband was confused and agitated but felt that he must say something. "It must have taken years," he observed.

"When they start," McNair said, "they never stop. Look." He pointed to another kauri from which dangled an innocent and lovely parasite. "That's how it begins."

By the time they reached the Big Nambas country John and the steward had fallen behind. They could hear McNair thrashing ahead to join Liz, who had already gained the plateau. Her provocative laugh came teasing back along the trail: "You're winded, Captain."

McNair breathed heavily and grunted, "I'll admit I was wrong. About women climbing, I mean."

Then John heard his wife scream, and he raced furiously ahead for the last twenty yards. He broke into the clearing just in time to see a chilling sight. From the jungle six brutally ugly savages had emerged with Winchester rifles, and across from them Liz Millstor had retreated to the protection of Alec McNair's brawny arms, where she huddled in real fright.

"By Jove, I'm glad you arrived!" the Australian shouted. "Here! Watch your wife!" Like a sack of potatoes he passed her along while he hitched up his pants and went boldly across to the savages, knocked down their rifles and asked, "You fellow savvy talk-talk?"

A monstrously ugly man dropped his rifle barrel into the dust and said grudgingly, "Me savvy good too much."

But at this moment the savage noticed Liz for the first time and made a rush for her. Millstor, confused by all that had happened, stood aghast, unable to bring either his mind or his body into action. His wife watched the horrifying creature bear down upon her and she would have fainted had not Alec McNair suddenly reached out and grabbed the Nambas warrior by the neck.

At this the startled savage broke into a riotous grin and, ignoring Liz completely, grabbed John Millstor affectionately by the arm. "You American!" he shouted with delight. He

355

pushed aside McNair's restraining hand and punched John in the ribs. "All Americans, he sitarong too much," he said approvingly. He patted John on the face and said, "You fellow ologeta come long me."

He led the visitors across the plateau and back into the jungle, his five companions forming a naked bodyguard. They wore absolutely nothing except a ridiculous leather belt eight inches wide. Around the edges of their massive cummerbunds were stuck those things a man normally carries in his pockets: a pipe, a knife, a stick for picking wax out of the ear, and a bit of cloth for wiping the face. John noticed that Liz tried not to look at the nakedness of the men. Laughing nervously she said, "They seemed to like you, John. Please be gentle with them."

Millstor looked closely at his wife to see if she were goading him about his indecision when the wild man seemed to be attacking, but she smiled frankly and appeared totally sincere.

The natives led their guests to a village where many old men sat sullenly on their haunches. A few women stared inquisitively at Liz and then disappeared giggling into huts while their men cursed them. Jungle children with great pot bellies peered at the strangers, who finally stopped before the chieftain, an old man who suddenly launched into a furious diatribe. Finally he stopped and the interpreter said, "Cheep, he want you talk-talk where he stop Mazinga Rule?"

"Mazinga Rule?" Millstor repeated uncomprehendingly.

"Marching Rule," McNair explained. "Like in the Solomons. The Nambas think America is leading a world revolution to Marxian Rule. Humor them."

"Why he no come, Mazinga Rule?" the interpreter shouted.

"Mazinga Rule he no come long time," McNair assured the native. "Suppose this fella pikaniny belong you stop old fellow too much, maybe Mazinga Rule he come."

The chief studied this answer for some time. He had been promised that one day the Americans would return with Mazinga Rule and all the Frenchmen would be killed. Then great cargoes of things—meat, refrigerators, axes, ice-cream stands—would arrive at Malekula for the Big Nambas. He rose sadly and went to Millstor, studying the American's eyes. He spoke rapidly and the interpreter said, "Cheep, he say Americans they good too much. He wait." John sighed with relief, and the interpreter added, "But, Cheep, he say you better come long Nambas soon. How soon?"

"Kid 'em along," McNair ordered.

"America, he come!" John said forcefully.

The chief broke into a broad grin and made several thrusts with his rifle, indicating how he would kill the French. McNair laughed and soon the entire gathering was chortling with delight at the prospect of unlimited murder, underwritten by the Americans.

The interpreter started to lead the visitors to a shack when the chief cried something, whereupon dozens of sag-breasted women streamed from the huts and surrounded Liz. Tenderly they touched her hair, her lips. One lifted her dress and studied the thick panties. There were cries of delight as the women smelled her handkerchief and tasted the lipstick which had rubbed off on her fingers. One very old woman gently pushed a forefinger into the white woman's breast. "Ahhhh!" the others cried approvingly. Then the chief screamed at the women and they disappeared.

The interpreter said proudly, "Long war I work Americans." He made believe he was driving a car. "Ford truck!" he explained with great satisfaction.

In the shack Liz showed no indication to challenge John for his confusion when the native charged. She whispered, so as not to offend the two Australian men, "Isn't it impressive? How everyone out here remembers and loves the Americans?"

"They also remember Santa Claus," John whispered back.

"John!" she laughed. "I mean it seems we command the respect of all the world."

McNair interrupted. "Don't let that Mazinga Rule fool you. Nor the Ford truck. Three years ago they ate a man in this village."

When night fell the natives gathered about the hut and beat huge scooped-out wooden logs that reverberated with maddening power. In the shadows women chanted. By the fire young men danced. Once Liz sang an old song, "Drifting and Dreaming." The natives cheered and McNair did some tricks with matches. Then the fires burned out and the travelers crawled into mosquito nets and shivered in cool breezes that wandered across the clearing.

Before they went to sleep McNair said, "You Americans have a fund of friendship out here. How astonished they're going to be when they discover it's Russia and not you blokes that's leading the revolution!"

"Damn!" the steward said. "Isn't that thunder?"

"It's a drum," Liz replied.

"It is thunder," McNair muttered. "A storm."

And before they got to sleep a slow, heavy rain fell upon the hut. At the doorway a lonely figure huddled, mumbling, "Me fella drive Ford truck. When you fella come back long Mazinga Rule, you bring plenty Ford trucks?"

The hike back to the *Roviana* became a nightmare for John Millstor. First a drenching equatorial rain flooded the trail and made impossible any attempts to keep dry, but at one swollen stream a haunting thing took place. John and the steward had forged well ahead to report on any difficulties and had forded a stream that came well up to their middles.

"Does it get better down there?" John shouted to the steward.

"No water in the path," the man replied.

"I'll double back and help my wife," he cried. He turned toward the turbulent stream in time to see big Alec McNair sweep Liz into his arms and plunge into the muddy torrent. Neither the Australian nor Liz could see Millstor, and instinctively he drew back behind a tree. He had the strange sensation of living in a dream, for when McNair swung Liz into the air, the man's big hands had purposely reached under her skirt and grabbed the bare legs in a passionate grip. And Liz, after a moment's shock, had deliberately placed her own hand on his. In this manner they forded the stream, and when McNair thrust her competently upon the shore, he caught one hand and pulled her back for a violent kiss. She did not protest. Instead she edged up on her wet toes the better to press her face into the tangled beard. And while John Millstor stood helpless, paralyzed by bewilderment, McNair passed his hand once more under her dress while she threw her arms with abandonment about his neck.

The spell was broken by the steward who came thrashing back along the trail shouting, "All clear ahead."

Millstor moved into the trail, stricken with indecision, but his next action came automatically. "Look at the tree!" he cried.

The four travelers stopped in the rain-soaked jungle and looked up at the kauri whose fate had concerned them the day before. The night storm had destroyed the jungle monarch at last. Some rampaging gust had snapped the decayed trunk. But miraculously the strangler fig, once the parasite, now lived a life of its own and in an affectionate embrace of steel kept the broken kauri erect as if it were still a living tree.

"Score one for the fig!" cried the steward.

"The tree was dead anyway," McNair grunted.

The travelers now moved along the trail in a group and came to the last formidable stream. The steward plunged into the angry water and cried with satisfaction, "No trouble here." He thrashed on to the other side.

There was a moment's hesitation and John mumbled, "I'd better carry you, Liz." He lifted his slim wife in his arms and felt his hand burn as it touched her leg. With a big stride he launched into the flood, but soon felt McNair's big hand supporting him.

"Better take it easy, John," the Australian warned, and in this way they forded the stream.

Then, once more aboard the *Roviana*, John Millstor began the lonely and confused battle with his conscience. He was appalled by his indecision. He was willing to have it out with McNair, even in a knockdown brawl. He correctly guessed that he was in much better condition than the paunchy captain, but deep within him there was no conviction, no motive power to keep his fists going once outraged vanity had started them. He simply did not know what he was expected to do. Was this merely another of Liz's modern attempts to keep marriage going? And how did McNair assess his adventure with the excited American woman?

Except for that lack of moral conviction, not even Millstor could have added any explanation of his puling vacillations. For most of one day he stood by the rail wondering what had happened in his life. In college he had been willing to fight anyone who threatened the inner citadels he had constructed. On Guadalcanal he had, as his commanding officer reported, "ignored the fact that there was danger." But here aboard the *Roviana*, faced with the debacle of his own life, he was lost in a fog of inanition.

Where had it come from, this sickness of will? He recalled that in recent years Liz had been reading a good many books about marriage, what it was that made a man and woman—especially the woman—happy. She had said many times, "John, I'm worried. About us." By that time he was disgusted with her clever gambit and had merely grunted, "What's it now, Liz?"

She had rocked him back on his heels by saying, "I'm afraid it's something dreadfully important, John. What I mean is, I'm afraid I'm not a good wife. Oh, socially I am, but what I mean is . . . Oh, dammit, sexually."

Then it became clear. She had come upon an outspoken article by a University of Iowa professor who said that twen-

359

tieth-century American marriages were different from all preceding ones in that the wife had finally won the right to demand emotional and physical gratifications equal to those previously enjoyed only by the husband. "I mean," Liz had said, "do I satisfy you? I mean really down deep?" And by professing her own embarrassed inadequacy she had let him know that according to the standards of the professor's article, he had never provided her with the gratifications she now learned had been her due.

From that day John Millstor had known no peace. It seemed to him that all aspects of American society—toothpaste ads, editorials, women's magazines, community gossip—were dedicated to the job of reminding men that in the American woman they had a treasure never before equaled in the history of the world and that only through the most meticulous attention could any man hope to retain his prize. Once, as a young man, John had naïvely considered marriage a rather delightful and normal prelude to having three or four children, a family pew in the Episcopal Church, a recognized niche in society and a happy home. It had seemed as simple as that. Now he discovered how ingenuous he had been. "Marriage," one of his wife's clippings had read, "is a social and psychological jungle in which only the eternally vigilant can find their way."

Liz agreed with this concept. "Really, John," she had often said, "I think marriage is the most difficult of all social relationships. It's something you've got to *work* at." And working, John discovered, meant sacrificing every normal, relaxed instinct he had ever known. It meant making the right friends, bucking for more pay, being a pal to his children and not just a father. Above all it meant that he had to be understanding when his wife dallied in mild flirtations with other men. Somewhere Liz had read that if marriage were to succeed, husbands and wives should take separate vacations, so he was miserable at the Millstor island in Maine, while she was bedazzled by an Englishman in Bermuda.

He looked at the dark sea and hammered his hands against the railing. He thought of his wonderfully attractive wife— the Australian newspaper woman had asked, "What do these American girls have that we don't have?"—and he concluded that the erosion of his marriage had not been Liz's acknowledged objective. She was too fine a woman for that. No. it was either the swift change of modern life or some inadequacy on his part. He tried to reconstruct his errors.

Had he been forceful enough? Hell, a man isn't supposed to play the tyrant, not in the twentieth century. Had he tried to make Liz understand his side of marriage? He had talked with her, but he would never have been willing to browbeat her the way McNair terrorized his frowsy wife.

Then, from far back in his courtship days, he remembered a warning his mother had delivered: "John, you mustn't marry Elizabeth. She's the new type of woman, the efficient American wife. But you're the old-fashioned type of man, and I don't think you'll be strong enough to battle things out with her."

Had that been the poison? Had those chance words caused him to avoid any arguments with Liz lest he be guilty of having allowed his mother to becloud his marriage?

Again he hammered the railing and thought, "Damn it all! Liz isn't fundamentally mean. There's nothing wrong with her. She's generous and honorable, and I love her!" He was about to rush in and discuss the impasse with her when a small voice came to his elbow and in the night shadows he saw Mrs. McNair. "Mr. Millstor," she said haltingly, "you may think ill of me, but I've got to say it."

"Got to say what?" John demanded.

"Please forgive me, but you ought to watch your wife."

No one spoke. The soft phosphorescence of the tropical sea rose quietly from the prow of the *Roviana* and slithered off into darkness. Great blobs of protoplasm scintillated in the night, casting an eerie glow upon the flying fish that sailed across the night.

"Mr. Millstor," the complaining voice begged, "I know the Cap'm. He's a weak man. Please watch your wife."

Finally Millstor spoke. "My wife? What do you mean?"

"Forgive me, but she's an evil woman."

The words shocked Millstor and automatically he drew back his hand as if to strike the Australian woman. In shame he dropped it and mumbled, "What do you mean?"

At last Mrs. McNair put her hand on John's arm. "You won't get angry? All right. Mrs. Millstor is in our cabin right now. Not completely dressed."

"Oh, hell," Millstor gasped. He bowed his head for a moment and tried vainly to reach some decent conclusion to his long hours of self-torment.

It was Mrs. McNair who broke the spell. "I know it's difficult," she said, looking up at him with eyes that suddenly seemed very large and important. "There have been times in my marriage," she confessed, "when I've beat my brains trying to figure what ought to be done."

"Look," Millstor said dully. From the bridge Captain McNair and Liz looked down upon the conspirators.

"Cap'm says we'll see Guadalcanal tomorrow," Liz announced gaily.

McNair boomed with some satisfaction. "You'll soon be on dry land, Nella."

"Are you really leaving?" Millstor asked quietly.

"Yes. That's why I spoke to you. Please don't let some tragedy happen."

"Look at them!" Millstor muttered as the couple above went forward. "They know we've been talking about them."

"The Cap'm don't let talk worry him," the plain little woman said, retreating in accustomed humiliation to her cabin.

Her parting words had a strange effect upon Millstor. Big Alec McNair didn't bother about talk. If somebody had been fooling with his wife, the brawling Australian would have knocked him in the head with a beer bottle. But John Millstor, the pasteurized American husband, had long ago surrendered such primitive reactions. Instead, he went to his cabin determined to talk this problem out with his wife.

She did not appear till several hours later, laughing a bit too obviously. She threw her hat on the bunk and said self-consciously, "What do you think? I've been conning the ship!"

"On the bridge?"

"Yep! Course is 349 true."

"Liz," he began quietly, "aren't you seeing too much of Captain McNair?"

"Why, John!" she laughed spontaneously. "He's only been showing me how a ship operates."

"Darling, let's not lie to one another. On the Malekula trail I saw him kissing you."

Liz turned an outraged scarlet. "That's dreadfully unfair, John. He carried me across the stream and kissed me against my will."

An argument like this was degrading and Millstor would gladly have dropped it, accepting defeat, but he had to continue. "No, Liz. It was you who kissed him. Darling, I saw you."

She whipped her lithe body about and slapped him in the face. "Don't call me darling," she snapped. "If you saw your wife kissing another man, why didn't you do something about it instead of playing the peeping Tom?"

"Liz," he pleaded, "I'm merely trying to prevent . . ."

Suddenly his wife became very cool. She stared at him and asked, "What are you trying to prevent, John?"

"I guess I'm trying to prevent you from making a fool of yourself."

"That's horrid, John. Truly, that's horrid, coming from you."

"It's not coming from me," he persisted doggedly. "Mrs. McNair asked me to do something. She saw you in her cabin."

Liz threw her delicate hands over her face and muttered, "That cheap, frowsy woman! Peeping through keyholes." She pushed her husband aside and went on deck.

Alone John tried to comprehend the inconclusiveness of the argument. He realized that Liz was right in demanding to know why he had not stepped onto the trail when McNair was kissing her. He searched the narrow Goal Poster looking for her, but he did not find her that night. Shortly before breakfast she appeared and dabbed her face with cold cream.

"Where have you been?" Millstor asked.

"Sleeping in a lifeboat," she said. He wanted to believe her but noticed that her clothes were not rumpled.

"Liz," he said earnestly, "if you're involved with Mc-Nair. . ."

She wiped the cream off her face and studied her husband. He sensed that she was assessing him ruthlessly as the spineless creature he had become. "John," she said with cool disgust, "we mustn't fool each other any longer. I did kiss Alec. I did let him make love to me. And I liked it. Because Alec McNair is what you never were. A man."

Millstor looked away. "But Liz . . ." he fumbled.

"It's all washed up, John. Now please get out of the way." With the confident precision of a general who has just handed down surrender terms, she pushed her way past him onto the deck. "By the way," she called back, "over there's Guadal-canal."

Millstor sat dumbly on his bunk. His wife was gone. His world was crumbling. He leaned forward and held his chin, aware of the ridiculous figure he represented: the modern husband who has been refined to the point of moral impotency.

He could guess why Liz preferred ugly, tough Alec McNair. The Australian retained, arrogantly, every distinguishing male characteristic that John Millstor had been forced to give up. After a beer, McNair belched as college students had done at Harvard years ago. (John had surrendered this repulsive habit in 1938.) McNair picked his nose. (John hadn't done so since 1939.) The Australian went unshaved. (There had been a real crisis about this in 1940.) And in bed McNair was a rough and ready bounder. (By late 1937 John had read all the books.)

Suddenly he clutched at his throat with both hands. He seemed to be choking, but quickly he realized what had happened. A cord from the curtains had dropped about his neck and for a moment he had imagined it to be a thin, beautiful creeper of the strangler fig.

Sick and dismayed, he went on deck to see Guadalcanal, the great brooding island, and as he stood by the rail he thought that in those jungles life had been simpler. The enemy was easy to identify. Your friends could be relied upon to the last round of ammunition. You could, if you had the patience, memorize where every shoal was, how far the enemy guns would carry, and precisely what you needed for victory. In the jungle there had been order and law. But in his own life John Millstor had been unable to discern the enemy. He could not even comprehend himself.

The *Roviana* pulled alongside a sagging structure John had once known well, and as the ship docked he felt that he was returning to a home he should never have left. This feeling increased when he saw a shriveled runt on the dock. It was Clarence Miller, and when he recognized Millstor he shouted in a nasal voice, "Hello, John. It's been a long time."

Eagerly, Millstor left the tangled problems of the *Roviana* and stepped onto the clean shores of Guadalcanal. Clarence Miller, as ugly as ever, took him to a jeep and they set off for a glass of beer.

It was a strange reunion. Three times during the war Millstor had rescued Miller from dark shores along The Slot, once in sight of Jap gunners. The two men had never mentioned the dangers, nor did they now, but on this hot day John earnestly wished that he might share with Miller the burden of his addled conscience. But that he must not do, for he recalled that Miller's wife had deserted him for a German planter. So Millstor said, "It's a bit different now."

Miller agreed. "Guadalcanal's a bit different now."

Looking at the prosaic planter, Millstor felt self-conscious. It was preposterous that the Western world should once have depended upon men like Clarence Miller and himself, for in the ultimate sense of the word neither could really be termed a man. Each had been unable to hold a wife.

"Well," Miller said, "got to be going. Have some coons to look after."

"You getting enough labor?" John asked.

The gnome-like fellow laughed. "Nobody is. The black devils'll fight for me, but damned if they'll work for me." He drained his beer and went along the sleepy roads where once he had been immortal.

The three days in Guadalcanal were blistering hot, and a kind of moral miasma settled over the *Roviana*. Sniffing into her handkerchief, Mrs. McNair moved ashore to stop with friends. Liz no longer even bothered to make believe she was sleeping in her own cabin. McNair avoided John on the grounds that if a man couldn't look after his wife the less said about it the better. And John stayed ashore at the dwindling American base, where he went over old trails with a fifty-year-old sergeant who said, "I don't give a good goddam if I never see the States again, because my old woman is on the bottle, but good."

Once, driving past the docks, John saw his wife standing on the bridge and an autonomic gasp caught his throat. He knew then that she had not intended this, that she had not wanted him to become the kind of man he was. It was all a mistake and he told the driver to stop. In the great heat of midday he ran along the crumbling dock and cried, "Hey, Liz. Wait a minute!" But his cry had brought McNair to the bridge, and the lovers went back to the chart room. The old sergeant asked, "That your wife, Mister?"

"Yes," John replied with no mask of shame.

"They're all tramps," the professional soldier said.

Finally the copra was loaded and the *Roviana* turned south for Lord Howe. The first day out of Guadalcanal was blistering hot and the musty copra began steaming in the sun. A sickly sweet odor settled upon the ship like an anaesthesia, dulling the senses. Along with the fetid smell came thousands of copra bugs, small pests that did not bite but which did crawl endlessly about the body, seeking deposits of salt. Sometimes John could feel a hundred of them touring his chest and the only alleviation was a cold shower. Once, when he was rubbing his shoulders with a towel, Liz entered the cabin. There was a momentary embarrassment while he covered himself as he might have done were she a stranger.

"I'm moving things topside," she said, using an old Navy phrase that he had clung to after returning to civilian life.

365

Methodically, for she had always been an excellent house-keeper, she packed her two bags.

"What's happening, Liz?" he asked.

"Nothing important," she said briskly. "We'll get a divorce later on."

"But, Liz!"

"John, please," she begged. "No scenes." It was part of the twentieth-century code duello that there must never be a scene. She clicked the bags shut and the steward came brazenly in to carry them aloft. When they were gone Liz said, "I'll not embarrass you, dear. I'll take my meals in my cabin." She left, and so efficient had been her rearrangement of their former quarters that no sign remained that she had ever been there.

On the second day south of Guadalcanal a heavy swell set in from south-south-east, followed by a stiff gale. The *Roviana* pitched heavily and the increasing storm diverted John's mind from the antiseptic modern tragedy in which he was playing so inglorious a role. He stood outside the cabin and watched thundering waves crash over the deck cargo until it seemed as if the diesel drums and copra must be washed away.

The radioman said that Noumea reported a hurricane moving up from the Antarctic. It was east of New Zealand but threatened to invade the Coral Sea. At first it seemed as if the *Roviana* might avoid it, but during the night a tremendous wind roared through the absurd goal posts, and by morning the full force of the hurricane broke.

Surging green seas swept the decks and hammered down upon the hatches. Once each minute the propeller wrenched itself clear of the boiling wake and vibrated sickeningly in the free air until the ship lunged bow-down into the next trough. There was a constant thunder of wind which forced the rain into each crevice, and a safety rope had to be rigged to permit seamen to pass from one part of the ship to the next.

Only Mr. Morrison remained calm. "I've seen worse storms," he muttered, but where he would not say. It was his opinion that the storm would last three days with no serious damage to the *Roviana*, but even so John heard him advise Captain McNair to jettison the deck cargo.

McNair studied his ship and said nothing. He kept his bow head-on into the mountainous waves. When the propeller screamed at the wind, he steadied himself for the following
366

shock, and as for the deck cargo, let her ride! Nothing wrong yet.

John studied the man with a macabre fascination. McNair was sure of what he was doing, oblivious to what he had already done. The brawny man seemed to have been fashioned for storms.

But Millstor was too generous in his judgment, for he had not yet seen the huge man oppressed by decisions which were difficult to make. John was standing forward of the bridge when two drums of diesel oil finally broke loose. "Cap'm!" Mr. Morrison shouted above the storm, "We better get those two overboard before they scatter the rest!"

McNair roared onto the causeway above the deck and surveyed the scene below. "They'll hold," he shouted. "They're the profit on this trip." He started back to the bridge but saw Millstor staring at him. In some embarrassment he justified himself. "Nothing wrong with those drums, Mr. Morrison."

But now a succession of devastating waves crashed down upon the ship and eight more of the perilous drums tore loose. They careened about the deck like roistering drunks knocking down beer bottles in a dirty café. Two of them hit the goal posts and one of the uprights broke off with a shattering crash.

"You there!" McNair bellowed at a young seaman. "See what you can do with those drums."

"No!" Millstor screamed, determined to countermand such a callous order, but before he could intervene, the lad had jumped onto the flooded deck. The *Roviana* lurched desperately and the heavy drums roared down upon the seaman. There was a penetrating scream, a body pinned against the bulwarks.

Without thinking John Millstor automatically vaulted over the railing and dropped onto the deck below. Captain McNair saw him do so and watched the mounting fury of the drums as they converged upon the American.

"John!" he shouted. "Come back, you fool!"

For a moment Millstor hesitated, and then with an old football skill sidestepped the crude projectiles as they ripped into the bulkhead. He dodged across the deck and knelt by the stricken sailor. "Thanks, cobber," the boy said. "They hit me with the hammers of hell."

There was an instant of intense identification between the two men as Millstor grinned at the broken legs. "We'll get you out of here," he said reassuringly.

Standing up, with the great storm in his face, he tried to pry loose the drum that wedged the seaman into a corner. The footing was precarious and from aloft he heard McNair bellowing, "For God's sake, throw a rope about the boy and get back here!" Millstor continued straining at the drum and McNair shouted, "Mr. Morrison! Get that damned fool out of there."

There was a moment's silence and then an agonized voice from somewhere near the bridge cried, "Oh, Jesus! Look!"

From the dark south, where the hurricane was most furious, a giant wave descended upon the *Roviana*. Its hungry lip was more than forty feet in the air and John could feel the dismal little ship hurry forward to meet it. He looked up, his hands still on the drum, and heard the crippled seaman cry, "Woolloomooloo! Here we go."

As the tremendous wave swept the ship and lifted Millstor high in its impersonal arms, he had a last fleeting glimpse of his universe. Mr. Morrison was hanging onto the gangway ropes. Captain McNair was bellowing confused and impotent orders to no one. And on the bridge, in her nightgown, her knuckles pressed against her white teeth, stood one of the world's desirable creations: an American wife, tall, straight, thin limbed, carefully beautiful. Above the disaster he heard her frenzied scream: "John! Oh, God, no! John! I love you!"

New Guinea

No island in the Pacific was so terrifying to American troops as New Guinea. Those men who landed at Port Moresby and crawled across the Owen Stanley Mountains to Buna and Gona knew war at its worst.

The jungle was almost impenetrable. Great gorges halted progress and rain was measured in feet. Malaria struck down many. Jungle itch was incurable. Often ninety men out of a hundred would be sick.

I remember flying across the Dutch end of New Guinea in a bomber. Around us towered massive peaks 16,000 feet high. Below stretched a dismal swamp. Unnamed waterfalls roared into sodden jungles that no white foot had touched. Great brown rivers crawled like snakes, cutting the land into impassable segments. Here was the most gloomy land I had ever seen.

It's surprising, therefore, to find that New Guinea today is one of the most loved sections of the world. All across the Pacific you meet old codgers with faraway looks in their eyes. They're obviously unhappy, and their friends explain: "He's an old New Guinea hand. Dying to get back." And on the island you hear again and again: "Me? Leave New Guinea? Not on your life!"

Lae, on the north coast, helps to explain this feeling of devotion. It's a rambling town of small houses, government buildings, Chinese stores and a fabulous airport that is said to be the fifth busiest in Australian territory.

Life is good in Lae. There's a large white population who live healthy lives. Malaria has at last been beaten by a miracle drug, paludrine. (No earache like quinine; no yellow skin like atabrine.) Most homes have conveniences, most have family cars, usually war-surplus jeeps, and air travel is commonplace.

In this jungle town, only seven degrees off the equator, there are telephones, electric lights, refrigerators, good stores, hundreds of cheap servants, a branch office of the Brisbane lottery and a bookmaker.

Lae is hot during the day, but never so unbearable at night as New York or Washington in a bad summer. There's ample food, but few vegetables. As for drink, the per-capita con-

369

sumption is beyond belief. Hong Kong beer is the favorite—Amsterdam second—and it's not at all unusual for a man to drink two gallons a day. When Anderson, the Rabaul sausage king, hits town I swear he drinks six dozen bottles. That's twelve gallons!

There's an active social life in Lae, built around the fabulous Hotel Cecil, an unimproved Army camp with few conveniences and excellent food. At a dance the women tend to be more carefully gowned than at an American country club. The men are handsome in tropic whites.

Socially there's one thing terribly wrong with Lae. There aren't enough women. Although many wives live there quite happily—no housework—unmarried girls are scarce. In peace time I've never before seen so many young men with so much money and no girls to spend it on. Said one quite homely girl after a visit to Lae, "If I didn't know I was ugly, I'd be convinced I was a pocket Venus." She married and stayed in town.

Eric Cretier is a typical Lae citizen. He's 25, a good-looking, tough young fellow with a ready wit. He drives a worn-out Army truck from Lae to the gold fields at Wau, 93 miles up in the mountains. The Road—the only one in New Guinea—clings to sheer cliffs, fords bridgeless rivers, plunges through jungle and rides across breathlessly beautiful kunai plains where a tree can't be seen. Eagles, hawks, parrots, and swallows follow him as he rides. Scarlet flame-of-the-forest and delicate orchids hang from the trees over his head.

Only vehicles with four-wheel drive can negotiate The Road, and men are constantly being killed by plunging down cliff faces into rocky gorges. The Road—built by Americans during the war—is a triumph of engineering skill and patient attention.

Eric figures he can average 10 miles an hour. Four of his buddies have been killed so far; so he takes it very easy. He makes two round trips a week, hauling supplies up to the gold fields, timber down to the coast. Everyone along the road knows him and he sleeps at any house he happens to be near. He makes more than $60 a week and picks up extras by letting natives cling to the cargo for $2.50 a head. He has no girl to spend his salary on and often hints that "maybe I'll go to Australia and try to win me a heart."

His principal entertainment is singing with a gang of drivers at Mark Schultz's half-way pub and drinking beer. He can drink more than two gallons in an evening but is careful not to drive when drunk. He wouldn't work anywhere but

New Guinea. "It's a big free land," he says. "When adventure here runs out, I'll find me some other backward land."

At the top end of his run he stays at the beautiful town of Wau. Here is New Guinea at its best: no mosquitoes, incomparable climate, fine houses, lovely gardens, good school, a rollicking hotel. Wau seems unreal. Even the airstrip runs uphill at an angle that experts said was impossible!

It is one of the fabled towns of the Pacific. Situated on a handsome plateau, miles from jungle, it was surrounded by gold fields. Edie Creek nearby contained an alluvial deposit of free gold from which more than 40 tons of bullion was lifted!

That was in the late 1920's, and a lusty crew of men and women invaded the highlands. They bought airplanes and started a unique service whereby houses, shovels, live animals and a hotel were flown into the crazy uphill airstrip.

In 1933 the gold-happy miners decided to have a horse race. They flew five fast horses in from Australia, set up a bookmaker who handled more than a hundred thousand dollars, and ran a fantastic series of races in which a thoroughbred named Harmony made a small fortune for her owner.

The next year Wau pooled its resources and backed a local boy in an air race from England to Australia. Their man got mixed up with some high life in Singapore and finished six months late. Toby Miller and his wife got news of a winning lottery ticket and chartered a plane to collect their winnings. They spent $890 to pick up twenty! In 1949 the tradition persisted. A child was strangling from a coffee bean in its windpipe. An airplane was chartered from Wau to Brisbane for $3,800. The child was saved.

Edie Creek was situated on a precipitous mountain that dropped into an equally precipitous gorge. A wise miner figured that much of the original gold must have washed away into the stream beds below. So on the Bulolo flats immense dredges were built of parts assembled at the seashore and flown in across the jungled mountains. No piece could weigh more than three tons, but the completed masterpieces, eight of them, weighed 3,000 tons each. They could cut channels fifty feet deep, and from the gravel beds of the insignificant Bulolo River these cavernous monsters still dredge huge finds of gold.

Among the wild men of the gold fields was one whose strikingly handsome face has never been forgotten. He was a young fellow quite adept with his fists. He recruited labor,

371

tended bar, worked sluice boxes and sailed small boats along the coast. At Busama he produced a hollow bamboo cane into which he tossed thrup'ny bits and out of which came bright new shillings. This so entranced the Luluwai that he traded forty prime boys for it, with the understanding that he must not work the magic bamboo until three days had passed. By then the labor contracts of the boys had been passed along to the gold fields for a profit of $4,000. The young trader's name was Errol Flynn.

He wound up at Rabaul where a news cameraman hired him for a trip up the Sepik to film headhunters. In order to start the fireworks, Flynn went ashore and launched a fine riot. The resulting films were so good that an Australian company hired him as lead in a picture "which might have dramatic interest": *In Wake of the Bounty*. Flynn played Fletcher Christian and then went to Hollywood.

The old hands say that New Guinea is divided into three parts—twice. The biggest third belongs to the Dutch. Papua once belonged to Great Britain, who gave it to Australia. The last third originally belonged to Germany, but in 1920 the League of Nations mandated it to Australia. For the present the United Nations have approved a single administration for Papua and the Mandate, which includes islands like New Britain, Manus and Bougainville.

The second division concerns people, not land. It divides all whites into three warring camps: B-4's, missionaries, goverment.

B-4's are old timers who lived in the Territory before 1935. They're planters, fossickers, traders. They can't speak of missionaries or government blokes without apoplexy. They drink tremendously, belt natives upon provocation, and assure one another that the world, especially New Guinea, is going to the devil.

Yorky Booth, from Yorkshire, is a B-4. He sits at a table in the Lae bar and drinks ginger beer. He has white hair, a big smile and penetrating blue eyes such as Coleridge must have seen when describing his mariner.

Yorky made a pile at Edie Creek—14,000 ounces in three months—but became involved in a historic court case with his wife. He's nearly broke now, but he keeps a copy of the High Court of Australia Proceedings. It's a tragic story of lives gone wrong on the gold fields. It contains an unforgettable bit of evidence on marital troubles: "I am a good revolver shot. I did not once with a revolver fire a shot

372

through my wife's hat while she had it on her head. Did it with a .22 rifle."

Yorky made several fortunes—his mines were Cleopatra, Helen of Troy, Queen of Sheba—and has no regrets. He lives with a mastiff big enough to saddle and often compares notes with another famous B-4, Jockey Jack Turner, who also made and lost an Edie Creek fortune.

Missionaries in New Guinea are often Americans. Lutherans, Catholics and Seventh-Day Adventists are common. They are rugged men, penetrating land not yet subdued by government. They suffer from a bad reputation earned by earlier missionaries. The B-4 accuses them of exploiting natives for financial gain. "They came out here to do good, and they've done very well." The government remembers that during the war only mission boys betrayed Allied airmen to the Japs. And many people recall certain German missionaries who worked subversively for a Japanese victory.

Most religious men, however, were like Father Glover. In 1942, when he had scarcely learned to fly, he escaped the Japs and flew to the central highlands in a tiny plane. He used it to evacuate planters. Then, remembering a larger plane, he walked 150 miles through jungle to get it. Soon he had collected most of the white people at a single station high up a mountainside. Then he set out to fly to Australia—an impossible trip—for help. He carried extra gas in a hospital bed pan and fed the engine with an enema.

He lost his way and crash landed on a jungle beach. There he found a canoe and crossed the ocean until rescued by a passing ship. In Australia he persuaded the Government to send a large rescue plane. He saved hundreds of lives. Then, after the war, on his last missionary flight, he crashed into the jungle and was killed.

As for the Government, nobody likes it. New Guinea is run by a dictatorship, benevolent toward natives. After generations of brutalization by Dutch, Germans and Australians alike, the black man is at last getting a break. (At this point the B-4 passes into a coma.) The new deal is caused partly by Russia's embarrassing questions at Lake Success, partly by the fact that honest humanitarians have been appointed by the Labor Government to stop mere exploitation.

The result is chaos. Reports a moderate minister, "Had there been a plan to create frustration, apathy and misery, and the destruction of civic virtues, it could not have succeeded better than the methods of this administration through three-and-a-half years of town planning." Old B-4's point out that the Government is doing everything to stifle enterprise. Australian meat dealers offered to establish freezer stores for each community. The Government would allot no land. At Port Moresby the butchers had to buy a ship and set up a floating market. Says one merchant, "The Government has made it impossible to invest money, difficult to hire labor, illegal to acquire land. Economic life is at a standstill." Contempt for the Government is unlimited. The Department of Works and Housing, which fumbles with one thing after another, is known as Works and Jerks.

Yet the individual official knows what he is doing. He appreciates that Australia must clean house—in a few years Germans accomplished far more than has been done since—or lose the mandate. Arthur Ewing, an assistant district officer, understands the score.

He's a slight fellow, hardly a man you'd pick to quell a native tribe. Yet when word trickled back to Lae that in a remote valley a gang of hoodlums had murdered four people, Ewing was sent inland to capture the murderers. He left by air and flew as far as possible. Then he started on foot toward territory that no white man had ever visited. Finally he reached the tribe that was being terrorized. He found that some young bucks had got hold of Jap rifles. His luck was good. He subdued the murderers without arousing tribal revenge. Then he started the long return trip with his prisoners.

This simple police case took six months. During that time Ewing had no comforts, was rarely dry, was many times surrounded by men who still practiced cannibalism. His experience was not unusual. He was merely an official on the world's least-explored island.

Mrs. Angelo, wife of a Works and Jerks man, also has dealings with natives. She is a pretty Australian woman with a wonderful sense of humor. She lives alone most of the time at the top of a steep hill while her husband, Michael Angelo—his real name, believe it or not—tends his portion of The Road.

She is famous for her piano playing and has a tremendous boogie beat. Sentimental truck drivers often stop by to hear her play "Tales of the Vienna Woods;" but her most important visitors are the natives from nearby villages.

Because of her good humor she has become their counselor, but she is handicapped because most of the natives are members of the fantastic Cargo Cult. These savages, looking at things like kerosene stoves, radios and good beds have been unable to understand how white men got them. Adapting the Christian teaching—"The Lord giveth and the Lord taketh away"—they have devised the belief that everything coming into New Guinea has been sent expressly to them, but that white men intercept it—for the time being.

They believe implicitly that within a few years all white men will be removed, whereupon cargoes which their ancestors now send them will reach their rightful owners. They were encouraged in this belief during the war by Australian Communists who worked out logical explanations of everything.

The natives are absolutely certain that pretty soon Mrs. Angelo's house will be theirs. She shows them pictures of cargoes being manufactured by ordinary human beings. The Government, to halt natives from rushing planes for their goods, has flown Cargo Cult leaders to Australia to let them see assembly lines. They returned convinced that God made the stuff—in Australia—and that venal whites frustrated His intentions.

Less grave is Mrs. Angelo's problem with the Wompit Dagens. War had a devastating effect upon these unhappy men because their women saw too much: (1) white men working like dogs at menial army jobs; (2) white nurses treated with delicate courtesy.

When war ended the women of Wompit Dagen refused to go back to the old ways. They wouldn't work while their men rested. The latter protest tearfully to Mrs. Angelo: "Maries no work long garden. Maries no carry water." The Maries had a high old time, and what was worse, relayed their discoveries to tribes farther inland. Now the men of Wompit Dagen, as they plow and lug water, curse war.

Mrs. Angelo conducts her discussions in pidgin, that astonishing language. The bane of scientists, it has been called "the wonderful confusion." Jack London termed it the language with no grammar and no dictionary. It flourishes in New Guinea and is disarmingly suited to blasphemous exchanges between impatient planters and illiterate natives. I tried vainly to tell a native boy that my tea was too strong. Finally, in exasperation, a tough old geezer shouted, "Monkey! Mastuh i no likim dirink. Dirink bilong mastuh sitarong tumas. Orait. Yupela kesim dirink hap tea hap water hot tumas. Mastuh no bloody Austrylian." (Boy! Man he no like his drink. Drink belong master strong too much. All right. You fellow catch him drink half tea half hot water.) The

375

closing insult meant that the American was a boy, not a real man.

The pidgin words I like most are tasol (that's all); gudpela (good guy); inogat (he doesn't have); tupela kirisimas (two Christmasses = two years); sapos (suppose = if); palanti (plenty); and liklik (little).

The vocabulary is painfully meager, but the range of possible ideas large, if you have endless time. I heard a planter sending for a book: "All right. You know house belong woman with dog? All right. Suppose you know house next door belong man he got no leg. All right. That man he good fellow too much. That man he got pass—anything printed or written is a pass—belong me. All right. Suppose you fellow run long man good fellow too much. Catch him pass belong me. That's all."

"And," concluded the planter, "I'd have saved time by getting it myself."

The Administration frowns on pidgin as humiliating to the native. Especially condemned are the words *mary* (any woman), *boy* (any man), and *monkey* (any boy). The last is not derogatory but a corruption of the German for little man, *mannki*.

Like many Pacific islands, New Guinea is a Babel. One estimate says there may be as many as sixty distinct languages and more than a hundred dialects. Natives from villages ten miles apart are often unable to converse, except through pidgin. This has led to the classic expression of brotherhood: "He me we wuntok." (H and I are one talk = speak the same language = come from the same village ∴ are good buddies.)

Ability to get along with natives is almost essential if you want to make money in New Guinea. Bob Day, owner of the Dauntless mine, is an example. He's a lean, good-looking Australian of about fifty. In 1936 he had a mining lease and some money.

His first problem was water, since his claim was a natural for hydraulic sluicing. Because he had a good reputation among the natives, he was able to get 135 boys to go with him more than two miles back in the hills. They built a water race which would deliver 54 cubic feet a second to an impound 180 feet above the workings. They tunneled 800 feet through rock and built many aqueducts. To prevent the water from running too fast and destroying the banks, Day built the course so perfectly that the fall was only two inches in a hundred feet.

376

Getting water took two and a half years. Then war came and Day went bankrupt. His boys went back to the jungle. After the war he assembled new funds and, while others screamed about no boys, he quietly picked up his old hands. They rebuilt the race, learned to sluice gravel for gold. In 1948—twelve years after he and the boys started—he washed his first bullion.

He hires 110 natives, some of whom have worked with him for twenty-three years. He pays them $2.41 a month plus bonuses for length of stay and ability. They get free food, clothing, shelter, medicine and tobacco. Their wage totals about $20 a month. One skilled mechanic earns $60 plus extra food for his family.

Day is one of six independent men left on the gold fields. Before the war there were 400. He describes himself as "a pigheaded fool, but I hate to work for a boss." Last year his boys won $30,000 worth of gold but his expenses were $36,000. He hopes to break even soon, but the cost of supplies may lick him. He used to pay $32 a ton for Indo-China rice; Australian rice now costs $189. South American beef was 11¢ a tin; Australian beef is 32¢.

Bob Day's life is that of the fossicker. His wife and three children prefer to live in Australia, where he visits every five or six years. He has a fine jungle house, kept clean by house boys, but it may fall down. Termites got in during the war. He eats well, enjoys what beer he can get, reads a lot, goes up to Wau—ten miles away—every two or three months. He's a citizen of New Guinea and as such has never had a vote in his life. His proudest boast is that "my boys sometimes walk 70 miles to work for me rather than work for someone else right at hand. I give them no contracts, don't baby them. But they know they can trust me."

New Guinea, with its million natives, is a prodigious place. Many areas of arable land have yet to be touched. Vast reaches of pasture land await cattle. Engineers predict that soon countless waterfalls will be harnessed for transmission of electric power across Torres Straits to Australia. There's more gold than has been found. Oil has already been hit in Dutch New Guinea, and if Australians locate some in their end of the island, the most acute raw-material shortage in Australia and New Zealand will have been solved. Fisheries, agriculture, local manufacturing and transportation have not yet been scratched. Whereas much of Australia may never prove habitable, the white population of New Guinea could expand a hundredfold.

A start has been made at Bulolo. There's only fifteen more years of dredging there. After that the vast establishment will have to turn to something else. It may be lumber. Already the company is cutting superb timber and prefabricating houses. They erect a four-room house, all conveniences, furniture, fixtures, even utensils—everything except linen—for less than $2,000. Some have been flown down to Lae and assembled for $2,600. There's talk of flying them right on to Sydney!

Several leads are being explored by agriculturists. Coffee and cotton are thriving, but the most spectacular venture is taking place at Nondugl, in the great highland plains toward the Dutch border. A rich Australian, E. J. Hallstrom, who invented kerosene refrigerators, has flown in large flocks of sheep. He hopes to prove that natives can herd sheep, clip them, weave their own clothes and live on mutton. If he can do this, and the ewes have been through one successful lambing, he may revolutionize New Guinea.

To accomplish any of these things will cost money—and men. For the present, Australia seems to have neither. Even the operation of the solitary and murderous Road is an economic drain difficult to justify. To build additional roads across rivers that destroy them in an afternoon is impracticable without additional revenue.

As a result, certain influential residents have suggested that Australia release the Mandated Territory to the United States. Such a request is silly. At any cost, Australia must retain New Guinea. The island is a noose about Australia's throat, and in unfriendly hands could be used to strangle the underpopulated continent.

In 1919 Woodrow Wilson recommended that Japs be allowed to settle New Guinea. He was opposed to the death—no American name is more reviled in Australia than Wilson's—by a brilliant politician, W. M. Hughes. Wilson was terribly in the wrong. Had Japs controlled New Guinea in 1941, Australia would have been subdued within two months. And America would have been denied an essential base. It must become an unwritten principle of American foreign policy never to let New Guinea fall into unfriendly hands, for when it does, our ally Australia is doomed.

Sensible and unsensational men in New Guinea say: "We can probably hold our half of the island another twenty years—at most. By then either China or Indonesia, working in through Dutch New Guinea, will have absorbed it." I asked, "Is there nothing that can be done?" They replied,
378

"Probably not." I persisted, "You know that the loss of New Guinea dooms Australia?" They said, "Yes, we know." I asked coldly, "But still you think the loss is inevitable?" The Australians looked me right in the eye and said, "It's inevitable."

Part of this fatalism grew out of what happened at Manus. No New Guinea man can possibly comprehend that action of his Government! At Manus Americans had assembled one of the greatest naval establishments in history. It was a city larger than Sacramento. It had naval stores worth a half billion dollars. I was at Manus when MacArthur was preparing the invasion of Leyte, and in the endless roadstead I saw twenty-six carriers, dozens of battleships, and actually hundreds of lesser craft. Yet the great anchorage—absolutely protected by coral reef—looked empty.

America requested permission to maintain this base, at her expense. Australia refused. Why, nobody knows. Manus was of only minor importance to us; it was absolutely vital to Australian defense. The vast naval stores, the incredible wealth of Manus was sold lock and barrel to Chinese wholesalers and carted off to make Hong Kong fortunes.

Now the once-great base is a shambles, an echo of the protecting bastion it might have been. I have heard men in New Guinea stutter with rage when speaking of this folly. There is only one saving grace: "If we ever get into trouble again, your blokes'll be able to use the anchorage—if somebody else don't grab it first."

It is strange, but on distant New Guinea I thought more deeply about America than I ever had at home. I wondered if we would be able to hold this island and Australia and New Zealand. I wondered if some day Americans would be back in the jungles of the South Pacific. But about one thing I did not wonder, for I was completely certain on that point: these islands are our concern. When they are lost, the Pacific is lost, and when that mighty ocean is lost, much of our way of life is gone.

I shivered in the intense heat and asked the Australians one more question: "Is there no way you could hold New Guinea?"

They thought a moment and replied, "With help, we might."

The Fossickers

Men in New Guinea say: "We can probably hold onto our end of the island another twenty years . . . at most."

All the way from Honolulu to Sydney I heard about The Queen Emma. In Tahiti an Australian said, "I guess I named it."

"How do you mean?" I asked.

"I was serving with the Yanks. Told them about Queen Emma. She was half Yank herself. Half Samoan. She became queen of New Guinea. Big, tough woman. They say she murdered her fourth or fifth husband. In Monte Carlo."

"What's this got to do with the hotel?"

"I was coming to that," the Aussie said. "This Queen Emma did the New Guinea Germans out of half a million quid. Oh, she was quite a girl." There was a long pause, the kind that occurs in tropic bars. Finally he said, "I told this Yank about her and right away he painted a big sign for his hut: The Queen Emma. 'It's me Broadway hotel,' he says, and he gives a coon ten bob to fix it up nice."

"So that's how The Queen Emma got its name?"

The Australian ignored my question. "Why you goin' to New Guinea?" he asked abruptly.

"Taking some pictures. I heard about a tribe. Up at the headwaters of the Sepik. But tell me. Is The Queen Emma as bad as they say?"

"Well," he said thoughtfully, "during the war it was a good place after a long patrol. In peace time . . ." He returned to his spirits and would say no more.

I didn't mind The Queen Emma. Reminded me of the Hotel De Gink at Guadal. Big sprawling lot of quonsets. I didn't mind the beetles or the snakes. And I was fascinated by those immense bumblebees that bore holes the size of dimes right through a wooden beam.

I could lie in my bunk and see the towering white clouds hanging on the Owen Stanley Range, and I enjoyed being back in New Guinea. You know what I mean. That great hot blast. The heavy smell of jungle. And over west—the Sepik.

I'd seen it from the air many times during the war, and I always said, "Some day I'm going up that river!" Have you ever seen it? One of the world's greatest. A huge brown mass of ugly water spewing itself out into the Pacific. Logs, brush, crocodiles, dead natives. Out they go, as if their brutal land could stomach them no more. The Sepik was my river, and when I read in a British magazine about a race of savage pygmies at the headwaters . . . Well, sometimes you get to do what you've sworn to do. Breaks, I guess.

On my first afternoon at The Queen Emma the old hands asked, "What you doin' out here, Yank?" I said I was trying to hire a boat for the Sepik and they said, "You must be nuts." But one old codger added, "The man you want is Shark Eye," and that night I met him.

He was more than seventy, a gnarled, skinny, hard-drinking Australian with no lower teeth. He was sitting alone at a corner table in the rusted quonset bar. "Name's Shannon," he said. "Folks call me Shark Eye." He ran his right forefinger down a gash in his face. "They say you want to go up the Sepik."

"That's right."

He rose to his full six-feet-four, pushed back his white hair and held out his hand. "I'm your man," he said. We sat down for the first time at that small table and Shark Eye shouted, "Hey, Monkey!"

A small native boy—couldn't have been more than ten— appeared with a huge oval tray. Shark Eye leaned back and studied the lad's blue-black shoulders. Then he snarled, "You're messy. Fix up your belt." The monkey became greatly embarrassed and tried to adjust the belt that held up his lap-lap. The tray began to slip and as it hit the floor Shark Eye gave it a kick so that it spun across the room. The monkey looked as if he might cry, but the old man raised his boot and shoved the boy after the tray. "Keep your belt fixed," Shark Eye growled. "And bring us some beer."

As the night progressed, that wonderful, quiet, heavy night, Shark Eye gave me a running account of his qualifications. "Been in these parts more'n sixty years. Used to live at Rabaul before there was even a volcano in the bay. I saw the eruptions, the floods, the native uprisings. Watched the Germans come and go." He stopped and eyed me suspiciously, then added softly, "Did a bit of fossicking, too."

"What?" I asked.

He would tell me no more. "Monkey!" he shouted. The little boy appeared and stood at attention, his immense tray under his left arm. "More beer!" The boy brought them, but I couldn't drink like these Australians. Shark Eye tossed the bottles down and reeled off to bed.

As the bar was closing I asked a stranger, "What's fossicking?"

"You Yanks call it prospecting," he said. "Shark Eye been bashing your ear? He's got a right to. One of the greatest. Made and lost three fortunes."

"Women?" I asked.

"There's always women," the stranger said, and he too stumbled off.

Next evening, after a fruitless day spent arguing with Government officials, I was on my way to dinner when Shark Eye stuck his head out of the bar and called me in. "Sit down!" he said imperiously. He was quite excited and huddled with me in the corner. "I've got me eye on a wonderful craft for this trip," he whispered. "We can coast it right into the Sepik."

"Do you know the river?" I asked.

He stopped cold, deeply insulted. "Monkey!" he screamed. The little boy ran up. "More beer!" We missed dinner that night, and several nights thereafter. We sat in the corner, this old man and I, and he'd tell me about his fossicking days in New Guinea. He'd been everywhere. Could almost smell gold.

"Then why are you broke?" I asked.

"Me? Broke?" He shouted for the monkey and spoke in rapid pidgin, after which he tossed a key onto the big tray. The little boy disappeared into the night and returned with a large box. The old man fumbled with another key for some moments, then hid the box below the table and began to produce papers. There was a bank book, showing some ten thousand pounds in Brisbane, news clippings about a fossicking trip into the heart of Australia, and a parchment citation for his work in rescuing citizens during the volcanic terror at Rabaul.

He fortified these records with verbal accounts of his adventures and I was beginning to be impressed when I recalled his cruel manner toward the monkey. I spoke of this and he guffawed. "Monkey!" he bellowed. "Come 'ere, damn you."

The near-naked little fellow stood before us, his belt straight, his lap-lap tucked in the way Shark Eye had directed. "Who's the best damn man in New Guinea?" the old Australian roared.

A tremendous grin spread over the monkey's face and he said, "You are, mastuh!" Shark Eye looked pleased and dug into his sweaty pocket for five marks.

"Get some bleach for your hair," he said. But he tossed the

382

coins viciously onto the floor, so that the frantic child had to crawl among the table legs to get them.

The bleach had quite an effect on our monkey. He dressed his hair into a ridge, like a rooster's comb, and the top half was bleached a bright red. Shark Eye said the boy looked disgraceful, even for The Queen Emma, and was about to belt him when he stopped and stared at the bar entrance.

There stood a remarkable woman. She was about fifty, sawed off, dumpy, red faced and scraggly haired. She wore men's army shoes and a rucksack. She looked straight at Shark Eye and said, "You still alive?" Several men at the bar stood to say reserved hellos. She ignored them and crossed to our table. Shark Eye remained in his seat and kicked back a chair. Then he said to me, in great disgust, "Meet an anthropologist."

She held out her hand, and I thought: "Here's a capable mitt." In a deep voice she said, "I'm Sheila Bancroft."

At this Shannon burst into laughter and said, "In Australia we call our whoors sheila. This here's my sheila."

I paid no attention to him because now I recognized this woman. It was her writing that had brought me to the Sepik. "Aren't you Dame Sheila?" I asked.

"Yes," she said, sitting down and reaching for a glass.

"I studied your report on the Danduras," I said. She was pleased, but as the evening wore on I had the strange feeling that both she and Shark Eye were maneuvering so that the other would have to leave first. I broke the impasse by going to bed, but before I got to sleep the gaunt figure of Shannon loomed in the darkness beside my head. "Don't have anything to do with that crazy woman," he whispered.

"Why?"

He pulled up a chair and hunched up beside my mosquito net. In a low whisper he said, "The most disgusting person you can meet is a woman scientist. They've ruined New Guinea—studyin' natives. They poison the Administration." He could have squeezed no more scorn into the word. "They want to make a coon utopia."

"What you mean is, she spoiled some of your plans?"

"My plans? I never have any. Just wait for what turns up." He lit a hand-rolled cigarette and crossed his long legs. "But this damn fool Sheila . . ."

"Wait a minute!" I protested. "This woman has been honored by the King. And by lots of scientists, too."

I could see Shark Eye's face only dimly. It had frozen into

383

a hard mask. "By God," he snarled, "you're one of 'em too! A coon lover!"

"Go to bed," I laughed. "I'm tired of you Administration haters."

"I won't go until I tell you something. For your own good." He leaned across my bed and whispered through the net. "I found out that this fine lady lived with a native man. Yes, right here in New Guinea. She was in the jungle, studyin' primitive habits—so she said." He filled the night with bitter scorn. Sheila Bancroft must have caused him much hurt to have incurred such hatred.

The old man left my bed and stood in the doorway. "She studied native habits all right. No wonder she fills her books with dirty stuff about sex. She should know!"

At breakfast he winked at me when Dame Sheila arrived. "She should know!" he cried in a whisper she must have heard. When she stopped to look at him, he stuck out his tongue at her and went, "Yannh."

That afternoon she met me going to the toilet, and although she must have known where I was headed, she stood in the pathway and said, "You'd be a fool to risk the Sepik with Shannon."

"I haven't agreed to—yet."

"Be wise," she warned. "Don't." I muttered something, hoping to break away, but she seemed to be weighing ideas. Suddenly she made up her mind and pulled me against the wall where no one could see us.

"What do you know about Shannon?" she asked searchingly.

"What everybody else knows. Rabaul skipper. Some experience with gold. He knows the Sepik."

"I suppose he showed you the parchment from Rabaul. He always does. But did he tell you why he can never return to Rabaul?" She pressed one hand against my chest and told in angry syllables how Shark Eye Shannon had fled the Japs in '42. He had run off with the last boat. Had stranded some fifty men who had fought on to cruel death or even crueler imprisonment and torture. "He got away to Australia. But if he ever went back to Rabaul . . . they would kill him."

I listened and found in her voice a freightage of disgust that was unnatural. "Did he betray a man you loved?" I asked.

"No!" she snapped.

"Then what did you do to Shannon to make you hate him so much?"

384

The powerful woman stepped back and digested my question. "What do you mean? What did I do to *him*?"

"Look!" I said. "Last night he came to my room to whisper what a monster you were . . ."

"What did he say?" she asked hastily.

"I won't tell you," I said. "But now you report the same about him. What happened between you?"

She was knocked off guard by this approach. Finally she said, as if at confession. "He was put in jail on evidence I gave. He debauched a native tribe. Terribly."

I thought this over for a long time and then said, "Dame Sheila, I like you. How's about us going up the Sepik together?"

"It's very rough terrain, where you want to go."

"I know that. Could we get there without Shannon?"

"No," she said. "I'm here to hire him for my expedition."

This one bowled me over. Even though my bladder was about to burst, I had to get this straight. I said, "Look! You despise the man. You say he's too tough for me. But you're going with him up the Sepik. I don't get it."

The tough little woman laughed. "Sounds silly, doesn't it? But I meant my warning. To my knowledge Shannon has killed two partners and betrayed dozens."

"You're still not afraid of him?"

"No." Then after a moment she added, "Sometimes you reach a point of involvement that insures protection."

That evening I had a further surprise. When I entered the bar Shark Eye and Dame Sheila were sharing a bottle as if they were old friends. Shannon's lean face was extra animated and the English woman's bobbed hair fell about her ears as she leaned forward to hear what he was saying. The Australian kicked a chair back for me and shouted for the monkey to bring more drinks.

"Look!" I said abruptly. "I can't hang around here much longer. Are we going to arrange a deal or not?"

Shannon put down his drink and said, "I bought the boat. We'll be shoving off shortly."

"Good!" Then to Sheila I said, "You coming, too?"

"She is like hell!" Shannon interrupted. "That's what we've been arguin' about."

"You'll take me," the Englishwoman said confidently.

"She thinks we can't get past the Danduras without her," Shark Eye gloated.

Dame Sheila laughed. "Nor can you," she said.

"Why don't we quit this stalling?" I cried. "Let's agree right now. We'll all three go. As soon as possible."

To my surprise Shannon turned almost black in the face and left us for another table. "Monkey!" he bellowed. The boy was slow coming and Shark Eye kicked at him.

"That dirty beast," Sheila gasped.

"More beer!" the old man roared. He drank three bottles—big, black quarts from Antwerp—but he wasn't even staggering when he entered my room late that night. "American," he said softly, "we've got to come to an understanding. You've almost wrecked things."

"How?" I asked.

He became very confidential. "We mustn't take that busybody."

"What goes on between you two?" I asked. "I know her explanation. About having you arrested . . ."

"And Rabaul. I suppose she told you about Rabaul?"

"Yes." I felt deeply involved with Shannon—for better or worse—and I wanted him to know that I was as tough as he. "She told me about you turning yellow belly. Deserting the ship."

I wasn't prepared for his reply. He laughed heartily, then went "Sssssh!" as if I were making the noise. "I wasn't the one who deserted the ship," he joked. "I ran off with the bloody thing!"

"She said they'd lynch you if you ever went back."

The tough old coot stopped laughing and said, "You're young. I'm seventy-three. I watched a lot of brave men insist upon committing suicide at Rabaul. They hadn't a chance. I told 'em so."

"They helped to stop the Japs," I said.

"Useless," Shark Eye said in disgust. "A sensible man knows when to fight. The Government had betrayed us at Rabaul."

"I don't like you, Shannon," I said. "I did my turn against the Japs."

"Look, sonny!" he laughed. "I've done more fighting than all the gallant men in New Guinea. Most of them are dead. I'm alive."

There was nothing I could say to this, and for some moments I could feel his tense face close to mine. Then I let him have it. "Dame Sheila tells me you murder your mates or desert them."

With no embarrassment he explained, "There's always two sides to a story. You've been giving me hell. I know why.

You want to test the kind of man you're dealing with. Now I've got to test you. Can I trust you?"

"Why not?" I asked.

Suddenly my left arm was gripped furiously above the elbow. I could feel my skin crinkling. "We're not playing a game now," he said harshly. "Yes or no. Can I trust you?"

I knocked his hand away and said, "Yes."

He pondered a moment, then lit a cigarette. He was afraid to speak, yet he could sense that his match had outlined the scar. He touched it with his finger and said, "It's crazy to call me Shark Eye. A damned native did that."

"On the Sepik?"

"Yes. Up where you want to go."

There was a long silence and I thought: "Well, I can wait." Then abruptly he said, "I'm an old geezer, and I've got to trust someone. I want to get back to them hills because a long time ago . . ."

He stopped and rose. I knew what he had to say, so I finished it. "A long time ago you found gold. Now you need it."

"I need nothing," he boasted.

"Don't kid me, old man. Because I saw the date on the Brisbane bank book. I'll bet you don't have a tanner."

He stood in the deep shadows above me and said, "I know where there's a treasure. But it's inaccessible. The damned rotten stuff is in Dutch New Guinea."

"But you think you can smuggle some out."

"I know I can!" His voice became impassioned. "Yank, I never miss on gold. Forget your pictures," he pleaded. "Come along with me! We'll make a fortune."

"No," I said. "You take me up to the Danduras. I'll pay my share. From then on you do as you wish."

He gripped my arm more violently than before. "A man can't do it alone," he cried. "Last time I had fifty thousand quid worth of metal. Strike me dead. But the cursed savages chopped me up."

"Well," I said, "that winds that up."

"What do you mean?" he cried angrily.

"We could never arrange a trip."

"But I know the Sepik!" he howled.

"You're an old fossicker," I said. "Mad for gold. Now you get any partner you wish. I'll find me a skipper I can trust. Good night."

"But, Yank . . ."

"Go to bed. You bore me."

Without another word he left the room, and in the morning I beat up and down the waterfront inquiring after various skippers who knew the Sepik. "That's funny," one of them said. "Short time ago a Dutchman was down here asking the same questions."

I met him that night at The Queen Emma. He was a chap about thirty, slightly bald, handsome and square in the Dutch manner. He was talking earnestly with Shark Eye and Dame Sheila. I was about to pass them when Shannon grabbed me and hauled me down beside him. "Meet Herr van Hoog." Shark Eye laughed with malicious gaiety. "Guess where he wants to go!"

"Up the Sepik," I said, and the four of us sat together and drank beer, as we were to do for three weeks.

The Dutchman took a keen dislike to me and one night finally exploded. "You filthy Americans!" he shouted, and it was apparent that he had been cherishing a grudge until he got safely drunk.

"Take it easy," I said.

"Easy?" he screamed. "When you ruined my country?"

"Oh, hell," I groaned. "Now we get blamed for Java, too."

"It was your fault," he ranted. "If you had stood with us, the Indonesians . . ."

"Take it easy," I said again.

But he raved on about how America had sabotaged the entire Western Pacific. The Dutch were kicked out of Java. Next they'd be run out of Dutch New Guinea. Then hell would start, because pretty soon the Indonesians would overrun all of New Guinea. Australia, with no defenses and no people, would be cut off. "Then," he bellowed in his stubborn Dutch way, "you filthy Yanks with your handsome white teeth will be in the fire."

He had risen from his chair to insult me further, but I'd had enough. I reached over and shoved my hand into his fat square face. I remember that Shark Eye looked pleased at this, as if he prospered on fights, but before van Hoog could do anything I began talking very fast.

"I wasn't going to say this, but you asked for it. So here goes. I agree with you that America was criminally stupid in backing the Indonesians. And we'll pay for that mistake. We'll pay for it in blood. But, van Hoog, I saw the Dutch administration. I saw it good. In a place you never heard of. Tanah Merah. A dump lost in the middle of a swamp fifty thousand square miles wide. Shannon, you've been all over. You ever hear of Tanah Merah? It's got a couple of big,
388

spacious buildings for the Dutch, and a hundred little two-by-fours built of corrugated iron. They're for the Indonesian prisoners. That is, they used to be. I was in one of those iron shacks. Temperature 130 degrees."

The bar at Queen Emma's was deathly quiet, but visions of Tanah Merah came back. I said, "There was an administrator there, a Dutchman. One of the kind we used to hear about in the States. 'The Dutch are the best colonizers in the world.' This one sure was. He beat and starved and baked anyone who opposed the Government. You know what the Indonesians from Tanah Merah told us after the Japs had liberated them? They said, 'If we get the Administrator we'll cut his legs off an inch at a time. With rusty knives.' Chickens come home to roost, van Hoog. So do Indonesians."

The Dutchman was very white. He took a drink of beer and said huskily, "All nations make mistakes."

"Yes," I said, "and when we do, we never get another chance."

"Don't say that!" the big, stolid man cried.

The four of us sat around for some time thinking of the nations that had lost their way. Dame Sheila said, "It's inevitable that all subject peoples must rise to the common standard. The Dutch in Java were unfortunate . . ."

Shannon banged down his glass. "You talk like a damned fool. It's you . . . Meddling old-women fools like you who talk savages into believing they can climb to our standards." He was actually quaking with rage.

The party ended dismally, but late that night my room door creaked open. "What the hell do you want, Shannon?" I rasped. I was sick of the old man.

"It's van Hoog."

"Turn on the light."

"Mosquitoes," he replied, and felt his way to my chair.

"I'm sorry about tonight," I said.

"No need, I've been to Tanah Merah."

There was a pause and then it hit me. That white Dutch face over the beer mug. "You were the Administrator!"

"No," he said with deep relief.

"I'm glad," I said.

"I was an assistant." Another silence followed and he said, "Some day tourists will be shown through your Alcatraz. And they won't believe it. All nations make mistakes."

"I said I was sorry."

Bluntly he changed the conversation. "Can I trust Mr. Shannon?"

389

"He'd cut your throat—if money's involved."

"Money is involved," the Dutchman said. "You must come along with us."

"You find a gold mine near Tanah Merah?" I hazarded.

He whistled slightly and said, "I took some convicts across the swamps. Up into the mountains near the border. That's why . . ." He paused and said in a terrible voice, "That's why I can never go back. It was a bad trip. I had to be harsh. The Indonesian Republic has named me a national enemy."

"Watch out for Shannon," I said.

"Do you suppose he knows about gold? Across the border?"

"No," I said.

"If I paid you, would you come along?" van Hoog begged.

"Nope," I said. My door opened and van Hoog was gone.

Next morning Shannon sailed his boat up to the pier. It was a sturdy craft with two engines, a dirty cowling and a deck house that would sleep four. It smelled of gasoline, and this may sound silly, but it looked a lot like Shannon, barnacled and weather-beaten.

"She was sunk by the Japs," he said. "But she's worthy, this one."

That night at the corner table he put it up to us. "Now make up your minds. Yank, will you join us?"

I studied the three partners: the Australian adventurer, the Dutch renegade, the English seeker. "All right," I agreed. "As far as the Danduras. You push on by yourselves from there."

"Good. You, Dutchman?"

"All the way."

The nasty old man looked at Dame Sheila. "There's no room for you," he said maliciously.

"I'll be there," she said with no concern. "Because without me you'll not get through. Has he told you, van Hoog, that last time he was nearly killed?"

The fossickers argued late into the night. They were like nations, each hating the other, each needing what the other had.

I thought of Sheila Bancroft's superb essay on sex in ultra-primitive societies, of the furore it had created. It was odd to sit with her in The Queen Emma and to catch a glimmer of what had driven her into the great jungles of the spirit. No man could have loved her. She had been a rejected girl, an unhappy woman. So she'd fled her society to study the ultimate beginnings of sex, the cruel force that had so punished her. Somehow, in some strange way, she had triumphed over those early rejections and had found reassurance in the savage jungles of our first beginnings. She had become a woman loved by the entire world. But the jungle remained her home, and she now proposed to fossick even past the boundaries she had previously reached. Once she told me, "Beyond the mountains you're always sure there will be gold."

Beside her, night after night, sat the stolid Dutchman. When he had boasted of absolute power over miserable brown men, he had pushed them through deadly swamps and up strangling mountains. He had written an arrogant book about it, *Beyond the Swamps*, and in each line he had signed his own banishment from all he loved. His family had ruled Java for centuries; now Java lusted to crucify him. He was an outcast, a fugitive from everywhere. Yet he felt certain that if he could only get back to that mountain of gold—the mountain beyond the swamp—he could rehabilitate himself. He had executed the only Indonesian who might have deduced the truth about the gold, but he was willing to believe that even such a crime was expiable if one could regain that mountain.

And to my right sat the old man of the islands, hatching his own plots. He had to abide the crazy Englishwoman in order to escape his earlier attackers. It infuriated him to think that a woman so despicable could, by reason of her disinterest, go where his rifle was powerless. He no longer tried to reconcile such absurdities. He'd seen everything: Queen Emma herself, the French settlers who had died like ghosts sensing the dawn, Tiger Lil of the imperial manner, the polite Jap trochus fishermen, the Australian Jew who had found the great gold fields, the whole lot of them. None of them was worth a damn. Men or women either. Once he'd carried a young married couple from Cairns to Rabaul, and five days after the marriage the girl was sleeping with him. He thought he might have as many as ten black kids, and there wasn't a decent one in the lot. Mewling half-castes, the lot. It was a rum world, but there was gold up the Sepik, and if you played your cards right you'd get your share, and maybe the Dutchman's, too.

It was midnight when we reached our agreement and the jungle was riotous with crickets when we went to bed. The next morning we said good-bye to The Queen Emma while castled clouds began to form upon the mighty mountains.

We were sixty miles off the mouth of the Sepik when Dame Sheila found the monkey. She dragged him from a hole so small you'd have sworn no human could have wedged himself into it. The little fellow bowed his red cockade and produced a remarkable document drawn up by some bush lawyer: "To all men, presents. Know that being of sound mind and body I do depose that my son may go on boat along Capt. Shannin. My mark."

"Well," Dame Sheila sniffed. "A fine thing."

"What do you mean?" Shark Eye demanded.

"We've got to put him ashore. That's obvious."

"We've not!" Shannon roared.

I was surprised when the Englishwoman backed down. "Very well," she said. "You're captain." Further, she took the legal document and endorsed it: "There was no way to put him ashore among his own people. We kept him with us."

The monkey was a tremendous help. I often talked with him and found that he considered Shannon the greatest man who ever lived. It was beyond me. Sheila and I treated the boy with respect, while Shannon bullied him, made him work like a slave. Yet the monkey had run away to be near the man who abused him. "Mastuh good man. Me like go ship."

I mentioned this to Sheila and she said, "I'd be stupid not to admit it. Many natives prefer brutal white men."

"Why?"

"Because such men conform to the stereotype of what a white man should be. The way Hitler, whether we like it or not, is most people's ideal of what a political leader should be."

"Then you can't educate people?" I asked snidely, meaning: "You admit Shark Eye is right about women scientists?"

She laughed. She knew what I was driving at. "No," she protested. "Look over there at tragic van Hoog. People who were once stupid caught up with him."

As we neared the Sepik—even the name haunts me, the great savage river, my Congo—I watched van Hoog with increasing pity. I could not even approximate the feelings of a man whose world had been washed away. For instance, I get terribly fed up with Chicago. It's one hell of a place. But no matter where I go, Chicago's always waiting, between Gary and Joliet. I would hate to think it wasn't there. Or that the enemy held it. Or that I couldn't go home.

I tried talking with the steel-brained Dutchman but there was nothing I could say. He never even laughed at the monkey. He was a man impossible to like.

Then we hit the Sepik. I remember the scene. I could never forget it. It was about dusk and we heard a shout far to starboard. The water was muddy and we couldn't see a thing. Then the glasses picked out a native riding a raft of logs. He was being swept out to sea. We tried to reach him, but it was no use. Drifting logs cut us off, and finally a wave washed him into the turgid waters. We heard him yelling. Something got him. Crocs. Sharks. Something snapped him in two.

"That's that," Shannon said, swinging our craft into the great river.

We went upstream about three hundred miles, moored the boat, and hired some canoes. Above us, around us, even growing from the bottom of the river, the jungle muffled all we did. Immense lianas twisted down like snakes, and pythons writhed away like drooping lianas. Parrots, birds of paradise and monster pigeons swept in and out of shadows. We caught strange fish and van Hoog predicted they'd all be poisonous, but no one died. The monkey sat in my canoe and chattered across the water to Shannon, who told him to shut up.

Natives skulked along the banks to watch us pass. White kiaps, who governed the disciplined tribes, stopped us and took legal notice of the monkey's presence. Soon we were beyond the places where white men dared to live.

This was the upper Sepik, one of the most fatal areas in the world. Headhunters still lurked here. Murders still went unpunished, and natives lived in deathly fear of voodoo, night mists and strange diseases that swept through villages like mountain floods.

I was ready to call it quits. I wondered if Amundsen and Scott had ever thought: "What a mess! Why did I come here?" Then I'd see Dame Sheila taking notes. She observed things I never even guessed at. And I came to the conclusion that the great explorers were like her. They pursued facts until they uncovered ideas.

When I watched Shark Eye shoot crocodiles and smack his lips after each good shot, it occurred to me that this man, too, had escaped fear. He hadn't scrammed out of Rabual because he was afraid of Japs. He wanted a more even fight. He said, "You draw stumps and wait for a better pitch."

On the thirty-eighth day we approached the Danduras, and Dame Sheila's nose dilated as if she were a race horse. I commented on this, and to my surprise she grew quite sober. "Everyone recalls that portion of earth where he grew up. When he finally discovered there was no cause to be afraid. It was in these mountains that I grew up." She pointed to where Shannon now led us. We climbed two days on that trail and each of us must have lost five pounds. I sweated until my fingers were a pale white. Then we hit the kunai plateau, and before us on the broad plain was the village of Lagui, close to the Dutch border. I fancied that van Hoog, staring across at the distant hills, was biting his lip.

Certainly Dame Sheila wasn't. A runner from the village had recognized her and now jumped up and down in giggling delight. He shouted some words which Shark Eye translated with mocking scorn: "Lady doctor come back!"

"Are you a doctor?" I asked.

"No. I used horse sense and cured some of them."

The villagers crowded out to meet us, and presently the Paramount Luluwai—a handsome brute—came toward us in stately measure. Behind him walked a girl of about sixteen. She was naked except for a small apron and was curiously appealing. Her nose was not broad. Her hair was curly instead of kinky. And I remember that she kept her feet one before the other.

She watched us carefully and it amused me that even a girl who had never seen white people before took only a quick survey of the woman and the old man. She divided her attention between van Hoog and me.

In the days that followed, while Dame Sheila assembled a crew for me and Shannon collected his, this girl Alwi spent more and more time watching van Hoog. The Dutchman was aware of this, and so was Shark Eye. He finally took us aside and laid down the law. "There's one rule up here. Learn by the gash on my face. Never fool with women if you've got to come back through their village."

Van Hoog showed great interest. "What happened?"

"I came back through the village," old Shark Eye laughed, "and the villagers came through me."

But van Hoog would not be warned. He shared a frond hut with me and one night I heard the monkey creep in and shake him. "Mastuh! Mastuh!" the little boy whispered. "Alwi say, 'You come 'long now.'" And the little conspirator led the Dutchman away.

I said nothing to Shannon, but after three nights van Hoog no longer pretended that he was living in my hut. What really surprised me was that the Paramount Luluwai made no complaint.

But I still had to come back through this village, and I had a bit of wind up. I spoke to Dame Sheila. "Will this mean trouble later on?"

The Englishwoman never batted an eye. She perched on a box of gear and said slowly, "You're young."

394

"I know. That's what Shannon said when he had dirty business to explain."

"You might call this dirty business," she said quietly. I recall that sweat stood at the roots of her bobbed hair. "But it's also essential business. The Luluwai knows that. Herr van Hoog is a sick man. His life has been cut away. You wouldn't understand."

"But I do!" And I told her about my sick feeling when I thought about Chicago lost.

"You do comprehend," she said with some surprise. "The moment often comes in a life when the world is lost. God doesn't exist. There's no good, no bad, no hope, no past. You're the basic animal, bewildered. You're dead." She now spoke with terrible intensity. "That's the moment I hope you will never know."

After a moment she unclenched her hands and said, "When such a time hits you, if it ever does, let the basic animal take control. There's a great cure in nature. The girl Alwi is that cure, and she's going with us. Van Hoog won't find his gold, and if he does Shannon will probably steal it. But he'll be cured."

And Alwi did go with them. This strange party set off one morning for the distant hills. Shannon led the way, with a rifle on his arm. Then came the bearers and Dame Sheila. The monkey ran up and down the line, swinging a machete. And behind them all trailed van Hoog and the naked girl.

Then like a flash of light, I saw it all! Dame Sheila had let the monkey come along to tie down Shannon's suspiring emotions. This way the old devil wouldn't bother the girl. And Alwi was going along so that if trouble came, van Hoog wouldn't have to face it alone. But where did Dame Sheila herself come in?

Then I understood. As the train disappeared toward the mountains—beyond the swamp—this naked girl Alwi walked in a strange way that I had seen before. I rushed like crazy into the Paramount Luluwai's hut and cried, "This girl Alwi! Whose daughter is she?"

"Mine," the big man said proudly.

This stopped me for a moment and I started to leave. But suddenly I began to laugh very loud. The Luluwai joined in, so I said, "Sure. She's your daughter. And who else's?"

He would not reply, so I took a long chance: "The lady doctor's?"

The Paramount Luluwai never stopped laughing, but he did say, "You savvy too much."

Rabaul

Before the catastrophes, Rabaul was the loveliest town in the Pacific. Lying near the equator, it demonstrated how idyllic tropical life could be.

It was a picture town. Wide avenues were lined with flowering trees. Handsome homes were surrounded with gardens of profuse beauty. A botanical park contained specimens from across the world, and the town was kept extraordinarily clean. There were no mosquitoes, no malaria and the nights were cool.

The Germans had built Rabaul in 1910 on a scimitar-like arm of mountains that cut off a bay of great beauty. The town was completed in 1914 and immediately lost to the Australians, under whose supervision it became even more charming, with a social life patterned upon archaic eighteenth-century customs.

There were two clubs, the Rabaul and the swanky New Guinea. Manners were impeccable. At formal dinners women wore gowns from Paris. Men were obliged to wear patent-leather pumps, black trousers, stiff shirts, hard collars, bow ties, white mess jackets. Perspiration was measured by the bucket and par was three fresh shirts for an evening dance. But "the conventions were protected."

Men visiting Rabaul who refused to wear tropical whites were asked to leave. Women who wore shorts were visited by the police and informed of the next ship south. The police also dealt ruthlessly with any white man who had visions of beachcombing with some dark beauty. He was tossed out of the territory, fare paid if necessary. It was all right, however, to welch on debts owed to Chinamen, many of whom went into bankruptcy because of unpaid chits.

Each family had five or six servants—ninety cents each a month—and no white man was permitted to lift or carry. White women often did no work at all. There was a good library, movies, a gay party life and a plane from Australia twice a week.

Everybody made money. One lawyer cleaned up $130,000 net in nine years. Citizens traveled widely, a favorite trip including London, New York, across America by Buick, and back to Rabaul with the car, which was sold at 100% profit to the taxi company.

Life had two focal points: copra and alcohol. Plantations on nearby islands were among the richest producers in the world, and when the price of copra was good—like cotton, the price is never good—Rabaul was a town of swaggering millionaires.

The consumption of drink baffles the imagination. It was common for a man to drink three or four gallons of beer a day topped off with a bottle of whiskey. Serious drinkers did better. Men who did not participate to the point of delirium tremens ran the risk of ostracism.

Yet the whole system was reassuring because it was founded on the principle that the white man—specifically the Anglo-Saxon—was God's choice to rule the world.

Natives addressed white men with a reverent "Mastuh." The numerous Chinese were ridiculed as being even lower than the natives. There was no social intercourse across barriers, no intermarriage, no admittance to movies, no stopping at hotels. If a Chinese could prove that he had been married for ten years, he might import his wife into Rabaul for three, after which she must return to China till she had built up another ten-year credit.

Rabaul was a tropical paradise—for white men. For white women it was even more so. If one was willing to behave in the stylized Rabaul pattern—a man trying to play tennis without a shirt was told by the police, "That costume is approved for natives only"—this town was one of the most gracious and charming ever built.

But near it hovered the volcanoes. Rabaul was surrounded by five cones. Six, actually, for the beautiful bay itself had once been a great volcano. It had exploded with terrific violence in some remote time, perhaps while still on the ocean floor. Eons later the eastern rim had broken down and the sea had rushed in to form a bay.

At intervals upon the remaining rim the other five volcanoes had erupted later, like pimples along the edges of a nasty boil. There was the Mother, with two jagged craters, the North Daughter, possibly the oldest of the newcomers, and South Daughter with a secondary crater called Matupi, from which steam and sulphur still escaped.

And if one forgot the volcanoes, gurias came to refresh the memory. They were violent earthquakes that rolled like waves. Sometimes they broke dishes. The worst ones knocked down houses.

397

The people of Rabaul knew that sooner or later their nest of dragons would lash out again. They reasoned that the gurias foretold volcanic action and that when enough pressure had been built up, something would have to pop. They recalled that apparently no Rabaul volcano had ever erupted twice. It was easier to make new ruptures than to force open old channels. Furthermore, it was known that the two most pronounced faults in the earth's rocky shell, one leading down from Japan and the other up from New Zealand, intersected at Rabaul. Vulcanologists—volcano experts—said, "In this region the crust is perilously thin. Catastrophe might strike at any time."

It struck in 1937. For twenty-eight hours there was a violent guria that shook houses. The people of Rabaul said, "Something's got to pop."

In the bay there were two rocky needles called the Beehives. Near them was an insignificant island used as a quarantine station. On May 29, 1937—a Saturday—this trivial speck of land exploded.

It started pumping ash and flame high into the air. The earth shook and within a few hours Vulcan Island became a major volcano. It wiped out three villages and killed more than 300 people. (Rabaul residents say: "Two people and 300 natives.")

Toward midnight the eruption became more violent. So much volcanic ash was ejected that the harbor was engulfed in a layer two feet above the surface of the water. Ships capsized. Vulcan became a mountain 700 feet high.

Ash so disturbed the atmosphere that an unparalleled electrical storm ripped across the volcanoes. Immense towers of lightning shot into the air "like diagrams of the blood system in a medical book," and thunder drowned out the eruptions of lava.

By morning the citizens of Rabaul wiped the ashes out of their eyes and said, "That wasn't so bad. Anybody who wants to evacuate can find boats up the bay. We'll stop here."

But now Matupi, the forgotten crater on the side of South Daughter, rumbled into very powerful activity. Belching huge clouds of noxious gas, Matupi threw out a vast eruption of silky mud. It engulfed the town. The gurias became worse, and the electrical storm continued.

That was enough. Rabaul was emptied. People were ferried to safety in anything that would float, and a second stormy, frightening, muddy, volcanic night settled upon Rabaul.

Within two days most of the residents were back. They found delicate mounds of mud on everything. One woman who had baked a cake for Sunday tea found it with a brown icing, baked hard. Flowers were frozen into shape with a coating of dried mud, and trees were frosted with volcanic ash.

The debris proved to be remarkably fertile and soon Rabaul's gardens were lovelier than before. Quickly life resumed its natural patterns, but with one change: from time to time Matupi belched a cloud of hydrogen sulphide that smelled simply awful. But even this curse was found to have a therapeutic value: it kept the air free of bugs. Within the week beer was flowing at the Rabaul Club. But now waiters did not plump the steins on coasters. They put the coasters on top of the glasses—to keep out Matupi's vagrant explosions of volcanic ash.

Now Rabaul was as placid as before. There was a relieved gayety. "It might not go off again for a hundred years!" But up from the Solomons came a strange white planter who used to sit at the bar and utter dire warnings. Ken Symes had always jabbered about odd things he was going to invent: new carburetors, a machine for husking coconuts, a trick for splitting the atom. Now he was on the booze and croaked: "Watch Java!" When fellow drunks asked why, he cried mournfully, "Java is the great enemy." A friend who had known him in the Solomons snapped, "At Tulagi you said, 'Watch Japan!' " Symes looked up condescendingly and said, "It's too late now to bother about Japan. Watch Java." Shortly he was executed—by the Japanese.

The men of Rabaul had often pondered the growing menace of Japan. But men who won't run away from volcanoes don't run from Japs, either. They organized a crude militia and begged Australia for planes. They got six.

Desperately, as if waiting for Matupi to explode, Rabaul awaited the Japs. They came. Women and children—no Chinese allowed—were evacuated, and the men of Rabaul hitched up their belts.

It is difficult to find a more hopelessly gallant behavior than that of the Rabaul garrison. Pathetically outnumbered, betrayed by the Australian Government and confused by conflicting orders, they marched out to oppose the landing. Their six useless planes waited on the airstrip till the last minute—to save gas—and then went lumbering aloft to meet ace Zero pilots. It was sickening, but the citizens below still marched on to their positions.

They met the Japs at a small beach, and for one day they irritated the invaders. Then they were overwhelmed. Many were shot. The rest were herded onto a hell ship, the *Montevideo Maru*. Some days out on the way to a Jap prison she was sunk, and there was hardly a family in Rabaul that did not suffer loss.

A few of the militia escaped into the jungle and tracked their way across New Britain. They were beset by fevers, by starvation, by the death of their comrades. Some of them, without shoes, reached New Guinea and Australia, where they enlisted in the regular army. One of these men became a notable hero. John Stokie looked and walked like a polar bear, a great hulk with a bullet head. They said he was too awkward to make a soldier, but they let him go back into the bush as a coastwatcher. The Japs sent many expeditions to capture him, but he set up a good system of spies and eluded them for three years. He rescued many Americans and was decorated by several governments. He lived through many hairbreadth escapes to become once more a prosaic copra planter.

Meanwhile the Japs had a great time in Rabaul. They started by serving the Chinese leaders a sumptuous banquet and then shooting them. They executed a few natives to scare the rest. The Germans who had stayed behind to welcome them were tossed into jail, and the Japs built themselves an impregnable base which was never taken by the Allies.

They intended to conquer Australia from Rabaul and moved down more than 100,000 of their best soldiers. They assembled an immense arsenal and a full invasion fleet.

In March, 1943, they launched their armada. Eight warships, eight transports, between 20 and 30 planes, and more than 6,900 invasion troops set out for a quick run across the Bismarck Sea. But this time Allied search planes spotted them. From bases in Australia and Port Moresby fighters and bombers roared out to begin one of the world's critical air battles. First the Jap planes were eliminated. Then, in sickening power the bombers swept back and forth across the fleet. They destroyed it. More than 3,000 Jap soldiers drowned. Others, on rafts, looked up to see machine guns blazing at them, fired by American pilots whose friends had been beheaded in Jap camps. It was, up to then, the most one-sided defeat ever suffered by the Japanese nation. It was, up to then, the most astonishing victory for air power opposed to a defenseless fleet.

But Rabaul seems to breed courage. The Japs assembled a

new fleet, new stores. Then one day from the Pacific itself carrier-based aircraft swooped in and started the total destruction of Rabaul.

Soon, after a ring of wonderfully placed airfields—Munda, Sterling, Bougainville, Green, Emirau, Manus, and great Nadzab with its dozen fields—the town was mercilessly annihilated. For days on end there were bombers over Rabaul almost every hour in the twenty-four, sometimes a single nuisance visitor to ruin sleep, sometimes fifty searing Mitchells.

No more ships from Japan entered Rabaul. No planes flew down from Truk, and now no Zeros were left to contest the skies. Day after day the shattering bombs came down. It was of Rabaul that the phrase was coined, "We'll bypass it and let the Japs wither on the vine."

Many of them did perish, but those that were left held on doggedly. They did something that had never before been done. They moved their entire town underground. In soft rock they dug deep caves, some three stories high. All were interconnected, and along the shore huge caverns were constructed for hiding ships in daytime. Trucks and guns were moved inside mountains, and it was said, "Rabaul has the largest underground force in the world."

When war ended the Japs were still holding on. Some had gone mad. Others had been sealed into their caves by Allied bombs. American investigators studied the fortifications and said, "We might have been able to take Rabaul. It would have been terribly costly."

Completely disgusted were the old residents of the town. For three years they had predicted that the volcanoes would explode and destroy the Japs. There hadn't even been a guria, although Allied bombers tried bombing the craters to get things started.

It is difficult to imagine how Rabaul looked at surrender. Not one major building remained. Not one. There were not even foundations left to show where homes had been. Often there was not a stick of wood, no trees, no cement floor—absolutely nothing. It seems impossible, but many families could not determine where their homes had been.

The stately trees had been bombed away, the wharves, the warehouses, the schools, the gardens, the botanical park. In proportion to its size Rabaul had led the Empire in four categories: "Number of volunteers. Number killed. Number of decorations for bravery. Extent of war damage." The last is misleading. Rabaul was not damaged. It was erased.

Now it is once more a flourishing tropical town. Two banks are doing business. The harbor welcomes ships from many nations, and the roads are jammed with jeeps brought in from Bougainville.

The scars of war have been bulldozed away. Jap prisoners did the work at first but were too expensive to feed. They were shipped home, "where they could starve in their own language." An occasional pillbox still hides in cruelly clever position to remind Australians and Americans how costly it would have been to storm this town. But along the bay there will be ugly reminders of war for generations: more than 160 big Jap ships lie wrecked and rotting in the sun.

And the houses! Probably nowhere else could you find so many attractive people living in such awful housing, not even in the United States. Temporary shacks, monstrously ugly, have been thrown together from scrap iron and discarded wood. In Chinatown, still segregated, the housing is a civic disgrace.

The hotel is typical. A converted army building, its cast iron roof collects a broiling heat. You've heard of hotel walls that were paper thin. Here the walls really are paper! They start one foot from the floor and stop three feet from the ceiling, so that a whisper in one room becomes a brass band in the next. Said one planter, "It's worse than a goldfish bowl. There you can see what's going on. Here you've got to guess." At five in the morning boys begin to sweep the rough concrete floor with stiff brooms that sound like cannon, and at six tea is served in cups with built-in sound. Some rooms have no windows at all, and there the temperature stays at a reliable hundred. Toads hop in at night, birds explore during the day, and any man wishing to use the toilet has to walk a good city block, smack through the middle of the lobby. There's only one consolation. It's a magnificent hotel compared to the one at Lae.

And yet life there can be deeply moving. That man in the corner is a tropical alcoholic, hopeless at 47. His friend says resignedly, "He can either go to the poorhouse or commit suicide." The pretty woman at the table lost her husband on the *Montevideo Maru*, her son at Tobruk. She's running a plantation by herself. The tall man bought disposal jeeps at 24¢, sold them for $860. The young chap at the bar has written a play but is afraid to show it to anyone. It might not be good. The old codger too drunk to sit up is a remittance man with a hot idea for making a million. I know that similar

402

types abound in any city, but in the tropics I seem to have more time to listen to their stories.

For example, my last night in Rabaul some Swedish sailors started a ruckus, so the woman who runs the hotel hauled off and planted a right hook to the leader's jaw. The rioters retreated. I started to exclaim, when an old man said, "Take it easy, Yank. Rabaul has always had capable, strong women ready for anything. The toughest of them all was an American. One of your consuls in Samoa took up with a native girl and had a slew of children. One became Governor of Guam. But the prettiest girl, Emma, came to these parts. She had three or four legal husbands, a string of plantations, a fleet of ships, many stores. She settled along the bay and became known as Queen Emma. When the Germans came she fleeced them and wound up with millions. She was a law to herself and had a string of beautiful Samoan girls attending her. Remind me to tell you about one of them that went to the Mortlocks. Finally she took her last husband off to Monte Carlo. He died suspiciously. There was talk of murder, and shortly after Queen Emma herself died. In Rabaul we've always liked women like that."

Today Rabaul is unforgettable. To it come men from the plantations to sell their copra. Fred Archer has a plantation about 170 miles from Rabaul and he is often seen about the streets. Lean, handsome, unmarried, he always has two desserts and hates whales. "So far as I'm concerned," he says, "every whale in the world could drop dead."

When war threatened he marched into the government office and plunked down his savings of four thousand dollars. "Use it as you see fit," he said. The Government couldn't find any regulation that would let them keep the money. "Besides," they said, "Hitler can't possibly attack Rabaul." Archer volunteered but was rejected as too old.

When the Japs landed near his plantation he tried to impress his native boys with his British aplomb by eating soup as the cruisers went past. "But when I got the spoon to my mouth, there wasn't any soup in it, so the boys lit out for the bush, followed by me." He became a coastwatcher and saw two men killed on either side of him as he led a scouting party into Green Island.

His plantation covers 500 acres and yields a good return. His trees bear coconuts six years after planting and if tended will continue to do so for nearly a century. They are planted about 30 feet apart in squares. To keep the earth between free of weeds, Archer cultivates a nitrogenous creeper called puraria, which makes it easy for the boys to find the fallen coconuts.

The average tree drops about five nuts a month—4,500 make a ton of copra—and the crop falls all the year round. Coconuts are never picked, but do fall most heavily during stormy seasons, when they must be gathered at least every six weeks to forestall sprouting.

The dirty brown husk is ripped off and in the Ceylon system the shell is split in half. (The milk, bitter in old nuts, spills on the ground.) The half shells, still containing the oily meat, are placed in a kiln and baked until all water is driven out. By this time the meat—now called copra—pulls away from the shell. If no smoke has reached it, the copra is nearly white and commands top prices.

In order to keep smoke from staining the copra, the kiln burns only the thoroughly baked shells of the previous day's run. It takes about four days' constant baking to dehydrate copra, which is of course quite inedible. It is used solely as a source of oil, chiefly for margarine, soap and glycerine. Coconut for eating is dehydrated in a different way.

Copra is packed in expensive sacks made in India, and if properly ventilated may keep for six years. Crammed carelessly into heaps, it turns rancid or bursts into spontaneous fire.

Many pests and about a dozen diseases attack coconut palms, but to humans the most unpleasant is the copra bug, a small insect that likes to leave copra and scramble madly over human beings. Two dozen in the hair can drive a man crazy.

To keep his trees clean Archer employs about forty native helpers—no white men—and would like to find twenty more. It costs him about $300 a year to pay and feed each boy. (The Government hates this word and especially forbids the old term for a house that has bars, "boy proof." The recommended phrase is "burglar proof.")

Like all planters, Archer is a confirmed individualist, yet he works in a business which is completely government-controlled. He may not hire natives without permission. When he does find some willing to work, he must conform to the rigid labor code, which protects natives from the gross abuses of an earlier age. His copra he must sell to the Government, transport it in government boats, and house it in government warehouses. And out of each dollar he gets, he must turn 20 cents back into a government fund to insure against price fluctuations in some future depression.

Archer doesn't like socialism, but he does prefer the present $144 a ton for his copra—break-even point $94—to the old days of free enterprise when whales drove copra down to $9 a ton and planters went broke.

As for the whales, somebody discovered that their oil made just as good margarine as copra did. Besides, it was cheaper. Archer says, "Anyone who wants to eat whale oil can." He quotes a lot of Omar and says that at fifty a man oughtn't to live on a remote island any longer. "Too many of my friends commit suicide." What he would like is a secure job where he could take things easy, preferably in Rabaul.

The Macdonalds were my favorite volcano people. He's an eager little scientist who works in the medical laboratory. She's a very pretty Sydney girl who says, "Only a crazy person can live in Rabaul." Too many volcanoes, too few good books. She finds one of her husband's habits very annoying. He jumps out of bed each morning, rubs his hands excitedly and studies the horizon. "Wonderful day for volcanic activity! Lots of rain last week. Not a breath of air. Heavy atmospheric pressure."

He's a nut on volcanoes. He gave up a good job to get service in Rabaul. He loves to recount the great disasters of the past. He figures the best explosions have been Mount Pelée, where the loss of life was terrific; Krakatoa, which was heard for three hundred miles and also killed its quota, and Vesuvius, "where untold numbers perished."

He's afraid Rabaul may not go that way. "More like Port Royal. Bottom dropped out of the harbor and the whole town fell a hundred feet into the bay, wiping out everybody. Of course," he adds, "they were mostly pirates."

Mrs. Macdonald says she's seen her catastrophe-starved husband slowed down only twice. He has only one eye and heckled the Army for twenty months before they accepted him. Then in the jungles of Dutch New Guinea he went exploring and ran out of food, so he popped out his glass eye to amuse the natives into feeding him. "It interested them," he says, "and they followed me back to camp." It developed that they were avid head hunters and wanted to know what they could trade for the "skull belong look-look he come out."

The second stopper came when Macdonald had been predicting something unusual, "maybe a real whopper guria." He was delighted with the prospects when at seven one morning it arrived and knocked things silly. For three days he made no more predictions. Then Matupi belched a particularly odorous cloud of gas and he ran up to me crying, "Smell that! An explosion here might be worse even than Krakatoa!"

Another kind of violence menaces Rabaul: the ferment in Asia. But to hear the white citizens talk, you'd never know they are aware of it. They seem to have forgotten that only a few years ago the Japs kicked all the whites out of Rabaul. Citizens yearn for "the good old days when a German trader had the right to knock a native down in order to establish discipline." Even yet there is resentment over Chinese who dare to attend the movies. ("They wouldn't have done so before the war, by God!") And there are many who say, "The only hope for this country is to give the white man a free hand."

There are some, however, who know what the score in the world is. Mostly they are government men who say privately, "Wouldn't surprise me if the U.N. took this place away from Australia. We're only piddling around with government." I was much impressed with the government men, although one planter said proudly, "Don't underestimate our government blokes. They're well up to the world standard in stupidity." They wasted a much-needed ship to send a cargo of coconuts to feed natives on Bougainville, one of the biggest producers in the South Pacific! They set up an expensive committee to see if cattle could be raised in an area that pre-war grazed 20,000!

Fred Archer knows history and is aware that Rabaul, strategic key to strategic New Guinea, may become a Japanese possession or a Chinese stronghold or an Indonesian center. Like most white men he hopes that Australia will be able to hold it. Sometimes he doubts it. "Not enough settlers. Not enough money to invest."

John Stokie has a more dramatic solution. "Australia can't hold this place. And she won't give it to America. Our only chance is to import two million Japs. Make them turn Christian. Make them practice democracy. Give them such a stake in the country they'll have to remain true. Then trust in God."

The land about Rabaul is worth saving. New Britain, New Ireland, Bougainville, and Manus are rich in resources. At the sprawling native boong (market) in Rabaul produce of all kinds can be found. Corn yields three big crops a year. String beans bear all the time. Pineapples, sweet potatoes, paw paws, cucumbers and peanuts grow abundantly. At elevations of more than 2,500 feet even potatoes and tomatoes can be grown at any season, if fresh seed is introduced yearly. Otherwise the rate of reproduction is so rapid that strains deteriorate.

One of the most popular items at the boong is betel nut, which grows on the fragile areca palm. The nut, about the size of a lemon, is covered in a thick, rubbery skin. The core is a fibrous, heavily veined, gelatinous mass. When chewed by itself, a betel nut tastes like much-diluted alum. It is mildly toxic and astringent. The juice is colorless and narcotic. It has no effect on teeth.

Alone, the betel nut is pretty drab stuff. But natives burn coral to get lime, a pinch of which makes the betel juice slightly effervescent and quite pleasing to the gums, which it ultimately eats away. However, the combination is still colorless.

In order to make the mess palatable, the native pops in a couple of inches of daca, the string-bean-like product of a creeping vine. Daca tastes like pepper and yields a red juice, which stains the mouth and teeth. In time, the red on the teeth turns black and becomes a sure cure for tooth decay.

Most natives spit out this witches' juice, but others swallow it and become mildly drunk. For this reason the triad betel-daca-lime is called "grog belong native." Tough characters swallow big doses and pass out cold.

Betel juice makes even placid natives look ferocious, with red slashes for lips. But there is one tribe near Rabaul which needs no such paint. The Mokolkols—called the Irish of the Pacific—were originally a seacoast tribe, but they liked to fight so much that neighboring villages decided to exterminate them. But a handful of the Mokolkols escaped and fled to the hills. They inbred, nursed their grievances and vowed terrible revenge.

They acquired heavy axes with six-foot handles. At unknown intervals they still swoop down on lonely outposts and kill everyone they meet. They don't rob. They don't collect heads. They simply kill.

Three weeks before I reached Rabaul the Mokolkols fell upon a coastal village. Screaming mad, they swarmed upon the unprotected natives. The axe-men did not stop to murder individuals. They slashed out at anything they saw. The raid lasted only ten minutes, but when the wild men had left, twenty-eight villagers were dead. Some had only one fatal slash. Others had more than fifty.

What makes the story absurd is that there are only sixty Mokolkols altogether, men, women, children. Dozens of expeditions have been sent against them, but no Mokolkol man has ever been taken alive. A long time ago a woman and two babies were captured. The woman killed herself and the children were reared in coastal ways in hopes they would return to their tribe and explain the necessity of law. When they grew up they were afraid to go back.

The Mokolkols have no home, no known leader, no specific area of operation. Their last three attacks were at locations more than a hundred miles from one another. There is new talk of "an expedition against the Mokolkols." Old-timers laugh and say, "Why waste the money?" It's provocative to think that Germans, Australians and Japanese with airplanes, guns, radios and medicine have been unable to find one small band of murderers in an area about the size of Rhode Island. Says the old hand, "Gives you city dreamers some idea of the fact that this is a savage place. Won't be civilized in another hundred years!"

During the war I had seen Rabaul from a Navy bomber, and I had from that moment wanted to visit the violent town that had known so many disasters. I wanted to know what it felt like to live under a volcano. I lived under six of them and in the bosom of a seventh. I climbed the lava sides of Matupi and stood at the rim watching that magnificent crater spit smoke along bright, lime-yellow cliffs two hundred feet high. The smell of sulphur was oppressive, and from the muddy lake in the heart of the crater twisting steam rose like a forming cloud.

Six days before I reached Rabaul there was a violent guria, another on the day I landed. It was interesting to feel the ground wobble, and even Mrs. Macdonald, who hates volcanoes, said, "Too bad you missed the big one. You'd have enjoyed it."

Life under the volcanoes was like life anywhere else. Men with money were making more. The Government was fumbling with a half dozen ideas, some of which might one day save the territory. And women cried at weddings. Nobody bothered much about potential disasters, either volcanic or historic. Mr. Macdonald kept saying hopefully, "In Rabaul anything can happen!" Fred Archer said, "I'd hate to live in New York now that Russia has the atomic bomb."

One day in hot Rabaul I asked my wife, "All sentiment aside, would you be willing to live on the islands we've seen?" We considered the worst aspect of everything and came to these conclusions.

We would be willing to live on almost any Polynesian island. We'd think ourselves lucky to be able to live on Tahiti or Rarotonga. We could enjoy a year or two on even the loneliest atolls. The inconveniences would be offset by the joyous life-patterns of the people who would share them with us.

As for Australia and New Zealand, if we could grow to ignore certain colonial pettiness—formal dress for men; nineteenth-century customs for women—life in either of those countries would be very good. My wife would choose New Zealand of the beautiful vistas; I'd take rugged Australia, especially if I could learn to drink beer like water.

That leaves the forbidding islands of Melanesia. We considered Fletcher's lament written in 1912: "I don't think the South Seas is a good place to earn a living in—especially for a fool who is cursed with the smallest grain of sensitiveness. The *dolce far niente* may or may not be good. Personally, I am inclined to think it would pall quickly except in congenial company. You see, sweltering heat, mosquitoes, flies, fleas and other pests are all against quiet enjoyment. . . . I should not stop in the New Hebrides another day if I could get away."

We would add: "It's difficult to live without plumbing, fresh milk and meat. The noonday heat is enervating, and we don't like living so near to beautiful water without ever getting a chance for a swim. The libraries aren't much good. Tropical diseases are unpleasant, particularly prickly heat. And we hate sleeping under mosquito nets."

But in spite of all that, we wouldn't hesitate to live on any of the Melanesian islands we've seen. If we could earn some income, have screening, some kind of lighting system and some native boys willing to work for a decent wage, we'd live anywhere. We like hot weather. We have liked most of the people we've met in Melanesia. We especially appreciate the release from tension that tropic life encourages.

Only two things might keep us from the islands. We would want to be assured of good medical services. And we would never willingly adopt the attitude toward natives that is prevalent among many white people in Melanesia. Only with great restraint have we been able to keep from brawling with people like the New Guinea planter who roared, "It's a disgrace! The bloody Government says I've got to stop knocking down my niggers. They're nothing but animals. It's the only way you can train the swine." Sooner or later we'd get into a fight over that.

The South Pacific is not a paradise, in the sense that Eden

wasn't either. There are always apples and snakes. But it is a wonderful place to live. The green vales of Tahiti, the hills of Guadalcanal, the towering peaks about Wau, and the noon-day brilliance of Rabaul have enchanted many white travelers who have stayed on for many years and built happy lives. Often on a cool night when the beer was plentiful and the stories alluring, we have envied the men and women of the South Pacific.

What I Learned

It would be folly for a man to spend almost a year knocking about islands if he proposed to learn nothing from the experience. The tropics taught me something almost every day.

First, I learned that white women enjoy the islands as much as their husbands do. On every island I met some woman who had found a home which was lovelier than she had ever known before. An inexpensive house of native materials, airy verandahs, local women to help with the chores, and endless flower gardens made many white women happy. On Tahiti there were many such women, tolerantly amused at the havoc caused by native girls among male tourists. My own wife was approached by a dazzling beauty who asked bluntly, "Your husban', he is very rich, yes?" My wife recalled her allowance and corrected the impression. The Tahitienne shrugged her shoulders and asked, "But he is very strong, yes?" My wife replied in that tone of voice recognized by women the world over, "Yes, *chérie*, but I am very strong, too. You understand?" Apparently the girl didn't, for she asked, "Would you be angry with me if I asked your husban' to dance with me on Saturday night?" Unmistakably now my wife replied that she would be mad, whereupon the dark beauty sniffed and said, "Madame does not trust her husban', yes?" In spite of such disarming propositions my wife liked the South Pacific even more than I did. Once in deathly humid Bougainville she wavered, but for the rest of the time she loved the quiet restfulness of the tropics.

Second, I learned what I believe is the secret of the South Pacific. Here nature is so awesome that it compels attention. Other things being roughly equal, that man lives most keenly who lives in closest harmony with nature. To be wholly alive a man must know storms, he must feel the ocean as his home or the air as his habitation. He must smell the things of earth, hear the sounds of living things and taste the rich abundance of the soil and sea.

The South Pacific is memorable because when you are in the islands you simply cannot ignore nature. You cannot avoid looking up at the stars, large as apples on a new tree. You cannot deafen your ear to the thunder of the surf. The bright sands, the screaming birds, and the wild winds are always with you. The great writers, Conrad, Maugham and Melville, spent only a few years in the South Seas, but their memory of those waters was indestructible; for the nature of life in the islands commands attention to the vivid world and its even more vivid inhabitants.

I have often been mildly amused when I think that the great American novel was not written about New England or Chicago. It was written about a white whale in the South Pacific. This part of the world sharpens the perceptions of a man and brings him closer to an elemental nature. It may seem contradictory, but in the languid tropics one spends more time contemplating those great good things of sound and sight and smell.

For example, this time I saw some things I had missed before. The mountains of New Caledonia, great glowing red hills rising from green valleys, were brilliantly beautiful. On the Australian Outback, across absolutely barren wilderness, I saw from aloft a herd of wild horses galloping with their heads stretched forward and their plumes flying. Or the lagoon at Bora Bora, nestling beneath the volcano, sleeping within the protecting rim of coral. Or that curious and half-revolting sight in Tonga where entire trees were covered with sacred bats, squirming, furry, flying creatures whose chatter was never silenced. And the gay color of the provincial square in Noumea where the flamboyant trees were aflame and where Canaques danced beneath them, shuffling for hours at a time while frenzied natives beat upon gasoline tins until the night throbbed.

There were strange things to feel, too. There was the brain coral that grows along the edge of the reef, a huge ball of rock covered with softly convoluted folds, living and delicate to the touch. I used to lie upon them and they would clutch my belly and keep me from slipping down the face of the reef. Less pleasant was the feel of that stubborn hypodermic needle in the French hospital, striving to force its blunt way into my arm, then leaping in triumph right into the bone—oh, horrible memory! Or the giant Rabaul snails, bigger than my fist, crawling over my fingers, no part of them moving, yet with everything in motion. Or the indescribable shock of those cold tropical shower baths where you would expect to relish anything cool—but not that cold! Or what my wife liked best, the cold fresh-water pool in Tahiti with the water plummeting down in a cascade. I know they've done it a hundred times in the movies. I know it's a cliché. But I also know it's a superb experience. And what I liked best, the feel

412

of the kava bowl in Fiji, a coconut shell worn grayish-brown by many hands over many years, cool to the touch yet containing a bite as the kava hit my gums.

Of the tropic sounds none can compare with the thunder of surf upon the distant reef, where the coral halts the vast waves in full flight so that they writhe into the air like monstrous horses along the rim of a Greek bowl, neighing and thrashing their forefeet. The most unbelievable sound, of course, was the laughter of the kooka-burra birds in Australia. I heard them at least a hundred times but never without wanting to laugh along with them, for their shattering cry is totally boisterous. There was a subtler sound that came in time to represent the jungle. A crowd of Sepik natives had been flown down to our plantation in New Guinea, and in their homesick huts they played endlessly upon their reed pipes of Pan. Sometimes they played for twenty hours at a stretch, four plaintive notes weaving a haunted spell. If I were to hear that monotonous tune tonight I would be back in New Guinea—and I would like that.

There were good things to taste, too. You can get pretty fond of Australian filet mignon, at 29¢ a pound. Or the juicy mangoes in Tahiti that drip bright yellow stains upon your chin. Or those fantastically good meals served by the Tonkinese cook on the edge of the Santo jungles. The classic taste was the sun-sweet pineapple of New Guinea, which was more acid and memorable than any I've ever known before or since. It clung to my fingers for a day as if reluctant to let me forget how good the feast had been. The most longed-for taste was that good, cold Hong Kong beer. The Chinese ship it across the Pacific, and a good refrigerator stocked with bottles can be a wonderful end to a journey, or a torturing memory when you are inland upon some trail.

But in human beings it is the sense of smell—least regarded of the senses—which is most powerful in evoking memories; so that now if I smell burnt chicory I am in Fiji. If I smell clean ocean fish, I'm in the Tahiti market. Or a whiff of burnt sulphur can pitch me back into the sugar factories of Queensland. But there are three Pacific fragrances I can never forget. I have tried to imprison the smell of ripe vanilla oils as they drift across Raiatea on some dewy morning, but I have probably failed. At Tonga there is another odor of which a traveler said, "Well, at least it's strong!" The Tonga reef stretches far out to sea and low tide exposes vast expanses of flat coral, where pools of stagnant water collect. Each pool contains its delicacies, as the pot of a famous chef

413

contains oddments for the stew: a fragment of dead fish, a fractured clam, a leg torn off a wounded lobster, an old shoe, some jetsam, and some rotting sea weed. All day the blazing sun cooks this delectable brew so that when the tide returns at evening a rich ambrosia awaits its probing fingers. When an off-sea breeze is blowing, you can stand along the shore and watch the smell come in. In the distance a kettle of stew is stirred up and swept along to another kettle closer inshore. Finally the whole powerful broth is thrown at the shore as a furious cook throws out a stinking mess. You have to brace yourself when the aroma hits, but strangely enough it does not smell offensive. It smells mightly like the ocean, and that is always good. But the queenly fragrance of the tropics is the tender perfume of frangipani blossoms when dew is on them. The frangipani is a miraculous tree which bears a multitude of creamy white flowers whose petals shade into a golden amber where they join the stem. And there they hide as lovely a fragrance as we know.

But rejuvenating as it is to feel one's self close to nature, that alone is never enough. Along with the timelessness of natural things must go a concern with temporal events if a man expects to live with any decency in his world. If the South Pacific were merely an escape from reality it would be nothing but a pleasant grave; but that is not the case, for when I am in the South Pacific I am each day more keenly an American. And from that restful vantage of islands and coral I sometimes discover things I did not know before.

For example, this time I discovered what I think about America. I was not on a single island but what someone with good sense and responsible years approached me with this direct question: "Did the American Government send you out here to report on whether or not we want America to take over this island? Let me tell you, my friend, we dream of nothing else. When will America adopt us?" Even in Australia—north of Brisbane in the country that was to be abandoned to the Japs in 1942—this question was asked.

These questions did not make me arrogantly proud of America. Often I explained to my questioners that if they studied the history of Puerto Rico they might not find the prospect so alluring. I also cooled them off by pointing out that my nation doesn't have too good a record in dealing with colored races. Finally I explained that during the war they had seen us at a rare advantage: our finest young men, with money to burn, and machines to waste, and hearts for any lovely girl. I told them we Americans were not all like that.

Of course, they didn't believe me. They knew I was painting a rather dark picture because I felt it improper to visit a foreign country and then encourage sedition among its citizens. Yet I can honestly say that never was this vital question asked—"When will America take over?"—without its awakening in me a tremendous appreciation of my native land. We can laugh at our weaknesses, and surely we've got to learn to accept it with good grace when others ridicule our faults, but a residue remains. Across the world that residue is known. I discovered it in the South Pacific.

I also discovered what I think about certain aspects of life. When I first explored the Pacific I was bowled over by the volcanoes. I climbed a full dozen of them, watched them explode at night, listened to their majestic growls as they spit forth ash. There was something awful and final about these Pacific volcanoes—more numerous than anywhere else on the globe—for they represented the fundamental earth asserting itself in violence.

But since that first exploration I have known enough of violence, and on this trip I was surprised to find that volcanoes bored me. True, it was interesting to see how old friends were getting along—Bagana in Bougainville and Ruapehu in New Zealand—but I had lost my taste for violence. Now what delighted me were the waterfalls, those poetic threads of light leaping through the quiet air and finding rest below. I was weary of gigantic horrors and relished the prospect of peaceful movement to some green haven. I have never seen a waterfall that did not bring spiritual restfulness; and once when I had turned my back upon a volcano to study a waterfall I thought that in his heyday Hitler would have screamed that I was degenerate. I found that I was all in favor of such degeneracy.

But not even the loveliest cascade could put me to sleep, for I kept seeing one vision across the Pacific that kept me fitfully awake. On Hawaii it was the Japanese storekeeper, alert and wise. In Rabaul it was the Chinese shipping magnate, quick and industrious. In Espiritu Santo it was the Tonkinese I used to know as a laundryman's helper's helper. Now he owns a store. In Tahiti it was the wonderful Chinese-Tahitian basketball team, lithe and tricky on the pivot shots. Wherever I went I saw the face of Asia, and it was unforgettable.

The South Pacific was once the playground for ship-sick

European sailors. Then it became the roistering barricade of the last great pirates. Next it was the longed-for escape from the canyons of New York. Then the unwilling theatre for an American military triumph. But now it has become the meeting ground for Asia and America. Wherever you go in the South Pacific you find present wealth in the hands of white people and most of the business energy in the control of Chinese or Chinese-natives. The exception is Fiji, where the Indians play the role of the Chinese, and play it more effectively.

In New Guinea the pressure of Asia is enormous. Indonesians claim the former Dutch half, and if they acquire that surely they will absorb the eastern half and perhaps Australia, too. In Rabaul fatalistic planters make wry bets as to how soon Japan or China will occupy that magnificent harbor. In the New Hebrides the Tonkinese bide their time, remembering that the French have broken a dozen promises regarding repatriation and listening with somber joy to the secret radio reports of French defeats in Tonkin-China. Asia is everywhere.

There is only one sensible way to think of the Pacific Ocean today. It is the highway between Asia and America, and whether we wish it or not, from now on there will be immense traffic along that highway. If we know what we want, if we have patience and determination, if above all we have understanding, we may insure that the traffic will be peaceful, consisting of tractors and students and medical missionaries and bolts of cloth. But if we are not intelligent, or if we cannot cultivate understanding in Asia, then the traffic will be armed planes, battleships, submarines and death. In either alternative we may be absolutely certain that from now on the Pacific traffic will be a two-way affair. I can foresee the day when the passage of goods and people and ideas across the Pacific will be of far greater importance to America than the similar exchange across the Atlantic. Asia must inevitably become more important to the United States than Europe. That is why we must all do all that we can to understand Asia. That is why it is stupid folly to look upon the South Pacific as a lecher's paradise or a wastrel's retreat. It has become, especially as it leads to New Zealand and Australia, one of our highways to the future.